State of War

State of War

A NOVEL

Ninotchka Rosca

W. W. NORTON & COMPANY

NEW YORK   LONDON

The text of this book is composed in Avanta,
with display type set in Cochin Black.
Composition and manufacturing by The Haddon Craftsmen, Inc.
Book design by Margaret M. Wagner.

First Edition

Library of Congress Cataloging-in-Publication Data
Rosca, Ninotchka.
    State of war / Ninotchka Rosca.
        p. cm.
    I. Title.
    PR9550.9.R64S7 1988
    823—dc19

ISBN 0-393-02544-6

W. W. Norton & Company, Inc.
500 Fifth Avenue, New York, N. Y. 10110
W. W. Norton & Company Ltd.
37 Great Russell Street, London WC1B 3NU

1 2 3 4 5 6 7 8 9 0

Contents

The Book of Acts

1

Twelve hours after sailing from Manila, the ship dropped anchor three miles off the island of K——, one of the thousand or so odd-shaped and odd-sized isles and islets dotting the Central Philippine Sea. Adrian Banyaga, who had watched dawn define the island with disconcerting swiftness, was roused from his contemplation of its rather drab waterfront by a volley of laughter in the ship's lounge. Turning from the bay windows, he saw Eliza Hansen at one of the tables, cheerfully rolling down the sleeves of her blue *camisa de chino*, the cotton man's undershirt which, with blue jeans and blue sneakers, had become casual costume for young adults in the last two or three years. Around her, a dozen men and women laughed, gesturing with admiration at her truly magnificent dusky olive arms. She had just bested, it seemed, the last female to challenge her at arm wrestling and was inordinately pleased with herself, her laughter spilling in little bubbles from her mouth as her eyes darted among the faces about her, the tip of her tongue now and then licking her underlip. Two tables away, in an identical costume, and with right cheek leaning on a loosely clenched fist, her elbow on the table, sat Anna Villaverde. Adrian blinked his tired eyes. Were it not for their color, the two women could have been twins. But where Eliza was of that rare fortuitous sienna skin, accidentally bred by a mingling of Caucasian and Malay blood, Anna was fair, of a golden tint that testified to an indefinable mixing of Chinese, Malay, and other strange bloods. A true child of the Philippine archipelago.

There were other differences as well. Although her reputation did not go beyond the fifty or so top businessmen in the country, Eliza was acknowledged to be a useful acquaintance, by virtue of a back-door alliance with an equally obscure colonel who controlled the head of state's calendar and the traffic of documents in and out of the said leader's office. Anna, on the other hand, was among the powerless of powerless, even her daily movement subject to military audit, by virtue of certain entries in her dossier folders at the military headquarters. Her vulnerability, Adrian thought, had marked her. Even now, as the others' laughter and raucous words broke about her, Anna remained quiet, her face without expression. She merely nodded when Eliza, mockingly flexing her biceps, threw her a boastful look. She had been watchful, quiet, the whole night—a still point in the boil of noise and mirth that constantly erupted about Eliza. She had been that way as the ship had moved, with terrific noise, from the mouth of Manila Bay and across an oily, black sea, while on the deck, under a giant canvas awning, the ship's band had tuned up and launched into an endless stream of dance music and the passengers, rushing up from the cabins below, had crowded and jammed every inch of the deck, their bodies swaying to the music.

Eliza, tiring of the dancing, had indulged in one silly whim after another. For a few hours, she had held court at one end of the dance space, a dinner napkin about the curls of her dark brown, shoulder-length hair. She had been the Swami then, or "Her Royal Swaminess," as she'd insisted, grabbing hands and peering into the palms of men and women, promising outrageous fates and fortunes. Anna had stood behind her, throwing in a suggestion or two as Eliza had pretended to read this or that palm line. Not even a smile had crossed her face. By the time Eliza metamorphosed into Rosie the Wrestler, both Anna and Adrian were red-eyed and wrung out by fatigue. But dutifully, they had stayed by Eliza as she collected her inevitable retinue. By then, Adrian had given up on seeing Anna laugh. It was his peculiar fate, he had thought, to be accompanied to the Festival by two fairy-tale women. The laughing princess and the princess who could not laugh. He had wondered vaguely if anyone, anywhere in the world, had ever created a story for the two. Or for the three of them—for there was no doubting his own role as fairy-tale prince. Perhaps, the Festival would weave it for them, he told himself wryly.

The definitive title was unfair, of course. The Philippines, with its seven thousand one hundred islands, held an uncountable number of festivals throughout the year—from the May parade of flowers and women to St. Claire's seed dance of women, to the brief dawn tree-walk of the residents of a small barrio in Laguna Province, to the evening fire dances of the mountain people. But such was the power of the ceremonies at K——, on the windward side of the island, that whenever festivals were mentioned, K—— sprang readily to the mind. Perhaps because the Festival here was a singular evocation of victory in a country of too many defeats. Or perhaps because the first celebration went beyond the memory of the grandfather of the grandfather of the oldest grandfather at K——, which made it no one's and yet everyone's personal history. Perhaps—. No matter. This year, when Adrian Banyaga, Eliza Hansen, and Anna Villaverde boarded a ship for the Festival, they had known they were joining a pilgrimage of a quarter of a million men and women.

A sharp cry from Eliza. She had risen to her feet and was fumbling with the straps of her waist pouch. With a slight lift of her chin, Anna indicated the sea outside the lounge windows and Adrian, turning, saw three flat-bottom boats crest a wave, sink, only to hover into view once more. The World War II relics were coming to ferry the passengers to the island whose harbor was too shallow for the ship. Already, the lounge was emptying as men and women made for the doorway.

Adrian felt his pockets; he had his wallet, his keys, and his toothbrush—all he would need for the island where, during the Festival, every house door was flung open, every room available to the pilgrim.

There was the minor confusion of boarding the ferryboats. He and the women missed the first two, such was the crush on the deck, but they managed to make the last one, backing into it from the rope ladders down which they were guided by sun-burned sailors who skillfully soothed tremulous women and challenged the men into deft passage. Powered by a sluggish-sounding engine, the boat veered at sea and headed for the island. As it rose with each sea wave, the boat gave the passengers a glimpse of K——: its single drab pier thrusting into the sea from a low, gray cement building and the crescent spread of white sand that horned an abrupt pile of rocks at one end of the island and thinned into a white line at the other, directly below a sudden crag which bore the weight of a grass-bearded tower which seemed to tremble with the groan of a two-hundred-year-old warning bell.

Beyond this was the Festival and the town proper had arrayed itself for it. Multicolored paper buntings had been strung overhead, straddling roads and the gaps between house roofs, while at every street corner bamboo stalls had been set up and piled high with necklaces of boars' teeth, death masks, spears and shields, red, blue, and green skulls, and whittled bamboo whistles on leather thongs. Each intersection was guarded by a panoply of bamboo, studded with nipa fronds and flowers—red hibiscus, white sampaguitas and jasmine, red and orange daisies, sheaves of white St. Joseph's Cane flowers, and pink tendrils of *cadena de amor.* In the midst of this riot of equatorial hues and smells, the townspeople walked, themselves arrayed in palm fronds, flowers, feathers, and seashells. The men's bare chests and the women's faces and arms were coated with an oily mixture of soot and the juice of *achuete* seeds—hallucinatory masks whose black and red strips rippled and writhed in the liquid light of an amber sun as the crowd pranced, hopped, and ululated to the alternating fast and slow rhythm of pagan drums whose beat seemed both distant and near, coming now from one end of the main plaza, now from the sky overhead, now from the central kiosk, and then again from the side streets radiating from the town's center.

The rites were simple. In the first celebration, a local chieftain had ordered a parade of his warriors and those of his allies who had helped carry the battle one morning at the edge of time. Though he had himself long gone on to death, here were his warriors still, dressed more gaudily with the artifice of the intervening centuries, though they did their march now not in the open fields of K—— but through the paved and dust roads of the town, between desultory houses bleached by sea wind and the sun, to the town's boundaries and back again, wending their way to the plaza whose northern end was held down by the church, a massive construction of stone and wood whose baroque facade had been so eroded by the elements one could no longer tell whether the saints or Arjuna's army were carved there; and whose southern side was weighed down by the town hall which, as though to challenge the church's prominence, was set on a raised cement promenade with wide terrace steps, though the structure itself was hulking and squat, its portico columns disproportionately massive. Images of a dream, Adrian thought as he steered the two women through a crowd already drunk despite the early hour.

Hand in hand, the three wove their way through the Festival, amidst the restless mass of bodies. They came upon a flock of transvestites who ambled along calmly, as though taking the sea air. They wore iridescent gowns of peacock colors, silver and gold sandals, and their shoulders were draped with lace shawls. They eyed the crowd haughtily, swinging their crocheted handbags and paper fans. Eliza's mouth dropped open at the sight. In such a disguise, she thought, man-woman, woman-man, one could live safely in illusions and avoid all confrontations.

The mortals followed—the blue denim crowd, visitors who owed no allegiance to any tribe and were therefore designated the invaders. Though the label had been whimsically adapted from a television series, it was accurate, for the great mass of the crowd were as alien as could be. There were the Japanese, the Chinese, the Caucasian, the urbanite with his short-focusing eyes and pallid discontent. They walked quickly, with self-assurance, and it took a while before the drums subdued and merged them with the town's rhythm.

Of the three, Eliza was the first to be snared by the Festival. Her arm was hooked by a young man waving a bottle of rum and shrieking with laughter, and Eliza ran off with him, half dancing to the drums' four-four beat. The crowd swallowed them quickly. Adrian's fingers tightened about Anna's hand and he bent his head closer to her ear, telling her not to break loose as it would be impossible to find her again. No problem, Anna murmured back; she could then be a member of the lost tribe.

He did not find that funny and glanced at her face to see if her words meant anything. But a woman, blond strings of hair flying about her head, whirled out of a wall of bodies, dragging two men after her. Adrian tugged on Anna's hand, pulling her away and the woman, body and limbs jerking in separate movement, stood in a cleared space while the two men her dancing had snatched from the crowd circled her. They slipped through the windmill slashing of her arms; their fingers dug into her flesh. She arched her back, offering them her torso and, shrieking, went on dancing. The two closed in on her.

A voice called out Adrian's name and he barely managed to catch a wineskin which seemed to have appeared in the air. He unstoppered it, held it aloft, and, squeezing with both hands, let the wine spurt into his mouth. His throat worked as he swallowed while a half-dozen men broke from the crowd and circled him. They began counting out the seconds as Adrian drank. Wine spilled from the corners of his mouth, down his chin and throat, and painted lilacs on his white T-shirt. Applause rang out—thinly, at first; then, in rhythm as the seconds count went up to thirty. *Arriba, letran!!* a man bellowed. Adrian choked. The wine spewed from his lips to the ground. Hands snatched the wineskin away and the group swerved, abandoning them for the next contender.

"Idiot," Adrian muttered, wiping his mouth with his hand. "It was the wrong school."

"Did it matter?" Anna asked lightly. But when Adrian held out his hand, she stepped away.

Embarrassed, he clutched at his shirt front, lifting the cloth from his skin. "Mothermine, I have purple blood," he said. "I'm royally dead. Yecch, it's sticky."

"Not quite dead," Anna said, watching as he stripped off the shirt and tied it like a turban about his head. His cheeks were flushed from the wine. "Never mind," she went on, after a while, "you're still the handsomest man around."

To confirm her words, wolf whistles shrilled out and Adrian grinned sheepishly at three girls who had stopped to look at him. He struck a pose, arms akimbo. Anna shook her head, took another step back as though to examine him fully, and bumped against the man behind her. She was about to apologize when the man extended his hand, palm up.

"It's quite simple," he said. "Four-four beat and we'll go around the plaza."

He seized her left wrist and before she could say anything, they had speared through the crowd to the middle of the road. The man paused, head flung back, one arm held out, fingertips barely touching her shoulder. Then they took off, diving into the rhythm of the drums, shoulders and feet marking time as they danced down the length of the road toward the church. Instinctively, her feet found their niche in the drumbeats; she was hardly conscious of the intricate pattern they wove on the asphalt, a pattern of small steps and halts—one-two-three, one-two-three, one-two, one-two-three—while the young man twirled on his toes and danced to her right, to her left, behind her, in front of her like a moth circling a flame lick. She had the disquieting thought she was dancing the pattern of her life and though the young man followed his own choreography, somehow they managed to keep in step, obeying the drums. It was a long journey; dancers joined in, breaking loose from the line of onlookers, only to drop back again. Borne by the stream of dancing men and women, they rounded the corner and passed in front of the church where they overtook a formation of warriors. They threaded through the ranks of the bare-chested, g-stringed, and painted men who, true to the code of braves, ignored their presence. To amuse herself, Anna played catch with the tribe's pennant, jumping to touch the red and blue crepe paper ribbons wriggling in the air. One of the warriors smiled at her and she was suddenly afraid.

"My love!" her partner called out, panting. "You dance well. Let me take you back before I collapse."

She shook her head, shot away from the hand he held out, and crossed the street. She walked aimlessly, wedging herself through clusters of men and women who, lost in their own little festivals, sang, danced, and labored to get drunk. She looked back once and saw she had lost her partner. Still, she spent another quarter-hour in wandering through the crowd before she leaped over the foot-high cement ledge that separated the plaza's lawn from the sidewalk. On the grass, exhausted dancers lay like scythed stalks. They called out, their hands languidly waving. "Come," they said, "don't be a stranger." But she ignored them and went on walking, circling back and forth, drawing closer to the kiosk that stood white and inviolate at the plaza's center. Abruptly, as though on a sudden whim, she turned and mounted the kiosk's broad steps.

After the sunlight, she found the interior dim. She blinked rapidly, forcing her eyes to adjust. But a hand had already found her wrist; she was being drawn deeper into the room.

"Easy, wasn't it?" The voice was Rafael's. "I thought you would take longer to break away."

"You saw me?"

"Here, there, everywhere." He shook his head. "You are stubborn. You aren't supposed to be here." He squatted down and gestured for her to follow.

"Let's not argue," she said, tucking in her legs yogi fashion. "I hadn't known about your plans when I made mine. Have yours changed?"

"Not to my knowledge."

"I had hoped otherwise." She rubbed her hands together, trying to warm them. "But why are you here? If I can't be here, why are you here?"

"To warn idiots like you. We hadn't anticipated that some of us, of our kind, would be attending the Festival. Fortunately, *you* tipped us off."

"How many are here?"

"Fifty!" He spat the words out. "Innocent souls. A man here, a woman there, a couple . . . It was too late to chase after them in the city. So here I am, a reception of one."

"And what are you—here, now?" She nearly smiled as she asked. She had known him as a priest, a traffic policeman, a professor, a pickpocket.

"Fisherman," he said promptly. Leaning forward, he added that the Commander was expected at the Festival, on its last day. He would address the crowd.

Anna shivered. "I have to confess I'm scared," she said.

"If it's any comfort, so am I," Rafael said. "And if it will make you feel better, *he* is here."

She was silent. After a while, she nodded. "I feel better—yes—and yet, I don't. Where will it be?"

"At the stage. One of the posts is hollow. The gift lies within, timed to the second. A few minutes' allowance for the crowd which would slow down the vehicle. It won't stop, though. It never does. As you know, the Commander is a madman for punctuality."

"I wish it were simpler," she said. "Any message for me—from . . . ?"

"Not yet. But why don't you make for the other side of the island? There are friendly fisherfolk there. They'll take you to the next island, turn you over to other friends who'll take you to a third island where you can catch a plane for Manila. You can be home by evening."

"I came with friends."

"Rot. They'll be safe. They won't go near the stage."

"Should I warn them?"

He made an incredulous sound. She shrugged.

"Then I have to stay."

A pause. Then he shrugged. "Suit yourself. But remember who you are, what you are. You're in no position to be generous." He began to unfold his body but changed his mind just as quickly. "Do me a favor. When things begin to happen, head for the other side of the island. The pier here will be secured at once. No possibilities there at all. So head for the other side. No, no; cancel that. Better yet, make for the cemetery, just beyond the town, away from the sea. Stay there until I come for you. Be there alone."

"But what about—?"

"The well-fed pig?" He spat the words out. "If you keep thinking of that being as a well-fed pig, you won't have so many problems. And if you kept in mind what you are, who you are, you won't even have a well-fed pig to worry about."

"That's not fair," she said fiercely.

"So, what is?" He rose now, not looking at her, and threw the rest of his words over his shoulder. "The cemetery. Remember."

He walked away quickly. She did not try to stop him; she knew he would know where and how to contact her—if she was needed. She waited, forcing herself to breathe slowly, calmly, giving him the time he needed to disappear. It was cool inside the kiosk and odd that, despite the crowds on the lawn and the streets, no one came. Even the drums were muted. She glanced at the ceiling's arch; the kiosk was obviously quite old. Perhaps, its stones had been glued together with egg whites. The Spaniards had favored such masonry.

She chose to leave by the southern door, sighing as she did so at the scene before her. The town plaza was a riot of confusion with walls of bodies blocking a view of the roads jammed by the parade and dancers. The sun, a white blur in the blue, cloudless sky, was relentless. She blinked her eyes. She caught a flash of olive green; a soldier, barely glimpsed between the crowd and the dark bole of an acacia tree. She sighed again, wondering how much longer the war would go on—this elusive, almost illusory war that was everywhere and yet was nowhere. By some quirk of fate, she had managed to thrust herself right into it. Somewhere, sometime, she had committed herself to what had seemed to be proper action and that was it. All it had taken and all it would take. And the vow she had made, while still a vague child, that she would never, never be involved in any war, whosever

war, was broken. All it had taken was the conviction that she knew
what had to be done and that she would do it. That was all.

She cut across the lawn, shifting the pouch tied to her waist to a
more comfortable position. Voices rose about her, calling, offering
wine and food and companionship. It was a rule of the Festival that
no one should be left by himself to laze away. She accepted a cigarette
from a young man stretched out on the grass and as she smoked,
scanned the shifting mass of bodies beyond the trees fringing the
plaza. There were no uniforms as far as she could see. Perhaps, it had
been a stray soldier, assigned to the island and savoring the celebration.

"Don't sigh too much," the young man said to her. He patted the
grass beside him, asking her to lie down.

She shook her head but squatted down anyway. "I have to find my
friends," she said.

"Can't I get to know you?"

She snorted. "If you did, you wouldn't like me."

He made a doubting sound. "Are you a whore?" he asked happily.
"A party girl? A tourist?"

She cut through his words and rose to her feet. "A widow," she said
abruptly. "With a widow's woes."

"I love the way you say that," he said but she was already walking
away.

A ball of anger tightened in her. That wasn't it at all, not at all,
she scolded herself. A widow in the archipelago had freedom equal
to a whore and more respectability. That hadn't started it—but how
it began, why it happened, no one could answer. The drums, which
answered all questions, merely laughed. It must have been a stranger,
they said, a man who one day raised his head from whatever work he
was doing and said he had had enough. Of the price of salt, perhaps,
the cost of rice, or, maybe, of the five perpetually agape mouths of
his family. Or of this or that. No matter. One morning, seven thousand one hundred islands awoke with an ominous roar and the Festival
began.

The mountain warriors heard it the day three lowland merchants, pleading the cost of fuel, tried to take away their cabbage harvest for a song. G-strings flapping in a ravine wind, the warriors took counsel with one another and chose one able-bodied youth to deal with the merchants. The young man in turn called on his sworn brothers and, together, they decapitated the traders with machetes while the others rolled cabbages down cliff edges and wished the worms the good fortune of eating.

The youths stuck the merchants' heads on their spear points and danced back to their village, an impromptu song about death and celebration on their lips. Along the way, they gathered the orange blossoms of the firetrees and wove victory wreaths while the village gongs announced the coming of the ritual feast that would mark the end of peace. The little thunder of the gongs smashed against the mountainside, bounced on itself, and rolled down to the sea edge where fishermen, sitting before their evening meal, heard and deciphered the message. Their eyes grew wary.

Upending their boats on the beach, the fishermen abandoned the sea. A melancholic wind blew through towns and rolled inland. Milk disappeared; piles of tomatoes, lettuce, and eggplants putrefied into a liquid mess at railroad stations as the farmers, unable to pay the cost of transport, abandoned their produce.

In the midst of this disturbance, the Noble and Ever Loyal City of Manila, hemmed in by the Magellanic and Chinese seas, lay lost in its dreams. So long as the city was at rest, nothing could be wrong. Wise men knew this and one such bureaucrat, feeling the dogs of desperation skulking at the city's boundaries, spent a sleepless night pondering whether or not to raise the cost of public transportation. He tried to soften the blow by decreeing that fares should be computed, on a graduated basis, by the mile. Thus, his conscience eased, he congratulated himself for making it possible for his countrymen to deal with the terrible increase in oil prices and went to sleep.

Alas, distance was reckoned in kilometers. And alas, he who could rectify the error took off for Europe to try for a cure of his headache at Lourdes. Such a simple mistake—which blossomed rapidly into a monstrosity as fistfights broke out amidst yelled mathematics. How much from Quiapo to Diliman, from Cubao to Diliman, and from Cubao to Quiapo? From the boulevard to the market, from the city hall to the cemetery, and from the cemetery to everywhere? Such a simple error—and yet, along with innumerable other acts of stupidity, it became the final insult in a long string of insults. The man in the street, walking about and scribbling sums furiously with his pencil, sulked and pouted and seethed and remembered all the small grievances of his life which, taken singly, were tolerable enough but when added up—

Some son-of-a-goat had better do something, a bus driver said. A passenger heard and, upon getting off the bus, picked up a stone and hurled it toward the road. To his delight, a barrage of stones and empty bottles followed his virgin throw. In five minutes flat, the boulevard was stubbled with rocks, pebbles, concrete chunks, stones, and broken glass. Now the schoolchildren dumping their books, joined in, filling their satchels with ammunition. By early evening, the main avenues were barricaded and a few thousand men and women warded off the night chill with a bonfire of buses.

Anna and her husband, Manolo Montreal, were eating mooncakes at the intersection of Quezon Boulevard and Recto Avenue when a half-dozen military trucks came careening down the road, screeched to a halt, and disgorged soldiers. The two forgot that mooncakes were mandatory when one was young and newly married. They watched enthralled as the soldiers formed groups, fanned out, and disappeared into the side alleys of downtown Manila while a force of maybe two hundred lined up across the boulevard and turned their faces to the distant bonfires. Another hundred positioned themselves behind garbage bins, parked cars, and lampposts. At 10 P.M., the order to fire was given. A wind blew through the silence that followed the command. In Anna's hand, the mooncake shriveled to pellets as M-16s, .45s, tear-gas canisters, and grenades brought an unexpected New Year's Eve to the city. The first body to stretch out on the cement cried out for the wrath of God.

Through Molotov flames, pillbox fumes, and pools of blood and oil, the soldiers marched forward, step by step. With precision learned from the firing range, they pumped bullets into the crania of young men and women betrayed by burning vehicles. By this time, Anna and Manolo had dashed up a building's fire escape ladder and from its safety watched the impossible war. *Amazing,* Manolo said over and over again, *they're fighting back. Amazing.*

And creating music all the way, Anna wanted to reply—for there it was, over the contrapunta of gunshots and the *whoomph* of tear-gas canisters, the delicate shattering of glass as the crowd retreated, smashing display windows of unaffordable merchandise. They scattered, regrouped, gave way and regained lost ground, dragged out the wounded and the dead, crawled through debris to hurl pillboxes with their makeshift shrapnel of nails and glass shards, and yelled from time to time, in bitter humor, at the soldiers. *Surrender now,* they shrieked in half a dozen languages, *we are the people!* Hearing this, Manolo burst into laughter though tears were streaking down his cheeks and Anna's nostrils dilated, savoring the words along with the smell of roasted corn for this was October, the time to eat corn still sizzling from the red-eyed coals fanned by iron-haired women squatting at street corners, war or no war.

2

The toke had barely touched Adrian's lips when the soldier appeared; he could only raise his eyes to heaven and curse his childhood friend and schoolmate Julius who had found him in the Festival and had steered him into an alley flanked by the gray backsides of houses. But Julius flicked a glance at the uniform and grinned. The soldier shrugged and moved away.

"How did you manage that?" Adrian asked, impressed.

"I bought the stuff from him." Julius laughed.

The others, three young men whom Julius had introduced as junior stockbrokers, nodded knowingly. Adrian exhaled audibly and mumbled something about finding his lost women.

"Trust you to come with not one but two," Julius said.

"Doesn't matter. I lost both."

"I wouldn't worry," one of the young men said.

"Adrian never worries," Julius said quickly. "He was born on the proper side of morning."

Laughter again. Adrian, embarrassed, wondered what the proper side of morning was to Julius. He awoke each day to the stain of sunlight on the windowsill and cooing from the dovecote in the garden below his upstairs bedroom. Invariably, when he reached the kitchen of his parents' house, there would be the scent of fresh bread and chocolate. All were a confirmation of his well-being and he had never questioned how it was possible that all his mornings were on the proper side. He was after all heir to seven major corporations, had been an athlete in college, and was all of twenty-three years old. He eyed Julius, noting his Chinese *mestizo* face and his slim, undeniably Asiatic body.

"Remember the girl you went after," Julius asked suddenly, "the one you used to say looked absolutely transcendental?"

Adrian made a noncommittal sound.

"She had a spectacular career, friend," Julius went on. "Taken in a gun battle in Malabon. Rat-tat-tat. Three soldiers killed, two wounded. On the partisans' side, two killed, one wounded. And there was your lady, cool as anything, shearing a hedge of violets with M-16 bullets. The soldiers barely managed to subdue them, the crazy kids. So they strangled one of the leftover boys, just to even up the score. Your friend went berserk."

Adrian shifted uncomfortably. "I don't understand."

"Neither do I," said one of the young men. "Can't see why people can't simply live with it—with all these changes. Everything's been fine so far."

"True," said another. "Kids taking on the entire government. Madness."

"Yeah," Julius said. "Anyway, they got her. Disappeared. Thought you'd like to know." He took a last puff on the toke, eyed it before dropping it to the ground and grinding it under his right foot.

"Who knows what I want to know?" Adrian blurted, his voice harsh. He threw a curt look at Julius. He could feel himself flushing as he clamped down on the memory of a sixteen-year-old body drowning in a loose blue-and-white school uniform with only a foot-long rosary for decoration. He had been young and foolish then, and was still young and foolish now—for the eyes in the face that rose before him were Anna's: intent yet vague, distant and yet precise. Transcendental.

"You had a genius for nicknames," Julius said, as though divining his thoughts.

He waved a dismissal at the group and walked away, his shoulders rigid. Around the corner, he came upon a dwarf in a miniature cardboard tank. The dwarf aimed the tank's turret at Adrian, stuck his tongue out, and fired away, a tinhorn rattle nearly shaking the gun loose. Adrian laughed.

A boy came running, holding up garlands of bamboo whistles on leather thongs. Adrian chose three and paid for them. One he slung about his neck; the others, he pocketed, thinking he would give them to the two women if and when he found them. As he moved closer to the plaza, the crowd began to thicken. A laughing Japanese girl caught him in a pirouette; he danced a measure with her before she ran off, drawn by sudden screams from the crowd. A transvestite appeared, holding aloft a bottle of Archangel beer, and Adrian obliged by taking two swallows. The beer was cold and good. As he handed the bottle back, he was nearly knocked down by a blond woman who, sprinting from nowhere, sprang on his back and dug her heels into his thighs. He obliged her as well, carrying her toward the noise of the Festival until his breath ran out and his heart thudded against his ribs. He did not hesitate. He shook her off without warning, throwing her into a knot of male teenagers who, with great cheer, caught her in their arms. At that instant, the rhythm of the drums changed; the packed bodies before him shifted and he could see clear across the road to the plaza lawn. Anna and Eliza were sitting on the cement ledge, their arms on each other's shoulders, their heads touching. Eliza was whispering into Anna's ear and Adrian could almost feel her moist breath. Anna looked incredulous, the fingers of her left hand half covering her mouth.

He quickened his step but the crowd surged forward and caught him. He rammed elbows and shoulders against the wall of flesh, trying to push his way through. It was useless. Something had wedged the onlookers into a compact mass. The drums drew closer, the whistles grew shriller, and curses began to ring out in the translucent heat. Adrian closed his eyes and shook his head. It wouldn't do, he told himself, to pass out in that crush. Beer and wine fumes boiled behind his eyes. A current caught, bore him forward.

When he opened his eyes, he found himself standing at the edge of the road. A mini-van was passing in front of the crowd and through a window misted by air conditioning, an oval face looked out—a face perfectly made up, perfectly groomed, the sole concession to the Festival being a red heart stenciled on its left cheek. The mascaraed eyes seized Adrian, lifted him, weighed him indifferently, and, after a second or two, dropped him back into the anonymity of the crowd. The image was gone; the mini-van had moved on and there were other faces in other windows. Adrian felt the uneasy stir of people behind him and, hardly thinking, labeled what he had seen: the Commander's wife. Of course. They never traveled together.

He had seen her before, some time ago, when he was young and foolish and suffering from lust for a sixteen-year-old girl with luminous eyes. It was the year of the Great Flood, at the height of the monsoon season, when cloud furrows overhung the city for thirty-two days, turning the air so humid that fish jumped out of the canal murk to walk on grass. Adrian had ambled along then, with the clink of authentic wealth at his heels, wearing the mandatory jeans (Calvin Klein) and T-shirt (Lacoste) of radical chic, while five typhoons chased one another across the skies, the last one roosting over the South China Sea, between Kwangchou and Manila, lashing with her tail of rain and wind the Noble and Ever Loyal City, threatening to return it to the sea of its birth. Not to worry, his grandfather, Old Andy, had said at the time, for Adrian was still living at his namesake's villa; the city came out of chaos, lived with chaos, and would survive any chaos. The question was, cackled Old Andy, whether it could survive order and reason.

Over the destruction, like a moon of a witches' sabbath, the girl had hovered, her fragility emphasized by the sack of a uniform she wore, her powerful neck rising from the white round collar to culminate in a face of impeccable youth. She moved in a translucent light—or so it had seemed to Adrian—which held her above disaster's tragedy, above the bloated carcasses of cats and dogs and the maze of upended ice cream carts festooned with seaweed, above cars and jeepneys stuffed with mud and worms.

For her sake, Adrian painted slogans on walls, on fences, on the church belfry, and on his tennis shoes. Politics, he discovered, was simply a declaration of love. The Poor Are Hungry! His masterpiece of two-foot red letters was the only epistle of romance he would write for her and he bit into a hamburger sandwich as he surveyed his work and dreamed of her approval.

She came; she looked at the school wall; she examined him.

"Should I do another?" he asked in great humility.

"Please," she said, her lips curling, "don't strain your imagination."

Years later, Adrian would understand that her school uniform concealed a body as passionless as hamburger, that quite early in life she had gone beyond common vanity and was locked, even at that moment when he was dying of lust, in a fierce struggle to attain sainthood. His gestures of affection, extravagant though they were, could not touch her for she was a creature of despair, beatified by the pathetic shoes, moth-eaten shirts, and worn blankets that she and other students sorted out and tied into relief packages for the flood victims.

Nevertheless, in his innocence, he chased her through that geography of destruction, wrecking his jeans by wading in black waters to reach the amphibian vehicles which carried him from the sleekly wet school compound to the workers' districts where the water rose even to the rooftops of row houses and apartments, carrying a debris of existence which should not have been made public: used condoms, broken syringes, plastic tablecloths, torn pillows, muddied bedsheets, and chairs and tables that floated with the ease of boats. He helped pluck a girl off the back of her mother's corpse, which had borne her safely through the flood for six hours. He was there when the amphibians spotted a man clinging to an electric post and he was among those who beat sewer rats off his thighs. Though he cringed within himself, he had managed a smile and did not raise an eyebrow when the amphibian nosed out two boys, barely ten years old, on a roof, calmly launching toy boats of sardine cans. Finally, back in the refugee tents, Adrian had fended off, with due compassion, the lascivious offer of a nine-year-old girl, handing her instead coffee and buns. At this point, the Commander's wife had arrived, neat as a pin in her pale peach suit, and had talked to the relief workers with tears trickling down her cheeks. At the edge of the crowd, Adrian had followed an old woman beckoning mysteriously. My son, she said when he had drawn close enough, is as handsome as you are. At which, she picked up something swathed in a faded blue blanket and Adrian let out a terrific yelp at the sight of the dead cat nestled in its folds, its gray fur matted down on its tiny skull.

What grief the girl had caused him. Adrian had vaulted out of the refugee camp and, still shaking, had found his car and driven away, convinced that nothing but nothing could be done for the miserable hordes of the calamity. By the time he reached his parents' house, he was over the flood, over the girl, over politics. Moreover, he was convinced that poverty was the only way of life for a certain category of people; they would die without it—as surely as it would kill people like him. He never looked back, electing to return to the proper side of morning, though from time to time his heart would stir restlessly, would slide into despair as though mourning something valuable which had been irrevocably lost.

Lost, it had seemed, until that day of Eliza's frantic phone call and he, cursing silently and steadily, had left his office, taken his car out of the parking lot of the business district, and driven through narrow and winding streets to a nondescript apartment building. He had berated himself for having gotten mixed up with Eliza Hansen, mistress of the head of state's aide-de-camp, no matter how advantageous the relationship had been to his own finances. He had regretted it even more when he discovered that the building had no elevator and he would have to climb six flights of stairs to reach a room where Eliza's inexplicably dear, dear friend "lay dying!"—she had screamed over the phone. Adrian's mouth had twisted wryly at the thought that this same dear, dear friend was, in truth, *his* employee and what boss in this godforsaken land abandoned his office and his work to come to the rescue of one unimportant documents clerk? At that, he rattled the knob of the filthy door that bore her family name. It was locked, of course, and in a fit of anger, he let loose with a kick. The door sprang open. Something stirred on the sofa and he was walking in, his eyes on Anna who lay amidst the blankets of her fever, her long, long, long hair loose for the first time in his sight. Her eyelids fluttered open and he had found himself looking into the lost tranquility a sixteen-year-old saint had once possessed.

His knees had turned to water and he had had to sit down on the sofa edge, his hands automatically taking her hot, dry hands while his mind, for some strange reason, instantly dredged up from his store-house of memories his grandfather's tale of Magellan crossing a name-less sea in a still young world. He had seen, as he had looked into her eyes, the sea; depths beyond depths, and the tiny ships and white sails of grace moving along the rim of time. Almost without knowing it, without being aware that he was doing so, he kissed her fingertips one by one, as he told himself that this was what it meant, that to love was to regain the capacity to remember a world without names, to recall by virtue of the whorl above the beloved's knucklebones and the blue of the veins beneath the skin the unbearable fragility of mornings in this country, to find October odors trapped in the skinfolds between her toes along with the scent of talcum powder and soap and human sweat. He moved then, without willing it, helplessly, and sank himself into the swamp of her delirium, as her fever broke and her bones melted in a cold sweat that drenched him and the bedsheets, soaking his chest, his legs, his armpits so that he thought he was making love to the monsoon and was himself dissolving into a needle spray of rain and the pungence of washed leaves and cleaned tree bark in a festival to end the dry season. Sometime during that febrile day and evening when he could not leave her, he was reconciled to the impossibility of not being with her, beside her, on her, beneath her, under her, in her—if he were to remember anything at all, from the dawn when Lapu-lapu, half naked, bare feet slipping on the wet sands of Mactan, had skewered with a bamboo lance that vagabond poacher Magellan, to the day the Commander's wife showed up, impeccable and exact, at the refugee center to inaugurate an era when dead cats would masquerade as babies.

Twenty-four hours later, Anna, hair still plastered to her skull, lifted her head, shrouded his nude body with a horrified glance as he stood by the sofa holding a cup of tepid cocoa to his lips, and said: "Your parents will kill you." Her eyes rolled into her head and she fainted.

Will kill you, will kill you, will kill you . . . The drums repeated her words, delighting in their rhythm. As Adrian forced his way toward the two women, he had to admit the truth of her warning. His father's glance in the last weeks had turned shy while his mother, at his appearance, would veer away, ducking her head and pretending to croon over orchids, ferns, and imagined dust on the furniture. It was no accident, certainly, that his father had terminated abruptly a telephone conversation with some colonel when Adrian walked into his library. He shivered at the thought; he knew vaguely that Anna had been snagged in one of those eternal military raids and that her husband had perished in some accident where the military had been involved.

It was Eliza who noticed him first and nudged Anna. She turned her head and now the two watched him with heavy-lidded, almost Moorish eyes as he crossed the street, dodging a formation of warriors who marched past, brandishing spears.

"Where have you been, Lord Adrian, my son," Eliza sang out. She held a rum bottle in her free hand and, smiling at him, raised it to her lips. She drank daintily, licked her lips clean, and giggled. "Have you been to your true love, darling?"

"We're into English songs now," Anna said. She and Eliza began to sway from side to side, in time to their humming.

Adrian straddled the ledge, ignoring stray comments from the crowd. He had grown used to the reaction that Eliza's presence provoked. She was so regular of features and limbs the very air about her seemed to delight in wrapping itself about her body. She was not unaware of her effect on passersby and from time to time threw an ironic glance about her, never stopping her singing though, taking Anna into snatches of Spanish, English, and Tagalog, mixed with some mathematical language Anna seemed to understand. Her feigned indifference merely emphasized her consciousness of her beauty and was so provocative that not a few men halted their peregrination about the plaza to stare at her.

She had been that way, too, the first time he saw her, three years ago, in the resort city of Baguio. She had sat on a boulder underneath the park's pine trees and, humming, singing, had detached herself from the fury of colors and sunlight about her, and from the anger of a young man who paced back and forth before her in obvious frustration. She had raised her eyes at Adrian's appearance, smiled gently, and remained still for a moment. Then abruptly, she had risen to her feet, walked forward briskly, her right hand raised to take his arm.

"There you are," she had said, pressing against him suddenly.

Over her head, he had met the other man's eyes and had recognized him almost at the same instant he was himself recognized. Though the young man belonged to the city's wealthiest clan, it was an uneven match—and the challenge died in the other's eyes before it was even born.

That had been the beginning of a week of learning, as Eliza had locked them both in the summer house, with the fireplace in the living room spewing heat day and night, as she led him through the labyrinths of love, making him understand the extent of his aloneness. On Sunday, returning from the supermarket, he had found Julius sitting at the patio. Eliza was gone and so were certain irreplaceable bottles in the usually well-ordered shelves of his father's wine cellar.

"Holy cow, friend, you look done in," Julius had said.

They had scoured the city for replacements for the missing wine, with Julius muttering bitterly about his friend's propensity for strange women. *Strays,* he had called them. Adrian had kept quiet, himself bitter about the knowledge of how Eliza had managed to work her magic those seven days. But Julius had reason to complain for they had to steal two bottles from *his* father's wine cellar, but there was no helping it. The old man wasn't due in Baguio for another year while Adrian's father was arriving in three days. Adrian had never been mortified.

When he chanced upon her at the Hotel InterCon in Manila, he had sworn to get even. She was having a breakfast of toast, bacon and eggs, and a margarita and looked up without surprise when Adrian pulled the empty chair across the table and sat down. He had told her that she owed him five thousand pesos. Her eyebrows had lifted but she had said nothing, merely sighed, picked up her purse, slid out a checkbook, and wrote the amount in. Having signed it, she had detached the check and pushed it toward him. It was only then he realized she had known who he was from the very beginning.

"I could bill you for services rendered, of course," she had said as he had tucked the check into his shirt pocket. "Seven days, six nights . . . Uh, uh. Expensive. Tell you what. There's the matter of a drydock your family wants to build in Negros. What happens if you don't get government permission?"

His heart had skipped. "You're kidding."

"I have a friend who sits outside the Commander's office. He is a little absentminded. Once he wrapped his lunch leftovers and the national budget was lost. It took three months before they could get another copy signed—even though government was disintegrating."

"You're kidding."

But she had picked up her fork and resumed eating. Adrian had known it was over. He had drawn out the check and flicked it across the table. She had laughed then.

"Take it," she had said, her mouth curling beautifully. "Triple it for me in three months and we'll call it quits. You can do it. Stocks, money market, whatever . . . I believe in giving young men a chance." At that she had cracked up, laughing over her plate.

The drydock permit had cost his family ten percent of its capitalization. All in all, it had been an expensive week. But he had never regretted it.

"Stop dreaming," Eliza was saying now. "Wake up, wake up."

He saw that Anna was eyeing him strangely.

"We're hungry. It's noon. Even the warriors are taking a break."

He stirred himself. "We're expected at the governor's for lunch. My father and some friends . . . Well, we can walk."

The women looked at each other—quickly, warily. Then Eliza smiled and Anna nodded. They rose. Adrian untied his T-shirt and slipped it on. He led the way through the thinning crowd, down emptying streets. Along the way, all the front doors were open and faces leaned out of windows and called to strangers to enter and eat, along with impertinent requests to Adrian to share his women. Some called to Adrian by name—former schoolmates, he explained to Anna and Eliza, at which the two wondered why they found none of their former friends in the crowd. For a few minutes, Adrian expounded on the advantages of attending a Catholic school; one was able to set up a grand cabal of one's own, always a help in business and govern-ment matters. But Eliza, impatient, dug her elbow into his ribs and asked why everyone wanted to share his women and not him. She was still laughing, teasing him and asking who would give him away—she or Anna—when they reached the broad cemented road leading to the governor's palace.

At the foyer, a maid in white told them that lunch was being served upstairs, in the state dining room near the verandas. Already, they could hear ebullient male voices as they climbed the marble stairs. The crystal chandelier overhead tinkled delicately from the sea wind. Eliza muttered that she could just see herself, slinking down those steps, making her grand entrance.

A thirty-foot-long table had been set up near the wide open french windows. The governor sat at one end, presiding over the conversa-tion and the meal. Adrian saw his father and his associates, including the corporation lawyer and accountant, clustered near the governor. He scanned the rest of the crowd and could almost hear the dry chuckle his grandfather would have given at the sight. *It would seem we never had the Revolution,* the old man would have said—for among the crowd of pedigreed *mestizos,* with their imperial noses and casual arrogance, his father's Malay middle-aged man's fleshy jowls were an affront. Strangely enough, he himself had escaped the injustice of his genes; though dark brown, he had patrician features. As he introduced Eliza and Anna to the governor's social secretary, his father shot him a warning look. The men's response to the women's appearance was old gallant—they bowed to the women—while their females palpitated, waved fans, and began subtle inquiries into the two's origins and family connections. Anna, pitilessly polite, put on such naivete that Adrian was surprised though he barely kept himself from laughing when he heard her explain that, indeed, her father was an ice cream vendor and her mother took in laundry. Eliza ended the inquisition by declaring, in a loud voice, that she was a nobody and who cared, anyway; certainly not, to her knowledge, the male folk. At which she favored the governor with such a lascivious look the man stuttered.

Room was found for the women at the lower end of the table while Adrian was seated near his father. The bar, said the governor, was at the other side of the room and if it pleased the men to drink, they'd have to get it themselves. The house was short of hands because of the benighted Festival. Adrian rose and his father joined him.

As they walked to the bar, his father flung an arm about his shoulder and drew him closer.

"Why'd you bring the women?" he whispered. "We're discussing business."

"I couldn't leave them; they don't know anyone on this island."

"Don't call attention to them. That's Hansen, no? The beautiful one. She could be useful." He glanced at Anna. "But the other one . . ."

"Anna."

"Villaverde," he said firmly. "Out of place, out of place, son. Shouldn't mix your pleasures with your public life. Well, what shall we have? Gin and tonic."

Adrian considered bringing wine to Anna and Eliza and thought he'd better not. The women near the two were already fanning themselves too energetically. He asked for Archangel beer.

"I suppose she is satisfactory in a way," his father said as they made their way back to the table. "Lots of experience, I must say. Got a report from Colonel Amor. She was his—what shall we say?—his ward for a time, you know. A year, to be exact."

His father's nostrils trembled. Confused, Adrian looked away. He took a swig of the beer, his eyes on Anna through the mug's distortion. He remembered how malleable her flesh was, curving to his every curve, fitting every line of his body. He felt a sudden chill. His heart, he told himself, was breaking. For whom, over what, he didn't know. He forestalled further conversation with his father by moving to his seat.

His plate had been heaped with pieces of lechon, puchero, and rice; his coffee cup and water glass had been filled. The governor favored him with a benign smile and said it wouldn't be too bad if the Festival could be made to last the year, instead of this annual bash which drove people crazy. Perhaps the resort would help . . .

"A consortium, Excellency," said the accountant quickly, "could be set up. Government and private capital. Minimal risks for everyone. We provide the preoperation costs—studies, plans, surveys—and government loans can provide the rest."

Adrian's father leaned forward. "We have one area in mind," he said. "This section of the waterfront is almost a hundred percent public lands. They could be leased at minimal cost, perhaps a peso per hectare per year. We can build a hotel, beach cabanas, a major pier, docking for yachts and small boats. Overseas promotions will bring in tourists and there you have it: a major industry for the island."

The governor nodded.

"We'll have to dredge the sea, comb the beach, and build breakwaters. But that will be up to the board of directors, which should have representatives from both the national and local governments. At a suitable remuneration, of course, since public service is a thankless task."

"Conflict of interest, gentlemen," the governor said, "conflict of interest. We do have such a clause in the constitution or something." He sighed. "However, we don't want to seem uncooperative, especially since the national government is involved. It is involved, isn't it?"

A glance around the table. Adrian's father hesitated and then gave a curt nod. The governor sighed.

"Understand, I'm subject to public accountability," he said. "However, my eldest son is not—and he has just finished college . . ."

Smiles all around.

"We didn't mean to put you on the spot," the lawyer said most humbly. "We can only plead the benefits that will redound to the town. Modernization. Progress. Contact with the world. Employment."

"True," the governor replied, his pink lips stretching into a smile. "Half the town can go on with the Festival for the tourists. Think of that. An endless fiesta. The other half—well, we can train them to work in the hotels."

"A true cash economy for the island," said Adrian's father.

The governor laughed and a sigh of relief went around the table. Separate conversations started up again. Adrian felt his father's elbow in his ribs.

"You put me to shame, Excellency," his father was saying. "You are committing a son to the project. I shall follow your example and have Adrian on the board. Perhaps your son and my son—they are the same age, aren't they?—will learn together, become friends. Who knows? They have years, decades before them."

"Oh, indeed! The line shall go on—to our children's children. Shall we have champagne now, or are there other problems?"

"A minor matter, Excellency," the lawyer said. "We have spoken to almost all government officials and their enthusiasm has been remarkable. However, we do have to get the Commander's approval—without which, as you know, nothing else matters, enthusiasm or no enthusiasm. We have to get an appointment through his aide. A certain Colonel Alejandro Batoyan."

Adrian had to swallow his lechon quickly. He glanced in Eliza's direction but she was gone, an empty chair marking where she had been. Anna shook her head slightly, answering his unspoken question. He scanned the room, rose, and went to the windows to peer at the commotion in the front yard. She was not there. When he raised his eyes to the sea, he saw two soldiers in combat uniform strolling on the beach, their M-16s slung harmlessly over their shoulders.

3

The devil of mischief rose in Eliza as soon as she had caught the drift of the conversation at the governor's table. She had slipped away, bowing apologetically to the women about her, her expression pained and embarrassed as she muttered about "the curse." They had been quick to sympathize and had discreetly pointed toward the stairway. Away from their eyes, Eliza had inhaled deeply, thrown back her shoulders, and dashed down the marble stairs: la-di-da. She had divined that at some point Colonel Batoyan would be mentioned. She had to admire Adrian's old man. Shrewd and tough; not above manipulating his own family. He must have known that both Eliza and Anna would be with Adrian and had maneuvered his own son into bringing them here. Then, of course, when the matter of an appointment came up, Eliza would have been in a ticklish situation. The faces there would have turned to her and out of courtesy she would have had to offer to make the arrangements. It would have been impossible, of course, in that social gathering to demand payment and since Batoyan was simply inept—oh, quite inept—when it came to dealing with the rich, they would have gotten off cheaply. The nerve. Now they'd have to chase her up and down the archipelago. Or perhaps, she could disappear for two weeks in Tokyo, another two in Taiwan, a week in Hong Kong, and so on and so forth. She could decide to visit each and every island of the seven thousand one hundred while executives suffered fits and heart attacks and tore their hair off their heads—for Batoyan, forewarned, would deflect every inquiry, would evade every question, and drop her name each time. When she was good and ready, she would hit them—really hit them, the whole asinine bunch with their courtly bows and their fluttering females and their noses perpetually pointed at the horizon.

She found her way back to the plaza, which was filling up again. She was about to cross the street when a voice—low, breathy—stopped her. *What do we have here,* it said. A creature of fantasy smiled at her, one hand holding aloft a pink parasol, the other the hem of a long pink gown.

"Shall we take a *paseo?*" the transvestite asked. "You be the male. You're dressed for it; I'm not. We will saunter through the plaza. I want to be seen in the company of the Festival's most beautiful woman."

Eliza demurred as she allowed the transvestite to take her arm. "I'm not really," she said. "You're prettier." He inclined the parasol to shield both of them and pivoted on the stiletto heels of his pink shoes. She thought he was taking an awful chance; only the Commander's wife went around in matching parasol, gown, shoes, and handbag.

"Let's not quarrel," he said. "We don't belong to the same league."

Eliza laughed. "I'm hopelessly outclassed."

Cheers broke out when they crossed the street. The crowd, now pouring out of houses and side streets, seemed drunker than ever. Eliza hesitated but the transvestite pressed her arm and she had no choice except to wear a face of stone and brave the catcalls.

"There, there," the transvestite crooned. "Don't let the bullies scare you."

Indeed, a group of men came running but stopped five feet away, rocking on the balls of their feet, as though held by an invisible force. Enraged, they taunted the transvestite and clapped their hands to their crotches, their groins thrust forward. Their shouts hinted at rape and violence and pleasure—at which the transvestite rolled his eyes in mock delight, forcing the onlookers to laugh and applaud.

"They are envious," he said. "Of all that's available, you find me the most charming. An insult to the men."

"No. They're angry you find *me* acceptable—even though I do not have their equipment."

"Dear, dear. Let's make a vow never to separate."

Eliza laughed. "Someone irresistible may yet come."

The transvestite halted and placed a hand over his heart. "To you or to me? I hope we won't have to compete." He pinched her forearm delicately.

"I am really outclassed," Eliza said, laughing. From the corner of her eyes, she saw the men had not dared follow. Now, the two of them, still arm in arm, stepped over the cement hedge and faced the center lawn. The light, so amber and happy that morning, had splintered into a million razors lying among the grass blades. Eliza shrank back at the thought that the grass would flay her feet. Where was her car, her chariot, her horse? The transvestite drew her forward relentlessly.

They passed through a cloud of talcum powder squirted from plastic bottles two men held against their loins. The powder settled on their hair and clothes. Eliza found it amusing to think she had grown old in an instant.

"And what are you, my dear, outside the Festival?" the transvestite asked.

"I'm—oh, I don't know. You'd probably call me a coffee shop habitué."

"A sanitation inspector or something?"

"Something."

"Ah. Caught in a time warp like me." The transvestite twirled his parasol. "I was a professor once, I think—or don't like to think, God help me. Until the day I entered the dormitory's shower room and found this naked young man admiring himself in the mirror. Vanity killed the professor, darling. Since then I've not moved away from the shower room's twilight where I'm constantly being filled by the sweet length of that brilliant young man. I'm not really here." He laughed modestly.

"And he is with you now?"

"Oh, no. He was a shrewd young man. He made use of me the whole semester; it was his last in school. Then a week before graduation, he reported me to the rector. It was a Jesuit school, child, and so that kind of thing, though common, once it was made official, was difficult to tolerate. I was fired." He laughed. "But you have loved one of your sex?"

Her heart contracted. "Yes and no."

"Don't explain," the transvestite said quickly. "I know all the permutations of love, my darling. I love you now."

"Thank you," she said, humbled. "But I am able to love only one person. Always and constantly, from the day we discovered we were to share a room at the college dormitory. We went to the state university together."

She saw Anna at sixteen again, already deadly serious, studying the list tacked up on the lobby bulletin board, her battered suitcase in one hand, a worn leather purse slung over a shoulder. She looked so woebegone, Eliza had thought, with her loose black dress and her straight, brown-black hair falling nearly to the back of her knees. She had sized up Eliza quickly, the long, almost reddish lashes of her pale brown eyes shadowing her cheeks momentarily.

"Anna Villaverde," she had said, offering a formal handshake. "Majoring in history."

Taken aback, Eliza had shaken the small hand, noting how strong the fingers' grip was. In her circle, women kissed upon introduction— first the right, then the left cheek. She said she was taking economics, or rather would be, once she completed the first two years' general curriculum.

"I'll take you to the room. Holy cow, I haven't fixed the bed yet," Eliza added, quickly.

Anna had bent down, her right hand feeling for a black music case, and Eliza suffered her first qualms. The girl would play day and night and drive her out of her mind. But Anna picked up the case firmly and followed her to the corridor.

"What is that?" Eliza had asked, already weaving arguments in her mind to convince *this* girl to move out. She would not be able to find a roommate with that instrument.

"A saxophone."

"You play it?"

"No. It was my father's—only thing he left me, aside from my college money. He was a musician."

Eliza had exhaled with relief. "What did he die of?"

A short silence. Then Anna's voice, reluctant, careful: "I don't know. He was always away—Hong Kong, Tokyo, Taipei . . . My mother died at childbirth. So I grew up with my aunt. So. Anyway, we got a letter saying he was dead and his body would be arriving at the airport at a certain time and day. I was twelve years old. My aunt chose what clothes I would wear, what everyone should wear. We went all in black, with veils."

"Here we are." Eliza had unlocked the door and flung it open. The room was actually a small cubicle with two single beds set against opposite walls. Two study desks and two tiny bookcases formed a short partition near the windows. "You can have that," Eliza had said, pointing to the naked mattress on the iron slat bed near the built-in closet. Striding to her own bed, she had sat down and said rather indifferently: "I hope he had a nice funeral."

"I'm not sure," Anna had replied, straining as she hoisted the suitcase onto the bed. She had fiddled with the locks in silence. Suddenly, as though she had reached a decision, she had turned around to face Eliza.

"There was no corpse, really," she had said, frowning. "He had been cremated in Hong Kong. So the purser—I think it was the purser—just offered this urn to my aunt, who promptly went into shock. We're Catholics, much like everyone else and cremation was— well, it wasn't acceptable."

"Oh, boy! What happened?"

Anna had sighed. "She kept shouting for the body, to be given the body. I suppose she had prepared herself to swoon over the coffin and all that. It must have been such a disappointment. Anyhow, there was this terrific commotion and my aunt bit the purser's shoulder and he tried to shake her off and her teeth fell out. Uh, they were false. Suddenly, everyone was laughing and my aunt, to get out of it, chose to faint. We kids—we were a half-dozen or so, I and my cousins—were so mortified. My uncle tried to faint as well but we beat him to it and started dropping like flies to the floor. My uncle had to drag us out of the airport, one by one. At the last minute, the purser shoved this urn at my lap as I sat in the taxicab. Yeech. My aunt refused to accept that that was all that remained of her brother. I carried the urn home though—and she ordered me to get rid of it. I went to our backyard rose garden and took out handfuls and scattered the ashes among the roses. The urn, I kept—"

Eliza had stopped listening for she was howling with laughter, bent over by spasms of laughter as she sat on the bed. It had been the weirdest story she'd ever heard, she had told herself, seeing the kids dropping—*plonk!*—on top of the ridiculous old woman. She had howled on until she caught sight of Anna's face in the vortex of her mirth. Anna had remained standing, as though backed against a wall, her chin up, her mouth and eyes intently watching Eliza.

"I'm sorry," Eliza had said, wiping her eyes with her hands. "I couldn't help it. I didn't mean to offend—"

"Don't worry," she had answered quickly, turning to her suitcase again. "It is a funny story. Only I can't laugh. Never have." And with her back to Eliza, she had added shyly: "That's the first time I've talked about it. You're nice. I like you."

Eliza's mouth had dropped open. She was no stranger to compliments but always it had been "beautiful," "magnificent," "lovely," and so on and so forth. But nice? And from a girl who could not laugh? She couldn't help giggling again.

"It took a while before I understood," Eliza told the transvestite.

"She couldn't cry, either. Emotions froze her, made her rational. You would think she was indifferent. She'd stand there like a statue, her face a mask—but behind that, her mind was raging, pacing, tearing through one thought after another, calculating desperately."

"Some are that way," the transvestite said. "I would prefer that to extravagant displays—though, of course, you should see *me* in distress. Hey, grand opera. Would you care to dance? We could do a slow waltz under the trees."

"But there's no music."

"I'll sing," he said, facing her and raising his arms. "It will be our homage to this festival of memories."

She stepped closer to him, wrapped her right arm about his waist, and, with her left hand, made a cradle for his right hand. She led him gently, carefully; he closed his eyes and began to hum. "The Blue Danube." Eliza had to smile. They danced under the acacia tree, their feet crushing fallen leaves. She didn't know when exactly a circle formed about them—young men and women, beer bottles in hand, who merged their voices with the transvestite's humming.

"We should really be dancing the tango," the transvestite murmured, smiling happily.

She remembered how Anna had been when she had confessed finally the reason for her month-long morning sickness and afternoon lethargy. She had been so scared, she had told Anna, she would flunk biology—so scared that when the young instructor had made advances she had surrendered without precaution among the comatose snakes in the formaldehyde bottles, among the dried sea urchins and snowy exoskeletons of water creatures, under the watchful eyes of three fetuses in varying degrees of arrested development floating dreamily in their glass jars.

Failure had frightened her, she had told Anna, her tear-limned and swollen face buried in her pillow. She had seen by accident, when she was eight years old, a photograph of her mother on the front pages of one of Manila's scandal sheets because some frumpy wife had picked up a gun and shot at her while she was having dinner at the Casa Español, emptying the gun's magazine and sending the black-tied and befrocked guests diving to the floor, hitting one tuxedoed waiter, a windowpane, a flower vase, a candlestick, and the band's large drum. It had been an embarrassment so harmful to her mother's discreet but wanton profession that the woman had sent Eliza off to the Franciscan nuns and herself boarded a plane for Paris where four years later, dying in a hospital in the South of France, she had written, begging her daughter to come for a last look. The letter had been answered by a creature of desperation, on the mother superior's instructions, to the effect that she had no wish to share her mother's immoral existence. At which, the older woman had written back saying she was leaving the bulk of her estate to the Church which didn't care how it got its money and all Eliza could expect was the cost of her upkeep until she finished college, calculated to the last centavo and with allowances for inflation; furthermore, that the child should always remember that destiny was destiny, fate was fate, there was no quibbling about it, and while the nuns may have managed to give her a prim head, her own mother had given her a whore's face and a whore's body. If the child had any brains at all, the note had ended, she would realize soon enough that the last two were better capital for a woman than a rigid mind.

It had been a mother's curse, Eliza had shrieked, the first indication of its fulfillment being her inability to pass a turd of a subject like biology! So, there. Anna had said nothing, merely massaged the weeping Eliza's nape. Over the next week, Eliza would feel cold waves of rage radiating from Anna whenever she was around; she would catch the other studying her intently, as though weighing something in her mind. Perhaps, Anna would ask her to leave? But one Saturday, clutching a piece of paper in her hand, Anna had told her, as she had lain in bed cradling her miserable belly, to get dressed; they had an appointment. Anna had steered her to downtown Quiapo, to a building a stone's throw away from the cathedral, into a doctor's office where Eliza was stripped naked, slipped into a hospital gown, and taken into a room with a cold iron bed with stirrups. A doctor and a nurse, both impeccably professional, had ministered to her as Anna had stood beside the bed, holding on to her hand throughout the process. Eliza had wanted to free her hand, to let go, to free Anna, afraid that in the convulsive pain that wracked her thighs and belly, she would crack the other's fingerbones but Anna would not allow it, her fingers twisting with incredible strength at every tremor of Eliza's body. Afterward, when she was rested and normal again, Eliza had watched as Anna had counted ten-peso bills (twenty of them) onto the nurse's palm. She was thoroughly nonplussed.

Anna had never referred to the incident again, never disclosed how she had come by the information and the money. Eliza would find out by accident—first, when a girl accosted her in the dormitory shower room, asking if it were true that her roommate was in trouble and had she tried the doctor downtown; and second, at the semester's end, when the biology instructor had given her her grade (an A— could less have been expected?), snapping at the same time that he hoped her friend was satisfied and would leave him alone. It had been a good lesson, he had added, for both of them, though a little expensive for him.

Despite her silence, Anna had not forgotten. Each night, as soon as Eliza walked in, she put aside her own books and notes and demanded that Eliza tell her about her lessons and classes. Saying that since she intended to be a teacher anyway and might as well practice now, she then coached her through the intricacies of mathematics and history, sociology and literature, philosophy and physics. It had not fooled Eliza, who sought to repay her by studying indefatigably and never again getting into trouble. They remained together through the four years of their college education, moving from one dorm to another, until the very last semester when Eliza had bloomed into an authentic beauty and was corps sponsor, lantern parade queen, sorority head, and betrothed to a handsome nineteen-year-old heir of a wealthy clan. She and Anna had relaxed then, for she could coast along on the accumulated knowledge of the previous years and the ties between them loosened a little. Anna herself was "seeing," as it was said, a young man by the name of Manolo Montreal while Eliza spent one evening after another partying, dizzied by the sudden respect and adulation that came her way. She had felt then that she could afford to forget a dying old woman in the South of France. She would never be afraid again, she had told Anna on graduation night, when she had staggered home still in her fiancé's gifts of chiffon and diamonds. Anna had pursed her lips and had lain washcloths soaked in vinegar on Eliza's forehead. After a while, she had bent over Eliza, brushed away stray locks from her face, and, sitting on the bed's edge, shushed her, saying, "Eliza, my friend, my only friend, do not tempt fate by saying never. Never again this, never again that—for you can never be sure of never and that's the only thing you can be sure of. Better not to call attention to yourself, better to live like the trees, better to be merely there like the plants, with no desire except to eat, sleep, and work, have a few thoughts, a few moments of happiness, not joy but happiness, better to exist without destiny, only to exist. This is what I learned from all the books and all the lectures—the virtue of mere existence."

Eliza had burped wine fumes and laughed, teasing Anna on her dismal view of what the future held. Did she not have, had she not ever had, any wish at all, any desire? At which Anna had looked even more serious than before. "Desires do not have to be magnificent or large scale," she had said. Her voice dropped to a conspiratorial whisper. "I did make one vow—a self-aware one, on which I staked all my joys. While I was tossing handfuls of my father's ashes among the roses, I wished for, I vowed that henceforth I would have—not extravagant but decent at least—funerals for my dead." At which, folding her hands on her lap, Anna had done a remarkable thing, sobering Eliza almost instantly. She had smiled.

"Really?" The transvestite asked. But he had stopped dancing and his incredulous eyes were fixed on something behind her. Turning, Eliza found a soldier in camouflage uniform, his M-16 slung over one shoulder. He grinned and pointed at the transvestite and, without waiting for Eliza's reply, stepped forward and seized the man in the pink gown about the waist. The onlookers shifted but the soldier froze them with a look. The singing began again—reluctantly, with foreboding. Eliza pushed against the spectators until the bodies gave way and she escaped.

Back in the street, she danced arm-in-arm with a Caucasian wearing a plastic phallus over his nose, keeping time with the drums that went one-two, one-two, one-two-three. The man offered to teach her how to square dance and soon they had a dozen couples walking, hopping back and forth, bowing to one another, linking arms and shouting *hey!* She and the Caucasian drained his hip flask of scotch and threatened to brain a television crew which had trained their cameras on them. One of the dancers collapsed abruptly, scattering the square dance. She seemed to be no more than a girl and two men picked her up by the arms and legs and carried her off, nodding and laughing at the bawdy suggestions of the crowd. Eliza felt the sun leaning too heavily on her head. She walked away, thinking of Anna, of how she had been lost for six years—or maybe, it was Eliza who had been lost. For some reason, the ground beneath her heaved and she was forced to concentrate on her feet, bumping into men and women who shoved her away gently. Then a hand gripped her upper arm and steadied her. It was Adrian, drenched with sweat, his T-shirt now tied by its sleeves about his waist.

"That wasn't nice of you," he said, "not nice at all."

She focused her eyes on his face.

"What?" And burst out laughing.

"You abandoned us."

She pushed his face away. "I was bored. I am bored." Her heart contracted suddenly. "Why did we come here? What are we doing here?" she whimpered.

He shrugged. "To laugh."

"At what?"

His eyes avoided hers. "I thought Anna would like it. She had never been to a fiesta."

"But where is she?"

He shook his head. "I had to join my father and the governor in the library. When I came out, she was gone."

"I left her in your care."

"No one can take care of her." He felt in his pocket, drew out a whistle, and slipped it over her head. "Here. Whistle for her. Or for a breeze. This god-awful heat."

"Our wanton is smarting!" She placed the whistle between her lips and blew. A shrill note pierced the air. She laughed. "Don't worry. If worse comes to worst, I'll kill for her."

He was shocked. "Kill me? What ever for?"

"Go away!" she screamed in anger. "Find yourself a nice girl. You're too young. Too young. Twenty-three years old. Holy cow! I'm twenty-seven and so's Anna but we're three hundred years older than you!" She made an obscene gesture, hooked the arm of a passing stranger, and laughed. "Let's go, love," she said to the man, "find us a man to kill. Can't kill boys. Christ!"

The man grinned and pulled her into a tangle of bodies. See, he said, there are little eddies here, tiny whorls, festivals within the Festival. As they danced, making a chaos of a warrior formation, they passed groups of men and women engrossed in their own celebrations. What are we celebrating, Eliza asked the man. Life, he screamed and pranced. Death, he said, bending and arching back. He hopped to the beat of the drums, one-two-one-two-three. He rushed at her and threw his arms about her body and squeezed her. He kissed the laughter in her throat. How right, how proper, she thought, to celebrate death.

She had known at once, the morning she met Colonel Urbano Amor, that she would have to kill the man. Punch him full of holes from his armpit to his groin; slide a razor across his throat; erase his face with her fingernails. She shivered with the thought as he had talked. His voice was carefully modulated. Twilight, he had said, was never allowed in his buildings; a decree protected his domain from that nemesis.

He had offered her a tour of the compound, gallantly, showing her the light meters, the automatic switches, the computers, the electricians on patrol, the soldiers at attention even as he had pointed out the network of bulbs and lamps embedded in the walls and ceilings which provided a subtle but nevertheless pitilessly clear illumination. The whole system required vigilance and dedication, a discipline no less tenacious than that of the Albigensian fanatics exiled seventeen years in the desert, undulating their torsos in perpetual prayer.

"Do you like the explanation," he had asked, interrupting himself, his voice changing. "I had it worked out by a university professor. As his penance."

She had nodded. He was pleased.

"I don't keep prisoners," he had gone on. "Except for my staff, everyone here is—just passing through. Back to freedom or the detention centers proper. Of course, they can always be recalled."

She had cleared her throat. "No one ends up in the morgue or cemetery?"

He had made a sad face. "Always regrettable when it happens. The dead don't cower. Don't talk. Don't twitch in pain. Ah, yes; here's something interesting . . ." He had stopped before a glass window; it looked into a room filled with file cabinets. A half-dozen men were within, reading, shuffling through what seemed like documents.

"Traitors." He answered her silent question. "Oh, I shouldn't call them that. Patriots. Maybe. But the truth is a man who betrays is simply a traitor. Period. One can't have too much respect for him. Despite his help."

"No women?"

"Women, like children, can be absolute in their loyalties. Very rare indeed."

"You don't free them?"

"I could, I suppose. But after they've talked, even the world outside becomes a prison. Extremely dangerous. This is the only safe place for them. We let them stay, out of charity. We give them jobs—as consultants. We let them go over the files and write endless memos and analyses. It's all useless, of course. The files contain mostly their own confessions."

Through the glass, Eliza had studied the curiously ordinary faces. Touching the glass with his forefinger, the colonel had explained it was a one-way mirror.

"So," Eliza had said finally, "there are organisms that feed on their own waste."

"Oh, don't be contemptuous. It's charity. The data are obsolete, the men's knowledge is obsolete. If there's anything at all I've learned in my years as—well, as an expert on conspiracies—it is the living nature of resistance. It exists in a constant flux, changing, breeding, metastasizing. All information about its internal processes is rendered obsolete by revelation." He had smiled. "How do you like that explanation? It came from the same professor."

"It's really good."

"Thank you. The glass is to make sure these men do not harm the files. We have traitors' confessions in there twenty, thirty years old—and if we could find others older, we would be ecstatic. Ecstatic, I tell you."

"But why? You said the data are old and useless."

"From time to time, in the complexity of its growth, the resistance evolves into a structure similar to predecessors we have in the files. Then, it's easier to piece together its modus operandi. Not exactly the same but close enough. Of course, the traitors don't do that. We do that. For some reason, they can't seem to go beyond their experience—like they're caught in a time warp."

"You're saying it's not easy to deal with the resistance?"

"Oh, God, no. Rather, thank God, no. Otherwise, I would be bored to death and ask for a transfer."

Christ, Eliza had said to herself, an aberrant intellectual. She had smiled at him, masking her thoughts, and he had smiled back, a gold tooth glinting in the left side of his mouth. He had taken her elbow and guided her away from the window.

"There are other places here. Isolation units. The box, we call those. The interrogation room. We call that the romance room. And the sleeping cells, some of which are occupied. But you did not come for these. You want to talk about your friend. Let us go to my office."

She had let him take her to a corner room, toward the back of the building. As soon as he opened the door, a familiar scent had reached her. Brut men's cologne, she had told herself, smirking. Oh, she knew him well enough, immediately and thoroughly. Imported cologne. A frailty of those enamored with power and yet not quite so powerful. A glass-topped black desk occupied the lower end of the room.

There were three folders and a vase with a single spray of purple vanda orchids on it. Quite in character, she had thought.

She had taken the seat in front of the desk and waited for him to arrange himself in his own chair.

"As you have undoubtedly noted, I had her files brought here as soon as you mentioned you were Colonel Alejandro Batoyan's—ah, friend. The colonel is my esteemed colleague and worthy of his uniform. He holds a most sensitive position, of course, being aide-de-camp to our commander-in-chief, as well as his personal bodyguard. I envy you your—ah, friendship." He had picked up the topmost folder but let it rest, unopened, in his hand.

She had vowed that for his "ahs" she would kill him slowly. "Did the professor also—ah, devise your way of conversation?" She could not help mocking him.

His eyebrows had risen. "How sharp you are! As a matter of fact, he did. He assured me it would be most impressive. An edge of threat to a most civilized tone. He trained me himself. You are clever. Do you approve?"

She had snorted. "He must have overdosed on World War II films."

He had laughed—a truly frightening sound, midway between a squeal and a giggle. Then, his other hand had made a gesture of dismissal. "Forget the professor. He's dead, anyway." He had flicked open the folder, glanced at the contents quickly as though refreshing his memory. "You're Colonel Batoyan's friend but it doesn't say here that you are Villaverde's associate."

"We were in school together. I'd lost track of her."

"Hmm." His face had said memories had no value. "How did you find out she had been here?"

"A phone call. I assumed it had been from one of her friends. I checked and discovered it was true. Since I owed her some favors, I could not ignore the information."

"True. Otherwise, where would civilization be? Villaverde, Anna. Never used her husband's name. Twenty-five years old when . . . What's the matter?"

"She is married?"

"Was. Widowed now. Degree in history; high school teacher. Arrested on suspicion of having committed or being about to commit subversion. Stayed here one month. Turned over to detention camp. Investigation pending. Possibly implicated—oh, dear!"

"Problem?" She had leaned forward.

"An escape. Three men, two women. Manner unknown. Interesting. She befriended a man in the camp. Fellow by the name of Guevarra. I remember him. Thin, dark; black hair, black eyes. Bullet wound in the thigh, calluses on hands and feet. A field man."

"A what?"

"A warrior. Takes to the field and shoots. Not like your friend and others who hang around the city and shoot their mouths off. She was returned here for a week after the escape—but nothing." He had raised his eyes to her face. "We may come to an arrangement, I think. Since she has been processed twice, I don't think anything more could be gotten out of her."

"You trust your methods that much?" She had been unable to resist showing her disdain.

He had bristled. "Miss Hansen, you live in a world of wealth and order. We maintain that world, understand. Our ways may not be known to you but believe me, they are both scientific and necessary. You may find them strange but I can assure you, they are based on a precise knowledge of the human capacity for pain and—oh, drat! I'm speaking like the professor again."

She had to laugh.

"You have a lovely laugh," he had said. "Very classy. I wish I could have that much class. But I will stop whining. I will show you what I can't explain—at least not in my own words. That stupid professor drilled me too well. Oh, I'm happy he's dead."

His hand had groped under the desk. A few seconds later, a soldier entered and saluted.

"Take someone to the romance room," the colonel had said. "Five minutes."

"Yes, sir." The soldier had saluted again, pivoted, and left the room.

The colonel had glanced at his wristwatch. Eliza had waited in silence, wondering what charade she would witness next. Just when she was making up her mind to rise and walk away, the colonel groped under the desk again. The curtains near the door rustled, slid apart on noiseless pulleys. A glass sheet was embedded in the wall, allowing a view of the next room. Sterile tiles, metal instruments on the shelves, black boxes, wires, and a metal bed on wheels. An emergency room, she had thought.

Four men walked in. Three were bare-chested; the fourth was naked. As Eliza realized what she was about to see, the colonel left his seat behind the desk and moved to the sofa. By shifting his eyes, he could watch both the other room and her face.

"But he is so young," she had blurted out, peering at the fourth man's face as the others began their work. "He is only a child." By then, she had known enough to know that that was the only protest she could make.

"As I told you, children can be dangerous."

Fifteen minutes later, when the first spatter of blood and urine stained the room's tiles, Eliza had looked at the colonel.

"Enough," she had said. "Stop it now, please." She had found the strength to say it gently, seeing Anna in that room. She had wondered then whether Anna had felt that same terrible nausea and anger during the abortion.

Colonel Amor had inclined his head in agreement. He walked to the desk and, a few seconds later, the curtains were drawing close. She had had no way of knowing whether the session in the romance room had gone on.

"To resist such methods . . ." The colonel had sighed. "I am therefore inclined to believe in your friend's—innocence? No, ignorance. We will reach an agreement."

Despite that, it had taken three more months before the colonel called. He said Anna could be fetched from the detention center now, this minute. She had jumped into her Mercedes-Benz, not even

combing her hair, and had heel-and-toed on accelerator and brakes
through the traffic, all the way across the city to the suburbs. She had
congratulated herself for having taken all the necessary precautions to
ease her friend back to normal life: a furnished apartment, cheap
enough so Anna could pay for it; a job in one of Adrian's minor
corporations.

The reception area, a gray cage stuck close to the barbed-wire
fence, was manned by a lieutenant convulsed with irony. Well, well,
well, he had said, here we are, Miss Hansen; here is Anna Villaverde,
safe and sound and ready to go home.

And there she was, indeed—standing in a corner of that unspeak-
ably pitiful room, her three paper bags of clothes gathered about her
feet, a wire hanger or two sticking out of one bag and snagging the
hem of her skirt while she turned wary eyes at Eliza, wary in a face
so blank that Eliza's heart contracted.

Eliza had taken her hand, led her out of that room, out of the
barbed wires and gray walls, and, once near the white car that seemed
to become a chariot of liberation, she had surrendered to her impulse
and thrown her arms about Anna, causing her to drop her bags and
spill the paraphernalia of her imprisonment: dresses and slippers, soap
and toothpaste, a washcloth . . .

"I moved the very day I received your friend's call," Eliza had
whispered hurriedly, her voice breaking. "But it couldn't be done
sooner."

Anna had raised her head and peered into her eyes. "What call?"
she had said. "What friend?"

The cold truth of it had seized Eliza then. She had had to lean
against the car door. The infernal Amor, he whom the outside world
called the Loved One, had known about her and Anna, had indeed
made the call himself and was after something that Eliza had, something she valued.

She would have to kill him—certainly, no doubt about it, she said
aloud and to confirm this bit of wisdom, she looked at her dance
partner. But he was gone; she had lost him. Instead, a soldier stood
before her, awkward in his combat uniform and heavy boots, his M-16

banging against his knee. He grinned. "You and I will do so, my love," he said in a sepulchral voice. He jumped; his fingers raked the sky. "You and me. Bang. You and me both. Bang." He pranced around her, his knees jerking almost to his chest. "You and me!" he shouted. "Bang! Bang! Bang!"

4

"*Message,*" Rafael said, panting as he ran beside Anna. She had to detach herself from a circle of six dancing women, bidding them good-bye with a hand wave. She whirled with Rafael, pretending to dance.

"Pest!" she said. "We were trying for a record. We'd gone six times around the plaza, nonstop."

"Fuck the Festival. It's insane. What do you think *I* was doing when the message came? It wasn't even for *me!* But for you! For you!"

"All right, all right," she said quickly. "This thing's getting to us. Where do we go?"

With his chin, he indicated an alley. Swiftly, they walked away from the crowd, stopping first at a corner store where Rafael bought a Coke. He was dying of thirst, he said, and had been offered nothing but Archangel beer and gin. "The biggest cash crop for a nation of alcoholics," he added wryly. "Want one?"

She shook her head. "And what were you doing?"

"Flirting with a transvestite." He grinned. "We've lost our minds. Remind me never to go to another fiesta." He paid for the Coke, took a big swig, and resumed walking.

She trotted at his heels. "The message, the message."

"Will need time," he said. "Time. Come." He pointed now at the end of the road. It was the beach—a rough section of it, the sand studded with pebbles and bits of coral. "Should dissuade anyone from trying to listen," he said. "Also the surf's loud. You'll be sorry you refused a Coke. National drink, this one."

When they reached the sand, he squatted down.

"He wants the rest of the story," he said without preamble. "You promised him. Tale for tale. I don't know why he's so interested. I find it boring."

"What about his? I haven't received anything."

Rafael shoved a hand into his T-shirt, brought out a plastic-wrapped package. "Two tapes," he said. "In code. His voice. You're such trouble. History, you say; history. *Leche!* You keep one eye on history, one eye on your enemy, and you get wall-eyed. You are the pest. Come, give."

She was unperturbed, knowing his roughness was a mask. She crossed her legs, placed an elbow on a knee, leaned her chin on her hand. "How come he gets to tape his story," she asked, "and I have to tell you mine?"

"Because he doesn't want me to know his," he replied. "I don't know why not. If he could trust you with it— In any case, I have eidetic memory. And would probably never talk. Also, you don't have to work with him; I do. And your tale is harmless while his— Will you tell me someday? When everything is over? Or half over? Or before I die?"

Anna laughed. "I promise. What can be told of it."

"He saved my life once," Rafael said. "Now, give. I have to spew details into his ears, about your late husband, especially—if we are to find out what happened to him."

"His favorite word was *amazing,*" Anna said.

"You think he called himself Commander Amazing?" Rafael asked. "Don't laugh. The underground has had weirder names."

"Pest! Stop kidding. He said it over and over again, that time at Recto Avenue, and he would go on saying it through that year, the year when everything happened." She shifted her eyes to the sea, inhaled, saw him again—a slight young man with black button-eyes. It had been an amazing year, she thought; by mid-morning of the day following the massacre at Recto, the first handful of hibiscus flowers had floated down to the street still littered with glass shards and oil and blood and the burned frames of buses. By that time, it had become known that twenty-seven students, three teachers, one worker, and an ice cream cart man had been killed and that nearby hospitals and clinics were clogged with the wounded. The hibiscus were followed by pink *cadena de amor* flowers, by daisies and lilies, by bougainvillea and a few luxurious red roses . . . Wreaths, bouquets, single blossoms came flying out of bus windows, jeepney windows, car windows, apartment windows, turning the cement road into a flowered carpet in memory and in defiance.

Manolo, watching the metamorphosis on television, said once again: *but it is amazing . . .* For days afterward, he went around with a holiday air. Later, Anna was to find out that he had gathered his friends, all science teachers, and had set up a Committee which had declared war on the Seven Pernicious Crimes: Arrogance, Banality, Corruption, Exploitation, Falsehood, Ignorance, and Nepotism. The Committee's founding ceremonies had included a chanting of Einstein's relativity equation and an oath never to surrender, come hell or high water. "Nothing," said Manolo, "could be more serious than E equals mc squared!" And when Anna taxed him with the foreboding in her heart, he had explained: "This way, I can show what I'm made of. Otherwise, I will be a physics instructor all my life. Now, I have a good chance of being department head. Think of that!"

Seeing him in the midst of a crowd, speaking into microphones, standing atop empty oil drums or van roofs, Anna could only shake her head. "Of all the bad luck in the world," she muttered once, "I had to marry a rabble-rouser."

He was happy. And seeing him happy, she laid a quieting finger on the worm of foreboding in her heart. In the first place, he made light of her fears, laughing and reminding her of how he had been in college. "I had no money," he said, "remember? I was poor. I had a tiny scholarship, half of which I sent to my parents. Remember? And remember my hydroponic garden in the dorm bathroom? I survived on that for four years! And remember all that fresh salad I fed you. You married me for the greenest lettuce you ever had, for the juiciest tomatoes, for . . ." She waved him to silence. She had married him for his nickname: Manolo, the Survivor. The other students had called him that and he had seemed to her indestructible, the kind of man who would be with her forever. And she had been alone all her life. "Don't worry," he said, resenting her silence. "If anything happens, you can always have a funeral for me." At which, most gravely, she looked him full in the face and said: "You will have that at the very least."

To herself, she said they were still young, that his current fancy with politics would pass, that the keel of their marriage would right itself again for a smooth, unremarked passage through the rituals of life—weddings, baptisms, fiestas, and funerals. It was a story she had woven for herself, this simple narrative—one which could not be found in her history books with their tales of epic battles and complex colonizations, of galleons and cannons, and the walls of Intramuros which had so drained Spain's treasury that the King, *El Rey,* had demanded to see their shadow over Madrid, of the strangers from across a turbulent ocean called the Pacific who had broken through the barricade of typhoons into a young world which had names only for virtue and none for property.

She had elected to ignore the warning printed in each page of her books, trusting instead in Manolo's invulnerability. It seemed indeed that he had read the times correctly, for disorder was becoming general over the land and his name began to appear, more and more often, in handbills announcing this or that symposium, in news reports and magazines, for the Committee had managed to calculate the rate of profit of various corporations—including those of oil—at every stage of the manufacturing process and had proven miraculously that prices everywhere should have been going down, not up. The Committee was hailed as the new center of the intelligentsia, leaders of a coming rational and scientific age, and there was a lot of talk about development and equality and so on and so forth. Once, she and Manolo awoke to find a man standing at the foot of their bed—a man holding his black hood in deference, a bloated jusi sack snuggled against his legs.

"Don't be alarmed," the man said, "I'm not a thief. That is—I am, but I'm not stealing from you. I came to give you something."

It seemed that someone had broken into the Securities and Exchange Commission and had hauled off a sackload of documents, thinking they could be sold. But it was no go; they were only paper—signed and stamped, sure, but of no value. The King of Thieves, for there was one, had gotten interested, had looked over the documents and struggled with their English and figures and names, and, in exasperation, had decided to send them to Manolo Montreal who was, at that instant when the King was agonizing over his decision, a guest on a television talk show. The King had caught sight of his face and had pointed his beautiful pliant forefinger at the television screen and said that was him, yes, certainly; Manolo was the one. Henceforth, the man said, all Manolo had to do was sort of say something in public like "I wonder what's going on at such-and-such an office" and the King would send someone to jimmy locks and cart away the documents. Because, the man had said, there was no helping it; we were all in this thing together, having only one country and nowhere else to go.

The thieves turned out to be a rich lode. Manolo dug into the papers and read and read and read. "I shall die here," he told Anna once, "buried underneath these papers and still not be through." After sorting out the documents, he took them to his Committee which promptly set up a research-and-study group of some fifty students who, after thirty days, unveiled an awesome chart of interlinked corporate executive boards, all controlled by a dozen men and women, all relatives of the Commander's wife. "Holy shit," Manolo murmured, "from steel to coconuts!"

Anna, terrified, stared at the chart. "You can't go public with that."

"It is not the worst," Manolo said, his voice sad for sackloads of documents had appeared every day at their back door since the thief's visit. "They've worked out an even bigger chart—from housing subdivisions to gin. And the fifty families who control everything and anything are shown to be interrelated, by blood or marriage. They have been since the turn of the century. The whole population serves one gigantic clan."

Anna dropped her face into her hands. Two days after the publication of the first chart, the Committee and practically everyone they knew were on the run. Manolo was not at home when *they* came: two jeeploads of soldiers, bristling with M-16s, sidearms, and even a grenade launcher. Stomping through their house, they smashed all the crockery, ripped up chair seats and the sofa, fractured all the lamps, and trampled books and papers underfoot.

When Manolo arrived, he found Anna bundling together three pairs of pants, five T-shirts, two changes of underwear, three physics books, and all the money in the house. Tears streamed down Manolo's cheeks as he tried to piece together their first-ever conjugal property— a cheap, clay vase.

"It's embarrassing," he finally admitted, dumping the clay shards into a trash can. "They only found things to destroy, nothing to steal. It's terrible to be poor."

"They will be back," she said, handing him the bundle. "Go. They said that in a list of five thousand names, yours had only two digits."

"Really?" He was flattered.

Outside, a jeep waited. Anna kept her eyes away from the driver and offered her cheek to Manolo's kiss. He leaned over her, pulled her close, and whispered.

"Take this," he said hurriedly, thrusting a piece of paper into her hand. "Memorize it. Never give it to anyone. If anyone should have need for armaments—oh, no more. Just guard it well. Let no one have it."

She closed her eyes. "Never," she said, bitterly. "Don't take a field wife."

He kissed her then. "My Anna. My quiet Anna. I will see you soon."

Liar, liar. How could a man be so terrible? When the jeep was gone, she took out the piece of paper and committed the Hong Kong address to memory. She tore the paper crosswise, lengthwise, burned half in an ashtray, the other in a bonfire in the backyard. Liar.

Oh but *they* were so stupid, she would whisper to his memory, so stupid indeed that it took them weeks before they realized what the one thing of value in the house was. When they returned, they had to step carefully over the relics of the destruction they had wrought for she had refused to clean the house again, deeming it already lost. Everything was lost. Schools were closed; radio and television stations were shut down; there were no newspapers. The house was lost, for the bank foreclosed on their mortgage. There was only the constant news of arrests and more arrests, more and more each day.

She was standing in the living room that twilight, wishing she could cry, when the front door's hinges snapped apart under a blow. *They* had poured in even as the world became translucent to her eyes and she had the feeling that her hand would have gone through the sofa's back had she dared touch it. Still calm, wondering why the objects about her had turned opaque, she watched them pour in through a door half-hanging off its hinges. They split into two streams of dark green and brown patches and hard black lines—a pair of horns, it seemed, that stretched and stretched until its ends reached her, had drawn close to her. At that instant, she lifted a hand to touch the sofa, to see whether her fingers would go through the upholstery and the wood but something dark and hard clamped down on her wrist and when she looked, she saw a man's hand holding her, the fingers bony and brown from too much sun. She did not scream.

They took her to Colonel Urbano Amor. He had her sit on the sofa, had a silver coffee service brought in and placed on the low table, and urged her to help herself. It was going to be a long night. She dutifully poured herself a cup of coffee, mixed in milk and sugar, raised cup and saucer, and leaned back on the sofa. As she was taking her first sip, Colonel Amor rose to his feet, towering over her, and dropped on the silver tray a dozen black-and-white photographs. Oh, Jesus, Manolo looked like a poor rabbit. A poor rabbit with his innards hanging out. The coffee spilled over her hands, her wrists to her lap and through her skirt to her thighs and she was grateful the liquid was so very, very hot.

It wasn't her fault, she tried to tell the Loved One, not hers, not Manolo's. Not theirs at all that the world chose to crack up just when she had thought everything had been settled.

"Did you really know him?" Colonel Amor asked.

"Quite," she said, cursing herself for not having the wisdom of Peter who had denied Christ three times.

"You didn't go with him." His tone was accusatory.

"I wasn't invited."

"Did you say you wanted to go?"

"No."

"Nothing more was said?"

"He said good-bye."

"Just like that. No promises of return. No way of getting in touch? Of communicating? No meeting places? No names?"

"There was no time. For anything."

"I wish you would stop lying," he said sadly. "I really wish you would. After all, he's dead. Dead."

"Can I have his body?"

"Bah, who cares about bodies? His body!" His right hand waved a dismissal. "Left to rot somewhere. Probably. I don't concern myself with the dead. Bodies. Pah! Carcass, you mean. Stinking, putrefying carcass. Look at the photographs. They are the truth, the reality."

"Can I have them?"

"No. But tell me what he wanted."

She thought for a moment. "He wanted—he wanted to give his people hope." Her voice broke.

Ah, the colonel said, that was a mistake. A mistake. Hope was too painful, too painful, for anyone. That was an error. Thus, properly sympathetic, he turned her over to two soldiers who stripped her carefully, attached electrodes to her nipples, and proceeded to crank a field battery to life. The current of pain stenciled the meaning of error into her cells. Screaming, arching her back and head in a parody of passion, Anna could see the tiny letters on the canvas sheath of the generator. It was an imported piece of equipment, blue seal as they would say, made in the U.S.A. A continent half a world away. Someone, she thought, must have made a joke because she could hear laughter bubbling through her screams.

Days, nights, disparate images. The lieutenant with the smelly armpits who subjected her to odoriferous love for who knew how many times and for how long. The fake doctor with his syringes. Pain was better. Blows, slaps, kicks. Cigarette burns. Her hair wrapped about some man's hand and pulled again and again. But pain was better. Better than the lieutenant; better even than the Loved One's questions—the interminable questioning in his office during which, like an automaton, she would spill things on herself: sheaves of paper, Coke or coffee, glass of water . . . It drove the colonel wild but, at the same time, a strange expression would dawn on his face until, finally, he asked if she was trying to baptize herself all over again. No, she had replied, truthfully enough; her body was anticipating the spill of her blood. Back to the romance room for lying, he stormed. He could not bear to be lied to. Sometime during those terrible hours she learned to create a sinkhole in her head—a sinkhole that swallowed her tears and her screams. Toward the end, the most terrible of pain would only set her sighing. But pain was better—better than the Loved One's prying and asking and peering into her life and Manolo's life, sifting through every minute, every second, of their existence. It was exquisite rape, the colonel admitted when she told him this truth; unlike his men, he preferred to fuck the soul. After that, Anna let the sinkhole swallow her words as well. She only sighed and sighed and sighed.

There was no helping it. She had to be turned over to the detention center proper. She was handcuffed, shoved into a jeep, and driven outside the city to a fenced stretch of land where long, low buildings stood. To call it the detention center was a joke, she found out; it was

the stockade where errant soldiers had been kept. Barbed wires and
gray walls; iron bars and dim rooms. Cool interiors. She gathered what
clothes she had managed to bring and hobbled to her assigned bunk
in a room of forty women. She did not look at anyone and when a
doctor appeared, distributing vitamin pills—Lord, he wanted the
prisoners healthy—she asked for a checkup. He gave her an incredulous look but he was a fat and kindly fellow and, three days later, he
took her to the clinic next door, escorted of course by three heavily
armed guards. He cleaned her, tested her, treated her burns, douched
her, counted out pills into her palm, and said she had suffered no
permanent damage. She was glad, she said; she wanted to survive. She
thanked him and he looked away, his eyes ashamed.

After a month, the doctor stopped his visits. She was grateful she
had forced him and herself to go through that. Now, she could settle
back in peace and wait out the days. The weeks. The months.

Days before *his* appearance, the center had hummed with stories
about a man who had drawn the line with the very first question the
Loved One asked. He had forced a life-and-death struggle over his
name—only his name, which Colonel Armor wanted simply to keep
his files in order. Guevarra—for that was how he was known—simply
said "Guevarra" and, like a moronic parrot, had repeated that over
and over again, maybe a hundred thousand times. The Loved One,
said the rumor, was livid, stomping and yelling that Che was dead,
who the shit was this man trying to fool? Anna, listening to the story,
could only admire the man's wisdom. In the Loved One's domain
where there were no rules and the only limits were imposed by the
torturers' sweet satiation, it was easy to go from one answer to another, from compromise to compromise until betrayal was total. From
one's name to others' names—it could be a short leap. But the man
had remained silent, even when Colonel Amor had had the camp
doctor dig out the bullet in his thigh without anesthesia.

When she saw him that day, coming into the mess room, carrying
overhead a ridiculous cot and stopping by the guard so he could be
untied from the stupid piece of furniture, she thought she was young
again. He would remain tied to the cot for another month more,

subject to the indignity of having to carry the thing around if he wished to move, to have his pants unzipped by the guards, his private parts laid open to view, each time he had to go to the toilet. But he never missed a meal, though the others offered to smuggle the food to him. Sometimes, as they ate, Anna would see him looking at her over the bowed heads of his companions and she would stare back with flat eyes, unwilling to let him see the hope she felt. Colonel Amor had been right about that; hope was painful.

Summer was ending when the Commander, by a strange quirk, suddenly decreed the nobility of work, of labor, and the prison inmates were gathered in the mess room one afternoon. The officer-in-charge said that, by the grace of the commander-in-chief who made the sun rise and the roosters crow, the back gates would be opened and the two hundred or so inmates of this center—as in all other centers—would spend three hours each day cultivating a rose garden, if they wanted to, so long as they were engaged in noble work.

The Commander's Day of the Dignity of Labor did not begin auspiciously. The inmates, ordered to form two lines before the back gates, found themselves snaking through the corridor to the mess room, past the lavatories, the cells, and even to the building's front gates. The soldiers paid no attention to their protests and issued them plastic garden tools, nothing with a keen edge to it, as they passed one by one to the backyard.

Sunshine. She had to blink. She could have sworn her clothes steamed with six months of dampness and that baby spiders scurried out of her hair. Around her, there was a muffled noise of joy as the inmates scattered like children. She scanned the yard. Her eyes were halted by fifteen-foot adobe walls festooned with barbed wires. She saw the guard towers; she forced herself to turn away, to look at the sunlight, the earth, and the impeccable green of grass. She would survive, she told herself; she had to. She had a burial to carry out.

She chose the most inhospitable spot in the yard, thinking the thick cogon would shield her solitude. Squatting like a peasant woman, her skirt tucked between her knees, she wielded the trowel they had given her. She would clear the ground for her garden. But it seemed futile;

though she whipped the trowel back and forth, the cogon merely bent beneath her blows and the scars she inflicted on the earth were shallow. After a while, as the sun touched her nape, she found herself hugging her knees, shielding her face with her hands, and crying. The tears came and ran down her cheeks though she made no sound and did not even feel like weeping.

A rustling in the grass. She uncoiled swiftly and raised the trowel but the man's voice warned her. He had lifted his hands to protect himself and she saw raw wounds on old scars where the ropes had flayed the skin repeatedly. She lowered the trowel and said the first thing that came to her mind and in a tone she would use with a student, a slightly nagging maternal tone: "You should paint those cuts with iodine." The next instant, she realized who he was and her tongue stuck to her palate.

"Why are you crying?" he asked.

She shook her head. "Not crying. Just tears. Nobody weeps here."

He was puzzled. "Why not?"

She could not answer. Her body was being shaken by tremors of happiness. Looking at his face, she found again the hope she thought she had lost forever that day Colonel Amor had said: "He's dead." In the silence, his face rippled. Was he blushing? She realized her own face had said too much.

That was how it was. She could no longer remember when exactly they started to speak to each other. But she could recall vividly the day her trowel struck something in the ground, something so unyielding that the tool had almost flown out of her hand. Guevarra, she called out and he was there, his fingers rooting at the soil with knowledge. It was a drainpipe. Their eyes raced along the ground, tracing its possible subterranean route, through the yard, under the seed beds, past the tomato plots, to the edge of the wall and underneath. Hallelujah!

A month later, two men, three women, and Guevarra picked the locks of their respective cells, broke the chains wrapped about the back gates' bars, and slipped into the night of All Souls' Day while a typhoon hovered at the edge of the city and the damp air sent candlelights sputtering in the town of the dead. They merged with the crowd, which preferred to face the dangers of the weather rather than the anger of the departed, and moved swiftly through what looked like a field of fallen stars. A limousine picked them up at the cemetery's parking lot and drove them through the camp's barriers. Only one of them returned—a labor organizer who had been betrayed by her brother. He had thought it better that she serve her time, so to speak, though she had had neither trial nor sentence. Later, when he found out what happened to her, he ran amuck, killing three policemen with a machete before the entire force of the Northern Police Command gunned him down.

It took eight hours for his sister to die. Her moans and delirium and the sight of her blood and matted hair and her nailless fingers and toes drove the women in their cells to lunatic rage and hysteria—for the soldiers had dumped her without ceremony on the corridor floor. That was not as bad as the flies and her odor, three days after her death, when *they* refused to remove her corpse, the flies, dear God, the restless specks crawling over eyes, noses, mouths, breasts, pillows, bedsheets, the walls, while Anna hammered four food trays marked *Made in U.S.A.* bang against the floor one after another, discarded the twisted and bent in favor of an intact one as the others tore their pillows and mattresses open, smashed basins, and hurled spoons and forks, icons and rosaries or simply kicked the walls, banged on the walls with their fists or their heads—doing anything at all, anything to escape that smell.

That same day saw the rebirth of Guevarra who, in his twisting retreat toward his mountain stronghold, demolished three military outposts, crashed through half a dozen barricades of patrol jeeps, and left a trail of uniformed corpses smoldering in the aftermath of grenade explosions. He did not forget. Somehow a letter reached the camp commander, appearing mysteriously atop the man's office desk. His life was forfeit, Guevarra wrote, if the officer failed to have the corpse removed and buried within four hours after receiving the note. The colonel had turned as gray as the ash of his cigars; there had been a terrible row, as intelligence men arrived to interrogate his own soldiers, but the corpse had been taken away.

Truly, Guevarra was magnificent. All the inmates said that as they sewed their pillows and mattresses, bedsheets and towels, and gathered once more in the mess room now free of flies. Anna, of course, was taken once again to Colonel Urbano Amor who, this time, contented himself with questioning her and not letting her sleep for days on end. But they both knew it was an exercise in futility; she would not tell him anything, not even how she had thrown a fit for days when the prisoners' committee had decided she could take the chance, she would be left behind. How she had railed at Guevarra, for it was she who had found the drainpipe after all; it was hers. She threatened to escape on her own, relenting only when Guevarra promised to find out what had happened to Manolo and promised as well, when she went on sulking, that he would tell her one day the most fascinating story she would ever hear.

"Satisfy my curiosity," Amor had said once. "What is his name? It can't harm him; he's escaped."

Anna had nearly laughed. "Guevarra."

A foul word exploded from the colonel's mouth. "His real name!"

"Where did Manolo die? How did he die?" She looked at him flatly. "Where is his body? Name a province, just a province. I will look for it myself."

He cursed again. "Are you proposing a trade-off? What is his name?"

"Guevarra," she said sadly. It was such an ordinary Spanish name.

The colonel had given up. She was returned to the center and there whiled away the weeks with learning how to sew for the guards abruptly ended the campaign to dignify labor and all the vegetable seedlings in the backyard died of thirst. She went on as before, jealous of her solitude, resisting the efforts of the others to draw her into prayer circles, discussion circles, knitting circles. When the others were occupied, she would lay out a game of solitaire and plan and plan again how she would find him, how she would force *them* to tell her where he was. Then, she would bury him—simply, quietly—and thus establish her connection to the earth, this earth, into which she would descend happily at the end of, hopefully, a short and quiet life, God help her despair. And shuffling the cards, laying them atop one another, turning them over, she thought of what she would need outside, what would be needed to see to her plans, and reading the signs from the cards she created a mask, her other Anna, and worked on it, giving it all the virtues required to survive.

She used the mask to hide what she felt when the guard came with the news that she was to be released. It hid well her surprise and confusion when Eliza Hansen, still the beautiful creature she had known years ago, walked into the receiving room. And it hid her anger at the hitch in her plans when Eliza first took her to the apartment she had reserved in Anna's name and then insisted that she see a certain Adrian Banyaga.

When Eliza asked about her husband, Anna saw that she had forgotten Manolo. She sighed with relief; she would not have to share his memory.

"Didn't he leave you anything at all?" Eliza demanded.

"No. He died suddenly."

"Young?"

"Twenty-seven? No, twenty-eight."

Surprisingly, Eliza echoed her words. "Ah, what a rabbit. What did he die of?"

"Forty-two bullets, I think."

"What a rabbit." And there the matter had rested.

5

A phalanx of young men, legs scissoring, arms on one another's shoulders, scattered the crowd near the Town Hall. *Hala, bira! Hala, bira! Hala, bira! Hala, bira!* On the sidewalk, a band of women ran alongside, one or two breaking off from time to time to dart across the street, daring the men to trample them underfoot. "Off, off," the young men shouted in harmony, footfalls marking time, "get off the road! We'll crush you! Hey! Smash you! Hey! Slam into you!" Safe on the other sidewalk, the girl-women fanned themselves with their fingers, chirped their excitement, and chased after the men, dodging and slipping through the crowd.

Sweat streamed down Adrian's face, his chest, as, held by the vise of the next man's arm, he marched along. He caught a glimpse of Eliza sitting at the sidewalk edge, her mouth open with laughter. Faces—young and old; brown, golden, and fair—swirled past him; the sky itself, blue with a relentless white blur of heat for a sun, seemed to pivot on its axis. Waves of masculine odor rose about him and he raised his voice happily, roaring with the men. *Off, off . . .*

Someone grabbed at his free arm. Adrian ignored the hand; lifting his knees, he tried to tear himself away but the man was already keeping pace with the group, his fingers tight about Adrian's arm.

"Your father wants you," Julius's voice reached him. From the corner of an eye, Adrian saw his friend's face flushed with the heat.

"Your grandfather called," Julius went on, panting slightly.

Smash you, crush you, slam into you . . .

"I'm having fun!" Adrian yelled above the noise.

Julius hung fire for a moment. The group passed the road's midpoint; now, the church hulked on the horizon.

Smash you . . .

"You could call your grandfather," Julius said.

Off, off the road . . .

"You are a pest," Adrian said. "We're trying to set a record: six hours nonstop about the plaza."

Crush you . . . !

"There's a telephone at the shipping line's office."

"Oh—!" Reluctantly, Adrian pulled away his arm, dropped out of the parade, and, to the women's taunts, followed Julius through the crowd.

"It took a while to find you," Julius said, stopping to regain his breath.

Adrian exhaled in exasperation. "I can't even be away from the family for three days," he said.

"Your grandfather's not feeling well."

Adrian snorted. Old Andy, after whom he was named, hadn't felt well in twenty years. Maybe, more. No one knew exactly how old he was or how his mind worked. He was already a wizened monkey in a wheelchair when Adrian, at ten years of age, went to live with him. It had seemed a perfect arrangement; he was the only grandson and his own parents were busy with overseeing the expansion of their various businesses. The old man, on the other hand, lived by himself in a mansion on ten acres of prime real estate, in an exclusive millionaires' housing subdivision.

But no one could have prepared Adrian for the confusion of Old Andy's house, with its labyrinths and corridors, its cavernous library, art and collection rooms, and the forty-two servants who exercised the half-dozen horses in the grounds stable by riding them and dashing through fruit trees, jasmine vines, and gardenia bushes. The *clip-clop* of horses' hooves had gone on interminably during his first weeks in the mansion. After some time, though, he divined that a mad sort of schedule kept the household operating.

Here, grandfather was simply Old Andy to visitors, servants, and family members alike. He had been called "old so-and-so," he assured Adrian when the latter had demurred, since he was fourteen or fifteen or even older—who the hell cared?—when he ran away from an orphanage in Bulacan, after painting Spanish cuss words in turd on the convent walls. He hoped the Castilian nuns had been properly scandalized. In any case, he was still "old so-and-so" when he surfaced at the Parian, the Chinese district in Binondo and hired himself out to a melancholy celestial as a used bottle collector and buyer. "Old so-and-so!" the young maids of Intramuros would call out from the wrought-iron balconies of their masters' houses. Being farm girls conscripted from plantations around Manila, their thighs were plump with the sun's sap—a virtue they made sure *he* noticed by lifting their skirts and pretending to fan their lower limbs, moving their petticoats to and fro. Old Andy would curse beneath his breath; he knew that they knew that for him to swing up the trellis vines for the balcony without the owner's permission was certain death.

"I was poor then," Old Andy said to the discomfitted Adrian, chuckling. "And since you're rich now, you should never neglect women, when you're the proper age."

He'd picked up "Andy," on the other hand, from another master, a *norte americano* who had swum into Manila in the wake of Commodore George Dewey's flagship, that vessel of war which surprised the Spanish armada as it lay hallucinating at the mouth of the bay of sunsets. With merciless efficiency and paying no respect to daydreams, the American commodore had riddled the ships full of holes, thus ending a war begun in Cuba. The Castilians surrendered the city and sold the entire archipelago, all seven thousand one hundred islands, for twenty million dollars. Or to put it crudely, the Americans paid two silver dollars for each native head, considering the islands' population at the time. The "monkeys without tails," as the *indios* were referred to mockingly, already skittish with thoughts of revolution and independence, turned pale at this terrible insult and threw themselves into a suicidal war, though the last one was not over yet, and in the amber afternoons, towns sank into silence as all the males disappeared into the hills and the women began a strange set of calisthenics: squat, stand, squat, stand.

Old Andy guffawed. "It was to stretch their vulvas," he had hollered while Adrian's eyes widened. "They thought that way they could survive rape by the *americanos* who were rumored to have penises as huge as their noses."

The new invaders, of course, could not quite understand why anyone would object to being benevolently assimilated by the great North American nation and sent half of its army to the archipelago, scattering them among the islands. Their presence bred corpses: corpses in the streets, on rooftops, hanging from coconut trees—for by the glory of God, the *americanos* dealt with the insurrection with great efficiency, torching villages and shoving two hundred fifty thousand corpses into mile-long graves, both men and women, for though the latter did survive rape, they could not survive the shame and committed suicide by the hundreds, opening their bodies from the throat to the groin with six-inch butterfly knives of the truest steel, or climbing to the roof and the church belfry to hurl themselves to death in the streets below as the hooves of the American cavalry slipped on the pungent mud of earth, brains, and blood for so many women killed themselves the air seemed filled with monstrous bats shrieking all the way down from the clouds to the ground.

"I was safe, though," Old Andy had told Adrian. "I stood by the side of my dyspeptic master and fanned his pink scalp with an anahaw leaf as he sent guerrillas, my unlucky compatriots, to the hanging scaffold and to exile in Guam. My master called me Andy, short for

Adrian—which is why you must never, never allow yourself to be called anything else but Adrian. It is bad luck to allow strangers to tamper with your name. If you want to change it, find a new one yourself."

And deeming Adrian sufficiently educated, Old Andy had let him have the run of the mansion though, in the end, because the old man was given to sudden monologues inspired by scraps of memory, the child preferred to play near the wheelchair, the drone of a quavering voice in his ear. It was only after graduation from college that Adrian moved back to his parents' house, to be taught the intricacies of business. Once a week, he still visited Old Andy and went over the mansion's budget as well as attended to odd tasks his grandfather laid before him.

But he had to admit that for Old Andy to call *his* father was unusual. The old man thought his sons were comical.

"What did my father say?" he asked, turning to Julius, who was hard put to keep up with his long strides.

"Nothing else—just that your grandfather called."

"Rats!" Despite himself, his alarm was growing. But the office of the shipping company was already in sight: a gray squat building near the wharf. Though it was only a short distance from the town plaza, the area was deserted. Someone had switched on the single bulb in the building's front room and, in the failing light, it shone harsh and naked. Through the window jalousies, they saw a man at a desk, his back hunched.

It was Julius who spoke to the man and arranged for the use of the telephone. Adrian would call collect, he hastened to add; the man could listen until the connection was made.

"I shall leave you here," Julius said to Adrian. "I'd like to see some of the ceremonies myself."

Adrian nodded and picked up the phone. The man in the office eyed him without interest. When the operator answered, he gave his grandfather's home number, his name, and asked that the charges be reversed. It took a while before the maid—Adrian was sure it was the parlor maid, the youngest of the bunch—understood who was calling.

More minutes passed before Old Andy's creaking voice came, borne by static currents and the whistling of the wires.

"Father said you wanted to talk to me," Adrian cut into the old man's mumbling.

"Your father's a comedian." Old Andy laughed. "Where are you? What are you doing there?"

"I'm at the Festival."

"A fiesta? The October harvest must be in. Does blood still stain the rice?"

Patiently, Adrian explained the ship, the trip to K——, the festivities. "I came with two friends," he added, hoping Old Andy would take the hint and cut the conversation short.

"Two!" The chuckle crashed against Adrian's ear. "Two women, I bet. The sun and the moon. Son"—Old Andy always called him that—"come home. I had a dream of omens last night."

"Must be something you ate," Adrian said quickly.

"Could be. This goat-of-a-cook you found me's no good at all. Keeps feeding me vegetables. If I wanted to eat chlorophyll, I'd graze on the lawn. I keep telling him that but he won't listen. Last night, I saw the sun and the moon together, at the horizon. Both were in full strength—one red-orange; the other, golden. I did not like the sight, I tell you. The sea all around was on fire. Who are the women with you?"

"Now, Old Andy—"

"Give, my son. An old man can only have vicarious delights. Your father sounded worried. He wouldn't give me their names. He said I should ask you. Such circumspection in an otherwise gossip is curious indeed; curious."

"Andy . . ."

"You'll be calling me grandfather next. Give, my son."

Adrian shuffled his feet, glanced at the man behind the desk. He lowered his voice. "Eliza Hansen."

A grunt of dismissal came over the wires.

"Anna," he said reluctantly. "Anna Villaverde."

A silence.

"Hello. Are you still there?"

"At the Casa Español."

"What?"

"I met your grandmother there." Old Andy's voice quavered and Adrian could see him, his lower lip quivering. "The minute I saw her, I lost my ability to eat and sleep. That night, the muslim bedsheets suffocated me; they were that heavy from the weight of moonlight. The next morning, I found myself weeping at the corner of Azcarraga and Avenida Rizal."

Adrian sighed, leaned his elbow on the desk, and resigned himself to listening to yet another off-tangent story from the old man.

"I went to see my old master *americano.* He had grown old and complained eternally about how food passed through his intestines like a toothpick. He blamed it on coconuts. We ate them, drank their juice, and sucked on their meat, you know, when we were traveling up and down the archipelago condemning all the men. It was a bad time, son. My master, who was no longer my master for I had become a journalist, said it was impossible; the lady who had launched the lightning bolt of her glance at me came from a family of lawyers. *Abogados de campanilla.* You savvy?"

"Sure, *abuelo.*" Adrian craned his neck and tried to catch a glimpse of the clock on the wall. The sunlight was fading fast.

"*Abuelo* yourself. I learned English, gaddamit. Her father was a lawyer, her seven brothers were lawyers, and a dozen or so cousins were practicing in as many towns around Manila. They would not take kindly to a former bottle collector turned columnist who wrote 'gaddamit' every other sentence. What could I do, son? I threw myself on the floor of his house and had a fit. You know what he said?"

"What?"

"He said: 'Fact is, you ain't no lawyer.' Then, he paused, inclined his head, and aimed one eagle eye at me. After a while, he said: 'That doesn't mean you can't be one.' "

"Good advice."

"Good, my foot. After reading the first three pages of the first volume of the sixty-three volumes of the *Proceedings of the Supreme*

Court of the Philippine Islands, I knew I would never walk through the front doors of the Justice Department. But that didn't mean I couldn't go in through the back door. So one night I hoisted two gallons of rice wine and a sack of hard coins to the building, found the janitor and the security guards, had a high old time with them until four in the morning. When I left, they were asleep and tucked in my pockets were the answer sheets for the bar exams. Two months later, I scored the highest on those fucking tests."

"You were a genius, Old Andy."

"Genius, my ass. I cheated. And the entire country went wild because I hadn't had a stitch of law school. Hee, hee, hee. The night of the celebrations, Miss Estela came and I cornered her on the terrace of the Casa Español and poured into the shell of an ear she neither offered nor withdrew all my passionate hopes. It was a good thing I married her. She had memorized the fucking sixty-three volumes of the *Proceedings.*"

"Grandma's memory was legendary." Adrian sighed.

"A lot of good it did her. She was so afraid she would forget during the American carpet bombing of Manila, at the end of World War II, she was so busy reciting everything aloud she did not notice the air raid warning. A piece of shrapnel, triangular like a shark's fin, sliced through her thighs. She expired somewhere among the words *in deference to.* It was an end one could not imagine for the compact lady with delicate wrists and spiteful eyes I saw at the Villaverde wedding at the Casa Español." Silence; then almost diffidently: "I didn't know they were still around."

"Who?"

"The Villaverdes. You must bring her here, son. They would never have me at their dinner table."

"She's just a namesake, Old Andy. She doesn't look like her family could afford weddings at the Casa Español."

"Bring her here, you son of your benighted father. Do I look like I can afford to breathe?"

Adrian laughed. "All right. All right. As soon as we get back to Manila."

"Wonder who the moon was and who the sun? We condemned them all, you know."

"Who?"

"Those in the Revolution. My master and I did. When will you ever get your history straight?" And without warning, he hung up.

Adrian could only shrug. It wasn't the first time Old Andy had done that. He thanked the man, offered a tip which was refused, and, untying his T-shirt from about his waist, slipped it on. When he stepped out of the office, he saw that twilight had descended, accounting for the sudden cool in the air. Two men stood at the corner of the narrow street leading off the main seaside road to the town plaza. Adrian considered walking along the beach for a while but the women must be looking for him by now, frantic over where to bed down for the night. He quickened his steps, approached the street corner. The two men moved apart to let him pass and, as he stepped through, the one to his left swung back an arm and punched him in the solar plexus. It was a short, exact karate blow. Air exploded from his mouth; his muscles clamped down in a massive spasm and his knees buckled. But the two were already holding his arms, bearing his weight and dragging him forward. They patted him solicitously, lovingly, murmuring their regret that such a handsome young man should be so drunk, so drunk, even as they half-steered, half-carried him inexorably toward an open and shadowed doorway. As Adrian saw that maw coming closer and closer, he recalled Old Andy's dream.

He was being guided into a room. Hands on his shoulders forced him into a seat of red velvet. Behind him, a door closed and silence thickened. Even the sound of waves pounding the nearby beach was muffled. As the pain in his body eased and he was able to gulp down air, he twisted his head to look about him. The men were gone. Black curtains sheathed all the walls while overhead a massive chandelier coruscated, spilling light on the entire room. Except for a white Japanese lacquer screen behind a white-and-gilt writing desk and chair, there were no partitions; the room sloped down to a lower end occupied by a long, white-clothed dining table and chairs. The table was fully set with gilded plates and cups, silverware and crystal glasses, embroidered napkins, a massive silver coffee and tea service, delicate curls of pastry, and an ornate centerpiece of purple and white orchids. A red Taiping rug, florid with pink and red roses, covered the floor from wall to wall. *Holy bananas,* Adrian thought and whistled to himself.

From behind the screen, a man in white appeared. He looked like a doctor, though of course he had no stethoscope about his neck. He crossed his hands behind his back and smiled at Adrian.

"Would you like a drink?" he asked.

Adrian gave him an incredulous look. The man smiled encouragement. Adrian opened his mouth to snarl. Deftly, the man raised a hand, palm toward Adrian, and shook his head.

"No alcohol," the man said. "The colonel gave explicit orders. Coffee, tea, mineral water, orange juice. I recommend the juice— fresh squeezed from fruit flown in from Taiwan this morning."

"From Taiwan?"

"Oh, they're not as good as Japanese or American oranges. But we have to make do. You understand, don't you, sir?" The man's tone was ironic, mocking. "Perhaps, a slice of cheesecake?"

"I don't understand . . ."

"Because of the medication—sir. We wouldn't want anything bad to happen, would we? Excuse me. I'll get your orange juice. The colonel has been delayed but—momentarily. Only momentarily."

The man ducked behind the screen swiftly. Adrian rose, hand to the knot in his belly. He turned and scanned the room. He couldn't even tell where the door was. He sat down again and tried to compose himself. The man in white reappeared, this time balancing aloft a silver tray with a crystal glass of orange juice and a brandy glass filled to the brim.

"Please be patient," he said. "The colonel . . ."

"I'm here," a mild voice cut in and another man stepped from behind the screen. He wore a khaki uniform which rustled as he moved and the insignia of his rank plus three medals whose significance escaped Adrian. The name tag was missing. It wasn't necessary. His identity leaped to Adrian's mind immediately: Colonel Amor.

The man his father had spoken to on the phone. If his father had had dealings with this officer, then there was nothing to worry about. Automatically, Adrian arranged himself in the chair—leaned back, crossed his legs, and raised his chin.

The colonel smiled, gold glinting briefly in his mouth. "But I am—was—your client," Amor said, settling himself behind the writing desk and waving to the man in white to offer the drinks first to Adrian. "Your warehouse; the one that—ah, burned down. I leased it. Oh, I know, I know. A private corporation recommended by Miss Hansen—what a delightful woman—held the lease. But I used it and the rent money came from my office. Too bad about the arson. We handled that pretty well, I think. Cleaned up the place. Made sure the insurance company paid. And lo and behold! You have a brand new warehouse where an old, rotting, and useless one had stood."

"The construction's not finished yet," Adrian said, taking the glass of orange juice and sipping to wet his dry mouth. "But surely, we can discuss the lease after the Festival."

The colonel waved his words away. "I'm not interested in the warehouse anymore. Goodness, no. Though business with you does have its moments. When my men had to remove one corpse from that spinster's bathroom. Ah, that was superb. I laughed my head off for days. It had zoomed in right through her window and was standing in the shower stall, leaning against the wall. Stark naked, of course, minus half its head and one arm. And she thought it was a pervert, waiting to rape her. We had to rush to her apartment building in three minutes to ward off the police. My men laughed themselves sick."

"What are you talking about?" Adrian blurted.

The colonel gave a small, pained cry. With one hand, he half-covered his mouth. "Dear me, I've violated security." His eyes closed and opened with delight. "Of course, you didn't know we stacked our corpses in the warehouse. In body bags or coffins. Dead soldiers from all over the archipelago—before we buried them or shipped them to their families in Luzon."

Adrian did not dare move a muscle. Near the lacquer screen, to which he had retreated after delicately putting the brandy glass on the writing desk, the man in white nodded at Adrian. Whether in confirmation or encouragement, he could not know.

"Your father asked me to watch over you." The colonel sighed, lifted the brandy glass, and took a hefty gulp. His face tightened as he swallowed, the thin bluish lips pursing. "That's why I had you brought here."

"I could have been invited," Adrian said.

"You wouldn't like my kind of invitation. So far, I've invited about three hundred men and women to my office. None of them liked it. Don't make me angry, Adrian. Be the gentleman you're supposed to be."

"I gather you don't like gentlemen," Adrian said.

"Not much," the colonel admitted. "I have to serve them constantly and yet I can never be one. Nevertheless, your father did ask me to keep an eye on you since you're so young and so—ah, rich. Wouldn't do to have you fall into the wrong hands. All that money. What do you think of this room, by the way? I had it furnished for you. I didn't want you to think I was a barbarian. I also felt it would make you more comfortable—to be in familiar surroundings."

"We do not exactly live in such an environment, Colonel."

"Hmmm." The man scanned the room slowly, raised the brandy glass again, and abruptly threw it across the room. "Wrong again, shit!" He stood up, took one step toward Adrian, and thrust his head forward. "Now, tell me. What are you doing here with Miss Hansen and that Villaverde woman?"

"Attending the Festival." Adrian could not help his amazed tone.

"Miss Hansen belongs to a colleague of mine."

"Eliza?" Adrian snorted. "She belongs to no one."

The colonel relaxed abruptly. He smiled. "That's true. Such a beauty. Can't be owned. How unfortunate. Though one may try. One may try."

Adrian had to laugh.

"And the other one?" The colonel's voice was careful.

"She came so she could dance, make merry, sing, laugh. Just—

that." He raised the glass again, nervous all of a sudden, and discovered he had finished the juice.

"Her kind doesn't do"—the colonel mimicked Adrian's dismissing gesture—"just that."

"What is her kind?"

"Listen, this is important. Your name—*Banyaga*—it means foreigner. Yet, it is a native name; I have a Spanish one. But look at us. Ironic, isn't it? Where does your grandfather fit in all this?"

For a moment, Adrian wondered who was crazier—the colonel or he for even considering the question. "I don't know where my grandfather got his name . . ."

"Idiot. Not that. What was that phone call all about? What has it got to do with your being here, with Eliza's being here, and with the Villaverde woman being here? And most of all, what has it got to do with the fact that the commander-in-chief will be here in less than forty-eight hours?"

"Holy shit," Adrian muttered. He wanted to hurl the glass in the man's face, suppressed the impulse violently, and lowered the glass to the floor. Just to be on the safe side. "There's—no connect—my grandfather . . ." He stopped, inhaled, and began again. "My grandfather is an invalid. For all we know, he might be dying at this very minute."

"He doesn't leave the house, true. We know that because we watch him. But he can still make phone calls."

"You watch him? Whatever for?"

"His agents go up and down the archipelago buying all this relicary. Of the Revolution."

"The 1896 Revolution, Colonel. Against Spain. And the 1902–1908 Philippine-American War. You weren't even born yet."

The colonel shook his head. "And of the 1930s uprising. The 1940s anti-Japanese resistance. The 1950s Huk rebellion and, of course, the current insurgency. Posters, documents, underground publications . . ."

"What?" Silence. Adrian thought of the old man in his wheelchair, the blind eyes. Old Andy, help! "I had no idea, Colonel," he said truthfully enough. "Maybe, he thinks they'll be worth something. Or maybe, he's trying to trace something. He's talked about finding his family. He was raised in an orphanage, you know. And he's talked about that, the possibility of finding out who—maybe; but I don't know. I really don't know . . ." The rush of words stopped. He raised his eyes to the colonel's face.

"Ah, another child." The colonel jerked away. "Absolute loyalties. Bah!" He wheeled about, faced Adrian again. "Wait here. Don't worry. Everything will be fine."

Adrian, dazed, remained in the armchair. The colonel left, followed by the man in white. Nothing moved for a few minutes. Then a dozen men and women in formal evening clothes marched from behind the screen. They did not look his way. Conversation erupted—in English, Spanish, and Tagalog. About the latest Woody Allen film, the proper size for pearls, the fantastic adventures of a guerrilla, surfing, the latest hit songs, the best dance place, and some internecine squabbling among the generals. Coffee and tea were poured; the pastries and cakes were eaten amidst the clatter of silver and the tinkle of crystal. How long it lasted, Adrian did not know for he was held frozen to his seat by the fact that all the men and women wore surreal makeup: demon faces, serpent skin, witches' noses . . . Abruptly, as though at a signal, they moved away from the table and filed to the screen. They disappeared without a sound.

Silence again. By this time, Adrian had to acknowledge that he was afraid. His pants were soaked through behind his thighs; the back of his shirt was wet. He wiped his palms on the chair's armrest. He wished he were home—at his grandfather's house, sitting on the floor at his feet. Old Andy, help!

The man in white came into the room. He had a book tucked underneath his right arm and Adrian caught a glimpse of the word "quarks." Something "quarks." Old Andy laughing sounded like a duck quacking. He was losing his mind, he thought.

"Nice party, no?" the man said, smiling. He put the book down on the writing table, opened a drawer, brought out a stainless-steel case.

"First, a sample," he said and, seizing Adrian's hand, jabbed at his forefinger.

"Hey!" He could not loosen the man's grip.

"Be grateful," the man said. "He's not this careful with others. Thank your father." The man caught Adrian's blood in a small vial—a thin red thread suspended in clear fluid. Then, the man released his hand and shook the vial. "There you go. Don't move now."

He left again. Six men in camouflage uniform crowded from behind the screen. Four walked to the table and picked at the leftover pastries; two approached Adrian. He saw they were the men who had brought him to the house. He sighed, hoping they were there to return him. One went to his left, pivoted on his heels and stopped; the other took the same position to his right.

Another wait. Then the man in white came again. He was grinning, his arms held close to his sides. He walked past the desk and stopped when he was in front of Adrian, so close that the tips of his shoes nearly touched Adrian's sneakers. He raised his right hand and the two soldiers reached down, pinning Adrian's arms to the chair's rest.

"Hey!"

The man held a syringe.

"Just a little shot," the man said.

Adrian arched his body off the chair but it was too late. The needle broke through his skin; the pain flared on the inside of his elbow and coursed through his arm. Just as quickly, the needle was withdrawn and the man was dabbing at the hurt with an alcohol-soaked cotton ball.

"Easy there, easy."

The soldiers backed off. Adrian's eyes stung. He was going to cry, he thought. He couldn't even fight. Eighteen months. This madness began only eighteen months ago and here he was, the habit of subservience already ingrained. As Old Andy would say, it was as though we never had the Revolution, never really went through that war that stained the October harvest bloody, amidst the *clip-clop* of horses' hooves and screams of *fuego, fuego,* the boom of caskets, the wheeze of artillery wheels. Old Andy, poor cripple in his wheelchair, assured him that it was true, son; no one remembered the totality of it, its entirety, only bits and pieces, that battle, this confrontation, that siege—but not, no never, the monstrous carnage of four hundred years, from the very first dawn when Lapu-lapu skewered that vagabond poacher Magellan to the most recent twilight when the forty-five caliber was developed to stop the Moros of the south in their maddened dash at the enemy whose corpse was the key to the gates of paradise . . .

"It is taking," a voice said and Adrian looked up.

The chandelier lights were blurred by halos of multicolored mists. They were beautiful.

"Now, about the Revolution . . ."

The voice sounded familiar. Adrian forced his gaze away from the lights and found the man who had spoken. It was the good colonel—Adrian waved at him cheerfully, seeing him from a great distance—and he wore a tuxedo with a red rose in his lapel. Old Andy, whose wheelchair had appeared beside Adrian's chair, winked and said to the colonel: "You look like a cruise ship steward—which you should be, perhaps." Adrian laughed and went on laughing for a long time.

6

When she saw who was waiting in the buffet room, Eliza cursed herself. She had let down her guard and been maneuvered most skillfully, passed on from group to group, laughter to laughter, all leading to this house, this room where Adrian's father stood near the french windows and bowed formally when she walked in. He gestured toward the food-laden table.

"What would you like?" he asked.

Eliza glanced over her shoulder. Her companions had disappeared and the door, which had stood open, was now shut. She inhaled, drew herself to her full height, flung back her hair, and untied the pouch about her waist. It was always better to negotiate in comfort. She peered at the food and said: "Everything."

Later, watching her chew on the barbecued spareribs, the prawns, the lechon, and the salad, he said: "You have a magnificent appetite."

She smiled, deliberately arch. "In everything, sir. But do proceed. You don't have to wait on me." She had perched herself on the sill of the side windows from where a backyard garden of roses and gladioli, daisies and jasmine, was visible. Whoever owned the house lived well.

When the man—whatever was his name?—remained silent, she went on eating, keeping her eyes on the rice noodles she was twirling about her fork. She said abruptly: "The permit." And punctuated her challenge by filling her mouth with food. Good, good.

"It has to be signed as soon as possible," the man admitted, sighing. "So we can begin to work . . ."

"Cabanas on the beach, eh? Japanese tourists? Money?"

"All that. Think of what it would mean for the town."

She belched delicately, covering her mouth with her right hand. "If I did, you wouldn't get anywhere."

"Pardon?"

She put down the plate, picked up her wine glass. "Well. Fart," she said, "what happens to the fishing grounds, the huts, the garden plots? Your hotels would swallow all the food in the island, drive prices up, and impoverish everyone. But that is no business of mine. So I won't think of the town at all. Only of you." She saluted him with the glass. Drank. Licked her lips. "My problem is coming up with a fair price for my intercession. And a scheme to distribute God's windfall among the odds and ends of the Commander's clan. You have thought of this?"

He nodded, his eyes noncommittal. "Fifteen percent of total capitalization has been set aside for public relations."

"Some may prefer stocks; some, cash. The wife will take jewels, of course. Or foreign currency. Whichever is convenient. That can all be worked out. My fee is another matter."

"Name a price."

Eliza smiled. "I may not want money."

"Information? A promotion for the colonel? Or—?"

"You know something I'd be interested in?" Eliza was intrigued.

"Your friend. She has been looking for a body?"

"Oh!" Eliza shrugged. "I'm not. I don't think a corpse would do her any good."

"Her papers, then?" The man walked to the table, poured himself some brandy.

"No assurance there won't be copies lying around." Eliza shook her head. "I'm not a novice, sir."

"I did not think so. But if you would name a price . . ."

Eliza thought rapidly. "A service, perhaps. Or rather, a pledge not to act."

The man mulled that over; he nodded, his fingers restless among the wine and brandy glasses.

Eliza watched him closely. "A guarantee of noninterference? So that what is taking place"—she chose her words carefully, testing for limits—"between my friend, my two friends, can proceed to its—proper conclusion. Whatever that may be," she added quickly for the man's eyebrows had lifted.

He was quiet for a moment. Then, almost sadly: "Adrian is too young."

"I am not—note, please—not asking for, not expecting anything to come out of it. But simply to give everyone a—shall we say—a sporting chance?"

The man turned away, considering. Eliza saw that the glasses he had fiddled with were aligned now, not one askew by even a millimeter. Rats, she muttered to herself.

"Adrian is an only child," he said after a while. "The only child of our family. My brother has—" He shrugged. "But you know that."

"*She* is my only friend. And I'm not asking for anything beyond letting what is happening proceed normally."

He clasped his elbows. Looked at her. He seemed an extremely sad man. "But where is the satisfaction in that?"

She smiled. "It is *difficult* to explain. Especially to one who has never been interfered with. You have always been in control."

He shook his head. "Inaccurate. However, go on."

"I myself do not know what will happen," she said, realizing at the instant the words left her mouth that that was true. "Chances are my friend will back off. They are too different. On the other hand, it could go the other way."

"And if it does?"

"Then my friend becomes an heiress." The thought was so absurd she laughed.

The man's face rippled. A shark surfacing, she thought.

"Oh, don't look so grim," she blurted. "Money will cover any defect you think my friend has. Of course, it is speculative. If nothing comes out of it, I lose."

"Has Adrian—do you know something we don't?"

She shook her head. He sighed and approached the table again, picked up his glass of brandy, and sipped. Very carefully, Eliza observed.

"What is the time limit? How long do we wait?"

She thought for a moment. "Six months, maybe," she said at last, reluctant. "A year at the most."

"If we refused?"

"It won't make any difference. Whatever's going on will go on. All I want is—Colonel Amor should be, and you should be, interested observers. But if you do refuse, I can assure you no work will begin on these beaches. At least, not until my friends say they have reached a decision. Not a stitch of work. Not until then."

The man nodded. "We could ask Colonel Amor to make the arrangements with the Commander."

She clucked her tongue in exasperation. "You do that, sir. And let me go back to the Festival. Really, I came here to have fun; not to do business. For that, you can always find me at the hotel coffee shop."

She brushed off his apologies. As she had expected, his face had flushed; he had not been dismissed summarily by another human being in a long time. She placed plate and fork on the table, tuned him out as she retied her pouch, strode past him, and made for the door. If it were locked— But it wasn't and she was sprinting lightly through the living room where a dozen men and women, almost sinking in the overstuffed cushions, looked up. She ignored the question in their eyes and headed for the front door.

Amor indeed! That asexual creature who delighted in holding her hand and watching her face as she watched his men wreck one prisoner after another. Adrian's father knew as well as she did that Amor would not touch the deal. The colonel prided himself on his "professionalism," as he would say. He had marked off a territory for himself, he would say, within the Commander's domain. He concerned himself with nothing beyond it, though he might not be averse to taking down an officer or two. Moreover, outside his world, he admitted freely enough, he was incompetent. So much for Amor. He envied and hated those who grew fat on his labors.

As she wandered through the Festival, searching for Adrian and Anna, the sun pressed against her shoulders and back. The crowd clogging the road was a mass of colors—blue-green, red, yellow—which translated into a dull, drumming pain between her eyes. She had eaten and drunk too much, though she had known she would pay for such recklessness. She had been careless with Adrian's father. She realized that, knowing her price, he might force the problem to come to a head. Undoubtedly, he would use Amor.

Dealing with the Loved One had made the past six months difficult. She had made her first mistake by sending him a rare purple orchid plant after Anna's release—a statement that she had gained something of equal value. Amor had telephoned and asked her to pay him a visit; he was so very lonely, after all, lonelier even than her friend. That had begun it. Each time she arrived, Amor had a gift for her, always elegantly boxed and wrapped, which he handed to her after the curtains had swished shut on the romance room. A Dior scarf, a bottle of perfume, a gold bracelet. Once, he gave her a rose, the color of clotted blood, still half open. It was the first flower of a garden in an island-fort where his wife, ah, lived. He had grimaced while saying it and Eliza divined that the woman was alone in the godforsaken spot, guarded by soldiers.

Throughout those months when she had suffered the colonel's odor, she had nagged Colonel Alejandro Batoyan about the danger. But Batoyan was a simple man. Eliza sighed. In the normal course of events, he would have been content with an ordinary life, an unremarkable career that assured him a promotion in rank every six years or so. He had had no thoughts at all of going beyond what had been ordained and was proceeding to old age, retirement, and death without regret, in the company of his wife, a large woman with magnificent square teeth, and six big-boned, unhandsome children. But the wheel of fortune turned of a sudden and bingo! According to the pseudo-science of head measurements his commander-in-chief subscribed to, Batoyan had the proper skull girth, slope of the forehead, and nearly nonexistent nose bridge that spelled fortitude, loyalty, and utter self-effacement. His file photographs were shuffled, his records studied, and in no time at all he found himself installed in the anteroom of the Commander's Palace office with a gold telephone, a crystal ashtray, a white desk and chair, and a secretary who seemed to suffer from lockjaw.

The unexpected assignment created a furor that was silenced by a terse statement from the Commander himself. Colonel Batoyan, he intoned, was an honorable man, worthy of his uniform; in addition, he was dim-witted and dull and his ambitions did not go beyond having three meals a day. Moreover, he had passed the combined scrutiny of the Palace's top scientists and astrologers. In any case, should the good colonel displease the Commander—why then, gentlemen, he could always be sent to do battle with the Moros of Jolo. So much for that.

So dim-witted had Batoyan been that it had been six months before he understood what awesome powers had been placed in his hands. In due time, he acquired a new wardrobe, four houses, and two Mercedes-Benzes and a taste for ten percent of everything. He was not stupid enough to hog it all but studiously distributed God's grace among the Commander's relatives and his wife's relatives. It was simply good policy, this cultivation of the clan, particularly since the Commander more and more fell prey to melancholia and would spend weeks at a time seeing no one, save for his wife and his aide.

But the evening Batoyan saw Eliza, as he said later, drunk and divine and dancing by herself at a raucous nightclub, the fringes of her Spanish shawl having swept everyone else off the floor . . . that evening he saw her, all his possessions had seemed nothing more than crumbs, pitiful pickings, and he had been driven mad with dissatisfaction. It was such a class act, he told Eliza, her dancing there by herself and, unnoticed by her, he had followed her night after night, watched her even through the bottom of his brandy glass so that it had seemed he was drinking her and the liquid fire of whatever he drank was the molten fire of her limbs. He had not rested until that morning Eliza awoke to the reek of nausea in her nose and a hammer of pain in her head and saw Batoyan—pink, soft, and satisfied—emerge from under her bedsheets.

It had not been a bad deal, Eliza thought as she went through the town's market. Not bad at all. She marched through a ring of vendors, ignoring death skulls, whistles, red rattlers, tin horns. Fate was fate; there was little one could do about it—though one did try, until the day her father-in-law, silver-haired and patrician-featured, entered her bedroom to tell her that his son was tired of his Arabian horse, his London-made wardrobe, and his wife, all at the same time. The servants no longer recognized her; the dining room table remained empty and the swimming pool had been drained. The bunch of keys she carried in her purse could no longer unlock familiar doors. Worse, there were no records at all of her marriage. She had taken what her husband's father had offered—mostly, her clothes and jewels—and resorted once more to that building near the downtown cathedral, for she had no wish to carry to full term the child of her husband's wayward seed. Then, pawning her jewels, selling her clothes, she had drifted from day to day, wondering where Anna was and why her mother had written such a harsh fate for her.

Batoyan treated her well. That alone would have kept her by his side. But he also shared what power he had, bringing home, so she might admire his cleverness, documents, proposals, and decrees and bragging about the *squeeze*. Men born to wealth pleaded their cause before him, *him*. She had discovered the pleasure of it by accident. Once, thumbing idly through his papers, she had found her ex-husband's name in one of the proposals. Immediately, without even thinking of it, she had picked up a pencil, marked a huge **X** on the folder, thrown away the pencil, and, seizing the papers with both hands, ripped every sheet to pieces. How much of a coward everyone was, she discovered then—for no one asked Batoyan what had happened, where the papers were, and so on and so forth. No one, of course, dared approach the Commander who, during that period, was in the grip of profound sadness, convinced that his most recent facelift had slanted his eyes too much so that he looked like an adult mongoloid.

If the truth be told, Eliza said, laughing as she danced to the rhythm of the drums one-two, one-two-three, he did look mongoloid, even before the facelift.

The transvestite, opening and closing his eyes with delight, said but of course, it was so much fun, finding her once again; and everyone did whisper about the Commander's looks, his wife's looks, and his mother's looks.

In due time, Eliza said, she installed herself at a table in the InterCon coffee shop and thrice a week, over breakfast and three margaritas, disposed of the fates of various individuals. That young man, for instance, she said, pointing to one of the many handbills stuck on the town's walls and storefronts. He had been a new graduate when he had brought her his American diploma and had begged for a teaching position commensurate to his degree in education. Despite his protest, she had put his name down as a possible assistant executive vice-president of the Science Center. "Don't be stupid," she had told him. "What does your degree have to do with it? There are no scientists at the Center—only positions and money." Months later, while listening to the radio, she had heard the young man pontificate on his theory of a cosmic rip in the atmosphere over the islands, a hole which allowed radiation from the Sagittarian constellation to bathe the Palace, conferring miraculous abilities and powers on the country's leaders. That had snowballed. Sometime later, the Commander's wife assured a visiting foreign dignitary that she and her husband could focus a mysterious cosmic energy to zap all the nuclear weapons in the world, if they so wished. Eliza had to remind herself to close her mouth; at least, her protégé had been creative.

"But he is speaking tomorrow, isn't he?" the transvestite said, looping his arms about her as they prepared to tango down the road.

Eliza nodded brightly. "The Commander's wife thought it brilliant to include an educational component to the program." She laughed and swept her eyes through the spectators, expecting to see Anna and Adrian.

"Sssh!" The transvestite hurriedly pressed against her and steered her to the middle of the road. Two soldiers in combat uniform appeared, disappeared, appeared again, threading through the crowd.

"Oh, it was such fun," she said. She had altered what she could. A nuclear physicist became administrator of fish ponds in Laguna province; a dyslexic, chair of the Board of Censors (Print); a fashion designer, head of the Museum of Modern Arts; a law school graduate who had flunked the bar four times, director of the Film Center with its enormous budget and unaudited grants; a real estate broker, chair of the Land Reform Program . . . These were not really part of the *squeeze* which so delighted Colonel Batoyan: those papers begging for the Commander's signature which opened the public treasury and poured money into private enterprise. Batoyan, by this time, had acquired the nickname "Colonel Ten Percent" and Eliza would tease him. Laughing, he would shove his cap on his head, salute her, and pick up the new swagger stick she had given him. Then, he would strut in the pink living room of the pink mansion he had built for her in the suburbs. Up and down, to and fro, his short legs scissoring, his cap at a rakish angle while she laughed so hard her maids were scandalized.

"How absolutely delightful," the transvestite said, "but do lower your voice, darling. Here—" He snatched a bottle of rum from a passerby and offered it to her.

She took two swigs and handed the bottle back. The transvestite gathered her hair from her nape and shook it.

"You're sweating, love."

"It's hot. But let's please not stop dancing," she said. "Please, please, please . . ."

"Tell me the rest. We'll dance to the music of your words, love; only tell me the rest of it."

"He saw it," she said, pouting. She let the transvestite hold her again and swing her in a slow waltz. "He, of all people. He alone."

She had tried to explain. She was merely weaving a bright blue comic thread through the dullness of the Commander's reign. For her own private enjoyment. Nothing more.

"But laughter, dear, is *subversive,*" Amor had said.

"Surely no one takes his rule seriously!"

He had looked at her. "Who doesn't? The world? Washington? Tokyo?"

She could not answer. She felt abandoned.

"Haven't you noticed that *I* have no sense of humor?" he had asked.

After which, of course, as though to disprove his words, he took to sending her love notes in which he conjugated his name: amo, amas, ama . . . amaretto. Six ludicrous letters on creamy linen paper, each handwritten and delivered in broad daylight by a caravan of six military cars, sirens wailing. Unfortunately, the last one was handed to Colonel Batoyan who had assumed that the tumult was on his behalf. He had ripped open the envelope, scarcely noticing the name written on it, and in a few seconds he was looking so stricken Eliza thought he had swallowed his tonsils. The silence lengthened; Eliza munched on slices of green mangoes and sipped Coke.

Abruptly, the colonel stomped his foot. "You taught him Spanish," he screamed. "You wouldn't teach me Spanish!"

He whirled; his eyes darted about the room and found his gun belt. *Holy cow!* Eliza was on her feet, sprinting for the front door, as he lunged across the room. She was laughing so hard her belly ached and she had to run bent over. The first shot was a thunder at her heels. She was dead, she thought, and found that so funny she nearly stopped running. Then she saw the vase on its stand beside the door disintegrate in slow motion, shards and dust falling to the carpet. She tripped on her high heels, fell against the door, her hands clawing at the lock. She had whizzed through and had slammed it behind her when a second shot resounded. A tremendous crash followed. One of the bay windows was gone. She was screaming, by then, for the garden boy to open, open, the gate. The Benz was in the driveway, being washed and polished, and she nearly tore its door handle off in her haste. She dove in, sprawling in the front seat, pulled herself up, felt the ignition key in place, and turned on the engine. What obscene wish for death made her stop and look around, she didn't know—but there was Batoyan, legs apart, knees bent, both arms stretched out full length at shoulder level, hands wrapped about his .45 pistol. She stuck out her tongue at him. "You can't even shoot straight, you son-of-a-goat!" A third shot; the car's rear window exploded. She gunned the engine and rammed the car through the half-open gate, sending the boy scampering over the gardenia hedge.

She didn't slow down until she was at Anna's apartment. After parking the car, she had rushed up the stairs and thrown the door open. The silence in the room was so thick she froze. She was about to call out—*Anna*—when a fluid movement over the sofa drew her eyes. At first, she thought it was a black veil hung to dry and stirred by the wind. But the next instant, the image shifted. It was Anna's hair, loose from its usual knot at the back of her head, falling to her flanks, covering her back, and spilling to the foot she rested on the floor while Adrian's hand caressed the thigh that straddled him.

She didn't think she would see such a thing, she confessed to Colonel Amor later. Such beauty—in this day and age. No sound. Only the intensity of Adrian's eyes as he looked into that face hidden from Eliza by the black cascade of hair.

She was still in shock over the discovery when Amor's men found her driving down Roxas Boulevard and with their sirens and hand gestures had made her stop. The men, austere with words, had asked her to move to the passenger side of the car while a soldier took the steering wheel. Then, escorted by four patrol jeeps, she had been taken to his headquarters.

She had been served dinner. The colonel had appeared for dessert, apologizing for his lateness. "No rest for the righteous," he had said. She had blurted out what she had seen, at the time not knowing what to think of it, what to make of it. "Such beauty," she had said, savoring the words.

"Foolhardy," he said, "to leave doors unlocked."

The shooting had been reported to him, of course. "I'm afraid we will lose one extraordinary officer," he said, dropping a folder on her lap.

It was a listing of Batoyan's transactions: services rendered, amounts turned over, check numbers, banks, dates, signatures . . .

"We don't usually pay attention to graft," Amor said. "On the other hand, knowledge of it is pretty good leverage. Especially when the officer involved has something one wants. Such beauty . . ." In his mouth, the words became filthy. "It is a beginning," he added.

Or the end. She had not wanted to be involved at all, not at all. But there was no helping that now. The colonel, the more fool he was, wanted her, or wanted a version of her he kept in his mind. The fool. He had said quite bluntly that, first, he wanted the man Anna kept hidden. Eliza's lips had moved about Adrian's name but the colonel had twitched impatiently.

"Guevarra," he said.

She had never heard of him, certainly not from Anna. "Why not tail her?" she asked brightly, still playing the game—her game.

"Uh-uh. He's an expert. He'd smell it and disappear. It has to be you and through you, your friend. Worm it out of her."

"For what purpose?"

"So I can be promoted," he said, grinning. "And you'll be right by my side. After all, the professor's dead and I need someone to—"

"Feed you your lines?"

"How sharp you are. I will be the envy of everyone. Under your tutelage, I shall rise from pinnacle to pinnacle. Until I am the Commander." He drew himself up, raised his chin. "What fun. That shall be a festival to end all festivals."

Shit, she muttered, *shit.* "Are you sure I'm the right person to guide you, Colonel?"

He frowned. "Don't dissemble. I hate people who lie to me. Don't pretend you're stupid."

"What if I am?" She nearly laughed.

He held up his hand. "First"—he ticked off the words on his fingers—"you marry into one of the richest families in the country; second, you get him to agree to turn you loose with enough money; third, you latch on to the Commander's aide; fourth, you acquire more money and more power than his wife . . . Amazing luck for the daughter of a whore, I should say."

She turned deathly cold. *Triple shit,* she breathed to herself, *twist facts around a little bit . . .*

"You're wrong, you know," she said tiredly. "But I won't argue. I'll need time."

"You'll have it, dear," he said, throwing his arm about her shoulder. "We have plenty of time."

He made reservations for her at the Hotel InterCon. When she was alone at last, she could shake her head at the magnitude of his error. But there was no arguing with the man; he saw what he wanted to see. She slept that night and, the following morning, sat at her table in the coffee shop. She had no plans, none at all, and could only wait for the world's end.

She was halfway through her breakfast when Batoyan appeared. He bowed to her, asked permission to join her, sat down at her nod, and ordered coffee for himself.

"We've had a lot of fun," he said. His voice seemed to have aged.

She said nothing.

"But we have to be serious now."

She looked at him. "They have a dossier on you."

He nodded. "I've suspected it. Strange things have happened. People shying away; my phone calls not returned. My friends in the military suddenly unavailable for poker."

"Will you survive?"

He stirred milk into his coffee. "Not sure," he said, after a while. "I can liquidate all my assets. Stash cash abroad. Also, I can ask around for a possible mission abroad."

"The house, too?"

He nodded.

"The car?"

Again, he nodded. "Have to have that window repaired, though. Will you take it to the shop?"

It was her turn to nod. She waited for him to mention the bank accounts, the jewels, odds and ends in her possession. There was no need to be embarrassed, she thought. She gave him a look of encouragement. Everything had been bartered, traded, bought and sold in this country since forever. Any process necessary for survival was respectable. There was no need for him to look so confused, so tentative; she would give him back everything happily, if only he survived.

"I will need six months, at least," he said heavily. A pause. He cleared his throat. "Will you come with me?"

It was so unexpected that Eliza had to look around, wondering if she had heard right. She saw the dark-suited men, the handsome women, the white-clothed tables and red-upholstered chairs, the waiters in their white-and-ocher uniforms, and, finally, Batoyan himself in his simplicity. Sweat beaded his forehead.

"I don't think I can survive without . . ." His voice broke.

Eliza reached out then and, with her right hand, covered his left. After a while, her palm grew warm against his skin.

7

Day's end found Anna and Rafael still on the beach, watching as sea and sand turned into matching red-orange sheets and the shadows uncurled from the base of coconut trees to stretch inland. After a while, Rafael rose, inclined his head, and Anna followed. They traced the shoreline, walking into a salty wind. Anna did not ask where they were going nor how far; as Rafael would say, everything that had to be known was known in due time.

They saw the sun vanish; a wash of orange hung briefly in the sky before it darkened slowly into a luminous blue. The stars were already out when Anna saw a cluster of upended boats on the beach. Past the boats, inland, were bamboo houses, with thatch roofs, their doorways and windows golden with light from kerosene lamps. Rafael slipped past the first circle of houses and stopped before a hut deep in the fishing village. He called out a name softly. A girl in a cotton slip appeared, peered at them, and waved them up the bamboo ladder.

Inside, the family—old man, husband, wife, and three children—had gathered in the central room. A cloth hammock slung near an inner doorway bulged with a baby's shape.

The old man, smiling, gestured for them to sit down. Though two long benches were set against opposite walls in the otherwise empty room, he himself sat cross-legged on the polished slats of the bamboo floor. Rafael folded his legs, acknowledged the rest of the family with nods and smiles. They smiled back briefly before scattering—the children into what seemed to be a small bedroom; the woman to the kitchen in the back. The husband walked over to the cradle and, sitting himself on the floor, placed his hand flat against its side and began to rock it gently.

"All goes well with you, Elder?" Rafael asked.

The old man glanced briefly at Anna, then at Rafael. He sighed. "One shipment was intercepted," he said slowly. "The boat ran into a patrol and had to veer away. It docked here. We have taken it to the—the usual place." His dim eyes again darted at Anna.

Rafael frowned. "Who will do the delivery?" he asked.

"It is a problem," the old man admitted. "No one has papers. And there are checkpoints."

"Is it ready?"

The old man considered, his gnarled hands busy with a crumpled pack of cigarettes. "Not for two hours more. We have it guarded. But we can't work on it now. Soon. Soon."

"It has to get there."

"Don't I know it, son? We have managed to get a jeep and gasoline. We're still looking for a driver." He eyed Rafael pointedly.

Rafael sighed. Nodded. He leaned forward, resting his forearms on his thighs. "Shall we trade problems?" he asked. His head jerked slightly toward Anna. "This one should not be here," he said. "But being here, cannot leave at the moment."

The old man nodded.

"When you next see her, I may or may not be with her. In either case, she will have to be ferried to the next island to—but you know to whom. Will that be a problem?"

The old man looked a query at his son. The young man wriggled the fingers of the hand on which he rested his chin.

"We have a volunteer," the old man said. "But if she doesn't make it to the place, what can we do?"

"Your son will have to find her. It doesn't matter where. So long as she's on the island. But I would try the cemetery first."

The old man clucked his tongue. "Too close to the town. But so be it, if it is important."

"It is not important. But I would consider it a personal favor. Besides which, we traded problems, didn't we?"

The old man laughed. As though this were a signal, the woman came out with a stack of tin plates. Anna rose quickly, took the plates, and laid them out on the floor. The son stood up, moving to join his wife. Together, they brought out platters and bowls. The pungence of tamarind stew and of steamed rice filled the room. It called to the children who came bustling out of the smaller room and threw themselves to their knees. Husband and wife sat themselves on the floor presently, each carrying a small can of water. One was given to Rafael. He thrust his right hand in, swirled the water, took his hand out, and shook droplets off his fingers. He gave the can to Anna who mimicked his action. The others were also rinsing their hands. They would eat with their fingers. The old man ladled the food out, serving the guests first, urging them to eat.

Rafael peered into the tamarind stew. "Forgive me," he said to the family. "It is nothing but stupidity. But every time I'm served tamarind stew, I have to examine it. Anna, you might find this of interest. I know what happened to the thieves."

"No one else does," Anna said as she used her fingers to gather and press the rice on her plate into little balls.

"I used to work with them," Rafael said. "I was a very talented pickpocket."

"I thought you were a student."

"That, too. They sent me to college. Or rather, the King did. Sort of a long-term investment. The idea was for me to go to law school. I would never lack for clients." He laughed.

"I can't believe it."

"He was both wise and foolish. In that kind of a group, he should have expected betrayal. But— Anyway, *they* got him. Cost him all his fingers. They fed it to him in tamarind stew."

The old man jerked. The children grimaced and started laughing, peering into the bowl. Anna, who was picking busily at a small fish, stopped.

"He ate it?" one of the kids asked.

"They didn't tell him what it was until afterward. Then, of course, he vowed to kill them. So, they killed him. Then, they had to kill the rest of his men. Broke up the association and placed the teams under new management. Under the head of the police's theft and robbery division, as a matter of fact." He glanced at the girl who sat beside him. Her face was scrunched up in disgust. "Don't listen to me, child," he added quickly. "I always tell the story so I can have the stew to myself." He made a grab for the bowl and the children laughed.

"We breed unspeakable men," the old man said. "This one here"—he nudged the boy next to him—"he's ten, eleven years old. Time he learned something."

Rafael studied the boy. "Do you want to?"

The boy nodded. "I want to be like you," he said.

Rafael turned to the young man. "We will take him—with your wife's and your consent."

The two looked at each other. The mother smiled. "If he won't be in too much danger . . ."

The old man cut in abruptly. "How can anyone guarantee that? Even here, there is danger. He could drown anytime."

"That's true, Elder," Rafael said. "There are no guarantees. But since he's so young, care will be taken, of course. Even then, we can't be sure. One gives and one gives without reservations. One only hopes for the best." Rafael resumed eating and waited.

A short silence. "Oh, do let me go, Mother," the boy cried.

The woman nodded. The father nodded. Afraid to show his pleasure, the boy bent his head and scooped rice to his mouth.

"Let's hope we can save what we have," the old man said, after a while. "These plans being discussed in the island—hotels and money, money, money . . . We've seen this before in other places. People go insane over the thought of money. And always, the money goes—*pfft!* No one knows. The governor is a *pendejo.* Not content with whoring himself, he must have us whore for him as well."

"We'll try to stop it," Rafael said, "or stall it, at least. But it is not unique to this place. People are losing everything all over the country. Too many development plans, too little of which are for people like us. Dams and hydroelectric stations; nuclear reactors—you name it. But what happened to your neighbor, the one with the beautiful wife?"

The conversation suddenly changed into anecdotes about the neighborhood as the old man fell silent and the other members of the family took over. The children spoke of their friends, the young man of his sea journeys. Anna noted how deftly Rafael drew out information about the fishermen's society on the island. His voice did not betray undue interest in anything, merely friendly curiosity, even when the wife talked of those who had joined military-sponsored groups. "They go fishing sometimes," she said with a wry smile, "but at night. Midnight." When Anna glanced at Rafael, he explained that the soldiers were smuggling in drugs, using quasi-legal town associations.

In half an hour, simply by listening, Anna had a composite of the village—the fisher folk against those connected with the town government; the young fishermen against those who found easy living with the military camp; and a whole impoverished social stratum against market wholesalers and food distributors. She heard of how the women feared for their children who each year increased both in number and in needs. As the conversation went on, she noticed how Rafael seemed to count every mouthful he ate, chewing slowly and often stopping. The children, though, ate quickly, reaching out for the platters and the bowls until the old man berated them for not letting the guests eat. Rafael shook his head and said he wasn't hungry.

"Are you afraid we don't have enough?" the old man asked bluntly.

Embarrassed, Rafael took more of the stew.

After dinner, there was coffee brewed from toasted rice.

"But you are rich," Rafael exclaimed when the wife handed him a tin cup. "Last time I was here, your coffee was made from old coconut meat."

The woman grinned. "I made a little money," she said, "making Festival decorations."

"Who will be the Festival tribute this year? Do you know?" her son asked, huddling close to Rafael. "Last year, it was a son of the town treasurer. He was walking at the dock between his girlfriend and his ten-year-old brother. Then, a wave rose like this"—the boy lifted his arm, shaped his hand into a cobra cowl—"and hooked him into the sea. It was done so neatly the two with him didn't even get wet."

"Really?"

"Pray it takes someone really important this time," the old man said. He lighted a cigarette.

Anna glanced at Rafael but he ignored her. Instead, he rumpled the boy's hair.

"And did you see it, little one?" he asked, teasing him. "Were you there? Did you see the sea come out like this"—he curved his arm and let his fingers swoop at the boy's ribs—"and take this one, that one, this one?" The boy laughed, tried to evade him, and ended up wriggling on the floor. "Remember this or I shall tickle you to the death," Rafael went on. "Do not believe everything you hear."

Anna shook her head. Rafael mockingly opened his eyes wide. "I wish someone had said that to me when I was young," he said.

The old man snorted. "You're young!"

"Younger than me," Anna confirmed.

"I'm not kidding. Once this classmate of mine appeared at my dorm room, with a package, some money, and the key to his own room. He said *they* were on to him and he had no one he could trust. Could I deliver the package to a certain house in a certain town? It was important. Afterward, I could have everything in his room, he said, all his possessions. So like an idiot, I took the package and looked up the town on a road map. Got on a bus, bought a ticket, found the town, found the house, and found Guevarra. In a godforsaken little barrio no one has ever heard of. And guess what the package was? Books and papers. I was intrigued. Stayed three months and learned politics."

"What has that got to do with—"

"When I returned to the university, I made for my classmate's room. It had been stripped bare. *They* had gotten to it first. Worse, they'd set a trap. I had to throw myself out a window. If I hadn't believed my classmate . . ." He grinned.

A noise came from the outside. The old man tensed. He signaled his son and the young man left the house hurriedly.

"Should they meet you?" the old man asked Rafael, who shook his head.

They waited silently. After a while, the house quivered as someone climbed the ladder. It was the son. He looked at the old man.

"The jeep is there," he said.

The old man yawned. "It is late," he said to Rafael.

Rafael gathered himself. "We will go. Come, Anna. We have work to do."

Their farewells were short. Anna thanked the family and saw how the young man stared at her face, committing it to memory. She shook his hand.

Once in the darkness away from the houses, Rafael began to walk swiftly. He cut through an adelfa hedge, saying Anna should try to be as quiet as possible. When a twig snapped in her hand, he said *hush* under his breath. Soon, she felt a path under her feet—a strip of earth worn bare and hardened by many footsteps. It led under the coconut trees and from there through a wasteland of thorny weeds that clung to her pant legs. Beyond, two houses loomed, light from their open windows slicing the dark. Anna heard voices, laughter, the clink of glasses, remnants of the day's festivities. Then more houses. They had reached the edge of the town. Rafael tensed; he seemed to glide on cat's paws, his head turning now and then to check the night, to see if she had managed to keep up. The houses began to crowd together now and their path became filled with more and more light.

Rafael shivered, dodging the windows' illumination. Anna tried to walk in his footprints, peering about her. She could not tell where they were.

The distance between houses grew longer. A cloud overhead must have passed on for there were moon shadows now. Rafael straightened his body. He walked easier, with more confidence. Seeing him thus, Anna also relaxed. She heard the surf and soon saw a white line moving on the horizon. It was the sea, the foam of a wave shimmering in the moonlight. She kept the white line in sight, thinking of how vast the water was, the ocean of typhoons with the ironic name Pacific. She was recalled to the present when she slipped on a pebble. She heard the harsh intake of her breath but Rafael was beside her immediately, clutching her arm in warning. He pushed her forward gently. Something stirred in the shadows; a man slithered past, his eyes snaring them. He nodded. Behind him was a low wooden fence. Rafael swung a leg over and waited for her. Then they were walking through a backyard, toward a closed door.

It opened outward and, in the sudden light, Anna had to blink. She saw the tiny flame of a wick floating on oil in a coconut half-shell. Against the far wall, a young man stood, his hands held behind him. When he saw Rafael, he sighed, moved away from the wall, and brought his arms forward. His right hand grasped a .32-caliber pistol.

"We're nearly done," he said. He crossed the room and locked the door.

"The jeep?"

"Half a block away. No problem."

Rafael nodded. The man motioned for them to follow. He led the way to the kitchen, then to the dining room. They were well past the doorway before Anna noticed another man sitting on a tall wooden crate, his right leg propped on a smaller one. Between his knees was an M-16. The man stirred at their appearance and raised his chin in greeting.

"Nearly got you, eh?" Rafael addressed him.

The man cursed quietly. He jerked his head back, toward the doorway opposite. "It's all in there," he said. "I have to head back."

"Let's get to work," Rafael said. He pulled Anna back a little and, bending his head, whispered: "Don't you tell *him* I made you do this!"

"Do what?" But Rafael was already pushing her ahead. It was yet another room, empty except for a few crates and Styrofoam iceboxes. The latter were painted with soda ads: Pepsi-Cola, Coca-Cola, Mirinda . . .

The two men in the room, both young enough to be teenagers, picked up one of the iceboxes and carried it out.

Rafael took a claw hammer from among the scattered tools on the floor, looked at the man who'd guided them to the room, and raised his eyebrows. At the man's nod, he proceeded to pry nails off the top of a crate.

"That's the last," the man said. "The rest are blinds. Probably full of Coke."

"Bring an icebox, Anna," Rafael said.

She grabbed one at random and carried it to Rafael. He was lifting the upper side of the crate. He whistled. Underneath, laid in two rows as neat as eggs, were hand grenades.

"Frags," he said. "Vietnam type. Probably stolen."

"From whom?" Anna asked, wondering who would have such an arsenal.

"Who else gets American supplies?" Rafael barked a laugh. "Line the box."

She found old newspaper sheets in a closet. Rafael and the man were examining one of the grenades. She heard the word "lovely" muttered several times. Hurriedly spreading paper at the bottom of the icebox, she looked at Rafael impatiently.

"Don't try to steal one now," Rafael said, handing her the first grenade. "At the bottom, carefully and neatly."

She put it down, held out both hands for the next. They were fragmentation grenades, slick and precise, she thought. They would not explode by accident. She watched her hands arrange the monstrous eggs in the box and thought of how much havoc they could cause.

"It is only a thing," Rafael said as he passed another grenade to her. "Remember that, you with your madness . . ."

Anna flushed. So, he knew. She bent her head, pretending to be busy. Quite by accident, through Adrian's tattling, she had discovered Colonel Amor's warehouse. Adrian himself had no idea what was in the warehouse but Anna had perked up the minute the name of the client corporation dropped from his lips. It had been common knowledge among detention inmates that the military used that corporation as cover. She had hung around the vicinity of the warehouse, listening to corner-store gossip. And when she learned what was stored within, something had snapped in her. The thought of all those bodies piled atop each other, waiting, unburied, had haunted her. She had prayed for a typhoon strong enough to pry off the warehouse's roof to reveal the truth within; an explosion perhaps; a fire; some accident—an explosion . . . It had been conceived as a joke at first but, later, she had been amazed by what guile she was capable of. She had found a mail drop, written to the address Manolo had bequeathed her. Two months later, the package arrived, complete with detailed instructions. A child could have done it.

And the joke had become a reality—a spectacular cracking asunder of the rotting timbers of the warehouse, an eruption of a lava of dead flesh: limbs, heads, torsos zooming like torpedoes through the air to land on sidewalks, rooftops, patios. They had punched through windows to skid along tables, demolishing the dinners of the unwary; to settle on sofas among the living who were watching television; to snuggle on the bedsheets, disturbing lovers . . . a necrophiliac visitation that had driven the neighborhood hysterical.

Thinking of it, of how it must have been, she had laughed quietly, the laughter painful in the pit of her belly. Until, of course, that evening she had returned home to find her street cut off by police barricades. Her heart drumming, she had edged against building walls, her eyes hard and dry in her skull. But under the streetlight, underneath a policeman's cap, Rafael's face had beamed at her. He had signaled with his hand, his mouth working at assuring noises as strangers passed. Only then had she calmed down and walked home to find Guevarra dressed in a colonel's uniform in her living room. The instant she walked in, he had pinioned her with his eyes and had demanded the name and address of Manolo's contact. On the floor by his feet were the wrapped remnants of the plastique she had used.

That was how she had broken her vow to Manolo and traded her joke—oh, what fun it had been!—for a truth. She had said to Guevarra's anger: here, the name, the address, the code, all in my head where the Loved One couldn't reach them, yours if you will tell me what happened—ah, the poor rabbit—what happened to him, where, why, and how; for she would have a funeral for the poor rabbit, though it be only a scattering of ashes in a cramped rose garden. And she had thought all the time that Rafael had not known about the joke, that it had been a secret between her and Guevarra.

"Did you layer the others?" Rafael was asking the man in the room.

He nodded. "With paper," he said.

"No good," Rafael said. "Open that crate."

The man complied. It was filled with bottles of Archangel beer. Rafael scratched his head.

"I wonder if beer and grenades are volatile." He laughed, squatted down, and began handing the beer to Anna. "Layer the top with these. Two layers, maybe. How many iceboxes are in the jeep?"

"Two."

"All right. The two underneath, this one on top. In case someone wants to check. Anna, make sure the—things aren't visible."

"All right," she said, trying to align the bottles. She was sweating.

"That's fine. Masking tape? No. Too suspicious. As is, then. Call them. We'll leave shortly." He turned to Anna. "Come." He patted the floor beside him. When she was seated, he slid his right trouser leg up. Tied to his shin was a butterfly knife. "Know how to use this?"

"Yes."

"Let me see." He loosened the knife from its thongs and handed it to her. She rose to her feet, feeling the knife's weight. It was perfectly balanced. She looked at Rafael. The knife twisted in her hand; a tiny click and the hilt unlocked. She flicked her wrist and the hilt broke apart, the six-inch blade rose, and half of the hilt circled to her palm to join the other half. It slid into place. Another click and the lock snapped in. The dagger was ready.

"Held down, waist level," she said, reciting a catechism, "for the thrust. Held over the shoulder, by its tip, for the throw." The knife flew and hit the wall opposite; it quivered on its tip but held. Embarrassed, she retrieved it, noting the blade had gone in two inches.

"Awkward and slow," Rafael said, "but will do. Come, come." He was already untying the thongs from about his leg. "Will it fit in your waist pouch? No? Your arm, then. Up with the right sleeve."

He closed the knife and settled it against her arm, measuring. He stopped when the three men came in. Without a word, two picked up the icebox while the third signaled with his fingers to Rafael.

"Got it," Rafael said, and the three walked out of the room. "We have to wait. Check if the knife will snag."

Anna brought down her hand. She jerked her wrist against the thong. The knife, its blade nestled within its hilt, slid into her palm. She nodded.

"Now, the proper blow," Rafael said, bending his head slightly and tapping his nape. "Right here. You know it?"

She nodded. "Manolo taught me." She could still hear his voice: through the skin, straight to the medulla oblongata, severing the s.o.b.'s motor nerves. Quiet and efficient and wholly unexpected.

"Good. We wait now."

She sat on a crate, crossing her legs.

"Nervous?"

She nodded.

"I wouldn't take you if the others were . . . You have papers?"

Again, she nodded.

"Good. We're lovers—off to see the common festival. There are two on this island. One by day which you saw; one by night which the poor folks see."

"All right." She wished he would stop talking. She wanted to probe the edges of what she was feeling.

"Now," he said, getting up.

She was surprised. Nothing had indicated it was time. But she knew better than to question him.

"We're going this way," he said, indicating a closed door. Then he pinched the light wick and it was dark.

She followed his shadow. All the lights in the house seemed to have been doused. But Rafael did not hesitate. He found another door which opened to the smell of the sea.

The jeep was parked a few yards away. There was no one about. She had to wait under a roadside tree while Rafael approached. She came running only when he had gunned the motor. As soon as she was in the passenger seat, he shifted gears and let the jeep move. But it was still some five hundred yards before he switched on the headlights.

They hit a checkpoint an hour later. As he braked the jeep to a stop, Rafael inexplicably said: "You don't see such stars in Manila." She had to peer at the sky where stars blazed, winking in and out of the mist of the Milky Way.

Two soldiers peeled themselves off the shadows along the road. They approached, careful to keep the jeep between them. Rafael leaned out. He said something in a low voice. Anna kept still, watching the man on her side of the road. He was cautious.

"Good evening," the soldier on Rafael's side said.

"At ease," Rafael said. "I'm going to get my wallet so you can check my i.d. Okay? I'm on a reconnaisance mission."

"Yes, sir." For some reason, the soldier's voice had an undercurrent of laughter.

Rafael felt at his back pocket. Anna froze as the soldier on her side leaned into the jeep. But Rafael was already straightening up, opening his wallet, extracting a card. He hesitated, felt in the wallet again, and came up with a fifty-peso bill. He wrapped it about the card.

"Happy fiesta," he said.

The soldier grunted. He slipped the money off and studied the card. "CIS, sir?" he asked after a while.

Rafael nodded. "I have some men waiting out there," he said, "otherwise, I'd leave you some beer. But the—you know—should get you some, no?"

The soldier smiled, gave back the card, stepped back, and saluted. The other soldier fell away.

"Nice evening, sir. Have a good time."

Rafael guffawed obscenely. "Carry on, men!" He shifted gears and steered the jeep to the middle of the road. "Carry on!"

After a while, he said: "You can breathe now."

Anna exhaled. "What are you doing with a Constabulary Intelligence Service card?"

"Pretty good, no? I made it myself. Hell, how many soldiers have seen one, anyway?"

"Why was he laughing?"

"He thought I was taking you to a gang bang. Don't get angry, now."

She was nonplussed. They drove on in silence. Suddenly, the tree shadows alongside the road disappeared and a clearing stretched out before them, dark wings spreading to the horizon, its slopes covered by tiny points of light. Anna thought they were driving through a portion of the night sky, but the next instant she saw the fallen stars were oil lamps. There were hundreds of men and women in the clearing—sitting on stools, lying on mats, standing near their water buffalo carts. Their faces were turned to the sky.

"What is it?" she asked.

Rafael had stopped the jeep and was eyeing the roadside. "Do we dare?" he muttered. "Better not. Might get stuck. Don't know the land here." He turned to Anna. "The poor folks' festival. Down there are the island's peasants—coconut workers, actually, but peasants still. This is their festival. They call it the Procession. They believe angels parade up there"—he peered at the sky through the windshield— "with their own candles and torches."

She was amazed. "Does it happen?"

He shrugged. "They don't talk about it. They come here and wait for lights to cross the sky. From horizon to horizon. That's what I was told." He shifted in his seat, restless, uneasy.

Up ahead, more carts were coming, drawn by water buffalos whose horn tips glinted in the starlight. Each cart had a little lamp on the seat beside the driver and its light swayed with the rhythm of the water buffalos' lumbering gait. One by one, the carts turned off the road into the clearing, to the left or right of the dust road. But a steadfast one came down, almost to the jeep.

"That's it," Rafael said when the cart stopped a few meters away.

Rafael was already climbing out of the jeep. Anna followed, keeping her eyes on the cart. There were two men and a woman with a baby in the cart.

"We're too exposed," she muttered to Rafael.

"Sssh," he said. "Wait."

A boy suddenly sat up in the cart, gave a shout, and crying "Uncle! Uncle!" jumped to the road and came running. He threw his arms about Rafael.

The two men came forward, clapped Rafael on the back, and loudly asked how the Festival had been and where's the beer and what took him so long . . . Slowly, they edged toward the jeep and were soon reaching in for the iceboxes. Anna remained by the roadside and saw three meteors fall.

Then the silence was shattered by the distant cough of a motor. Rafael glared at the direction of the noise. A motorized pedicab appeared. It stopped, a Caucasian climbed out. Shouting "all right, thass all right," he paid the driver. The pedicab arced across the road and turned back. In a few seconds, it was gone while the Caucasian swerved for the jeep.

"A tourist," Rafael said quietly. "Better move fast."

The two men hauled out the first icebox. But before they could carry it to the cart, the tourist was upon them. "Beer, beer, I buy, I pay . . ." Lurching, he brought out a wad of money. The two men glanced at Rafael. Anna stepped forward, grabbed the man's hand, and tried to pull him away.

"Dance, Joe," she said, "dance?"

When the Caucasian scooped her up, she saw Rafael signal to the two men who promptly lowered the icebox to the road. Then the

Caucasian was pawing her shirt front. She let herself go limp, her right arm falling as though in consent. The knife slid out; she heard the double click of the hilt's opening and closing. Now, her attention shifted. She could feel his heart thumping and, bringing up her left hand, she placed it gently on his chest, pushing him back a little to give her the leverage she needed. The blade, she thought, should slip between her thumb and forefinger which marked the man's heart-beat.

He let go suddenly, springing for the icebox. The two men did not move. They waited until he had pried open the top, felt the beer, felt something else, and with a "hey!" was about to leap to his feet when the shorter man pivoted and, bending without effort, shoved the knife blade into his nape. Six inches, Anna thought, of recast ball bearings, right through his medulla oblongata. *Requisat in pace.* The Caucasian slumped to his knees, fell back, and sat down on the road.

"He's drunk!" Laughing, the two caught his arms and pulled him to his feet. They draped the limp arms about their shoulders and dragged the tourist to the cart.

"Don't worry, Joe, we'll take care of you. Sleep in our hut tonight, Joe. Don't bother our brother. He's got his girl with him. There, there, Joe. There, there."

"Unlucky, that one," Rafael said. He had stepped closer to her. "I thought you would. Why didn't you?"

"I didn't have the courage." She sighed.

"Stupid foreigner. Doesn't half-know half of what's going on." He sighed. "We must look pretty silly to them. Small and quiet and smiling. Always smiling."

"Someone should tell them our teeth are simply on edge."

The two men returned. They shrugged, opened their arms help-lessly, apologetically. Rafael made a dismissing gesture. The men picked up their pace and soon had the three iceboxes transferred.

"Well, have a good time," they said. "We'll see you tomorrow. Thanks for the beer. And don't worry." In a lower tone, one muttered: "May the Festival's tribute be just."

"Amen," Rafael said and embraced them one by one.

At that moment, a sound rose from the clearing, a collective sigh. Rafael pointed to the sky. Four, five meteors streaked toward the horizon. Then two more. Three. Quick as the blink of an eye, a shower of fire was upon them. In the clearing, the peasants picked up their lamps and held them aloft, greeting a star, flashing blue and white, as it moved from its post at the apex of a tree. A red-orange star detached itself from a cluster. It followed the blue-and-white one. Now six more appeared, describing a slow parabola across the sky. From the clearing, the voices came, floating singly, in twos and threes, some faltering over half-remembered words but rushing on nevertheless, until all the men and women were singing and a river of melody flowed between sky and earth.

8

Adrian fled from Colonel Urbano Amor through a terrain that mirrored his own anxiety. Beneath his bare feet, the steaming ground of compacted ash burned colder than ice; his lungs labored with gulps of air that was not air but an exhalation of tar pits. The motile earth quivered and shifted, breeding mountains and rocks, while from the horizon jagged cracks crawled into his path, yawned into fissures filled with gray magma in which familiar objects—the debris of some existence—floated and stirred with heat currents: a blue bundle, an old boot, a cat's head, a rosary of giant beads, toy boats of sardine cans, bottles of wine, trophies, medals, and bankbooks . . . As he ran, his heart tremulous, Adrian tried to keep all he saw straight in his mind, numbered and itemized like an inventory list, for Colonel Urbano Amor was but a breath away, stepping in his footprints nearly as fast as he made them. Adrian's throat was parched, the blood pounded in his temples, but the colonel walked cool and inviolate through the

soot of that undiscovered country. He wore a white ship steward's
uniform and an upended chamber pot on his head, and bore a lance
that was a four-foot syringe with a monstrous needle. From his open
mouth, a transparent ribbon issued, undulating like a wave and breaking into foot-long sections that rode the thick air. One floated to
Adrian's feet. Stenciled on both sides, like etching on glass, was the
word *remember.* When he saw that, such a grief possessed him he had
to cower, his hands cupping his naked genitals, and weep. On a crag
above him, a woman leaned her elbows on a low wall. She waved,
gesturing for him to come up to safety, and her concern was so visible
that Adrian's tears mingled copiously with the sweat on his cheeks.
By her hair, he knew her and tried not to look, for the colonel was
marching down the trail, his eyes searching the mountain ramparts
for enemies. From an eagle's nest suspended from a mast that was no
mast but the huge barrel of a rifle, a man in white lifted a hand and
pointed to Anna's den. Adrian shook his head no but it was done, the
colonel was marching forward, his needle-lance down and aimed at
the wall that protected Anna's home.

But it was no wall at all, merely books piled atop one another,
volumes of the *Encyclopaedia Britannica* which Adrian had ordered
for her one summer day. He tried to explain, running about the
colonel whose lower limbs had extended to become the body of a
horse and who now, hooves pawing the earth, made ready to charge
up the mountain trail. Adrian scurried about him, saying wait, wait,
try to understand. She had five dresses exact and wanted no more; two
pairs of shoes, exact, and wanted no more; a handbag, exact—and all
she could think of wishing for was the last half of the encyclopedia,
from R to Z. She had never managed to read it, she said, and had
always wondered what it contained, since her twelfth birthday when
her uncle had given her the first volumes from A to Q, saying *there,*
if you can't be beautiful, try to be intelligent. All her cousins had
guffawed at the remark but she hadn't minded at all and had taken
the books, setting them against one wall of her room above the house
garage. She had read them one by one, whenever she had the time,
often during dinner, the book propped up by bottles of vinegar and

banana sauce. But she had not seen the last volumes of the set—not until that afternoon Adrian had them delivered, himself following shortly after to find her bemused, barefoot, and in blue jeans, in the middle of her living room, surrounded by the entire, complete set of the *Encyclopaedia Britannica,* ta-ran!!!

She had risen to her toes and flung her arms about his neck and all he could do was mutter *my goodness!* The hours had seemed too quick, too short, between the end of office hours and the time he had to return home. Too swiftly did they fly though Anna and he never did anything except remain linked together, in bed, on the sofa, or, when the day was too warm, on a *buri* mat on the floor. They would sit face-to-face, arms about each other, the lunar sheen of her thighs about his hips until he began to feel that they were on a skiff, launched carelessly with the tide, to skirt shores of firetrees, yellow bell flowers, and woolly caterpillars munching on summer. Her face always had this detached, almost clinical expression, watching him try to absorb the unbearable blows of pleasure, and only his name escaping the quiver of her lips, *Adrian,* told him of how delicate ecstasy had seeped into the cracks of her soul. Her head on his shoulder convinced him, time and again, that this was the way his life was meant to be—to be set adrift thus, on a reed mat of a skiff, on a wayward current, to the songs of caterpillars.

Being an honorable man, he wanted to make everything official, so to speak, and found a half-carat solitaire for her. On Saturday, their last before the Festival, he hid the ring in a bag of peanuts and met her in the park where they sat on a bench and watched the waves play with the sun. He waited in silence as she popped peanuts into her mouth. When she froze suddenly, her right hand still in the bag of peanuts, he knew she had found it and answered her accusing glance by beaming foolishly, innocently. She brought the ring out and studied it, turning it this way and that, making the diamond flash and sparkle. It was some seconds before Adrian realized that a low horrible sound was coming from her closed lips whose corners trembled up and down, up and down. *She was laughing.* A truly horrible sound. He realized then that he had never heard her laugh. A few seconds more and she was bent over, howling with laughter like one demented as Adrian, not knowing what to make of the spectacle, wrung his hands and looked around helplessly. She stopped eventually, her eyes and cheeks shiny with tears, and she brought the ring close to her nose and sniffed at it. It smelled, she said, like spring water. And as her face smoothed out, the last of her hilarity disappearing, she slipped the ring into his shirt pocket, stood up, and walked away.

So, you tell me, Colonel—she was insulted, perhaps, because the stone was too small?

Colonel Amor smiled and nodded, smiled and nodded. He was pleased, he said, that Adrian remembered so well. His smile widened, became a slim crack through which a wet, purple orchid bodied forth, its petals trembling with the labor of its birth. The orchid bobbed before Adrian's face and he saw it was held by the man in white, who had a gigantic stethoscope draped about his neck. Adrian's heart, said the man, was doing fine; perhaps, it was time for another dose?

At which a thunderclap filled the sky; a cliff cracked asunder and, to the sound of trumpets, Old Andy charged forward, his wheelchair spewing smoke like a dragon. *You,* he said, *you!* The man in white fled. The governor drifted down from the sky, feathered wings flapping at his shoulders, a pillow of cloud beneath his sandaled feet. Clasping his hands and rolling his eyes to heaven, he asked if Adrian, having remembered so well, would also forget.

Old Andy was not put out in the least, not at all, he said as his wheelchair rocked back and forth, snorting flames and smoke. This was a revolution, he cried out. A sword materialized in his hand. In a terrible clang of metal, Old Andy met Colonel Amor's thrust with the syringe. A pity, the old man said, that the real protagonists in this war never met, would never meet—the men behind desks, the men who signed papers, issued orders, summed up costs and profits. His attack repelled, Colonel Amor shrugged while the governor, wings flapping, hovered six inches off the ground.

But Old Andy was rising from his chair, pushing his body up on thin arms and thin legs, and having made it to his feet, struck an operatic pose. This was the Revolution, he said again. His words echoed, re-echoed, nearly upending the governor. Adrian laughed. Old Andy was more than a match for anyone, he knew.

You tell 'em, boy, the old man said, looking at Adrian fondly. *I have told you often enough.*

Anxiety gripped Adrian again and, almost panting, he circled the colonel, words spewing out of his mouth. The colonel metamorphosed into a gigantic anthill with two eyes at its apex. Coldly, unimpressed, he stared at Adrian without blinking. But you must understand, Adrian cried out. He paced back and forth before the anthill, nearly stumbling on his own feet, so desperate was he that the colonel should understand.

Understand what, the anthill rumbled from its bowels.

Understand that it was a ridiculous thought at the time, though it was nevertheless true that Old Andy crawled out of World War II's second most devastated city with the means to build an empire. True though his waterfront house had collapsed into blackened bits of wood and loose roofing sheets and he was weeping bitterly as he sifted through the rubble, picking up bits and pieces of a vanished epoch: the ribs of Miss Estela's fan, the chin and neck from a Luna oil portrait, charred gilt-edged pages from books, the ear of a silver candy dish. All that, he thought then, so that son-of-a-goat MacArthur could strut through the flattened city of Manila and lisp "told you I'd be back," gaddamit. Everything—the city, the people—had been props to a farce; Douggie MacArthur never even smelled the corpses in Bataan and Corregidor, nor laid eyes on cadavers laid end-to-end for a hundred miles, yes, even to Capas, Tarlac; nor had he known how Old Andy had huddled in the basement of his house, unable to decide which was better, death by bombs or death by diarrhea. Phooey!

Old Andy saw his first blond GI after four years that bitter afternoon—an artilleryman taking a respite from the 24-hour cannonading of what was left of the 300-year-old walls of Intramuros. The blond was whistling *it's the loveliest night of the year* as he walked, his knees wide apart through the city ruins, his eyes searching the windows of the one intact house left of the block of adobe mansions and wrought-iron balconies, hoping for a glimpse of its frail *mestiza* resident, a woman in her late twenties, passing for a sixteen-year-old, such being the benefit of a protein-deficient diet.

For all his bitterness, Old Andy was no fool; he could recognize opportunity whatever its disguise and, raising his hand, two fingers pronging the air, he boomed out: *Victory, Joe! Liberation, Joe! Long live America! Cigarette, Joe! Don't be stingy, Joe!*

Alas, the habits of a lifetime. He cursed himself as he laid out the GI's gifts on the burnt dining table, two of whose legs had been replaced by adobe blocks: three loaves of bread, a can of peaches, a can of sardines, two candles. He and his two sons bowed their heads and, in the purple light of dusk, Old Andy prayed aloud to an indifferent god to whom he vowed never to pray again, saying that his last whine for survival had been heard, he would never, never, never grovel again before strangers, never again would he build and accumulate only to let everything be reduced to debris by another man's war, gaddamit. Never, never, never again. Before he became involved in another man's war, he would start one himself. So be it.

The governor seemed touched by Old Andy's words. He fluttered his wings and his eyelashes and turning to the colonel said something was wrong, why was the boy cackling like that? But the colonel patted his shoulder and said there, there; there, there, there; it's all coming out now, coming out, you will see.

He did see, Old Andy said proudly, though it had taken a while and though he had called his eldest son shitbrained when the morose engineering graduate, staggering about the ruins, rinsing tin plates at the water buckets, waved an opaque sheet before Old Andy, assailing his delicate nostrils with its chemical odor, and announced that this was the future. It was nothing but plastic—but it was the future. Twenty years later, when Old Andy's body and brains reeled with the seismic tremors of a stroke, the floor of Manila Bay was already rotting under an indestructible pile of plastic sheets, bags, tubes, and bottles, the waves heaving pestilential vapors and poisonous sprays of startling rainbow colors into the clear moist air—courtesy of the Banyaga corporation. Fish refused to enter the harbor and the fishermen had to head for the spawning waters of the typhoons and by the logic of their desire to survive, perished instead. Even wealth, Old Andy understood, had its price.

The governor gave an exasperated sigh. Adrian took this as indictment of his grandfather and he wept. Colonel Amor wiped the tears as they ran down his cheeks. There, there, there; about the Revolution . . .

Understand, Old Andy said on a pleading note, this was the time of reconstruction; fortunes were being made. A handshake across a desk, a whispered introduction, cash under the table and so forth . . . The most tenuous of agreements sufficed because capital was pouring in from across the seas, War Rehabilitation Funds from the great North American nation, funds whose disposition and distribution depended on the signature of one—two, at the most, perhaps— man, sending the clever and the sly scurrying to acquire heroic pasts, twenty-eight medals apiece, or sagas of having fought the Japanese Imperial Army, as well as losses in the form of houses, factories, plantations, all catalogued in detail in their nonexistence. Buying and selling triumphed once more in life—though there were no goods, no products. What was sold instead were sheaves of paper, agreements, quotas, permits and licenses, contracts, and government became the biggest business in the country. Assisted by his sons, Old Andy chose to invest in shares of men, staking small fortunes in this or that rising political star in the expectation that, in due time, the man would control all that paper, sheaves and sheaves of signed, stamped, and numbered paper. He optioned the futures of other men, since he was himself already bereft of one, being old now, old.

It was his eldest again who called his attention to a young lawyer . . .

Ah, we get to it, the governor said.

Get to it, get to it, get to it—the echoes rolled off the mountaintops.

. . . a newcomer to Congress who stood out because he was lean of body among so many fattened calves. Old Andy's curiosity was further pricked when the man boasted of having two medals of valor from the U.S. Congress—a sign certainly that the *norte americano* was up to his old tricks. He bought a quarter share in the man's political career, sold half of it at triple its original price when the man married a beauty queen. By the time the lawyer was Senate president, Old Andy's share had become both invaluable and a risk. As he rose through the levels of power, the lawyer had trailed in his wake a network of relatives, a locust horde, which gobbled up everything in its path: a paper mill, a bank, a shopping center, a land development corporation, a furniture store, a jewelry corporation, coconut and sugar lands, a beauty parlor, and a gambling joint. Old Andy, who had turned over his fortune to his sons, had only the years piling on his shoulders and Adrian, son of his son, who played at the feet of his grandfather and listened to all his stories and his monstrous monologue of unmeasured time, and who was too young to smell the old man's fear.

It had begun, one afternoon at an intimate banquet with the lawyer who was now head of state, his shoulders stiff with the title of commander-in-chief. He wasn't an impressive man, not tall, not handsome, his hair the impossible black of vegetable dye, but he made up for his unprepossessing appearance with pomp and ceremony, starting with his beauty queen wife who changed her clothes and jewels thrice in four hours and serenaded the guests with love songs. Old Andy, exhausted by her reedy coloratura voice, was seated midway down the table for thirty—not too close to the seat of authority, as it were, since the lawyer still didn't know that the Banyagas owned an eighth share of him, which was all to the good, said Old Andy, since the man was ruining everyone and anyone who'd invested in him.

The man had just emerged victorious from a confrontation with his erstwhile principal financier, a sugar baron whom he had stripped of sugar import quotas and whose letters of credit had been reined in by the Central Bank. The poor bastard was unable to sell his sugar to the U.S. while his creditors were demanding payment for his sugar mill equipment, the stupid so-and-so. The double squeeze had forced him to his knees and he had had to surrender part ownership of his Manila electric power plant, signing it away to the lawyer's relatives without a single peso changing hands, the old so-and-so.

Old Andy had kept track of the game, unsure whether to cash in on his share or to keep quiet. He had been amused by the shrewdness and voracity of this upstart who now denied his peasant origins and traced his genealogy to Alexander of Macedon, the shitbrained so-and-so.

But we're going away from the Revolution, Colonel Amor said. His eyes flashed red and orange and Adrian wept. There, there, there. There was a furtive movement behind a leafless tree and, startled, he saw Eliza briefly in the company of a phantasm dressed in peacock blue. She darted forward but her companion grabbed her elbow and drew her into a black mist that roiled out of nowhere and swallowed them. Adrian wept.

We're waiting for the Revolution, the governor sang in a piercing falsetto.

That afternoon precipitated it, Old Andy said, his arm slashing the air; listen to me, *pendejos* of the world. Revolutions do not happen without wherefores and whys. This very afternoon, as the plates were being cleared from the table, the silverware changed for dessert—*brazos de mercedes* and *sans rival,* I remember—two men brought up the matter of an empty land bordering the highway, outside the city—true—but close enough to feel the pressure of the megalopolis's burgeoning population. A subdivision to equal the old Forbes, a new Beverly Hills with free-form pools, Jacuzzi and saunas, greenhouses and fountains, roofs with skylights, and front doors made from the gates of century-old churches of which there were too many in the country, etcetera, etcetera . . . The two had planned for this, had discussed it, and were most pleased that the permits had been issued and construction could begin, for the good of the country, and *blah-blah-blah,* as a token of their appreciation, of their gratitude that the new head of state was such a *forward-looking man*—those were their words, Colonel—the corporation had decided to give a prime corner of the new town, a somewhat largish piece of real estate, not to the man, mind you, for that would be contrary to the law, but to his children that they may have something of their own, for everyone knew that public service was a thankless job, especially when it ended.

Old Andy had watched the lawyer's face throughout this speech and had seen that face darken, pulse with a violet, malignant force at mention of his retirement from power. He took in the black rage, marked it, and said to himself, *leche,* there could be another war and soon, holy shit, barely six years to go and Adrian was unprepared.

He was still muttering to himself when the two men handed over the leather folder with the land title. Now, the Commander's expression changed again. A half-second of silence when his fingers touched the folder and his eyes scoured the two men's faces. Now a serene light shone on his forehead, washed over his cheekbones, and his lips worked at something seemingly immeasurably sweet. Old Andy nearly pissed in his pants. He saw clearly, immediately, that the man didn't care about the gift's value, didn't care about the gift even, but cared profoundly for the act of receiving as though the gift were a tribute, a confirmation of his self, his being, his reality. He found no pleasure in what he was taking but in the act of taking itself. Old Andy cursed silently and steadfastly, right through a string quartet's rendition of a *kundiman,* an old love aria that spoke of infinite possibilities in a still young world which had not known Douggie MacArthur, the son-of-a-goat.

He was right, Old Andy was, Adrian said. Two months later, when construction did begin at the new subdivision, half of its holding company's board of directors were relatives of the Commander and each of his children, as well as his wife, held titles to several lots. The former owners were overseas in disgrace, having defaulted on government loans by some unforeseen accident.

Six years to go. Old Andy roamed the corridors and rooms of his mansion, the whine of his wheelchair a squeal of fear. There was hardly time to build a wall of typhoons about his possessions, to secure everything for Adrian, the last of his loins, the most perfect, the most innocent, the handsomest of the Banyagas; Adrian who was untroubled by doubts as to his origins and who, even when feeding on that unspeakable invention, the hamburger, was truly to the manner born.

He sent the slips which bore the Commander's signature—paper that acknowledged Old Andy's electoral contributions—to the Palace with a note saying *we don't have to have this between us now.* A month later, his eldest son received a logging concession in Palawan Island. Old Andy's mouth tasted of ashes when he heard about it. There was a message here, he thought, but he himself had not clawed his way up for nothing.

It was quite simple, Colonel. A few phone calls, a transfer of money from bank to bank, and Old Andy had a station in Hong Kong, outside the man's perimeters of power. Pity the peasant who could not afford a sanctuary. Three years more and the station was operational, having established links with the unacknowledged commerce of weapons and explosives flowing from country to country all over the world, mankind's most profitable modern enterprise. The plan was simplicity itself: to deflect the Commander's attention by creating a minor disturbance; to create a buffer between the Banyagas and the man who would rule absolutely and eternally. It was not difficult, for the man himself helped things along; he was well on his way to gobbling up the seven thousand one hundred islands, piling loans upon loans, printing worthless money, taking over one business after another in the name of his inept friends and relatives while his equally maddened wife, suddenly freed from the shame and ostracism of poverty, pursued her silly obsession with aristocratic titles and threw one party after another.

When one feared a man, one invested in his enemies—right, Colonel?—and by the fourth of the six years, the man had plenty. Old Andy nosed around, found a group here, chose a group there, and through intermediaries placed them in touch with the Hong Kong station. He was careful though in his selection, limiting his network to young professionals, a number of whom had intact memories of poverty. He preferred them young because the young were absolute in their loyalties. Weren't they, Colonel?

Oh, yes, yes, yes. Very good, very, very good.

It was all very simple, really, and each month, Adrian—dear, innocent Adrian who knew everything but never seemed to put one and one together, who listened with only one ear to everything said to him—brought checks to be signed and forwarded to a coded address overseas.

Ah, that was it, said the governor, beatified with contentment. The colonel agreed, saying *that was it, that was it, you may rest now, good boy, good boy, don't worry about it, we'll take care of the old coot while you sleep in the governor's palace in a beautiful bed and your father will be so pleased we are returning you intact—with all your faculties intact.* Adrian wept, certain now that what Old Andy had always thought was right, that his sons, Adrian's father and uncle, were comedians.

But he, Old Andy, never wept, never despaired, and went on mumbling and murmuring in his dotage, his withered head shaking with the effort of speaking, trying to teach Adrian the one lesson—so very, very important, Colonel, you should take it to heart as well— that he had learned when he was still a shrimp, a twit, prosecuting his first case, a handsome devil of a playwright accused of sedition. It had been simple, since the tribunal was staffed by American officers and all Old Andy had had to do was argue that, gaddamit, everything was an act of God and poof! The handsome devil was exiled to Guam even as Old Andy was rushing out of the court to purchase the last two copies of the poor unfortunate's book of plays. It was a good-looking volume, all leather binding, good linen paper, and gilt-edged. He had rushed to Intramuros, the dungeons of Spanish and now American infamy, the copies in his hands, to ask the elegant young man with the handlebar mustache and the European accent to inscribe them with his historic name. The young man had been amused and, despite his bruised and swollen face (for the blonds had played with him), he had signed twice with a flourish. Thank you, thank you, Old Andy had breathed out, his eyes loving the mementos of his first court case, his fingers caressing the leather covers as though his skin could absorb the words on those pages. It was then that he made a terrible mistake, gaddamit, because he had deemed himself worthy, having been a newsman, a bar topnotcher, and a victorious prosecutor, and having been civilized enough to show he respected the man he was sending off to exile by actually buying his book and asking for his autograph—because of all that, Old Andy had held out his hand like a true gentleman, saying no hard feelings, señor. The playwright had looked at him, looked at the hand he had thrust between the bars, and had stepped away, smiling with disgust. And in a voice loud enough for the jailer and the jailed to hear, in words of the crudest Tagalog (not even poetic), he had uttered the phrase that was to haunt Old Andy to his dying day. That was how he learned his lesson—the one Adrian should learn one day, if not today—to wit: that to own things did not necessarily mean one belonged; that possession was no guarantee of control. And when you came to the bottom line, sir, nothing—not beautiful gestures, not beautiful words—spelled the difference between whether one did or did not belong to the seven thousand one hundred islands except the willingness, indeed the capability, sir, to take risks on the archipelago's behalf. Risks and relentless action, sir; risks and steadfast action.

He learned that and more from three words, uttered with unbearable disdain by a playwright in a voice colder than a sword: "You old fart!"

Peace, Colonel; peace, Governor—old farts both.

9

Daylight was a knot of pain behind her eyes as she rose, stiff muscles protesting, from the mat on the floor. What room it was, in whose house, she did not know; gathered dimly behind the pain in her head were the previous night's memories: of the transvestite guiding her through a labyrinth of back streets; of herself cowering between the bamboo stilt legs of houses, watching soldiers round up a dozen or so men and women and prod them with rifle butts toward an army van; of a black-velvet-curtained room where Adrian sat in an armchair, twitching and quivering, his legs thrashing, as Colonel Urbano Amor and the governor watched; of a furtive flight through the dark accompanied by children's shadows, the transvestite at her elbow shushing her. What did it all mean?

Nothing of what had happened so far had been expected. Adrian, Anna, and she, Eliza, had come to the Festival for a measure of relief—to forget, they had told one another, the city and all its problems (meaning, of course, their own) for a little while, just three days. Instead, here were all the problems still, heartache and headache both, having stowed away in the overnight bags and backpacks and waist pouches, every single troublesome one. And the Festival's perimeter of safety had turned out to be no larger than a ten-block-long and five-block-wide plaza, with the church at one end and the town hall at the other. A step outside and, immediately, the stench of war was in one's nostrils, unmistakable, inescapable.

A bare-chested man sat up on the *buri* mat and Eliza recognized with a start the night's transvestite. He grinned, got to his feet, hooked thumbs into his blue jeans' waist, and hitched them up. He was a mature man, perhaps forty years old, and though he had shucked off his female persona, he still looked pleasant, his soft face an odd contrast to his muscular torso. Without a word, he left the room but was back almost immediately, carrying a tray of coffee and buttered *pan de sal*. The hot buns' fragrance cleared her head somewhat.

"Hungry?" the man asked.

She nodded, already reaching for the food. The coffee was hot, freshly brewed, and smelled divine. And the buns were obviously homemade.

"Mimay makes great bread," he said, reading her thoughts. He was eating as fast as she was.

"Who?"

"House owner. The one in yellow yesterday—uh, uh. You don't remember."

She lifted her shoulders apologetically, looking at him over the cup's rim.

"Are you and your friends with the underground?" he asked suddenly, tearing a bun and stuffing half into his mouth. He did not look at her.

"What underground?"

He shrugged, concentrated on his chewing. "Have it your way," he said after a while. "One picks up rumors here and there, from festival to festival. Whispers. Hell, everyone knows about it but no one wants to talk. We're all living it up in a fort, anyway, and the enemy's closing in."

Eliza remained silent.

"Funny but when one does come across such creatures—you know, from the underground—they're usually dead." He laughed. "Maybe they become visible only when dead. I've seen a couple, displayed at a town square on another island. They were only children: boy-man, girl-woman. I have never understood what the fuss is all about. Just children. A feast for flies."

Eliza returned the empty cup to the tray. "I don't know about the underground," she said. "It seems to me that if I—if you—if anyone wanted to do something, he or she would do it on his or her own."

His eyebrows rose in mock surprise.

"Because—well," Eliza chose her words carefully. "To resist is so dangerous one wouldn't wish to involve anyone else."

He laughed. "You have a generous heart." A moment's silence as he studied her. "This Festival—it doesn't feel right." He raised his eyes to the windows and sighed.

"I don't understand."

"When you've been to as many festivals as I have, you get a feel for it. This one now—too many things happening, too many soldiers, too many scuttlings in the dark. I get goosebumps when I think of it, when I *seriously* think . . ." With the tip of a forefinger, he drew an invisible line on the mat. "This was the house where your friend was last night."

"Is he—?"

"He's fine. They took him to the governor's house. He's probably sleeping it off, whatever it was they gave him. And here, here, here— houses where soldiers are billeted. Here, the house which was raided. All in a narrow arc about this space. And guess what this is. A stage. Where the closing ceremonies are supposed to take place." He frowned at what he had laid out. "I'm thinking of leaving. Want to join me?"

"No," she said. "My friends are here."

"But then again, I'll miss the fun, whatever it is. I won't

have stories to take back with me." His voice changed pitch, became higher, self-indulgent. "You know how we are. My friends would kill me if I came back without gossip. Lord, I haven't even made any conquest yet. They'd be so disappointed." He giggled.

"I wish they'd kill Amor," she said bitterly.

He ignored her. "I certainly don't want to miss this morning's event. And, chica, you shouldn't. After all, this slut's your protégé. I just love government functionaries. They are such sluts." He giggled again and, just as abruptly, changed his tone. "Perhaps you'll have your chance, child, in the confusion. I wish I could do it but I don't have the guts. I could help you, though, if you really want to do it. There are about a hundred of us here—you know, men like me. And we all are marvelous gossips."

"How will that help?"

"I should be able to tell you where he is at any given time. Or where to find—shall we call those things implements?"

"Why?"

"He killed a friend. A benign old professor, the only one who spoke up for me when I got into trouble at the Jesuit school. Not my friend, really. When he tried to defend me, I was surprised. I hardly knew the guy—and he wasn't, you know, like me. I suppose that was what killed him—his habit of speaking out when it's better to be quiet. Left six children orphaned. He was a widower. Nothing much I could do for the kids but—"

"All right," Eliza said. "I'll keep it in mind." She laughed. "I can't believe we're talking like this. I'm just an ordinary person. I feel ordinary, probably smell ordinary. But I'll keep it in mind. After all, obligations are obligations. You have yours, I have mine. Let's hope the twain meet." She shook her head. Foolish, all these dreams of death.

"I have to fix my face," the man said. He circled to the far wall and slid open the doors of a built-in closet. "Mimay has tons of gowns." He flicked a hand at the clothes. "Want one? She has pink, green, turquoise, garnet . . . Lord, you name it."

Eliza declined. She dusted off her T-shirt and jeans. "I'll wash," she said, "and remain what I am."

"Bathroom downstairs, near the kitchen. Ignore the maids; there's no one home. I'll use the bath up here."

Half an hour later, he came down in a towering silver wig and a red beaded gown. His face was made up, the eyebrows arched, cheekbones defined, and his lips a perfect pink moue.

"That's neat," she said, "neat."

"To the town hall, love," he said, crooking his elbow. "And be sure to introduce me to this lovely deputy so-and-so. I could give him ideas. Such ideas!"

Outside, a flock of children burst into laughter at their appearance. The transvestite stuck his tongue out. The children scattered, the voices shrill as bird cries. There were too many of them, Eliza thought as she peered at them surreptitiously. The boys wore nothing but T-shirts and their tiny genitals swung freely; the girls wore camisole slips, straps edging down their slim shoulders. It seemed hardly possible that in a few years they would fill out and blossom into stupendous beauties—dark-haired, dark-eyed, skin reddish-brown. Right now, they were pests, sprouting out of the earth to run barefoot on dust roads, harking to the Festival whistles, or materializing behind trash bins to ogle Caucasians.

The drums had not started and the sparse crowd milled restlessly through the plaza. A steady stream of people headed for the town hall. Eliza's and the transvestite's appearance occasioned some applause and giggles—but for the most, the air was subdued, crisp with expectation, still restrained.

The town hall's lobby had been transformed into a conference room, cracks on the wall plaster hidden by tall potted palms, the worn floor under a red carpet. Its mood of melancholic resignation contrasted oddly with the prefab seats with built-in audio systems which had been set up in the lower half of the lobby. Eliza shivered in the air conditioning, noting that the first seat rows were occupied by men in dark business suits. Half a dozen handsome youths, male and female, served as ushers and they were so impeccably polite not one

raised an eyebrow when the transvestite swept down the lobby and
announced his name. After checking a list on his clipboard, a young
man led them to the fourth row from the last. The transvestite, aware
of the commotion his appearance had inspired, thanked the usher,
smiled, and bowed to the left, the right, the front, the back, before
arranging himself in his seat. In a loud voice, he informed Eliza that
the speaker had seven Ph.D.s, two secretaries, and one translator in
a booth somewhere to reduce his high-caliber English to plainer
words—"for less gifted mortals like us." He beamed.

Eliza recognized businessmen, industrialists, intellectuals from all
regions of the country, this being—as the transvestite pointed out—
the cultural high point of the Festival. "So foreigners will know we
do know more than just eat, drink, and be merry." He learned closer
and whispered: "The man recommends projects to the Commander's
wife. An alternate route, you understand, when the barrier around
himself can't be pierced. So, don't be impressed, darling. Most of the
people here are failed businessmen. Looking for a way back to grace."
He giggled. "But there is your friend, way down front. Now, how did
she get there while we're here at the back?"

Eliza followed the direction of his look. It was Anna, in an aisle
chair to the right, her legs crossed, face watchful. She read her expression at once, recognizing it for what Anna called "observing but not
being engaged." She was about to call her friend's attention when a
man made his way to the platform in front, walked to the lectern, and
tapped the microphone.

"You have to use the earphones," the transvestite said. "Not now.
Later. Don't slip them on. Just hold one close to your ear. That way
you'll hear what the speaker says and what the translator says. Don't
worry. It's from English to English and back. You shall be most
edified." He laughed.

The man on the lectern greeted his audience. The lobby had filled
up, all the seats were taken, and a spillover crowd stood at the fringe
of the seat rows. After a few jokes, the man introduced the speaker
and Eliza, smiling, recognized her protégé—much changed now
though he was still a thin, dark man. Instead of the unpressed cotton

shirt and crumpled pants which had been his usual costume, he now wore a white sport suit over a lavender silk shirt which billowed over his pants' waistband.

"The strategic intervention of authoritarian democratic bureaucratism," he began, "could hasten the trajectory of the critical path of implementation of development plans."

Eliza's mouth opened.

From the earphones, a female voice issued: "Government support will ensure quicker implementation of development projects."

For thirty minutes, the man went on in the same vein, as expressions of alarm, shock, and then despair flitted across the faces in the audience. When the man in front of her jiggled his earphones impatiently, a squeal escaped Eliza. The woman to her left was cursing steadily under her breath. The transvestite, on the other hand, listened in obvious delight, his eyes opening and closing in barely contained ecstacy. Now and then, at a particularly vile circumlocution, he breathed out a "yeah, baby!" and blew kisses toward the stage. But when Eliza chortled, he was quick to seize her knee and squeeze.

There was bewildered applause at the speech's end, murmurs of *most edifying, instructive, very intellectual,* etc. An announcement was made that reactions from the floor were being accepted and no one should worry about his level of English for the translator could scale it up or down as needed. At this, a bearded man, miserable in his sleeveless shirt, stood up and tried to control the chattering of his teeth. He was obviously a stranger to the island, a Festival visitor.

After clearing his throat and hemming and hawing, he said: "I have observed that there is less and less land available, especially in the cities."

The speaker stopped him and picked up his earphones. From her own set, Eliza heard the translation: "There is ongoing reduction of prime real estate, particularly in the urban areas."

The speaker nodded. The man with the beard sighed.

"Even cemeteries are overcrowded. There's barely enough space to bury a corpse. And the chances are, this will get worse with time."

From the earphones: "Even space allotted for the disposal of matter which has lost organic relevance is reaching null point. It has become a statistical difficulty to entomb such matter as needs encryptization. And the prognosis is toward an increasing gravity of the situation."

The bearded man threw a terrified look at the earphones in his hands. But inhaling audibly, he went on: "I barely get orders for tombstones and angels anymore. There's no room in the cemeteries."

"Commissions for the production of elegiac sculpture are at a stage of nullity. Space for their proper display is not available."

"Perhaps, the problem is caused by our burying the dead lying down. If we could convince people that being buried standing up is just as comfortable, we would solve the problem." He sat down abruptly.

From the earphones: "The roots of our quandary lie in the tradition of encrypting remains horizontally. Astute re-education of our populace on the desirability of vertical burial can be a major step toward resolution of the problem."

Silence. The speaker smiled, considered the problem. He grasped the edge of the lectern and leaned toward his audience which nervously leaned back. The transvestite said sotto voce: *sock it to 'em, baby!*

"Our esteemed colleague," the speaker began, "has enunciated an illuminating summation and proposed resolution of a problem of significant proportions . . ."

From the earphones: "Our friend has stated a problem and a possible solution."

"However, if permission may be bestowed upon me by this aforesaid personality . . ."

"If I may be allowed . . ."

". . . it would be to my utmost gratification to pursue the relentless induction of his proposition."

". . . I'd like to follow his arguments to their logical conclusion."

"Why be content with providing only the alternative of vertical sepulcherization? There are other, justified, preferences—options which may respond to the citizenry's spectrum of desires while coincidentally providing resolutions to this quagmiric quandary. We could propose an edict, on the personal initiative of our most gracious Lady of Ladies, that our citizens be tendered the possibilities of vertical burial, or with knee joints folded, or in such a reposeful mode as would require the use of a piece of furniture for the posterior."

The transvestite was writhing in his chair; Eliza had to clamp both hands to her mouth. She barely heard the translation: a choice of being buried upright, curled up, or seated.

"As a preventive measure, we shall also propose that, henceforth, all government projects and structures shall incorporate a designated area for the encryptization of matter of null organic relevance. So be it."

A standing ovation. Shouts of *bravo*. The transvestite was screaming *I love you!* and blowing kisses with both hands at the speaker.

"Marvelous, isn't he?" he yelled above the noise. "As deceased as the subject." He turned his head toward the stage again and, raising his hands, clapped with great enthusiasm.

The audience poured out of the seat rows, some heading for the speaker while others made for the lobby doors. Eliza saw Anna walking away, edging through the crowd.

"Wait!" she yelled.

"Darling, darling," the transvestite murmured, scandalized, as she pressed past him, knocked aside the restraining hands of an usher, and ran.

She caught up with Anna outside, on the wide portico.

"Did you see that? Did you see?" she called out eagerly. "I was responsible. I gave that man his job!"

"Oh, Eliza," Anna said, turning away.

"What's the matter? Didn't you like it? A discussion of government policy?"

"Bodies and burials." Anna started down the stairs, dragging Eliza along.

"Same thing," she said, laughing.

"Don't look now," Anna said, glancing over her shoulder, "but a lady in red is making a beeline for you."

"Oh, no!" Eliza seized her hand. "Let's duck. Quick. I've had enough insanity for a while."

They fled down the stairs and dove into the crowd, moving like quicksilver, letting themselves become one with the sudden dancing that erupted along with the drums: *Hala, bira! Hala, bira! Hala, bira!*

"Loosen up," Eliza yelled at Anna. "Admit it. It was marvelous. As a phony, he was a genius. And I discovered him." She laughed. Eliza, talent scout of phonies. She danced that rhythm around Anna who swayed like a pond reed stirred by the wind.

"I don't like it when people monkey around with language," Anna said, raising her voice above the chanting. Step-step-step. Halt. Step-step-step. Halt. "Mess up language, mess up memory. People forget. Even what they are." Step-step-step. Halt. Step-step-step. Halt. She whirled slowly, keeping time to the drums.

Eliza thought that they—both of them—seemed to be two people each all the time.

The drums hit a new rhythm, faster. *Hala, bira! Hala, bira!* People sang and chanted. *Let me*—LET ME!—*hold you*— HOLD YOU!— *and I shall*—I SHALL—*smash you*—SMASH—*crush you*—- CRUSH—*run over you*—RUN OVER YOU!!! Laughter. Cheers.

Anna hummed a ballad. *Does anyone ever listen to what we say?*

Eliza added a second line. *Or do they just watch us, see us, little dolls in a sea of islands?* She laughed. The drums went BOOM! BOOM! Ta-ra-dyin BOOM! The crowd parted and a group of penitents appeared, their faces covered with brown hoods, their heads crowned with thorns. They lashed at their backs and one another with spiked ropes and thorny branches. Oblivious of the celebration, they murmured Latin prayers, grunting as the whips rose and fell, rose and fell. A soldier in combat uniform cut through their ranks, his eyes held above their bent heads and backs.

The two women had stopped to watch, hand in hand. "I've never understood why anyone would do that," Anna said.

"Pain to drive away other pains," Eliza answered. "Simple. And voluntary—unlike life's miseries."

"Stupid. Why not just remove what's causing all the other problems?"

"Oh, you're too logical," Eliza said, smiling at her fondly. "Look, ices!" Suddenly, the heat was unbearable, the sky and road blazing. They cut through the parade, made the other side of the street, and in a few seconds were queued up before the vendor's cart.

Eliza found a five-peso bill in her pouch. "Leftover wealth," she said laughing and asked for two mango-flavored shaved ices on cones. She handed one to Anna and, licking, they walked away, straight into a circle of mangy-looking children.

"There are too many of them," Eliza said.

"And each one beautiful," Anna said. She nodded at the nearest child, a girl, who hesitated before smiling shyly and extending a cupped hand.

"Now, you've done it," Eliza said.

"Just one, just one," Anna muttered, fumbling at her pouch and dropping a peso bill into the child's hand.

"Quick, quick. Let's go!" Eliza grabbed her wrist and pulled her into the crowd to escape the horde of children who, having witnessed the transaction, were preparing to besiege them. They ran past three soldiers clustered under a tree, each holding a rum bottle.

Licking ices happily, they walked through the Festival. The town decorations had not survived the first twenty-four hours of celebration intact. Some of the buntings were down, looping between rooftops; a bamboo arch had fallen and most of the flowers were withered. The nipa fronds had managed the heat though and glistening dark green, still rustled from electric posts and arches. The warriors, impassive as ever, kept their formation and marched round and about the plaza, in time to the drums, hurling war cries and chants at the crowd. A flock of transvestites passed, a dozen grinning soldiers trailing in their wake.

"You're too clean," a man said as the two passed the church. He stepped up to them and, before Anna could dodge, his hands had caressed her cheeks, leaving red and black streaks on her skin. "Tiger," he said, grinning, and turned to Eliza who, shrieking, tried to escape his hands. But he clawed at her, staining her clothes, her arms, and finally her face. "Now you're truly beautiful." He bowed and walked away.

"Pest!" Eliza screamed.

"Adrian would love this," Anna said.

Eliza shoved the last of the cone into her mouth, and chewed studiously while sneaking a look at Anna's face. She had not expected her to bring him up now. But there it was. She wiped her fingers on her pant seat.

She inhaled. "Do you like Adrian, Anna?"

A pause. "Yes."

She would get no more than that, she knew. She waited, gathering her courage. After a while, she said: "It would be nice to have a normal life."

Another silence. Then, Anna's voice, wistful, full of regret: "Ah, yes."

Eliza's eyes stung; her friend's voice said with finality that it could not be, could never be. Sadness filled Eliza like water in a new-dug well. There was no escaping it, Anna's voice had said. She flung an arm about Anna's shoulder and drew her head forward, letting their foreheads touch. She looked into her friend's brown eyes—paler than her own, certainly, but with the same heavy lids, the same hint of an upward curve at the outer corners, the same smoky fringe of eyelashes.

"What strange ways we've gone," she said to Anna.

With her right hand, Anna patted her cheek. Eliza saw the two of them when they were young—Anna in a cool gauze blouse and blue jeans sitting in the wrought-iron chair of the dorm's back terrace, herself in T-shirt and shorts also in a white wrought-iron chair, and, between them, on the glass-topped garden table, a plate of green mango slices, dewy with salt. Their chins and fingers itched with mango sap and spillovers from the Coke they were drinking as they played *sungka*, their hands scooping out tiny seashells from the carved hollows of the wooden board, swooping one by one over the other hollows, dripping seashells. The wind, the scent of azaleas, the delicate clink of shells—all that had spelled peace for two orphans those

Sunday afternoons. What strange paths, indeed, they had traveled.

"We should at least dance," Anna said in her gentle voice.

Eliza lifted her arms and as Anna clapped in rhythm to the drums, she danced. Heart, blood, limbs synchronized now. Careful, careful, she warned herself; instances of love were too few and far between, too fragile. A sudden gesture, a sharp noise, an unnecessary blink of the eye and banality returned.

There was music all about them; the crowd was singing. Snatches of a thousand songs mixed, segueing into one another's melody yet fitting exactly with the drums' rhythm. Anna took her hand and danced down the length of the plaza, across its width, up its other leg, and in front of the town hall—a peregrination through memories. The whole phantasmagorical Festival shimmered in heat rays; men and women writhed, twisting their bodies like snakes reaching for the sun. Eliza's hand tightened about Anna's; she drew her friend closer, saw wisps of hair escape from the tight knot at her nape.

We will—WILL—*crush you*—CRUSH—*smash you*—SMASH!

Oh, the anger, the hatred even in the laughter.

SMASH—*smash*—TEAR—*tear you*—APART!

"What does Amor want?" Eliza whispered, when Anna floated near, eyes half-closed, body given over to the music.

"Innocence," she said. "But he can't recognize it, the fool."

Eliza laughed. She stomped, arms akimbo, around Anna. She was a warrior now, showing off her courage.

"And Adrian?"

Anna shrugged. "A life to live," she said and breathed audibly. "As though someone could give that to him." She whirled away.

And because she was warrior of the moment, Eliza asked her last question, teasing her friend, who had linked arms with a stranger. "What does Anna want?"

Anna raised her face to the sky. "A burial," she said through gritted teeth. "An end to a story." She traced a pattern on the ground, a series of steps done over and over again, like a bird tied to a stake.

Eliza's heart contracted with foreboding. She saw herself caught like her friend, dancing in circles without beginning, without end. As she danced, the drums intoned: four hundred years of action without achievement; of movement without distance. She heard a cry—a sharp birdcall of distress. Anna had stopped and was staring over the heads of the crowd, her fists rigid by her side.

Eliza looked in the same direction. There, there, there. In a second-floor balcony of black wrought iron, his forearms on the rails. Colonel Urbano Amor, in his khaki uniform, faced the crowd, faced the plaza, and, Eliza knew with deadly certainty, watched her and Anna.

A hiss broke from her lips; her arms rose without her knowing it; her hands hooked like talons. She felt her mouth stretch as though she would bare fangs; Lord, the misery of not having fangs at all. She turned her head. Anna was still frozen. Eliza pounced, grabbed her right forearm, and started dragging her away toward the crowd's center. They could hide there, among the hips and backs, shoulders and elbows of the anonymous. But Anna resisted, digging her heels into the ground, twisting her head to look back. She was an impossible weight and Eliza finally had to use both hands to peel her away from the snare of the Loved One's eyes.

Then suddenly, they were running, Anna knocking aside everything in her path to scramble across the plaza for the shelter of the tree covens on the other side. They did not stop until the shadows closed over them. Anna leaned her back against a tree trunk, catching her breath, hands gathering strands of her hair from her face. Eliza bent over, gasping, right hand pressed against her chest, trying to quiet the pounding of her heart.

"Holy shit," she said.

"You brought him here," Anna shouted.

"Whoa, hold on there," Eliza shrilled back, but Anna had turned away, her nose in the air.

"You can't be trusted, you drunken—!"

"Anna!"

Silence. Anna's face did not relent. She threw a glance of disgust at Eliza, who bit her lower lip. What could she say? It was true enough. The Loved One had followed her spoor to the Festival. She waited, willing herself to be calm.

After a while, Anna sighed. "Never mind," she said. "It's finished. It's gone."

Eliza saw she was crying. She moved to her and took the shuddering body in her arms.

"He can't touch you," she said. "He'll never touch you. So help me, God. I swear to you—"

"Sssh." Anna broke away. She dug her knuckles into her eyes. "I wish I understood. I wish I knew. How, why, who, and what for."

"I tell you—"

She jerked back impatiently. "You can't tell me anything," she said harshly. "You don't know. I don't know. Too many things, too many details . . ." She slid down and squatted at the base of the tree.

There was nothing for Eliza to do but to sit beside her. Silent, they watched the parade, the milling throng. A soldier passed by, his eyes a dark mask. Then, two more. Then five. Six. Rifles slung about their shoulders or dragging behind them. In khaki or olive uniforms. Bareheaded and capped.

"There are too many soldiers," Anna whispered. "Too many. It's finished."

Eliza kept quiet, feeling she was on the brink of a great discovery.

"I never loved Manolo, you know," Anna said suddenly. "I married him because I felt safe with him. Hah! I could not keep him on this side of safety. I can't do anything at all. Can't even bury him. I've failed at everything I set out to do."

Eliza kept very still. The silence that lasted was long enough for her to become aware of the wind in the leaves overhead, of the chirping of a lone cicada. If Anna had failed, considered herself to have failed, Eliza thought, what could she say about herself? She had made a mess of everything, a fine, super deluxe, mess. The cicada sang on, oblivious to the commotion of the Festival.

Anna's shoulders slumped; her head bent forward. She was staring at the earth between her feet.

"What are you thinking of?" Eliza asked timidly.

Anna looked at her and, quite unexpectedly, smiled. "Something stupid. I had an emerald-and-diamond earring once. Found it in an old jewel box. Among heaps of junk in the garage of my aunt's house."

"Where is it?"

Anna frowned. "I hocked it so I could send money to Hong Kong. I needed to pay for—never mind."

"We'll take it back," Eliza said eagerly.

"No, I don't want it. I was just wondering where it came from, what it was doing there among the relics in my aunt's house. We never had money, were never rich—and yet there it was. I knew it was real the minute I saw it—half of a pair, the other one missing. And when I took it, not telling anyone, hiding it in the toe end of my shoe—why did I do that?—I had the strangest feeling. A touch, a memory of a story, not even a story, just the breath of one . . ."

"Can't you remember?"

Anna thought for a moment. She shook her head. "No. They monkeyed around with the language, Eliza, while we were growing up. Monkeyed around with names. Of people, of places. With dates. And now, I can't remember. No one remembers. And even this"—she waved a hand toward the Festival—"even this will be forgotten. They will hide it under another name. No one will remember."

Eliza exhaled loudly. She looked at the sky through the branches overhead, felt the heat come through like so many knives in search of flesh, saw the crowd jam the plaza roads like a snake biting its tail, heard the drums and the roar of voices, saw the house roofs blaze like mirrors under the noon sun. She thought of what had happened, what was happening, and what would happen.

She took Anna's hand in hers. "What strange ways we have traveled," she said. If only there was an explanation for it all. Still, how could anyone forget?

The Book of Numbers

1

One summer day, a widow and a young man fell in love. Had the times been otherwise than what they were, which is to say that no state of war existed, the occasion would have inspired no more than a spattering of ribald jokes about a widow's expertise and youth's inexperience before it was swept away by the current of life in a tropical country of fifty million people and seven thousand one hundred islands—tucked away and forgotten in the infinite details of existence. No one would have remarked on the unbearable fragility of that particular morning, or on the look that passed, short and direct as a bullfighter's sword thrust, between the two—he, worn out equally by ministering to her fever and to his love; she, freshly delivered from the swamps of her delirium and, in that clarity that came with the first touch of health, seeing past, present, and future laid out within the small boundaries of her lodgings, which inspired her statement of death.

Unknown to both, that morning's shock of awareness was merely
an echo, a duplication of a morning shrouded by antiquity, when a
middle-aged friar, condemned by his melancholia to service in the
heathen lands of the Far East, rose at dawn from an insomnia made
worse by the sultry heat that had brooded over his bed's mosquito net
the whole night and still squatted like a monstrous presence in the
room. Oppressed, his heart feeling the writhing of the worm of foreboding, the Spaniard had donned cassock and sandals and gone out
of the monastery for a walk by the river. The land he passed
through—from horizon to horizon—though still unnamed, was already owned by the Church, its tributes of produce and cash used to
maintain the cathedral built by Chinese artisans and to sustain the
Spanish priests' need for capons and wine, as well as the Virgin Mary's
requirement of silk and lace, diamonds and gold. The friar, who
belonged to the Capuchin order, measured the *encomienda* with his
eyes, expertly calculating the coconut harvest, even as a monologue
of despair went on in his mind. He saw himself dying in this forgotten
corner of the world, this archipelago floating in an ocean which, to
mock its name of peace, periodically unleashed the terror of typhoons
throughout Southeast Asia. He would die, he thought, and be buried
at the foot of the altar, his name engraved on black marble by slink-
eyed barbarians, his saintliness unheralded, his sacrifice unknown. His
bones would rot far from civilization and nothing would remain of his
memory, despite all his efforts, for time was impossible in this country,
existing in all the true meaning of eternity. Things fell apart with the
heat and the rain, and the incessant mastication of insects, and he had
no doubt that the great stone bridge he was building across the
seasonally rampaging river would, at one time or another, encounter
a torrent too strong to withstand and thus be swept away.

At the end of this thought, he reached the river and surprised a
woman leaving the waters—a dark, Malayan girl with an acacia tree's
sturdiness. Secure in the drowsy hour, she had taken off her clothes
to bathe herself and managed to equally surprise the priest with an
image of a brown Venus rising from the waves. There were no waves,
of course, only the eddies of a summertime river, but the scene was

close enough to the Spaniard's European memories to cause him to bellow like a bull and hurl himself, cassock, cowl, sandal, and all, at the girl, catching her as he tripped on the hem of his skirts and overwhelming her with his weight. The girl, who was fourteen years old, knew enough not to resist the priest, having grown up surrounded by the gossip of elders and taken to heart the admonition that the tenderest of thighs, whether of chicken or of women, belonged to the friars. She yielded her virginity on a bed of pebbles and curled arms and legs tightly about the pain of the unholy entrance, bit her lower lip, and thought of how much all this silliness should cost the stupid priest.

He gave her a gold coin, stamped with the profile of a king no one had ever seen, and having made arrangements for her weekly visit to the church, he turned around, humming the "Ave Maria," only to be struck by the enormity of his sin as he approached the shadow of the cross on the ground, laid there by the gold light of a morning of fragility with its cockcrows, scent of roasting corn, sparrow chirps, and all the musky smells of a land newly touched by the sun. He rushed into the church and woke his brother priest, an obese man of sixty, who received his confession of a transgression against the flesh with a fit of laughter. He was given absolution and told it was the most common failing of friars in the whole territory, this incessant rutting among the *indias* who seemed to have the devil's capability to incite and excite. Thus absolved, the young priest went his merry way, and six months later gave the girl enough money to go away. Her belly was beginning to swell. She was the first of a number of nubile *indias* who consoled the priest in his melancholia until, of course, a peculiar morning dawned again fifteen years later and the priest stumbled upon the wife of his cook in the monastery's kitchen as he was yearning for a cup of cocoa and a bite of *pan de sal.*

Her name was Maya and her blue-black hair fell to her ankles. Her exclusive use cost the priest two bags of gold coins. She lived with him openly, supervising the servants in the monastery, taking care of his mass vestments, fixing herbal potions to ease his dyspepsia, holding his hand as he lay in bed assaulted by heat or rain or other unspeakable climatic tribulations this land brought him. Living protected by his power and yet outcast by her status as a priest's whore, she was both in the center of and yet outside the half-pagan, half-Catholic society of the bustling city of Malolos, in the province of Bulacan, one of the wealthiest in the archipelago with its superb rice lands, its fecund fruit trees, and its rivers aswarm with fish, shrimp, and rock lobsters. As a consequence, she became a character, driving her caleche herself, the reins of a beautifully matched pair of black horses in her tiny, callused hands. Because she borrowed odds and ends of clothing and jewels from the life-size Virgin Mary, her saunter through the city and its towns was often a spectacle to rival the interminable religious parades with which the friars occupied themselves. Perched on the driver's seat of her caleche, her tiny hands with wrists of iron controlling the palpable power of her black horses, her small, hard body with its mahogany skin costumed in an extravagant embroidered blouse of woven pineapple fiber and a burgundy velvet skirt over lace petticoats, her neck weighted by a necklace of emeralds as big as hens' eggs, her lips clamped about the lighted end of a brown *cigarillo,* she drew in her wake men, women, and children who stared at, ran after, and hailed her passing, calling her witch, whore, saint, patroness, insane. She would stop at intersections and accept rolled-up petitions from peasants, petitions which, for a coin or two, she promised to bring to the attention of the proper saint, prodding the statue with whip lashes every twilight until the request was granted. In the course of these rituals, the peasants somehow inverted her idea of coercing the holy powers and began flagellating themselves instead, in the hope that such a sacrifice of blood would appeal to the white gods whom they took to be as murderous and rapacious as the representatives of the Royal Viceroy of Mexico which ruled the archipelago. Thus, inadvertently, the priest's whore invented the penitents' practice which more than a century later would become standard spectacle during Lent and which her great-granddaughter Anna Villaverde would witness at a festival confused by time and history.

She bore the priest seven sons and saw six of them scatter throughout the world, sailing with the ships plying the route between Aca-

pulco and Manila for the lark of braving the typhoons of the Pacific
and measuring with their own eyes the breadth and depth of the
ocean that surrounded the archipelago and kept it in perpetual isolation. Unknown to her, one of them would jump ship in Mexico and,
with six other *indios,* make his way to Louisiana to establish the
first-ever Malay community in North America. He never returned.

The other five roamed Europe and in a parody of the legend of
Martin de Goiti, who razed a Moslem city to erect the Ever Loyal,
Ever Noble Spanish City of Manila, rutted among the languorous
maidens of France, Spain, Italy, and other places which had borne the
same name for ages, leaving olive-skin descendants whose Malay
genes were explained away as Moorish. They never returned.

The son who remained, the youngest, Carlos Lucas de Villaverde,
was loved with such fierceness by Maya that he was assaulted forevermore by the need to escape the cloying power of her affection. From
the age of two, he'd felt her as a vine entwined about his soul, much
like the *balete* that began under the shadow of a mature tree and
slowly but inexorably wrapped itself about its trunk and branches,
letting down roots shaped like gigantic penises, until the tree died of
exhaustion in its embrace, withered away, and the *balete* took its
place, already fully formed. In his efforts to free himself, Carlos Lucas
caused his father's death—for there was only one way he could forget
Maya, the tobacco stench of her faded laces and gold-embroidered
velvet saints' skirts, her witch's eyes of wet coal which summed up
every cut, every scratch on his fair skin, every inch of growth of his
cells. He found his refuge among the peasant males who ran the
encomienda for the friars, especially in the company of Juan Itak, the
bamboo man whose duty and livelihood were to invade the mountain
groves and chop down the sinuous yellow boles which, dried and
varnished, held up the peasants' nipa huts until they were disassem-
bled by the year's first typhoon. Juan Itak, it so happened, was Carlos
Lucas's unrecognized brother, being the son of the priest's encounter
by the river bank one diaphanous morning years ago. Except for a
slightly aquiline nose, his Iberian genes had left no trace, having been
thoroughly defeated by the robust Malay chromosomes of his mother.

Nevertheless, Juan Itak found Carlos Lucas congenial company and initiated the youth of fourteen into many mysteries, including forty-two ways of self-indulgence, a few so subtle they fell within the loopholes of the code of sins the friars had made up for the natives. It was Juan Itak who, one morning, proceeded to teach Carlos Lucas the way to forget, hauling from its cool storage in the river a demijohn of rice wine. Unfortunately, the priest happened to be at the church belfry that particular morning, scanning the land with a pair of binoculars. The sight of Carlos Lucas thoroughly drunk and stark naked, and going through the motions of one of Juan's cruder ways of self-indulgence, drove the priest to such an apoplectic rage that he lost his footing on the belfry's planks, fell through the trapdoor amidst a mad clanging of bells big and small, and broke his neck on the landing below. As he had more than three hundred pounds on his six-foot frame, no one thought it odd that he should die this way.

Maya and Carlos Lucas were evicted from the monastery and their precarious status decided their fate. They moved to Manila, which was in the throes of breaking out of its cocoon to become the first truly cosmopolitan city of the Orient. Here, in the graceful district of Binondo, they made their residence, buying a cavernous two-story house, with a garage for coaches on the ground floor and curving steps at its left flank leading to the upper living quarters, a house whose backside balcony of fluted iron overhung one of the city's main canals. The Binondo *estero,* it was called, and it served as source of water for both bathing and laundry while functioning as a thoroughfare as well, with dozens of slim leaf-shaped boats paddling upstream and down-stream, carrying wares of wine, flowers, vegetables and fish, strange tribal handicrafts, and jewels.

The house cost them a fourth of the gold contents of the pirate chest, which together with the emerald necklace and Carlos Lucas's family name were the only legacies of the priest. Maya swore to keep the necklace to her deathbed—a vow which Carlos Lucas, in his new role of man of the house, acceded to with an amused smile, comment-ing that, if things were to remain as they were, he would even see to it that Maya was buried with the jewel. To which, the wise witch replied that it was unnecessary since, sooner or later, her darling Carlosito would dig it up again and she had no wish to have her bones handled by careless grave robbers.

Thus they set up a pleasant existence and Carlos Lucas applied himself to discovering a career. As it happened, all his knowledge, aside from forty-two ways of self-indulgence, had something to do with inebriation. He cleared the house's lower floor of furniture, set up a laboratory, and proceeded to mix and distill a vast array of liquors, from nipa wine to fermented sugarcane sap, causing the house to perpetually exhale a sweetish, drunken breath which floated over the *estero* into the poultry yards, the pigpens, and the stables of the houses on the opposite bank, driving cocks and hens, boars and sows, mares and stallions so crazed with desire they became a minor scandal of the city.

Maya took her son's family name, becoming herself a de Villaverde, and passed herself off as an accomplished osteopath—one who could set broken bones with such precision that it would seem afterward no damage had even visited the affected limb—and as a masseuse who could stroke and caress women's flesh back into an approximation of youth. She prefaced every curing mission by taking the short riding crop she'd hung on the wall over a St. Anthony icon and whipping the impassive saint about the knees and legs. Thus fortified by the saint's submission, she sallied forth in her lace blouse and velvet skirt, and with her brown *cigarillos,* her dark, determined face still beautiful despite her fifty-odd years or so, Carlos Lucas being a child of her old age.

The Spaniard died at a fortuitous time, it would seem, for he, as the other ecclesiasts didn't, would not have tolerated the new face of Manila, which buzzed from morning to morning, with taverns and pubs, and visitors from Britain, France, and even the old enemy, Portugal, brought thither by the mercantilism that blossomed in the wake of the construction of the Suez Canal. There were gentle festivals of beauty now, where women in gowns of the delicate quality of dragonfly wings vied for titles, to rival the splendor of the rites of St. John the Baptist, the month-long festivities of the Virgin called *La*

Naval de Manila, the cruel rituals of the Black Christ of Quiapo which increased its weight tenfold every January 9th so as to render more difficult the fulfillment of vows made by penitents who had to pull and push its massive wheeled stand through the city streets. No, the melancholic Spaniard wouldn't have countenanced these, least of all the travels of *indios* to Europe, from whence they returned with the language and knowledge of their masters, as well as with impossible ideas of turning the archipelago into a Spanish province with representation in the Spanish Cortes. Worse, they insisted on acquiring a name for the ridiculous mix of history that they were—Malay, Chinese, Arab, Hindu, Spanish, British—arrogating the name which hitherto had been reserved for pure-blooded Spaniards born in the islands. They called themselves Filipinos.

Carlos Lucas called himself Don Carlos Lucas de Villaverde and lived ensconced in the hallucinatory breath of his Binondo house, puttering with his Bunsen lamps and glass jars, venturing out only to search for and haggle over strange berries and fruits and sacks of malt and barley. These he would subject to a hundred and one chemical processes, noting each step in a notebook of fine linen paper, using a code based on Latin. He would not allow Maya into his laboratory and saw her only at breakfast and dinner which were served by the bastard daughter of a Chinese merchant and his Malay housekeeper, a tiny girl of ten, so quiet both Carlos and Maya forgot they were not alone in the house.

Maya added copper and silver coins to the pirate chest and always wore her necklace at dinnertime. She took the seat to Carlos's right, yielding to him the table's head as befitted the man of the household. Nevertheless, this did not prevent her from nagging him about finding work for himself and getting married. At peace, honorable again for no one in the city knew of their origins, they were quite content. Carlos Lucas no longer felt the stranglehold of the *balete* about his soul, not while gentle dusk filtered through the open wall-to-wall windows of the house and the scent of the neighboring gardens' jasmine vines fought with the alcoholic fumes of the ground floor. They would spend the next ten years this way, forever it would seem at dinner, with the soft clink of porcelain, glass, and silverware, and fresh sea wind blowing inland from the walled city of Intramuros where the Spaniards concerned themselves with saints, money, and a continent halfway around the world.

Indeed, the priest died at a fortuitous moment—for among the flotsam of *indios* threading their way among the warehouses and the piers of the harbor where the ships of the world docked prow to prow, a young orphan hawking walking canes and fans suddenly found himself able to understand Spanish and in possession of several books, including Hugo's *Les Miserables*. In his evenings' fatigue, with his mind in the grip of languages, he conceived the inconceivable and saw the Castilians driven back the way they had come, the archipelago once more a pristine Malayan one. The imprimatur to this dream was made in blood as the clandestine Society of Sons of the People sprang into being, each oath of allegiance inked in red, the thin white scar of the healed wound on a man's left arm serving as his badge of membership.

Maya Villaverde would remember to her deathbed, though she forgot so much else, the day knowledge of the Society reached her. A boy servant had appeared at her door, asking that she come see one of her customers, a young woman who lived across the *estero,* though a visit had not been scheduled. Said young woman was suffering from a nervous attack which, having deprived her of sleep for three nights running, left her bones feeling full of water. Maya dressed for the street, gathered her scented oils and scapulars, and, because she was in good humor, merely slapped St. Anthony's face twice. As she stepped out of the doorway, she noticed a peculiar quality to the sunlight, a tremulous feel to the air. She could not have known how this was merely a repetition of a morning which had twisted her destiny and left her with Carlos Lucas. The *estero* boats seemed to float an inch or two above the water; the houses on both sides of the street were unreal enough. She felt she could, had she so desired, push a palm through their adobe walls. The blue, clear sky leaned overhead, so near its breath ruffled the hair on the top of her head. Suddenly, the worm of foreboding awoke in her heart and, made uneasy by

successive omens, she drew the shawl tighter about her shoulders and
hurried after the boy.

Her customer greeted her with red-rimmed eyes. With the curtains
drawn in the living room, she stripped to her chemise and lay on her
belly on the sofa. Maya poured oil onto her right hand, rubbed her
palms together for warmth, and proceeded to work on the young
lady's shoulders. Suddenly, the woman burst into tears, heaving and
retching into the pillows and confessed, in a rush of words, how she'd
betrayed her betrothed by revealing to a Dominican friar his secret
membership. Today, at this very instant, the priest was leading a
squad of civil guards on their way to seize the hidden printing press
of the Society, as well as all its records. Arrests, incarcerations, executions . . . the woman broke into wails.

But Maya had sealed her ears. She was thinking of Carlos Lucas,
of his strange absences, his sudden quiet, the shy slyness of his eyes
at dinnertime. As if to confirm her suspicion, the curtains billowed
inward abruptly and as they whipped forward, sprang back, in a gust
of wind, one panel snatched a little St. Anthony from its cantilevered
altar against the wall and sent it tumbling to the floor. It was smashed
into a thousand pieces. Maya capped the oil bottle, thrust all her
paraphernalia back into her basket, and, without a word to the young
woman, hurried out of the house.

She was still two blocks away from her house when the rumble of
an explosion came down the street and she saw the front windows lift
themselves from their moorings and sail to the neighbor's yard. The
basket dropped from her arm; her feet scissored with sudden vigor and
she reached the front door before anyone had appeared. It was hanging from one hinge while white smoke spewed out of Carlos Lucas's
laboratory. Glass shards lay all over the floor while the tables, chairs,
and demijohns had fallen on this sides.

She said his name once, almost as a prayer, before stepping into
the room, her old woman's lungs screaming at the assault of pestilential vapors. She searched through the debris and found him, the
last of her brood, lying behind sacks of barley. He was covered
with soot, burnt in places, and moaning quietly, though he kept

an iron grip around a six-inch vial filled with clear fluid.

This was to become the Four Roses Gin, distilled, bottled, and marketed by Carlos Lucas himself, with a label designed by Maya which showed a doe-eyed woman wearing four blossoms in her hair. All through the three years of insurrection that gripped the islands, the gin sold—hawked by couriers through battle lines, carried by train, by horse, by water buffalo. It was said to have the ability to instill courage, to cool the spirits when the going was hot, to heat the blood when the nights were cool, and, when worse came to worst, it also served as a terrific incendiary when corked with a wick of rags, lighted, and thrown with precision.

The house along the Binondo *estero* became a distillery with a dozen men working the stills and a dozen women painting labels and corking bottles. There were eternal comings and goings as the factory's demand for bottles increased—used bottles, washed and rinsed, bought from Chinese merchants who sent a seemingly endless line of men staggering into the yard, on their shoulders bamboo poles balancing the weight of huge baskets filled with the bottle harvest of the day. Carlos Lucas, walking with the wide strides of a rooster through this disorder, never discovered that one of those Malay boys haggling angrily with his foreman was the son of Juan Itak, who'd been killed in the first volley of the Revolution—a pubescent youth with calluses on his shoulders and the worm of foreboding in his heart, a not quite man who'd been given by the nuns of an orphanage in Bulacan the rather surprising name of Adrian Banyaga. Carlos Lucas's nephew, actually.

2

All things considered, Carlos Lucas de Villaverde was to say to his new partner, the German chemist Hans Zangroniz, after everything was over, the twentieth century blew in with what seemed like half a dozen wars fought simultaneously and one after another, so that one couldn't tell whether the dead died for this or that cause, whether they belonged to this or that faction, or whether they gave up the ghost because they simply got fed up with living in such confusion. First, of course, the insurrection that burst out of the alleys of Manila spread like a seasonal flood until eight provinces were in uproar over a full-scale Revolution and artillery pieces were hauled hither and thither, by horse, by water buffalo, by peons, and the cursing Spaniards found themselves cursed back with due elegance and the proper Castilian accent by voices from fortifications, trees, cliffs. All the young men, it seemed, had returned from Europe and were busy shooting, digging war trenches, getting drunk on Four Roses Gin, and writing poetry. Then all the drunken young men from Europe got into a fracas with all the serious young men who'd stayed at home—so the war now had two fronts or were there two wars, no one knew. In any case, the young hawker of walking canes and fans was murdered and his followers, if not killed, were scattered all over the land.

Carlos Lucas recounted this at dinnertime, as was his wont— though dinners now were affairs of thirty people, the strangest assembly ever, as Don Carlos himself would admit. There were mad inventors and their women, crazed herbalists and their women, European stowaways, sailors who'd jumped ship, one lanky American who introduced himself as an anthropologist. Everyone spoke Spanish, even Maya de Villaverde enthroned in a rattan peacock chair and wearing her icon's clothes and emerald necklace. She had learned the language in a year's time, forcing herself to confer genders on inanimate objects—a world view that offended her sense of the intimate unity of the universe. She had difficulty with male/female pronouns and was surprised that such distinctions should exist based solely on sex and not upon class, status, aura of dignity, and respect, which were the criteria for pronoun distinctions in her native language. But there was no helping it; everyone above thirty was using Spanish—perhaps in defiance of the new colonizers—though as all acknowledged, it was too late, the children's voices in the street were already singsonging *one-two, bato; three-four, bapor* . . . Thus, with a feeling of doom, with great resentment at her own abrupt realization of what she, as female, was in this decaying world, she sat in the rattan peacock chair and brooded over Carlos's assembly, her dark witch's eyes jumping from face to face, studying, ferreting secrets, asking herself what else they had hidden from her all her life.

Because she was quiet save for a command snarled now and then at the servants, who were all efficient in any case under the Chinese-Malay girl's supervision, she managed to afflict Lucas Carlos with guilt. He wriggled in his chair, avoided her eyes, struck pompous poses of attention whenever someone mentioned a business possibility. He never listened, of course, knowing the peculiar frenzy that was war's immediate aftermath. Besides which, though he himself made as much profit out of the six-inch vial of the explosion, he couldn't believe that a three hundred percent return on investment—the most quoted figure—was possible. All he wanted to do was to preside over dinner, smell the moistness of the *estero*, rid himself of the suffocating embrace of Maya's eyes, tell his stories, and be Don Carlos Lucas de Villaverde.

Hans Zangroniz had two doctorates, one from Munich, the other from Zurich, and since Carlos Lucas repeated this wondrous fact as often as he was able, the German chemist came to be addressed as Señor Doctor Doctor. When he first heard the title, Carlos Lucas had grown livid, embarrassed by the ignorance of his countrymen. He had tried to explain that *x* number of doctorates still amounted to only one titular doctor but his foreman, an eighteen-year-old pure Malay, had merely inclined his head and said that a man was entitled to what he was entitled and since the *Señor Aleman* claimed two certificates, then he was a doctor twice over. Where was the harm in giving a man his just due? Thus, the thirty-five-year-old Hans who had sailed to the East to make his fortune suffered for his overeducation. When he took his constitutional in the morning, walking by the *estero*, in his black frock coat, hat, and swagger stick, adults and children alike hailed him as Señor Doctor Doctor.

He had spent nearly all his youth as apprentice in an apothecary shop in Munich, reading chemistry and alchemy, and experimenting with all kinds of liquids in his effort to discover the secret of the philosopher's stone. It never occurred to him that he was Europe's last believer in the myth; his poverty, the stringent diet of black bread and eggs which formed his only pleasure, would not allow him to abandon his fantasy. Finally, on his thirtieth birthday, when the shop mistress he had courted for ten years turned down his suit, fatally (he thought) wounding his heart, he had taken stock of his situation. For the next four years, he saved ruthlessly, to the level of stuffing his shirt and shoes with rags at wintertime, so he could have the fare to sail to the East. He had heard of instant fortunes made, of power and respect suddenly earned. More than this, he had heard of the strange exuberance of the elements in the tropics—a strangeness which resembled the bruited but never defined qualities of the philosopher's stone. Thus it was that he disembarked at the port of Manila one April morning of blistering heat. Having found a rooming house, he placed an advertisement in *El Diario* and hadn't even been surprised when his own landlord came to call. For he had taken lodgings at one of the four city blocks owned by Don Carlos Lucas de Villaverde— blocks of two- to three-story white wooden houses of grace with fluted iron balconies overhanging the *estero*. All on the outside, though, Hans Zangroniz would tell himself, for the old crone Maya had had partitions built within partitions and rented out the cubbyhole rooms to the itinerants who swarmed to Manila in the wake of wars upon wars: prostitutes, students, dockworkers, and even a lanky American.

Hans's guttural Spanish, two certificates (forged), and melancholia so affected Carlos Lucas that he had apologized for the boarding house, offered Hans both a partnership in the gin business and the hospitality of his home. Hans pretended to hesitate so that Carlos was forced to press him, inviting him on the spot to have dinner at the distillery and waiting impatiently for the German to gather his vials and don his frock coat.

That same fortuitous afternoon, in the midst of her shuffling among rows of bottles, upended baskets, sheets of paper, cans of paint, and all the litter of the distillery which had spilled over to a makeshift shed swallowing her front yard, Maya de Villaverde caught a sepulchral vision of two men in long brown robes coming down the road. The sudden thump in her chest lured her first into believing that Death's angels had come for her but, in the next instant, she understood that her heartbeats were merely the resonance of memory, for the two were Capuchin monks trodding along in their cowls, skirts, and sandals. They stopped at the gate and waited until their presence was noticed by the workers who, as one, rose and queued to kiss the hands of the two priests. Maya had to tuck her chin to her chest to hide the smirk she couldn't suppress; the two had accepted the obeisance with a mix of divinity and arrogance.

But they had indeed come for her, the foreman said, and Maya eyed them shrewdly, wondering how to deal with this unexpected honor. She gave orders for the main doors to be opened and for refreshments to be prepared while she retired to her bedroom. Her maid came running and tucked her into a gown so that half an hour later she appeared in the living room as Doña Maya de Villaverde, neck bent by the weight of emeralds. The two priests, shocked by the mirage, put down their cups of cocoa and forgot to chew *pastillas.* Maya had the satisfaction of having her hand kissed by the two. She waved them to their seats rather casually and arranged herself on the sofa.

They were Father Don Jose Saavedra and Father Don Luis Rigodon, officials of the Capuchin order. Father Luis was younger and thus had the responsibility of conversation. He asked after the health of Maya's body and soul, inquired about her confessor, and professed astonishment that such an illustrious lady should, like any ordinary mortal, line up at the confessional box of any neighborhood church. Indeed, they, the clergy, had been remiss. He offered his and Father Jose's services, promising to include the Binondo house in their calendar of calls, crammed as that was, for nothing was better for a *lady's* soul than the shared solitude of an afternoon with her confessor.

As he spoke, Maya and the older friar studied each other. His bird-beak nose, burning eyes, and thin rose-lips reassured her immediately. She was prepared to bet her emeralds he came from Madrid. She knew everything about Capuchins who came from Madrid. She closed her ears to Father Luis, who had insulted her by speaking in her language—an unforgivable error in judgment. Lazily, noting their empty cups, she stretched her hand out for the small bell that would summon a servant, but at that moment Father Jose chose to speak, lisping all his sibilants and confirming her suspicions as to his origins and his shrewdness. He used Spanish.

"The Capuchin Order is renowned for its austereness, its discipline, its vows of chastity and poverty, its missionary zeal," he said in a voice of sorrow. "We have many brothers and sisters in heathen lands who suffer unspeakable deprivations for the sake of a harvest of souls. We take the Lord's way."

"And the Lord has looked upon you with favor," she replied, wondering what was to come next.

"We have loved these islands—far more than the Yanquis who now seek to take apart what we have put together."

She shifted uneasily beneath the weight of her skirt. Sedition laws were still in effect and the *norte americanos* had no scruples about exiling to Guam anyone remotely suspected. But it was obvious that Father Jose was waiting for an answer. She felt around in her head, tried out and discarded several statements, and finally sighed. "The Yanquis," she said, "will be Yanquis."

The priest smiled. "Our collection grows leaner each day . . ."

She raised a hand. "For that, you'll have to apply to my son—as befits the head of the household." She couldn't help her disappointment. Alms! That was all they wanted?

"We will, in due time—but think of it this way, Doña Maya. You may give us a tithe but that will only go so far. Our needs are immense . . ."

"Even though you're poor."

"Exactly. And what we want is some assurance that we will be enabled to have a steady source of income."

She rang the bell, picking it up abruptly in the spurt of anger that possessed her. She already knew what was to come. "Bring cocoa!" she barked at the maid, and thus managed to diffuse her temper.

Father Jose was a true fanatic and would not let himself be distracted even by hot cocoa. He leaned forward, bracing an arm on his right knee, and aimed his eyes at Maya.

"The collection box has given us enough to buy a share in your business. As you know, we have a small brewery which had been doing well until . . . well, gin is stronger and cheaper and all the peons want is to knock themselves silly as quickly as possible."

"I do not discuss business. My son . . ."

"Perhaps the señora would like to think it over," Father Luis interposed. "Meanwhile, there is the matter—the greater matter—of her soul to attend to. My lady, have you considered burial within the cathedral?"

"We're honorable people, Father," Maya rebuked him. "It wouldn't matter where we're buried. The site would neither add to nor subtract from our honor."

"Still . . ."

But the two priests acknowledged that the courtship of Maya would be long and tedious. Indeed, all three of them realized this as the maid came in to replenish the cups. Maya consented to take a biscuit, catching as she did so the amused glance that passed between the priests.

Hans Zangroniz, therefore, was no less than a disaster when he arrived with Carlos Lucas that twilight. For the first time, mother and son had a real quarrel.

"Your partner? Why couldn't I be your partner?" she screamed.

But Carlos Lucas was adamant. He would not hear of his decision being questioned. "He's got two doctorates from the best European schools. His classmates were princes and dukes. They consulted him about state matters . . ."

"So why isn't he a prime minister? Your partner? What about the Capuchins?"

"They will not buy into *my* business. They will not come near me again." The *again* slipped out before he could be aware of it. Enraged by his own indiscretion, he knocked down her St. Anthony statue. "I might agree to buy into *their* business. Or better yet—better yet, I'll brew my own beer and bankrupt them."

"Sssh. Careful with your mouth. You don't know what you're getting into."

"I will brew a better beer. Hans, with his two doctorates, will find a formula so impeccable those Capuchins will pull their cowls over their heads in shame. I will have a better beer. I will, I will, I will. And I'll call it Lucifer. Hah! After all, we won the Revolution."

He would repeat that to Hans. "We won the Revolution—in a manner of speaking . . ." It was one of those things which defied satisfactory evaluation, as Carlos Lucas explained. "We won and yet—"

"Victory is always relative," was Hans's only answer but that was enough to send Carlos Lucas into paroxysms of respect for the German's wisdom. The statement took its place among his many set opinions about life in general—so much so that he would declare everything to be relative, thus antedating his own descendants in modernity.

But it took time for him to reach this equanimity. As with men of his generation, made conscious of their own mortality by the advent of middle age, Carlos Lucas became enamored of the past, tracing and retracing in his mind the maze of history and his own biography. He had had no part in the Revolution, as he told everyone, nor in the wars that followed, except through the Four Roses Gin. But he was attuned enough to the country's life to understand the sudden fervor that gripped everyone when all the young men from Europe who had agreed to the Spanish governor-general's request for a truce returned from Hong Kong, yelling once more about a Republic. This time, not only eight provinces took to guns and the hills but seemingly the entire seven thousand one hundred islands and, for one celebratory year, New Year's Eve went on and on with the boom of cannons, the clip-clop of horses, the ping and bang of muskets, and a confetti of newspapers and manifestoes done on the run, a printing press traveling by train from one battlefield to another. Noise and words for a whole year. Meanwhile, Commodore George Dewey had smashed the Spanish fleet at the Manila harbor and the city itself flew the American flag.

"Everyone was noble," Carlos Lucas said. He would add though that he discovered the futility of it all the day he escorted a shipment of Four Roses Gin to Tarlac where three prior deliveries had disappeared. There, the old sugarcane train whose tracks run through blighted fields was halted by two dozen peons carrying rifles and Carlos Lucas was taken out of the coach he had had attached to the locomotive and marched half a kilometer to a hut.

Carlos Lucas made the sign of the cross and declared himself dead. The men were *sacadas*—migrant workers who, before this war, moved from plantation to plantation, doing the muscle-wrenching labor of cutting sugarcane, hoisting bundles on their shoulders, and carrying them to the cargo trains which sputtered and clanked away, heading for the sugar mills. They had no homes, and were accompanied in their nomadic lives by their wives and children, their cooking pots and blankets—all of which they deposited in the lean-tos and makeshift barracks provided each planting and harvest time by the plantation owners. They were a mysterious lot, Carlos Lucas admitted; they lived in the most terrible poverty and had no affiliation to anyone save their own clan. For that matter, since they owned nothing but the most basic necessities, they had little attachment to their lives as well.

They walked stooped and with knees slightly bent, as though a load remained on their shoulders. But they were frighteningly polite, their eyes flickering in the customary way of peasants confronted by authority. As the leader—an extremely young man, a boy almost—parlayed with Carlos Lucas over the gin, the men waited, their gnarled fingers restless on their weapons. Carlos Lucas noted this with his peripheral vision and, sweating in his white summer suit, streaked gray by the coal-burning train engine, he gave himself up for dead once more. "I must have died a half-dozen times in two hours," he said later.

"Don Carlos," the leader said, "we do not wish to steal. We're peasants. We don't steal; we earn our living on this earth. You must understand the extreme need that forced us to confiscate your property. In the name of the Revolution."

Carlos Lucas nodded. He glanced at the others and this time noticed, with amazement, that all the sights had been removed from their rifles. But the leader was speaking again and he had to pay attention.

"We do not drink gin," the leader was saying. "We've had tragedy with it. Some men who went on three-, four-day drinking binges woke up blind. Sober but blind. So we have issued orders for the gin to be treated purely as ordnance."

"My gin had nothing to do with that!" Don Carlos shouted.

The leader studied him for what seemed to be an eternity. Don Carlos gave himself up for dead once more.

"Maybe, maybe not," the leader said after a while. There was a perceptible easing of tension in the hut. Carlos Lucas breathed. "In any case, what we take from you is accounted for. We cannot pay now—"

"No need, no need," Carlos sputtered. "My contribution—I didn't know—the Revolution . . ."

"But we can pay in due time," the leader stressed. "We will give you an eighth of this plantation once we've taken it over, as soon as it belongs to us. Legally, after the war."

"But the owners—"

"There are no owners. We fight for the land, Don Carlos—and it will be ours. We're stockpiling the gin; we need it to burn the enemies' camps."

"We already won. The Republic has been declared."

"The Yanquis are still here. They're as long-nosed as the Castilians. And they speak to sugar barons. We want the land. It will be ours."

Carlos Lucas was given a piece of paper on which some town scribe had written the promise of an eighth of Hacienda Concepcíon to him at the termination of the Revolution. The leader had made an X at the bottom, witnessed by two lawyers.

"We held pistols to their heads," the leader said, causing his men to smile. "They kept insisting it wasn't legal. Satan, what is legal in this world? You will send us more gin."

Carlos Lucas nodded. A shipment or two, perhaps watered down, he thought, though that would be compromising his pride in his product. The leader gestured; the negotiations were over and Carlos Lucas was alive. Two men approached and seized his forearms. Lord, they had fingers of iron. On impulse, he turned to the one on his right and asked: "Where are the sights on your rifles?"

"We took them off," the man replied. "They made us cross-eyed."

They were doomed. He knew it instantly, he said to Hans; doomed by their own passion and ignorance. Back in Manila, he had gone through the Revolution's documents and newspapers. Nothing there about land, nothing about the distribution of land; nothing but the setting up of a government which would allow locals to hold office. "Lord," he told Hans, "the leaders fought for one reason; the foot soldiers for another. A mess. I knew it!" Then a Yanqui shot and killed one of the Revolution's soldiers.

One morning, Carlos Lucas, coming down the wide stone steps that led from the upper main doors to the ground, was struck by the tremulous quality of the air, by the light that seemed to lend an opaqueness to things so that, for a moment, he was sure he had walked from the house right into a dream. He felt he could, had he wished it, push a fist right through walls, through trees, or even churn the sky that leaned so near clouds threatened to snag themselves on his hair. The distillery was already humming but the soft clink of glass, as the women corked and labeled bottles, echoed and re-echoed through that molten air. He had a sense of event—something was happening, had indeed already happened and there was nothing more to be done. He was seized by a desire to weep. Dazed, he braced a hand against one of the shed's posts and looked around. Everything was normal, except for his foreman's absence, and he couldn't see small Juan who tended the fires and Angelito who took care of the debris and . . .

"Where are the men?" he thundered at the nearest girl.

She lifted a face of mourning to his eyes. "We're at war again, *patron.*"

"Holy—! With whom, this time?"

"With the Americans."

Automatically, he turned his eyes in the direction of Intramuros, the Walled City built by Chinese artisans under the orders of the Spaniards. It was said to have so drained the Castilian treasury that one day the Spanish king—which one, no one knew—having received yet another demand for more money for the walls, had exploded in rage, saying that considering how much the walls were costing they should be visible from Madrid on sunny mornings. Carlos Lucas couldn't see Intramuros from his Binondo house but he knew, since he had seen it before, that strange flags, with stars and stripes, not the lion seal of Aragon, flew atop those walls. He observed a moment of silence, wondering how and why a war begun in Cuba—a place no one from the seven thousand one hundred islands had thought of, much less visited—had managed to cross the ocean of typhoons to roost here. He recalled the rifles without sights, the cross-purposes of wars, and the dark Malays who knew only the most simple, the most fundamental language of all—life, love, and liberty—and who now would find themselves within the coils of power and politics.

"Pray for the men," he said to the girls, his heart filled with lead, "and see that you all get pregnant. As quickly as possible. We will lose a lot of human beings."

Ten years and two hundred fifty thousand corpses. To make matters worse, all the young men from Europe caught war fever and began murdering one another. The mathematics of history passed like wind through Hans's ears. He thought his partner, Carlos Lucas, no better than the peasants he had such contempt and sympathy for, sharing with them both ignorance and passion. Hans had breakfast and dinner with his host and hostess every day, once a week with the strange assembly of Carlos's friends. He lived in an upstairs room, despite Maya's objections, and puttered about with malt and barley and test tubes and vials, his partner's words ringing in his ears: a better beer, an excellent beer, a brew to be called *Diablo.* He knew nothing about beer, could find no books, and couldn't buy secrets from the workers of the city's only brewery. They had all been placed under the confessional seal by the Capuchins, who threatened to roast their souls in hell forever should they even dream of the brewing process. Hans ordered books from Europe but they took forever to arrive or were lost or pilfered—no one knew. He was in a miserable state.

He lived in fear of his partner's patience coming to an end, for though he was treated as became a full partner and received a weekly allowance from the Chinese-Malay maid, no papers had been drawn up confirming the alliance. For two hours each day, from five to seven in the evening before the dinner bell rang, he trembled from head to foot as he packed away the chemicals of another failure, cursed both beer and the philosopher's stone in one breath, washed his hands, and changed to one of the six identical formal black suits he had had tailored for himself, preferring to keep his image as a serious German scholar rather than be comfortable in the silken pineapple-fiber dress shirts the natives wore. At the silver sound of the bell, he finished his toilette by dashing cologne on his chin and neck and entered the dining room, cowering in his coat at an expected assault of insults from Don Carlos Lucas de Villaverde. "Fraud," he waited to hear the words from his host, "cheap German fraud; *ladron;* give back the money I spent on you!" It never happened.

It could never happen, for, unknown to Hans, being a stranger to the culture of the Binondo house, Carlos Lucas had taken him as fair exchange for his six brothers lost to Europe. As far as Carlos Lucas was concerned, the younger man could spend a lifetime studying the secrets of beer and never come up with a formula. It didn't matter. All he knew was that in this house run by women, from Maya down to the ten-year-old who scrubbed the outside doorsteps each morning with coconut husk, there was at least one more resident male.

Hans was not relieved that Carlos Lucas never rebuked him for a year of research spent in vain. He still trembled from head to foot every afternoon, and suffered spasms of fear at various moments of the day. He sought to forget his predicament by pinching the bottoms of the innumerable and exchangeable maids in the house, running his hands up their backs, and feeling their thighs through the often threadbare cloth of their skirts, restraining himself only in the formidable presence of the Chinese-Malay woman. He guessed that she was Maya's twin and should not be disturbed, lest the house came crashing down on his ears.

The rest of the time he walked along the *estero,* anger rising like fever in his body at the sight of so much richness, so much wealth, and so much ignorance. The leaf-shaped boats bore unbelievable wares beneath his eyes—extravagant fruits and vegetables, flowers of excessive colors, a thousand kinds of fish, sometimes gold trinkets made by the northern mountain tribes, baroque pearls from the southern sea tribes, cloth of incredible patterns, and, of course, the men and women, brown as aged wood, skin varnished by the sun, dark eyes that smoldered, he could swear, with both deviltry and innocence. He cursed them one and all for not seeing the potential locked in their environment of no winter, no drought; he cursed them for being existential, so immersed in the pleasure of living in this moment and this moment alone, this drift of boats down the current of a canal whose clear waters spoke of mountain rains, while he, Hans, old soul from Europe, had to think of the future and sweat out all the possibilities of disaster before it even struck. If he could only learn not to anticipate . . .

Thus, when Don Carlos Lucas de Villaverde announced to his assembly, one Friday night, that he was to be married, Hans Zangroniz believed he had been given a reprieve. With a woman to amuse, his partner would not pay too much attention to the German albatross. He sighed, congratulated Carlos Lucas, and was about to tease Maya about grandchildren when he was struck full in the face by a glance of hatred from her eyes. He could not have known that the marriage had been engineered by the old woman; that indeed it had been compelled by the sight of him speaking to two Capuchin monks by the *estero*—a sight Maya caught one morning as she bent closer to the vanity mirror facing the wide balcony doors of her bedroom.

3

Her signature on the church marriage registry read Maya Batoyan and she was the daughter of the Chinese-Malay maid, though none of this was known to Carlos Lucas when he came upon her one peculiar morning. He was still in his nightshirt and robe, having been awakened by a portentous feel to the air, as though the house was breathing, its walls quivering and sighing, so he couldn't be sure he was no longer asleep, was not in fact caught in a dream. He had yawned, stretched his arms upward, and looked out of the bedroom window to see the boats which delivered milk and eggs to the *estero* houses sailing, as it were, on air, six inches above the water, which was so translucent the mud spurts of burrowing crabs at its bottom were visible. Because he had no wish to remain in this impossible mood, he had gone to the bathroom to wash his face and rinse his mouth, then to the kitchen in search of coffee. Instead, he found her, shrouded by her blue-black hair from head to ankles, wearing an

old-fashioned sheer loose blouse of woven pineapple fiber and a burgundy velvet skirt. Her feet were bare. She had her back to him and
the noise of his appearance caused her to half turn, to glance over her
right shoulder, with her lips pursed, for she was raising a cup of cocoa
to her mouth, ready to blow cooling breath on the blistering liquid.
He knew immediately, when her wet coal eyes fell on him, that he
did not want her, would have difficulties loving her, but would marry
her nevertheless, because this morning was so new it could only be
the future. As soon as he accepted this, the beams of the house
creaked their welcome to the sun.

That was all he knew; he would have found it surprising, had he
been told, that her presence in the kitchen on that particular day and
at that particular hour was the culmination of a series of events that
had begun with his mother, Maya, catching sight of Hans, "the putrid
German," as she mumbled to herself, deep in conversation with two
Capuchin monks on the opposite bank of the canal. The shock of that
treachery, the danger it signaled, was transformed in Maya's mind
into an omen: it was time for her to go outside the Binondo house
after more than a decade of isolation. By what circuitous logic she
arrived at this conclusion, she herself did not know, but having
reached it, she did not hesitate.

"Order my caleche and horses for tomorrow," she said to the
Chinese-Malay maid who was fussing with her hair, which was pure
platinum now. "We're going for a trot by the sea."

The maid dropped the gold high-comb she was using to rake
Maya's scalp. Retrieving it hurriedly, with her face hidden as she knelt
and fumbled beneath the dresser stool, she mumbled that such an
excursion needed planning, it wasn't going to be easy, there were a
thousand and one things to be done before they could leave the house
and the distillery with a clear conscience, the windows had to be
washed, the furniture dusted, the servants marshaled and set to
work—

"Enough," said Maya. "We leave at ten o'clock tomorrow. Have
some food wrapped. We'll have lunch by the sea."

"But—"

"I will not discuss it anymore."

The maid wrung her hands and finally confessed she was worried as to how Don Carlos Lucas would react.

"Since when has my son told me what to do? Don't worry. I will tell him." She settled down and allowed the maid to finish pinning up her hair. "Careful," she said as the comb snagged, "my hair won't grow again. My scalp is old." She wondered how old she really was but discovered that a fog had grown about her memory. "I must be nearly a hundred," she mumbled. "That putrid German!"

It was a morning of complacencies. With the land breeze came the voices of children, half-naked brats who fell in and out of the canal, taking to the water like brown dolphin pups. She heard the words, the insidious words of an insidious language—*one-two, bato; three-four, bapor*—driving her crazy with pickings of intelligibility. *Ferdinand Magellan, the crazy old coot; took five ships and circumcised the globe.*

"What are they saying?" she asked her maid.

"Fernando Magallanes went around the world with five ships," the maid translated.

"Not true," she said. "Only one returned to Madrid. Magallanes stayed here—in Cebu. The *indios* killed him. Maybe ate him. I don't know. Ferdinand? Where did they get this Ferdinand? Tell them it's Fernando. Fer-nan-do."

"Same thing, señora."

"It's not!" She was quiet for a moment, brooding over whether a word was exactly the same as its equivalent in another language. There was no answer to that so she found another question: "Do they really know English—the children?"

"I don't know, señora. I can barely understand it myself. Almost, you have to make a goldfish mouth to pronounce it."

Maya sighed. "You and I—we're becoming obsolete. We should take a look at the world. And to see the world, we have to look at the sea. I was right. I'll speak to Carlosito tonight."

Ferdinand Magellan, the crazy old coot; took five ships and circumcised the globe . . . Skip, jump; skip, jump; a rope, held and swung at both ends by two girls in braids, rose and fell and slapped the ground in rhythm with the limerick.

Carlos Lucas took it as a personal insult.

"You will not do any such thing!" he yelled. "If you wish to commit suicide, you'll do it in the privacy of this house."

Maya let the spoon in her hand drop back to the soup plate, spattering chicken fat and broth on the tablecloth.

"Far be it," she hissed at him, "far be it for me to even think of death. What will happen to you then? How will you survive?"

"I will not hear of your going to the sea. You wish to catch pneumonia, you can stand bare breasted at your window. You will not embarrass me by this public suicide."

"Stop accusing me of wishing for what you wish yourself. Enough. My caleche and horses tomorrow. I will go to the sea."

The blood left Carlos Lucas's face. He fixed dead eyes on her, plucked the napkin from his lap, and threw it on the table.

"If you go tomorrow, I'll have my lawyer draw up the partnership papers." He swiveled toward Hans who, as usual, had been reduced to a cower by the noise. "Yes, Hans. We shall be partners in fact as well as name. And if I die without survivors, which I assuredly will, since my mother is intent on aggravating me to the death, you will inherit the entire company. All you have to do is agree that so long as it exists, it will be known as Villaverde y Compania."

Hans's mouth opened and closed several times, his eyes darting between Carlos Lucas and Maya. Finally, he managed to croak his agreement. Whereupon, Carlos Lucas pushed his chair back, bared his teeth at his mother, and stormed out of the dining room.

"The Capuchins have always been crazy," Maya shouted after him. "And you're no different."

The outer door banged with such force that the chandelier crystals overhead tinkled.

"My dear German," Maya said with a disarming smile, "am I being unreasonable?" To her, Hans, like the maid, was his nationality. *El Aleman.*

He winced at this reminder of his alien status. "Certainly not," he answered with gallantry. Then, as always, caution prevailed. "On the other hand, my dear friend Don Carlos"—he stressed the possessive phrase, sensing danger in Maya's affability—"has reason on his side. It could be risky—especially with the humors rising from the sea and your bones . . . I mean, one could never be too careful with one's health; he's right to worry, I mean, though it may sound—"

"It sounds like shit," Maya said. "I'm going to the sea. And that's that." She rose, forcing the German to stand up, and flounced out of the room. What, she asked herself, were they hiding from her?

Her last thought that night, just before she slipped inside the gauze mosquito net and climbed into bed, was of the sea. "Do not forget. My caleche and horses tomorrow," she said to the maid.

All fight beaten out of her, the Chinese-Malay bent her head and murmured: "Yes, señora."

It was nearly dawn when she was awakened by a commotion in the living room. For a moment, she was confused by the veil of white that circumscribed her world; she thought she had gone blind or her eyes had metamorphosed into a bad pair of binoculars, perhaps in retribution for the bizarre death of the only man who had loved her without reservation and against everything and everyone. Carlos Lucas was bellowing somewhere behind that whiteness. Maya called out calming words, thinking he was weeping over his father's bier. Her voice cleared her mind. She swept aside one edge of the mosquito net and reached for the silver bell on the night table. Before she could ring, however, the maid appeared and, in a whisper, explained that Don Carlos was roaring drunk. He had been celebrating with two distillery workers who had brought him home and were now trying to make him stay in bed.

"So much for him," Maya said. "I'm not changing my plans."

Carlos Lucas didn't appear for breakfast and both Hans and Maya ignored the untouched plate on the table. She had a hearty meal, and asked Hans if he wished to join the excursion—which so frightened the German his refusal was incoherent. Maya shrugged, told him coldly he could do as he pleased, it was none of her business. At exactly ten o'clock, leaning on her maid's arm, she traversed the living room, the foyer, and the great stone steps at the house's flank.

She was dressed for the occasion in an embroidered blouse with loose lace-trimmed sleeves, an ankle-length lace underskirt over two petticoats, a short black overskirt hugging her hips, a shawl, and white leather shoes. She had considered the emeralds but decided that for such an early hour they would be vulgar. Instead, she wore three gold chains with saints' medallions. She would look beautiful, she thought, on the driver's seat of her caleche, holding the reins of her matched black horses—which she had had Carlosito buy for her as soon as there had been enough money.

"I'll take the reins," she said to her maid, as she slid one foot to the next step, followed it with her other foot, and kept one hand on the balustrade.

"No, señora, excuse me, señora, but no, no, no. We have a driver—"

"I don't need one."

"For your status, señora, and for this caleche—yes, yes, you—we will need him."

Outside the gate, there were neither horses nor caleche—only this man waiting beside a monstrous thing of metal and white paint, a huge box, it seemed, crouched on black wheels. It had square holes covered with glass at the front, sides, and back, windows which were held in place by a low-slung roof. A vast number of trumpet-shaped metal pieces stuck out from its body.

The man tugged at a handle and a section of the thing's side swung open. Maya froze.

"What is this?"

"This is an automobile, señora," the maid said, "a kind of caleche, without horses."

Inclining her head to one side, she studied the monster, glanced at the man. "And will he pedal us all the way to the sea? He doesn't look strong enough."

"No, señora, it has a motor. The motor drives the wheels and he"—the maid pointed to the man—"will use that other little wheel to steer it. It's quite safe."

Maya pushed her away. "WHERE ARE MY HORSES?"

The maid burst into tears. Don Carlos Lucas, she confessed, had sold both caleche and horses years and years ago, that's why he didn't want the señora to go to the sea, because she would have to use the automobile. He was so distressed at the thought of her distress he had knocked himself out with gin the night before. He couldn't face her.

"The sniveling coward," Maya said, grinning at the fright of maid, driver, and the distillery workers alike. "My lovely horses."

"They were getting old, señora."

"Like me. You will replace me, too? Traitors."

The maid covered her face.

"Really, señora, it is quite safe," the driver interposed. "Besides which, if you want to go to the sea, there is no other way."

"Very well," she said, calmly. "If I must, I must. I go in there and sit?"

The man nodded. She swept forward, climbed aboard, and arranged her skirts on the velvet upholstery. "The roof," she declared, "is too low." She noticed the maid, who had hung back. "Well, come on in, come on. We will *drive* to the sea."

It was to be a journey of revelations, from the sudden crackle of the engine, its ridiculous noise, to the bone-wrenching rhythm of the car's passage over the cobblestones of Binondo's streets.

"This thing will disintegrate," Maya said, hearing her voice waver and quake with every bump. "We will be left on our backsides in the middle of the street."

"It will get better," the driver yelled over the noise, "when we get to the asphalt roads."

"Bah! Asphalt is for roofs."

They wriggled out of Binondo's narrowness onto wide roads and the run became so smooth, so fluid Maya found it necessary to complain about missing her horses' trot. But she forgot her complaint immediately, for they were passing through the world's most crowded spot, certainly, the massed, rhythmic movement of thousands of men and women enchanting, reminding her of an infestation of swallows which visited the ricefields of her childhood.

"So many, so many of them—of us," she said and was glad, remembering how she had fished couples from behind sacks of berries and rye, turpentine barrels and demijohns at the distillery, to which hiding places they had been driven by the itch caused by the odor of fermentation. It had seemed but an instant ago when only swallows and women in mourning were left in the world.

"This is downtown Manila," the maid said.

"That's the Quiapo church, so it must be Quiapo."

"It's called *downtown* now."

She tried out the word, shrugged, and said Quiapo was easier. In any case, both maid and driver should hold on to something because they weren't sure yet this *automobile* wasn't about to fall apart.

"This is the Agrifina," the maid said as they swung into a circular road.

"Since when did we use Roman names?"

"Not Roman. From agriculture and finance—those two buildings . . ."

She looked. "They're ugly. They're new."

"They say the Americans build at every fart—excuse my language, señora . . ."

"So—where shall we put our trees, our flowers, our grass? Oh, there's the sea!"

And there it was, filling half of everything available to the eyes—the vastness of it, the depth of it, the weight of it, clear blue, like a mirror to the sky.

"This is Dewey Boulevard," the maid said.

"After the commodore?"

"He became an admiral."

They pulled over to the street side and stopped. The driver disembarked and opened their door.

She refused to move. "I want to go to Bagumbayan."

"This is Bagumbayan—or Luneta now. Over there is Rizal's monument. And you can see the sea."

"Bagumbayan was a place for executions. Why are there so many crosses with wires?"

"Electricity, señora; the Recollects and some American businessmen have formed a company to bring electricity to the city."

"What is electricity?"

"Uh—some fuel, señora. We don't really know."

"Business and religion. Bah! Religion and business. We used to have only one devil. Now—"

She allowed herself to be led to the seawall. Nothing had changed; only the shapes of the ships docked toward one side of the harbor were different. There was still the shadow of Corregidor in the horizon, that nondescript island no one save the Yanquis could find use for. She inhaled the sea, letting all its memories possess her bones. The sharp, briny smell brought her the words of her Capuchin monk, of his voyage halfway around the world, of the water and the waves and the terror of typhoons. Nothing remained of that, only a black marble marker at the altar's foot at the Malolos church. No one even remembered who had designed and supervised the building of the old stone bridge spanning with grace the mighty Bulacan River.

It was a kind of sin, certainly, to forget—but it was not easy to remember, especially when names changed, languages changed. A century-old name held that century; when replaced, a hundred years were wiped out at one stroke. Amnesia set it; reality itself, being metamorphic, was affected. "Soon we will forget everything," she told the maid, "and if we forget, how are we to proceed?"

The maid ignored her. She was busy with spreading a tablecloth on the wall top, anchoring it against the wind with bottles and jugs, and with emptying the picnic basket, laying out enamel boxes of food.

Irritated, Maya called her a fool. "When the German inherits everything, where will you be?"

The Chinese-Malay frowned over this. "Perhaps we should get the Don married."

Maya was surprised; her *chinita* had been mulling over the problem. She looked at the maid closely. The ten-year-old girl underwent a metamorphosis on the spot. She was no longer a girl; she was a woman, taller than average—or had Maya shrunk through all these years?—with the heavy breasts of her Malay mother and the slim bones of her Chinese father, sheathed in a severe dark blue cheongsam. But Maya noted the sadness settling about the woman's mouth and understood she was no longer young.

"I should have married you to him," she said on impulse and was shaken to see the maid's eyes brim over. So, she had loved Carlos Lucas—the reason for her constancy, her devotion to the household, her years of residence there broken only by a year's leave to care for her dying mother and by summer and Christmastime vacation. Moved, Maya took the maid's hand and patted it. "Too late now. He needs sons."

To her surprise, the maid fell to her knees on the ground and since Maya was seated on the seawall, it was easy for the Chinese-Malay to press her forehead to Maya's lap. Awkwardly, knowing she would reject the maid's desire, Maya stroked the woman's smooth hair and noted how gray mingled with its black strands. Then, from that bowed head, the impossible words came.

"My daughter celebrates her fifteenth birthday next month."

Maya's hands flew up; she felt she'd touched live coal. "Your what?"

The maid lifted her head and with her eyes upon Maya's face, repeated the words.

"But—who?"

She named a former worker at the distillery, long gone now. Maya was scandalized.

"He was a boy—so young!"

"So was I," the maid shot back. "Besides, one takes solace wherever one finds it."

Maya's heart creaked. She counted the years of pain the maid must have gone through. And neither she nor Carlosito had known; they hadn't even known her name. Still—

"She is a bastard," Maya said, forcing the words out, deeming a direct attack the best possible move.

"Not so. I married a peasant from Laguna. I bought his name for her. She is legitimate. Baptized."

"But untutored! Barefoot!"

"She has lived with the nuns of Calamba since she was five. She speaks three languages and plays the harp. Her embroidery is so exquisite the nuns auction off her work."

A moment of silence. Then, because she could not help it, Maya guffawed.

"Convent bred! So that's where all your money's gone. Well, well, well. Of course, she has no money and no connections but—what the hell? I was a servant, too, in the house of Carlosito's father." She chuckled. "We are a hardy lot, you and I. You must have planned this for years. You carry your father's genes well."

The maid smiled, rose, and dusted her knees. "I thank you, señora."

"How soon can she come?"

"In three, four days' time."

"It has to be before the fool Carlos meets with his lawyer." She accepted the plate of rice and chicken curry the maid held out. "You understand, of course, we can only propose this thing. Half of the doing of it rests with Carlosito, the other half with your daughter." She let the maid spread a napkin on her lap. "It is perfect, of course, for you have been raised after my own image. You can carry on after me. But—so much is uncertain in this enterprise, you understand?" She felt around in her head for the source of her trepidation. "Tell me, is she beautiful?"

The maid went on ladling food for the driver who waited by the car but a knowing smile played about her lips. Then, she gave the reply that decided the matter once and for all.

"Her name is Maya."

Her blue-black hair had not been trimmed since birth; her skin was as brown as the swallow whose name she carried but, because her blood was confused, a sheen of gold overlaid that earth hue, as though she bathed in pollen. Maya was struck speechless, though she had been prepared for such an apparition, having sensed the tension in her maid throughout the day, even through the evening meal hour and the after-dinner tallying of accounts when the two of them were left in the dining room. She had begun the session in the usual manner, mumbling that "someone has to attend to money in this house," and taking the head seat while the Chinese-Malay sat to her right. She had opened the cash box, counted out the distillery take, the houses' take, and all the crumpled and filthy paper money distributed by the Yanquis, the silver peso and quarter coins, snapping out numbers which were translated into a strange dance over the abacus by the maid's fingers. As usual, despite her paper and pencil, Maya entangled herself in her calculations and the correct total had to be read from the alien instrument that her maid used. She ended the process still in the usual manner, saying "that's that, what we've sowed, we shall reap." But as she snapped the box closed, the maid had placed a hand on her arm and murmured "wait." Maya had waited, watching as the maid left the room, watching the empty doorway even as she sensed a kind of fate coming toward her; she had waited until the maid was there, leading by one hand an exquisite creature.

Instantly, she saw herself as she must have looked that morning nearly a century ago, as she had stood barefoot in the monastery's kitchen, a cup of cocoa in a slim brown hand, her lips pursed to blow cooling breath on the blistering liquid, her face half turned to look over her shoulder at a tall Capuchin monk who had materialized in the doorway. She had worn clothes like these and her hair had tickled her ankles, though to keep its wild strands away her eyes she had run about her forehead, behind her ears and knotted at her nape, a ribbon of intricately designed beads, one of those woven by then still savage tribes in the forest. At the same time, she understood that this was exactly how Carlos Lucas should find this girl—at a particular hour of a morning of fragility, barefoot and reckless, a cup of cocoa midway to her pursed lips, both he and she in ignorance of how this had happened before, so they could believe this strange instant to be their own invention.

Maya wanted to weep but the years had not toughened her for nothing. She gestured for the girl to approach. The maid pushed her gently forward. She stood beside Maya, who swiveled in her seat and examined her: the high forehead, the wet coal-black eyes, the thin nose, the small mouth with its succulent slightly swollen underlip, the pointed chin with its tiny brown mole. Maya ran a hand over the girl's right arm. It was as smooth and firm as a tree-ripened mango. "Show me your fingers."

The girl lifted her hands. They were small, the fingers tapering to close-clipped nails, each bearing a half-moon.

"Show me your palms."

The girl turned her hands over. Suddenly, Maya struck out with her fists, pushing with all her strength against the smoothness of the girl's palms. But she felt the tremor of strength run through the girl's forearms as the latter's wrists locked and resisted Maya's downward push.

"Wrists of iron," Maya said, pleased. She nodded at the maid.

"She sleeps with you tonight? For instruction?" the maid asked, expressionless.

Maya hesitated. Her consent would set an irrevocable course for the household. She looked at the girl's face again, saw her own morning of destiny, and at last accepted that she was to die soon.

She nodded. "But let her come later. Let me finish my preparations first."

It was nearly midnight when the bedroom door opened and the girl came in. She wore a thin cotton chemise and, as she slipped inside the mosquito net, she filled Maya's world with the scent of wildflowers. She laid herself down beside the old woman, who rose on one elbow and felt her body, testing flesh and bones.

When she was satisfied that nothing was lacking, Maya began to recite what Carlos Lucas was and wasn't, what he liked and didn't like, what the business was, what was expected of the girl if and when she became the new señora. But as she spoke, her heart thumped and writhed in protest; this wasn't the lesson at all, not at all. Her mind divided between her litany and the wildness of her heart, Maya soon lost her way through her speech and drifted to silence and half-sleep, listening to the girl's light breathing, smelling her odors. A calmness possessed her, inspired by the girl's silence; she had the impression a length of time passed, with only the soft lapping of the canal waters audible in the room, its moist heat causing the mosquito net to sway gently, so that she began to think that she had boarded a skiff with her Capuchin monk, as they were wont to do, and the boat now floated on a wayward current while from the firetrees on the river-banks rose the song of woolly caterpillars chewing on summer.

She was nearly asleep, lulled by this vision, when the girl moved and before Maya realized what she proposed to do, the girl loomed over her, stooped, and pressed her body against the length of Maya's body, her hands on Maya's hands, palm to palm, pinning them to the pillow. The weight, the glint in the girl's eyes only two inches away from her own threw her into confusion and, before she could stop herself, she was back within the monastery, deep in the cellar, where among casks of Benedictine wine she and her monk had celebrated their alliance. She had dressed as the Virgin Mary for him, a blue mantle on her head; as St. Lazarus; and once, with a loincloth and a crown of stripped vines, as Christ with breasts, affirming through these fake visitations the Spaniard's dream of sainthood. Her memories vomited her shame—both public and private; the shame that had driven her to lash saints and horses with equal cruelty and that which had driven her to embrace the priest's corruption until he found himself unable to live without her contempt. She felt the pain of all her childbirths, equal to the pain of watching her six sons walk away from the monas-tery, each with a woven reed chest of clothes on his shoulder, on their way to unspeakable voyages so they could escape the recurrent ser-mons of their own father who, insidiously, condemned his own brood by repeating over and over again that the sins of fathers were visited upon their descendants even to the third generation. Her body con-fessed the source of her relentless affection for Carlos Lucas who, among all her sons, carried and expressed himself most like his father; confessed even her lifelong pleasure at his celibacy.

Finally, she was back to the eve of her wedding to the peasant who would be monastery cook months later—that dark night of heat when she had lain with her own mother in exactly this manner, absorbing the older woman's knowledge through this means, opening a channel to the past, and in the process, accidentally learning the moment when the woman beneath her would die. Through her mother's flesh, she had met her own grandmother who was still raving against what the Spaniards had done, her voice joined by the voices of other women who spoke of a time when the world was young, the sea was simply the sea, and names were but newly invented, and when women walked these seven thousand one hundred islands with a power in them, walking in single file ten paces ahead of the men, their gold bracelets and anklets tinkling, warning that the women were in passage so that strangers could stay clear, for women then were in communion with the gods, praying to the river, the forest spirits, the ancient stones, pouring out blood libations in evening rituals, healing the sick, foretelling the results of wars, quarrels, couplings, and the seasons. They walked with wisdom, dressed simply in an ankle-length piece of cloth wrapped and knotted about the hips, breasts left bare—until the Spaniards infected them with shame and made them hide their strength beneath layers of petticoats, half-chemises, drawers, skirts, blouses, shawls, and veils.

It must have been only a moment, this communion between Maya and the girl—a mere touch of the flesh, though it resonated with eternity. Then, it was over. The girl slid to one side, leaving her with such vigor Maya thought herself young again. Her legs twitched. The girl sat up, sliding her feet outside the mosquito net. Her eyes were half closed; her mouth, satiated. Maya gripped her shoulder, holding her back for a second.

"My death?" she asked.

"Three years, two months, and a week hence." It was said without mercy.

4

She bore Carlos Lucas two daughters and a son—or at least that was what the world knew—and she would cause the destruction of the precarious honor that the city's anonymity had conferred on the Villaverdes. At the time of the wedding, though, no one could have foreseen this despite Maya's and the maid's intense consultations with psychics and the *I Ching.* The seers could not be faulted for in the two old women's anxiety over this new alliance, though they provided the wise ones with all kinds of facts about Mayang, as the girl was called informally, and Carlos Lucas, the two forgot to mention the German. Whereupon, the stars, the turtle bones, and the book— standard instruments of prescience—failed to note an extra fork in the two's fate line and blessed the marriage.

Because of the number of guests, fifteen hundred all in all, the Casa Español had to be leased for three nights, and Don Carlos Lucas and Mayang exchanged matrimonial vows thrice. Two and a half, actually;

on the last night, Mayang was so worn down by the fever of the festivities, by her voluminous gown, the weight of the emerald necklace, and by the constant fussing with the wedding bouquet and the veil flowers, she fainted before she could say "I do." This time even the worm of foreboding failed Maya, who had become preoccupied with another problem. She had noticed the absence of the Capuchins at the presidential table where the American High Command and the Superiors of Religious Orders sat. The Recollects, the Jesuits, the Augustinians, the Dominicans, and even the lay clergy bantered with the Yanquis who were all in dress uniform—but the familiar brown robe, sandals, cowl, and austere disapproval of the Capuchins were missing. She made her way to where her son sat with a group of businessmen and hissed into his ear. He laughed, brushed away her fears, and said they had not been invited.

"Never mind," he said, gesturing at the table around which religious robes of all hues clustered. "We're well protected."

He spoke the truth, it seemed, despite Maya's three-day brooding over the problem, for an air of joy hovered over the successive gatherings and the weather remained impeccable for the duration of the feast. This was in June, when the monsoon should have begun its cavort over the city. Instead, the skies remained clear. Each evening, the dancing at the open azotea of the Casa was held beneath a swollen moon and stars as huge as a man's open hand. Even the sea hid the breath of its beginning decay and released gusts of freshness upon the city, stirring such longings among the wedding guests that a number of loves were consummated without the Church's blessing. For months after, the rumor went around that Don Carlos Lucas had had a barge of French perfume sunk at the harbor, because he couldn't abide the thought of anything as stupid as a fishy whiff of wind ruining his wedding.

Even each evening's two dozen roast pigs, racked against the wall behind the serving table and still hugging the bamboo poles of their demise, looked happy enough in their shiny reddish-brown skins that, truly, the Chinese-Malay maid had no reason to blame herself for having ignored the omens—omens which flashed, like quickly shuffled cards, before her mind's eye at the instant she kicked a stool from beneath her feet and felt upon her nape the blow of the knot of an awkward hangman's noose as her eyes had taken in the distillery's relics on the morning of her death. The day Carlos Lucas informed his mother of his betrothal, Maya had awakened with a massive headache and the start of a constant complaint about the disintegration of her vision. She could see clearly and in detail at the center of her sight, but objects at the periphery were blurred; their shapes bled into one another and hid behind a white haze. It would grow worse, hampering her scuttling about the distillery, though she remained indefatigable, testing each new batch of gin, opening a bottle at random, sure that a conspiracy was afoot to reduce the name of her house to shame. She could be forgiven for not having seen how, at the end of the first wedding mass, Mayang had placed a hand on her new husband's shoulder and, leaning her weight on him, had hoisted herself to her feet. A few of the guests did, though, and nodded knowingly at the wisdom of the bride who thus ensured she would dominate her spouse.

But the maid was present when half a dozen Yanqui sailors appeared at the Casa gates and in their eagerness to join the festivities had congratulated Hans. Because Hans looked astonishingly handsome in his white tuxedo and cane, his blond hair brushed and pomaded, his blue eyes aflame with whiskey, for Carlos Lucas had decided to serve imported liquor thus banishing his own gin from the table, the maid accepted as natural he should be mistaken for the groom. It was Hans, of course, who picked up the wedding ring when Carlos Lucas dropped it in his haste to catch his swooning bride.

None of these seemed important at the time, because a million things were going on simultaneously and the poor *chinita* had to rush from the Casa's kitchen to the foyer, to the azotea, and then back to the central dining room. There were the newspapermen who arrived en masse, the elite of the profession, including Don Adrian Banyaga, the star of the *Tribune*. Carlos Lucas and the erstwhile bottle boy failed to recognize each other. The first was too giddy with pride and the second had just been struck by the lightning bolt of his destiny, spying in one corner of the azotea a rather severe young lady by the name of Miss Estela.

The Chinese-Malay maid saw to it that the newsmen were pampered; she had to watch the señora as well, making sure she did not trip over her skirt; she had to check the guest list at the door—in short, she had to be vigilant and thus could be forgiven for shoving aside what seemed to be trivial, could be forgiven even for not having known, until three months later, that Don Carlos Lucas had managed to teach his bride thirty of his forty-two ways of self-indulgence, so she was a virgin all the while Maya and the maid were scrutinizing her for the first signs of pregnancy.

Horrified, realizing that a Catholic education had not included that esoteric knowledge, the maid took Mayang by the hand, sat her down on the dresser stool in her own tiny room, and tried to explain. She used so many euphemisms and circumlocutions it took the whole afternoon to make the bride understand, by which time both were sweating and blushing from head to toe. To seal the instructions in her daughter's mind, the maid then arranged for them to watch, first, the breeding of pigs, then of dogs, and finally of horses. The sight of the stallion's magnificent tool threw the girl into such confusion she remained open-mouthed throughout the proceedings and discovered, later, that a portion of her skirt had caught on the heel of her right shoe and ripped when she had kicked out in sympathy with the horses' thrashings.

When she deemed Mayang ready, the maid caught hold of her arm as she rose from the dining table. "Do it," she hissed into the girl's ear, "now!" That evening, as the house settled into sleep, Carlos Lucas felt his bride's caresses stop and when he lifted his head to see what the problem was, she gave him an enigmatic smile and shook her head. "Not that way," she said gently, "this way." And she proceeded to instruct him in the way of dogs, pigs, and horses, infusing the lesson with such vigor that Carlos Lucas forgot where his head was and where his feet, which his right arm and which his left, forgot even his name or that he was a human being, for he heard himself snorting, barking, and, at the end, whinnying as though he had run a tremendous race and was breasting the ribbon of victory. He fell asleep instantly, releasing a volley of snores, not even noticing that his bride made a face as she left for the bathroom.

Carlos Lucas was so bemused by the evening's experience he walked like a man possessed throughout the next day, absentmindedly approving everything his workers did or asked for. At breakfast, he stole glances at Mayang, wondering how she could sit there with equanimity, speaking about this and that to the others, never missing her cue: the tone of respect to Maya, the friendly distance with Hans. She was the same and yet not the same, and he couldn't reconcile her daytime grace with the previous evening's mystery. This contradiction so haunted him that, by dinnertime, his bones felt like soup and it was all he could do to finish his meal. When dessert was over and Mayang pushed back her chair, a sudden fear gripped Carlos Lucas. He thought she would disappear and in his anxiety, he caught and held on to the edge of her sleeve and said, unaware of how Maya and the maid exchanged looks equal to a handshake: "Show me that again." Thereafter, until he lost his strength, this was to be a signal between them. Carlos Lucas would say "Show me again" and, nodding, she would give that enigmatic smile.

Two months later, the house echoed with the moans of her first pregnancy. The Chinese-Malay maid ordered bushels of green mangoes which she pickled for the long siege of irrational demands that were a pregnant woman's due—yellow-green slivers, sour and salty, which Mayang chewed like peanuts, between sips of black beer. When Clara Villaverde was born, squalling with rage one Friday morning, Carlos Lucas bought out the entire stock of a candy store and had himself driven around Manila, peppering everyone with the red- and green-wrapped sweets. Hans, on the other hand, nearly swallowed arsenic in his frustration, for the once-promised papers of the partnership continued to recede to never-never land. He could not know that Clara Villaverde would see only the year of her menarche before the great cholera epidemic of the depression tore life away from her emaciated and pain-wracked body.

Two months after the birth, Carlos Lucas held his wife's hand and said: "Show me again." Maya and the Chinese-Malay maid uncorked a bottle of champagne that night and celebrated. Nothing, it seemed, would touch the perfection of their plan, though it had gone a little awry with the birth of Clara who was supposed to be a boy. But so long as Carlos Lucas could manage, the possibility of a male heir to carry the Villaverde name remained.

"Give them time," Maya said, "he's my son and I had nothing but sons."

The maid nodded. To herself, she vowed to guard against the untoward by making the rounds of all the churches once a month for this pregnancy's duration. She would light candles, give alms, and harass all the saints with prayers and promises.

All to no avail, alas, for the second child was a girl, Clarissa Villaverde, and she was so tiny it appeared she wouldn't even survive. By this time, the disappointment was palpable. Mayang felt herself in disgrace. Carlos Lucas contented himself with the purchase of an immense amount of clothing for the baby, a quiet baptism, and went about his business. Maya complained from dusk to dawn about her eyesight and pretended not to see her daughter-in-law even when she was merely three feet away, causing her to flee to her Chinese-Malay mother for comfort. Here she found impatience, instead.

"But your child was a girl—me," she remonstrated in vain.

"Don't make me responsible," the maid said harshly, "I'm not the one sleeping with the Don."

"He's not even doing anything anymore!"

At which, the maid threw up her hands, a gesture of surrender for neither she nor Maya knew the wiles of seduction and she had no advice for her daughter.

"Give him time," she said, "he'll get around to it."

But Carlos Lucas was entangled once again in his fight with the Capuchins whose brewery was showing recovery. He paid attention to Hans once more, which both buoyed and frightened the German for he had spent the years at the Binondo house not on beer but on the philosopher's stone, on rigorous exercise, and on seducing the young servants one after another, sending them away with money as soon as they showed signs of rendering his indiscretion visible. He thought vaguely of sailing on to China but comfort had made his soul lazy and he had no wish to risk a sure thing for what was at best a hope. Besides, the Capuchins still talked to him, asking about the gin; they were always oblique about it, so Hans never felt his loyalty compromised. When he asked about beer, though, the monks gave him so much information, so many details, that he lost track of the myriad of ingredients they named and had to hazard guesses. As a result, the one keg of beer he managed to brew smelled of old shoes and was rancid.

Carlos Lucas, though, grew ebullient and said it was a beginning. To make things easier for Hans, he bought a small warehouse. He had it stocked with kegs and barrels, with malt and barley, a long table for Hans's research, and a rocking chair for the hours the scientist needed to mull over his formulas. He even found ancient books on beer, mildewed, with pages missing here and there, no mean feat for the Capuchins were jealous of information. And to make sure that Hans would not be disturbed, he gave the German all the keys to the warehouse.

Thus, every morning, Hans rose from his bed, did his exercise while stark naked, slipped on his robe afterward, took a shower, returned to his room to dress, had breakfast with the household, and then left for the warehouse. He never varied this schedule even during weekends when Don Carlos Lucas urged him to go to the cockfights. These had replaced early Sunday mass as far as the Don was concerned. "No priests, no women," he would say. "Besides which, it's the best way to build a political constituency." For there was talk now of a Constitutional Convention under the Commonwealth and Carlos Lucas had received vague intimations from one party or another about his possible candidacy.

"You—a politician?" Maya snorted. "What do you know about it?"

"I'm rich," Carlos Lucas boomed back. "That's the only requirement."

Mayang hung at the edge of the conversation and others like it, poor lost soul, ignored by everyone. Clarissa was three months old already and Carlos Lucas hadn't given the signal yet. Mayang, on the other hand, could not bring herself to initiate anything. The very thought of it, of her taking the edge of his sleeve and saying "I want to show you again" or perhaps, "Let me show you again" or "Will you let me show you now?"—any of an infinite number of variations—caused her to wring her hands in horror. The nuns of Laguna had laid such strict injunction against the expression of desire that rather than violate it, Mayang bit her nails, hugged a small cushion to her chest, and moaned in her rocking chair. She had sleepless nights. Once, she spent hours listening to the canal waters lapping. She dozed off and on, hid her head under the covers to escape Carlos Lucas's snores, and woke up suddenly when the gray sky was translucent with tentative light. Like a sleepwalker, she rose, began walking through the house, breathing in consonance with its walls, checking on her children who were cared for by servants, wondering why at the age of seventeen it was her destiny to be imprisoned in this lay convent. From the children's room, she walked to the dining room, to the kitchen, through a tiny passage leading to the servants' hall at the back. The open door showed her a number of bundles on the floor—all the girls cocooned in blankets, stretched out on their sleeping mats. The sight filled her with unbearable melancholia.

She walked to her mother's room but its door was closed and though she pressed an ear to the keyhole, she heard nothing. Restless, her heart stammering its aloneness, she walked on and found herself in front of Hans's room. The door was open and the dawn's ghost light showed her the nude German engaged in a stiff dance, flinging his arms overhead, bending his body to the right, then to the left, bringing his hands down to his waist, to his knees, to his toes.

The sight transfixed her. It took a while for Hans to notice her presence, for he was half facing the windows at the lower side of the room. Then, gradually, perhaps her gaze nudging him, he turned toward the door, revealing to her the awesome size of his Teutonic equipment. Their eyes locked. But because she could not help it, could not control it for all her convent-bred modesty, her eyes wavered, slid down, down his body, while the image of a stallion rose in her mind and her jaw dropped in admiration. Her right leg twitched; she took a step forward.

Hans met her midway into the room—a force that engulfed her and bore her back to the writing desk against the wall. By the time her cotton shift had slithered up her hips and her thighs had spread apart, she had lost all consciousness of who or where she was, knowing only that this would be the biggest, the best ever in her life, that henceforth she would suffer if he were not in her, beside her, on her, under her, holy mother of God who must have known the same pleasure once, forgive her.

The instant of fate was sudden and swift. When they fell apart, breathless with pleasure and shock, both found it unbearable to be asunder. Hans, his rear end chilled by the floor, knew himself immediately for what he was and cursed himself, saying his daughters would be born whores. The self-loathing was not for the betrayal of his host, but arose out of the certainty, even at this instant of his being sure that he loved this woman absolutely and without reservation, that he would use and betray her for the sake of his own comfort. "I *am* a beast," he mumbled, at which Mayang said "yes" and slid off the desk, tumbling toward where he half-reclined. There was no resisting it. His body lunged forward, loving her independent of his volition, and he had to stuff strands of her hair into his mouth to keep from bellowing as she rode him, her hands with their wrists of iron clinging to his shoulders.

Panting, drenched with sweat, her gown stained by copious love, Mayang's first words afterward were: "The door!" It was still open, had remained open, with neither of them noticing, and anyone could have looked in on them. The danger alerted Hans at once. He went to the desk, took out a key, and gave it to Mayang.

"The warehouse," he said. "Afternoons. Vespers."

Mayang clasped the key and fled. Carlos Lucas's snores were still setting the mosquito net aquiver when she climbed into bed, stretched out beside him, and fell asleep, her fingers curled about the warehouse key. When she opened her eyes again, it was noon, Carlos

Lucas was gone, and the house floated in the heat rays of summer. Mayang sang under her breath as she took her bath, her limbs loose as she sat on a low stool beside the cistern and poured water over her shoulders by means of a small porcelain pitcher. She sang as she dressed, sang as she entered the dining room, and kept the silly melody in her mind throughout her meal. She was alone, served by a girl of ten who brought her a dish of fish stewed in tamarind shoots, grilled dried beef, steamed okra, and rice. Mayang ate everything. She had never felt as ravenous or as healthy in her entire life.

That day began Mayang's devotion to St. Francis, to whose Capuchin church she went Monday to Friday. A thunderous rage possessed Carlos Lucas when he found out but he was stunned and eventually overwhelmed by the cold fierce resistance of his wife. To make matters worse, Maya approved of it, saying that perhaps that would square things between him and the monks, whose enmity had grown with the years. Besides, this was the modern age; no woman should be as cooped up in the house as she had been. The Chinese-Malay maid, on the other hand, was puzzled. Her daughter had never looked as happy or as beautiful, her body so supple it recalled exotic fruits. The maid could only surmise that Mayang's rebellion had stirred Carlos Lucas's lust. So she threw the weight of her judgment on Mayang's side, giving her the freedom to come and go as she pleased. This was a period of great joy for the girl.

She did go to church thrice a week, to familiarize the parish priest with her presence. The other two afternoons—she made sure she staggered her disappearances through the five weekdays—she hurried to Hans, clutching key instead of rosary, taking the public bus, walking like a woman at home in the world through alleys and streets, arriving breathless with lust at the warehouse. She would open the pedestrian door carved within the larger gate, slip in, let veil, missal, crucifix, and purse drop to the floor, and hurl herself across the room, into Hans's arms.

Hans led her through the infinite permutations of love, himself stirred by her amazement that there was more to it than the ways of pigs, dogs, and horses. The stink of malt and barley in fermentation, the acrid odor of chemicals, mixed with the chlorine-sea scent of their exertions, taunted them with half-glimpsed, half-imagined pleasures so that as the days passed, they grew more and more inventive, Mayang's wild cries and Hans's bellows ricocheting back and forth between the warehouse walls. They played at being cats and licked and sucked each other from head to foot, until Mayang was convinced that one more minute of such intensity would kill her, while Hans wanted no more than to crawl into her womb, never to emerge again. He knew the talcum odors of the skinfolds between her toes, her armpits with their bristly black short curls, the secret indentations that defined her sex which gave off an almond exudation and tasted of amaretto. Mayang, on the other hand, ran her nose over his body, sniffing at his scalp's sweat, his jaws' bristles, his chest's tangle of hair, the dimple of his navel, and the soft hairs surrounding the base of his sex which, at the sound of the key in the lock, was instantly alert and remained so for the tryst's duration.

Once they sat linked in the rocking chair, swaying back and forth, murmuring to each other their desire to be able to do this in the open, in a boat perhaps adrift on a river, under the bluest sky God ever made—on one of those slender skiffs traversing the *estero,* seemingly propelled by nothing more tangible than the song of summer's cater-pillars. To float naked on a wayward current—the innocence of the thought brought Hans such desperation he began to weep and, be-cause he wept, Mayang was overcome and wept herself. Both realized they had no middle ground; there could be no compromise to this passion. Either they cleaved together forever and ever or walked away from each other's lives totally, completely, irrevocably. More, they knew what was and wasn't possible. Thus, clinging to each other, they rocked back and forth, weeping, interrupting their sadness with screams of pleasure until it was time for Mayang to go.

Hans, despite the warehouse madness, remained alert to danger. He was the more astute, finding excuses for her to remain even beyond the two, three hours that the supposed mass and the journey back and forth allowed her. He shopped for her, buying her clothes and shoes, handbags and underwear, so she could claim to have wandered through the business district during those inevitable days when an extra hour together meant more than life itself. Thus, slowly, Mayang discarded her peasant clothes and replaced them with fashions from America—convenient slim, one-layered dresses, with short sleeves hugging her beautiful forearms, and chunky white leather shoes. Finally, she had the stupendous cascade of her hair cut and permed so that Carlos Lucas, sitting down for dinner one night, was struck dumb by the sight of this stranger, a creature who seemed to have stepped out of any of the English magazines that now littered Manila. His heart turned over and, at the meal's end, he tweaked the edge of her sleeve shyly and said, "Show me that again."

She would not. She said so over and over again, calmly, without anger but also without pity, despite his storms of rage and pleas, his threats, his drunken bouts, his weeping. She would rather not. She gave no reason, finding none in herself, except that she was truly monogamous. She wasn't even aware she was paying him back for the months of neglect—for Carlos Lucas suffered the way she had suffered, finding himself at last head over heels in love with this woman, this strange woman with the pert clothes and haircut, this cold-hearted she-dog who simply said she'd rather not and turned over on her belly and went to sleep, leaving him to console himself with one of his forty-two ways of self-indulgence. In desperation, he learned to woo his wife, courting her with flowers and jewelry, with surprise weekend trips to the resorts of Antipolo and Baguio. She only had to hint at a desire and he rushed forthwith like a madman to fulfill it for her. Nothing worked, for Mayang did not even notice Carlos Lucas's despair, immersed as she was in visions of Hans and the warehouse, so much so that when her husband went down on his knees to beg her to tax him with some task, anything at all that he may prove his love for her, Mayang smiled and said she merely wanted to be left to her devotion to St. Francis.

"The Capuchins have corrupted you," Carlos Lucas said, his voice broken.

"Nevertheless, that is all I want. All I truly want, dear spouse," she replied with pitiless courtesy.

One morning she woke up with a lightness in her heart, a touch of inexplicable joy in her limbs. Leaving Carlos Lucas still snoring in bed, she walked to the window and glanced at the sky, at the houses on the opposite bank, and then at the canal. She did not know what had stirred her from sleep at such an early hour; perhaps it was the strange quality of the day, the translucent light which made everything so dreamlike, so ethereal, as though reality itself was nothing more than a play of colors. When she placed her hands on the windowsill, the better to lean out and see the boats, she half-expected her fingers to touch nothing, to pass through what was merely an illusion of wood. Down in the canal, the boats appeared to float a foot above the water, stirring a wash of varying hues of blue in their passage. It was a morning of intense fragility and quite by accident, though it may have been preordained, Mayang lifted a hand off the sill and caressed herself, her fingers sliding down between her breasts, to her belly, to her navel, to stop at the spot where her womb hid itself beneath skin and muscle. Instantly, she knew: she was pregnant, it was a boy, and his name was Luis Carlos.

5

Hans convinced Mayang that the better part of valor was to let Carlos Lucas believe the child his. It was a simple matter to arrange. One evening, Mayang let the enigmatic smile slip across her lips and heard the hiss of her husband's breath. "Next!" Carlos Lucas yelled, shocking the maids who had to scurry to and fro, removing the half-eaten fish, the meat broth, the vegetables, while the Don muttered "next, next, next . . ." No meal, it seemed, was finished as quickly. When he made the signal after dessert, touching Mayang's right wrist with the tip of his forefinger, her discreet nod was enough to cause his soul to sprout wings. He heard the windows of the house singing and thought he was walking in his wife's footsteps on a journey to the world's edge. He never discovered he owed his adopted German brother two joys: his wife's favors which, though grudgingly and sparsely given, sufficed to ease his love-besotted spirit; and his son, Luis Carlos, who entered the world too early and in silence.

The pregnancy dulled neither Hans's nor Mayang's appetites, though the latter grew shyer as her belly advanced. But Hans proved to be capable of such gentleness, such concern for her condition, that Mayang's tears often spilled in the middle of their embrace, wetting the hand with which he stroked her shoulder and held her steady as she sat on his lap in the rocking chair. In the last months of her pregnancy, her belly was of such size, the skin stretched so tight, that her navel pouted. Hans thought she was carrying twins. He laid his ear against her hugeness and tried to catch the beating of the theoretical fetal hearts. Instead, to his consternation, he felt the child pummel the inner walls of his home, fighting the pressure of Hans's head. He was so frightened that for a while, he wondered whether a gnome, not a child, inhabited Mayang's womb.

As the weeks passed and Mayang's confinement drew closer, hysteria assailed the two. It was, Hans thought, to be the moment of truth, the instant of the child's birth; it would appear with hair the color of autumn, with eyes the color of a rain-washed sky, and with the stamp of a German scholar upon its brow. He hoped it was a girl, the better to conceal its heritage, but Mayang was adamant, saying the child was a boy and his name was Luis Carlos. She could not know that this threw Hans into a panic, for he had studied Mendel's experiments and was convinced that a boy would be absolutely in his image.

"I'll have to leave," he said, already going through the motions of packing in his head. "Sail for China!" He imagined Carlos Lucas at the dinner table, screaming at his appearance: *"Thief! German ladron! You're no better than an Italian. Return my money; return my wife; give me back my son!"* He saw Carlos Lucas dismembering him with the aid of his distillery workers who would all gently say, *Beg pardon, Señor Doctor Doctor,* while they cut out his heart, his liver, his testicles, and threw them one by one into the distillery vats.

Mayang dropped to her knees, her belly spilling to her thighs. Weeping extravagantly, she kissed Hans's feet and begged him to stay, even if only as a friend, not as her lover, perhaps as his own son's godfather. She panted out the words between great sobs, all the while just as feverishly praying he would refuse. She knew love's course had been run and to go further would be certain death for all three—Hans, her son, and herself.

Hans, being a gentleman, did refuse. "I must sail for China," he said, gently. His heart shriveled; an unbearable chill hooked into his flesh. He sat in the rocking chair and stared at Mayang's lowered head, for she was still on her knees on the floor, amidst a scatter of mats, blankets, cushions, and clothes. He understood that this was a moment of finality, that he was dying, was dead indeed, and in the sudden welling of bitterness within him he swore that if there were any chance at all, any opportunity, for him or for his descendants to do something for Mayang and her family, it would be done at whatever cost.

"Come, my heart," he said to her, his vow making him feel better. "We have always known it was to come to an end."

Mayang, child that she was, lifted eyes almost blind with love. "He is older," she said. "He will die before you and me. Will you wait? Will you write to me from wherever you are so I can tell you when he dies? Will you?"

The German lied. "Yes," he said. "I will wait. I will wait and watch over you. No matter how many years—centuries even." He pulled her to his lap and held her, his fingers caressing the tender skin of her nape. "You'll always have me with you in our child."

"Poor Hans. Poor me. Poor child."

"I wish there was something I could do for Carlos Lucas." His eyes misted at the name. "Then, my debt would be paid and I can be at peace."

Nestling against him, curving herself to fit against his body, Mayang asked what he needed so he could settle his obligations.

Stammering, choosing his words, Hans moved on the path to betrayal. "I'd like to—to—I don't know—perhaps, do a history of the house which would—would—make Carlos Lucas proud—but . . ."

"Surely, you know enough about it."

"Ach, dear child, dear, dear child." He was quiet for a moment, gauging his own corruption. "Not enough. As you know, he won't let me examine the—the—the notebooks of his early experiments. The ones in your bedroom. In the wardrobe. And without those, there's simply no way I could—could . . ."

"Don't worry. You'll have them."

"My dear child, my heart, my love . . ."

Mayang found the notebooks, wrapped in tissue paper, under Carlos Lucas's folded undershirts. She removed them, trusting in her husband's absentmindedness, not even preparing a tale with which to deceive him. To his questions, if ever they came, she would simply look innocent and shrug, for Carlos Lucas knew she never opened the carved mahogany wardrobe which held his property. It was her mother's task to do so, to put away the clean and pressed clothes handed to her by the laundry woman.

A thin scream echoed from the house's interior when daylight struck the three notebooks. Hurriedly, Mayang tucked them into her woven reed bag, covering them with her crocheting, before she ran out of the room, her hands to her belly's sides. In the living room, she met her mother, the Chinese-Malay maid, hobbling toward the bathroom. She had dropped a pot of boiling water on her feet and was hurrying to douse them with cold water. Mayang helped, scooping frigid water from the cistern, pouring this into a basin, and letting her mother lave her feet.

"It doesn't look bad," she said vaguely, her mind already on the pendulum clock in the living room.

"No," agreed her mother. "Don't stoop so. You might harm the child."

Mayang laughed, as befitted her new self with the American dress and hairdo. "Nothing will harm the child."

"Nothing?"

She laughed again. "Not even a war."

Her mother was pleased. She felt Mayang's soft hair. "We have done well, haven't we?"

"Yes, 'Nay."

The use of the old honorific pleased the maid's heart. "I hope it will be a boy. The señora will be pleased. You have a name ready?"

For it wouldn't do, should anything happen, for a child to die un-named.

"Luis Carlos."

"Carlos—it's not too bad. But why Luis?"

"I don't know. He chose it so he'll have to explain it himself."

Her mother thought she was referring to Carlos Lucas, not the child, and so let the matter rest.

"It's nearly time for your devotion," she reminded Mayang. "It won't do for you to be late."

Mayang hesitated. She looked at her mother. "Are you really all right? You don't need me?" A twinge of anxiety made her search her mother's face.

"It's nothing. The skin will be red for a while. That's all."

Still reluctant, Mayang left the bathroom. She dressed quickly, in the tent-shaped maternity smock her mother had sewn. She put on lipstick, ran a brush through her hair, examined her eyes, wondering if her sins were visible. An inordinate fatigue settled on her bones; she thought briefly of not going to the warehouse, of staying at home, of sleeping, but Hans was waiting, would wait until the first star shone true and clear.

She picked up the reed bag, counted out change for the trolley car. Then, slowly, with many sidelong looks at the house that seemed to breathe, she crossed the living room with its wide windows, its fune-real Castilian furniture, its Italian crystal, and the flurry of saints, candles, and flowers on the small altar set against one wall. Everything was quiet, all noise coming from the outside, but the air was so musty the voices, the distillery's humming, even the laughter of children seemed to come from a great distance. She entered the foyer, with its porthole windows, its carved reddish-brown bench, its copper um-brella stand, and the hanging fern pots which on her first visit had made her think of lopped-off heads. She touched the inner knob of the front doors. Something crashed and broke in the house, startling her into twisting the iron knob. One door panel sprang open and the afternoon sun showed her the steps—the great stone steps—scrubbed white and impeccable. She took a step, then another, hearing the door swing shut behind her, feeling her dress cling to the sudden perspiration that drenched her chest and back. She half-expected a voice to cry out, for voices to shout *stop, thief!* but nothing happened. It was a most ordinary day.

She walked to Binondo's main street; she had refused, early on in her fight with Carlos Lucas over her churchgoing, the use of the automobile, saying the walk to and fro was good for her. Standing at the trolley stop, she had the disquieting conviction that the house was vanishing, had vanished even as she waited there, and when she returned it would be to a strange neighborhood where no one would know or even remember her. She could see herself beside the *estero*, which had inexplicably turned into a canal of thick-crusted mud. She was surrounded by children, none of whom knew where the Four Roses distillery was, nor even what it was, and deemed her half-mad. Her heart creaked with desolation at this image of herself lost forever, unable to return home, but at that moment from the distance rose the clang, clang of the trolley and she forgot the mirage. Hans was in her mind now, nude Hans doing his brittle alien dance.

It was unseasonably warm for February; by the time she reached the warehouse, her smock stuck to her skin, hampering her knees. She unlocked the door, stepped into the cool dimness that held Hans's odor, and saw him rise from behind his work counter, his eyes glinting like ice. She was too big now for the dash across the room and too tired today to do more than lean against the door. She held out the reed bag and said, take them, take them. Hans hurried forward.

"But what is the matter?"

He felt her forehead with his palm, exclaimed at the warmth. "You're feverish, child."

She gave a short laugh and sagged against him. He picked her up, taking her weight easily, and settled her on the rocking chair. Then, he rushed back to the bag she had let drop to the floor; he thrust his hand into it, ferreting, Mayang thought, like an animal intent on prey. For the first time, her eyes took in the warehouse, pathetic scene of her passion—the chipped gray paint, the old, piled-up sacks of failure, weathered barrels and rusting hoops, the disorder of the work counter, the lamps, the cracked test tubes, the mat on the floor with its desultory pillow, the unwashed blanket . . . She felt the shame of her betrayal. Hans was turning the notebooks in his hands, eyeing them with lust. *What have I done?* Mayang thought.

"Hans!" she called out.

He was beside her instantly. "You're ill," he said.

She nodded. "I must go home."

There was a moment of silence. Hans debated the wisdom of letting her go alone; on the other hand, if he took her home . . . The explanations! The suspicion! He paced back and forth, not looking at her. She moaned; his heart stopped. He realized what was happening.

"Holy mother of God, not now, not now," he muttered, gathering her things. "Child, get up. Get up. You must go home. Hurry. Hurry."

Listless, Mayang allowed him to pull her to her feet. Hans almost dragged her to the door.

"I'll walk you to the stop. But be quiet. Be very quiet."

Mayang nodded. She squinted at the daylight. "I'm going to be sick," she said.

"No, child, you're not," Hans corrected her firmly. "You will get on the trolley, you will pay your fare, and you will reach the house safely. Believe me."

"I believe you," Mayang said. "I'll always believe you." She began to weep. Hans handed her his linen handkerchief and hurried her on.

"I'll put you on the trolley," he said. "Go home and go to bed. You're ill, child." He dug into his pocket and gave her some coins. "That should pay for your fare. Listen, love, we'll see each other next week. But right now—right now . . ."

The trolley rumbled into view.

"I do love you, child," Hans suddenly said. "Beast though I am, I do. I do."

She saw him as through a haze, heard his words like the echo of distant thunder—soothing but unintelligible. The trolley came nearer, slowed down, inched to a stop. She boarded it, Hans pushing at her back. She handed the conductor some coins, shrugged when he returned two, and found a window seat. As the trolley began to move, she and Hans looked at each other. Somewhere within her, someone was closing doors, shuttering windows, drawing curtains. A smile of regret crossed Hans's face; her own face, she knew, mirrored it. Close the doors, shut the windows. He was gone and she was staring at buildings, houses, and the occasional banaba tree that broke the monotonous gray and white of the city.

She refused dinner that night, preferring the company of her humiliation. She couldn't look at Hans, couldn't watch him be friendly, normal, gracious, while the secret of how he had turned her out, turned her away in her moment of distress, gnawed within her. The thought of the long walk from the trolley stop to this house, with her knees buckling, the tears she had had to wipe away, oppressed her. There had been men and women at the corner store, children by the *estero* who watched as she had staggered past. Perhaps they thought her drunk like Carlos Lucas—the scandal of it, and in her condition.

After dinner, Carlos Lucas found her perched on the windowsill, staring blankly at the night.

"Don't do that, child! What if you fall?" He pulled her gently toward the bed.

"It's too warm to go to sleep," she said. "You rest. You have a long day before you."

He grunted and began undressing. His old man's body, with its barrel torso, offended her. She left the room, walked to where her mother and Maya were settling the day's accounts. They shooed her away, telling her she needed her sleep.

In the silence of the living room, she found comfort in her tears. She settled in an armchair, curled her feet under her, and inhaled the moistness of the canal. The sea came to her—that vast stretch of fluid blue across which, in some timeless time, the ships had come, those for which the crown jewels of the Spanish queen Isabela had been pawned. Mayang wondered if the queen had redeemed those jewels, wondered even if they had been as magnificent as the emerald necklace Maya had lent her for her wedding. Thrice—for she was thrice-married. And soon to be thrice a mother. She patted her belly. The child was very quiet, immobile. She crooned to him softly, and managed to croon herself to sleep.

The pain woke her—the familiar spasm of her belly, that bunching of muscles which, strangely enough, felt as though her body was being rent apart. She bit her underlip, broke into a sweat, and waited for the contraction to pass. After an eternity, it left and she rose gingerly, walked to the bedroom, and grabbed Carlos Lucas's leg through the mosquito net.

"Wake up, wake up," she hissed at him. "I'm giving birth."

Carlos Lucas mumbled and then sat up, stunned awake by her words. "You can't," he said, "it's too soon."

"Like hell it is," she said, sweeping aside the gauze net and laying her body down. She closed her eyes, settled her fists between her breasts. "Like hell it is," she repeated and laughed at the first curse she had ever uttered.

It was a sixteen-hour struggle, for the child fought his own birth. Mayang herself, shrieking with the contractions, oscillated between the wish to get the whole thing over with and the desire to keep the child inside her. Hans, she knew, would stay barely long enough for a glance at his son and the assurance that Mayang was all right. Then, he would sail to China. In her head, amidst the pain, she saw him boarding a folded paper boat which rocked back and forth on a painted blue sea toward a land where a row of paper dolls with slanted cutout eyes waited, their hands linked within their huge sleeves. "At least he won't find their women charming," she murmured.

"What?" Maya bent over her. The old woman eyed her strangely. "Be sure this is a boy now."

"He is. And his name is Luis Carlos."

"Carlos Lucas Segundo," Maya said, her eyes angry.

Mayang sat up and began to scream. "You will not, you will not, you horrible old woman. You will not!" Inside her, the child squirmed.

"Hush, hush," Carlos Lucas said from the other side of the bed. "Will you be quiet?" He shouted at his mother. "Luis Carlos, then. Luis Carlos. Or if it's a girl, Luisa."

Mayang fell back on the bed. "I am señora now," she said. "I am not a child."

"She is delirious." It was her mother. She had come in with six maids. "Come, we have to strip the bed."

The maids helped her to a chair. Then, they removed the bedsheets and spread out layers of linen paper, sweet-smelling and new, on the mattress while Carlos Lucas raged from one end of the room at what he called an incredible aberration.

"She's not comfortable," he shouted, "sitting there. Hurry up, for God's sake. What shit is this? Buy a new mattress tomorrow, throw the old one out. Buy four new mattresses! What do I care? Let her lie down!"

Mayang screamed as another contraction hit her. The maids clustered, one fanning her, another combing with her fingers the damp hair away from her brow.

"Don't let her hurt!" Carlos Lucas yelled.

The Chinese-Malay maid knotted one of Carlos Lucas's handkerchiefs. "Here," she said, giving it to Mayang, "keep it between your teeth. It's shameful, the way you're carrying on. When I had you—"

The bed was ready. The maids helped Mayang through the six tiny steps it took to reach the bed's edge. They helped her stretch out and then, as one, turned toward Carlos Lucas.

"What now?" he stormed.

Maya, wheezing with fatigue, showed him the enema bag. "You have to leave," she said. "Go. Wait in the living room. Send for the midwife, though what good that'll be, I don't know. I know more about childbirth than she does."

Thrown out of the bedroom, Carlos Lucas found himself pacing back and forth, back and forth, in the kitchen, his hand reaching automatically for a plate of biscuits someone had left on the table. He crunched the biscuits between his teeth, shivering to a stop whenever Mayang's screams came slithering through the walls, the doorways, the curtains. Why, he wondered, was it taking so long? The first two had slid out of her as though her opening had been greased—easy births, with nary a murmur of pain. Dimly, he saw the midwife arrive, hustled past him by a maid. She had come through the service entrance and was carrying a black bag. The dog-smile she aimed at Carlos Lucas hovered in the air long after she was gone.

After a time, Carlos Lucas noticed that someone else was pacing along with him, reaching one end of the room just as he reached the other. He half-saw the hand that picked up a biscuit a second before he did; it must have happened a dozen times before it registered in his mind and he lifted his eyes to the other man's face.

"Hans!"

The German gave a wry smile. "Yes, friend."

Carlos Lucas was moved. Hans's company in this long wait confirmed his trust. He held out his hand, which the German clasped in his own, his mouth twisting in the wash of strong emotions. Then, they resumed their pacing, each on his side of the dining table, their shoulders stooped, their hands crossed at their backs. From time to time they exchanged fond looks, and smiled to reassure each other.

The living room clock struck three o'clock, its notes resonating in the silence. Carlos Lucas counted backwards, to Mayang's announcement of her pains. Sixteen hours! Abruptly, the Chinese-Malay maid appeared, in her hands a cheesecloth bundle stained red. Maya followed, hobbling on her old woman's feet, her face ashen, drawn with fatigue. Her eyes flickered back and forth, as though she had trouble focusing them. She was mumbling.

"The clay pot is ready, señora," the maid reassured her. "Shall I bury it under the jasmine or the tamarind tree?"

"Yes, yes, the tamarind . . ." Maya stopped, placed a hand on her right temple. With her left, she held her skirts bunched, keeping the bloodstains away from her flesh.

The maid nodded and was about to leave for the kitchen when Maya called out suddenly, frantic. "No, no, no! Set it adrift—the *estero* water, to the sea. Yes, to the sea."

The maid hesitated, threw a glance at Carlos Lucas, and then shrugged. It was only when her back had disappeared through the kitchen doorway that Carlos Lucas understood; they had been discussing the afterbirth. Abruptly, he was seized with such a deathly chill he thought himself done for; there had been no wail of triumph, no sound at all, only silence after a series of terrible screams from Mayang. His child was dead.

"Was it baptized?" he whispered, shaking from head to foot.

"Right now? Don't you want a baptismal feast for your son?" Maya was indignant.

Carlos Lucas yelled in sudden jubilation. He did a dozen mazurka steps about the table, and threw his arms around Hans, screaming "we did it," while the German pummeled his back. He barely heard Maya complaining about the child's strangeness. The boy would not weep, she said, and merely frowned and grimaced each time the midwife smacked his bottom. His hair was stained red from lying in his mother's blood for so long and no amount of water poured over the thick curls could rid them of a reddish glint. Worse, he had the eyes of his grandfather—as gray as the ashes of Carlos Lucas's best cigars.

Hans stuttered and, without meaning to, shot a glance of horror at Maya. The old woman jerked back; her hands flew up to her neck, groping for the absent necklace. A terrible certainty possessed her, though Hans recovered swiftly and tendered his congratulations to his partner and friend, saying that now they would have to discuss his leaving the house; since his family was growing, he would need the space and so on and so forth . . . Carlos Lucas once more was grateful for the German's tact and, squeezing his hand, drew him into another embrace. Meanwhile, Maya watched openmouthed, the hair on her nape stirring like worms. She fought down the confusion rising within her and merely added to it. Her sorry state overwhelmed her, from the sour odor of her skin to the pungent blood on her clothes, to her shriveled naked neck. She shuffled toward the doorway and crossed the living room to the bath. Suddenly, she remembered the necklace, and retraced her steps to her bedroom.

The sun sat on the windowsill—a white, murderous ball of heat. She spat at it, hardly knowing what she was doing. Slowly, she took the pins from her hair, loosening its knot, shaking her head so that white strands settled upon her shoulders and fell to the back of her thighs, down to her ankles, like a winding sheet. Next, she unlocked the dresser's top drawer and brought out from its velvet box the emerald necklace. It caught the flames of the sun as she held it up, the Virgin Mary's legacy for which the friars had torn the monastery apart on the demise of her Capuchin, not knowing that she and Carlos Lucas had secreted the treasure away, together with the pirate chest of gold. She was about to slip it over her head when she smelled herself. "I stink of the grave," she said aloud.

She tucked the necklace into a folded towel, chose underclothes from the closet, found herself a bathrobe, and left the room. She ignored the putrid German who, with his back to the living room, was watching the *estero*. She could take some comfort from the fact that he would soon be gone and the stars of fate could right themselves again. As she turned away, she caught a glimpse of the canal and noticed how odd the boats looked in the white light of the afternoon. They seemed to have been painted black from prow to stern and were almost etched against the inordinately brilliant light. She shook her head and murmured that her eyes were playing tricks on her again, for the boats were plying a sky route.

In the bathroom, she undressed, sat down on the stool, and checked the soles of her feet for calluses, reminding herself that a woman's first beauty was her pink, soft insteps. She remembered the necklace, unfolded the towel, fondled the emeralds briefly, touching each of the eight stones with her forefinger before slipping the jewel over her head. She chuckled at how she must look, a withered assortment of bones and skin with an incomparable thing of beauty about her neck. She picked up the porcelain pitcher and tested the cistern water with her hand. It was cold. Quite inexplicably, the evening her Capuchin monk had done a *misa cantata* came to her. "Tonight," he had said, "I sing for you." And thus his voice, rising above the high tenor of the boys' choir, had a lambent undertone, a rather poignant Latin confession of love that moved the unknowing congregation that Sunday as they knelt on the pews, Maya among them, in a ceremony of candles, music, gold vestments, and incense.

No one missed her until three hours later, when Carlos Lucas was allowed to enter his own bedroom at last, to press a kiss on the mushroom-pale lips of his wife, who lay like a frazzled blossom, so near death that tears sprang to his eyes. Broken with pity, he held her hand and asked her what he could give her, what treasure in the world, to make her forget the pain of giving him a son. Mayang, as empty from her ordeal as from the loss of Hans, let two tears slither down her cheeks.

"My heart," she whispered through dry lips.

Carlos Lucas jumped to his feet and shouted for his mother. "She wants her harp," he yelled. "Get her the harp!"

The Chinese-Malay maid came running from the kitchen.

"Where's the señora?" Carlos Lucas asked. "Make arrangements to get her harp. Tell her Mayang needs . . ."

But she was not in her bedroom or in the dining room, not even in the distillery, and the mystery was threatening to drive Carlos Lucas crazy when the Chinese-Malay maid remembered the bathroom. She knocked on the thick wooden door gingerly, asking if anyone was in there, already wondering to herself why, if Maya was taking a bath, there was no light within. Gently, with her fingertips, she pushed at the door; it yielded and swung inward. Enough light came from the great windows of the living room to show the full-size mirror on the bathroom's opposite wall and, within the carved wood of its frame, Maya's image, stark naked save for the emeralds, her flesh already cyanotic blue.

6

Harp notes were Luis Carlos's earliest memories—cool silver music drenching the house in the evening, after dinner, just before the maids hustled them off to bed, the three of them, Clara, Clarissa, and himself, picking him up because he was the smallest, off the floor where they sat cross-legged, chin on palm, elbow on thigh, watching and listening to their mother play. That a woman with short, permed hair, wearing the shin-length shirtdress of current fashion, a white faux-pearl choker, and white stubby-heeled leather shoes should be coaxing German leider tunes from an ancient instrument did not appear to be incongruous. Indeed that was how his mother always would be in his mind: in consonance with the cool fall of harp notes, so that even in the midst of the driest day she seemed attended by the first rains of the monsoon, the earth's exhalation of relief from parchness.

His father, on the other hand, evoked constant panic, for Luis

Carlos could only remember the terror of the trolley bells the day Carlos Lucas had taken him for a walk. The walk had ended in a dim-lit place of many tables and a number of men, where Carlos Lucas launched a magnificent peroration against the Capuchins, their beer, and their superiors while imbibing glass after glass of whiskey, enjoying himself so thoroughly that when Luis set up a wail for home his father transfixed him with a glare of hatred. Staggering, Carlos Lucas led his son out of the tavern, through streets where daylight rendered him incapable of determining direction. They scuttled down one alley after another, in search of the house, until Carlos Lucas, exhausted by the perambulation, postponed the chase in favor of a nap and, letting go of Luis's hand, stretched himself out in the middle of the street, across the trolley car's rails. Luis Carlos, being well trained, squatted peaceably beside his father, shooing flies off his suety face, until a clang-clang of bells warned of the trolley's approach. In horror, he let loose a seagull screech and, grasping his father's inert hand, tugged with all the strength of his five-year-old body, trying to drag the old man to safety. It was useless. Straining against the weight, screaming, Luis Carlos in his valiant struggle was a pathetic and comic sight. So intent was he on saving his father, he did not realize his own predicament until he saw men in a corner store pointing and laughing enough to shake their heads off their shoulders as the trolley slowed, stopped six inches away, and the driver and the conductor, both bellowing with laughter, came down and hauled Carlos Lucas aboard. Luis, mortified, did not want to be rescued but there was no helping it; the driver slid an arm around his waist and hoisted him like a bag of sugar into the trolley car and seated him by his snoring father. The shame of it became a constant flurry of bells at Carlos Lucas's heels— noise which caused Luis Carlos to shudder whenever his father drew near. He couldn't know his aloofness confirmed Carlos Lucas's worst fears.

There was no denying the alliance between Mayang and her son. Carlos Lucas, appearing at the harp playing, would be seized by an almost uncontrollable rage whenever Mayang lifted her eyes from the music score to let them fall on her children. Clarissa provoked a smile;

Clara, pursed lips in an intimation of a kiss; but Luis Carlos. . . She looked at him with a stillness that confessed a loyalty unto death, an oath of fealty without words. The child watched his mother with equal gravity, his eyes unwavering. What Carlos Lucas saw was Hans and Mayang at dinner, exchanging looks so distant, so grave, that the very memory kicked at the inner walls of his heart.

It did not help that Luis's nanny, his *yaya*, bragged about the child's reddish hair, his gray eyes, ascribing the alien heritage to Mayang's obsession with St. Francis during her pregnancy. Carlos Lucas had to warn himself not to scrutinize Luis's features for traces of the putrid German.

In the tavern, though, with the sense of power alcohol brought him, he could summon his son's image with equanimity. "Ah, yes, the nose," he would murmur, belching fumes at his unknown audience, "the eyes, of course, the mouth. . ." The desire to weep clutched at his soul; he sang in a broken baritone, while other customers clapped and pretended to dance the fandango. Don Carlos Lucas, white-haired, bleary-eyed, felt his dog-jowls quiver with the melancholia of old peasant songs, those taught him by Juan Itak. He sang of a woman who kept saying she'd rather not, no, would rather not and crossed her legs, tucking her skirt between her knees. Throughout the performance, his hat sat without compromise on his right knee—a hat battered and soiled by the successive disasters that struck the house after Maya's death.

For a year after the funeral, the Binondo house settled into the routine of accomplishing in her absence what Maya, in life, had ordained. The business flourished; the Four Roses Gin was sold in three standard amounts: the personal half-pint, the pint for duo drinking, and the formidable quart for parties. Carlos Lucas installed a bar in the upper-floor living room and there mixed drinks for his friends who filled the Friday evening air with chatter and laughter, disturbing Luis Carlos who, fair-skinned and auburn-haired, lay face-down in his crib in Hans's former room. It seemed to Carlos Lucas he was proceeding complacently to old age, his fortune secure, his lineage indestructible. He ate and drank, puttered about in the distillery, met with politicians, and winked at priests. He had only to order his own cemetery plot to feel that everything in the world promised to be in its proper place.

One afternoon, as Carlos Lucas was preparing his reply to the Federalistas' invitation to join the party's political slate, a military jeep parked before the house gates. A uniformed Malay entered and, having sought him out with respect, handed him a summons to the American High Command. Instantly, he had no wish to visit anyone and would have demurred except no one said no to an American official. Having assured the sergeant that he would follow, he called the Chinese-Malay maid and ordered a change of clothes. He took a bath, lingering in that dim chamber, and came out only when a sudden sneeze warned him of dangers to his health. As his car carried him to the old summer palace of the Spanish governor general, now occupied by the Yanquis, the worm of foreboding stirred in his heart. He had intended to refuse both the Federalistas and their opponents, to live his life in peace, having his dinners with his friends, raising his children, and preparing for his return to Bulacan in his old age, so that he could be buried beside his mother, in the cemetery shadowed by the massive Capuchin church.

He was ushered in by white-suited Malay flunkeys, into the central banquet room with an oversized coffin-lid ceiling and massive chandeliers. He wondered briefly how many *indios,* or, for that matter, half-breeds, had stood in this inner sanctum in the three hundred years the Spaniards had stayed in the archipelago. Probably none, he thought and savored its luxury. But the flunkeys were already opening a side door and before he could collect himself, he was in a smaller room, furnished as an office, with a mammoth desk to one end, the American flag at a corner, and on the walls photographs of a Yanqui president and legislature no one had ever seen.

To his surprise, the American official was flanked by two Capuchin monks—Father Don Jose Saavedra and Father Don Luis Rigodon. Carlos Lucas crossed himself at the sight. The two friars smiled. The high official gestured to the chair before him and, without preamble, as soon as Carlos Lucas had seated himself, read in flawless Spanish from a sheet of paper on his desk. Quite politely, even elegantly, the words told Carlos Lucas to cease and desist from manufacturing the Four Roses Gin, aforementioned product being considered a hazard to the health of all who imbibed it, and totally unworthy of a market-place run under the aegis of the great North American nation, since it caused injuries to the brain, the kidneys, and the bowels.

Carlos Lucas half rose from the chair, his hat sliding from his knee to the floor.

"Understand, this is a direct order," the American said, "a private one. It could be made public—in which case you would be exposed. Who will protect you from those you have harmed?"

"There is no proof!" Carlos Lucas shouted.

The monks smiled. One drew out from the folds of his robe three familiar notebooks. Carlos Lucas stammered, saliva spraying on his chest. Dimly, he went over the faces of his household. One had betrayed him to his father's brood. Maya, Mayang, the Chinese-Malay, the maids, the distillery workers, the children. . .

Father Don Luis shook his head. "Your own notes on the effect of turpentine on blood vessels. We've made our own tests, of course. . ."

Father Don Jose flipped open one of the notebooks. "Oil of turpentine. No wonder it knocked out the peons quicker than beer. Tut-tut, Don Carlos, you know your countrymen's taste buds better than we do."

The American official rose. "We don't have to discuss this any-more. Your distillery will be sealed, of course, and all leftover stock confiscated. Beyond that—well, let's try to contain the scandal."

Carlos Lucas gathered himself together. He sighed. "How much did they offer you?"

The American official raised an eyebrow. The monks smiled.

"You can't match it," Father Don Jose said, "because we offered nothing."

"Really?" He jammed the hat back on his head. "That will be the day hell freezes over." He hesitated, weighing anger and helplessness. But he could not resist a last thrust at the American. "Sir," he said softly, "a revolution happened here once. There's no guarantee it won't again."

The American laughed. "Don Carlos," he said, coming from behind the desk to throw an arm around the distraught man's shoulders, "no one would risk his supply of Coca-Cola! Really! I suggest you retire from business and enter politics. That's where all the fighting's taking place. With words and paper and insults. No bullets."

The monks tittered, the American laughed, and Don Carlos Lucas exited the palace with the echo of mockery in his ears. That night, when Mayang said once more she would rather not, he let loose a string of curses and knocked down the living room altar. That did not suffice. As Mayang knelt to mop the spilled water of broken vases, Carlos Lucas kicked her between the shoulder blades. She sprawled forward, landing on the mess on the floor, lacerating her upper chest and arms on plaster and crystal shards. What Carlos Lucas saw, when she rose painfully to face him, was a life-sized replica of one of the Church's tormented and bloody saints. He yelped in fright and fled.

That night, Mayang moved to Luis Carlos's room, taking the bed once used by the putrid German. Carlos Lucas, staggering home at two in the morning, was too drunk, too heartsick, to care. Fully clothed, he dropped to his bed, collapsing the mosquito net, and fell asleep, only to be awakened by the commotion of soldiers breaking the distillery stills, demolishing the front shed, shooing all the workers home. He waited, his mouth working on the bitter film on his tongue.

It was the Chinese-Malay who rushed in, cheeks shiny with tears, hands clutching the paper of the official order. Carlos Lucas found he couldn't look at her, couldn't even listen to her, as she called his name and asked one question after another. The old cow, Carlos Lucas said to himself, blocking her voice, the old treacherous murderous cow, my notebooks, the old cow, after all these years. . . He began to tremble from head to foot, thinking of Maya, her tobacco-scented lace and velvet, her shrewd eyes. She would know what to do, he thought and, so thinking, began missing her in a way he had not since he was ten years old. He saw himself by the Bulacan river, half a century ago, watching as the current bore away his fishing pole. Dread, anger, sorrow, grief at the loss. . . Buffeted by the wash of emotions, he could only think of Maya and her fierce affection. He forgot the Chinese-Malay who, despairing, tugged at his arm.

"Don Carlos," she said in her timorous voice.

"Whore!" Carlos Lucas spat out. "Don't touch me! Go rot with the Capuchins!"

There. Carlos Lucas closed his eyes. An inordinate silence possessed the room. When he looked again, the maid was gone. He did not know she had fled downstairs, had watched the soldiers close the old coach garage's gates whose unused hinges moaned, had gone on watching as they looped a stout iron chain through the curved door handles and snapped a padlock into place. When all was quiet again, she remembered the side door no one had ever used, recalled the key among the bunch Maya had entrusted to her. She dashed upstairs, pursued by the certainty that all the years and all the plans had gone awry. She plucked the keyring from the nail on her bedroom wall, ran downstairs again, found the little door just to the side of the stone steps, unlocked it, and stepped into the rancid air of the destroyed distillery. There, in the artificial twilight of the shuttered garage, she tripped on a length of rope and instantly realized what she had to do. With a ladder, she managed to reach a ceiling beam, over which she threw one end of the rope and, tugging, pulling, ran it until it could be tied to a leg of the work counter anchored to one wall. The rope's other end dangled six feet in the air. Carefully, she fashioned her hangman's noose. She had to search for a high enough stool to reach the loop, eschewing the ladder for fear her hands would cling to its steps and betray her. *There, now,* she said, *there, there* . . . She was thinking of Maya when she pushed her head through the noose, thinking of Carlos Lucas when she bent her eyes to the floor that seemed so far below, and having thought of him, thought of Mayang now, the child she had borne just for the pleasure of witnessing a morning when the odors of eternity mingled with steam from a cup of cocoa, a morning that foretold a wedding, three births, and even this instant of death, and more besides, which couldn't be foreseen since time's end was as shrouded as its beginning. . . She smiled and kicked the stool away.

With her death, Carlos Lucas discovered her identity. Mayang, cradling her mother's body, screamed the old honorific—*Inay! Inay!*—again and again, her mouth twisted by sobs and syllables. Ashamed, Carlos Lucas would have spent gladly for a splendid funeral but the Church would not allow a suicide to be buried on hallowed ground. Carlos Lucas had to purchase a plot in the Chinese cemetery, at the city's edge, and there the tiny cortege wound up on a Sunday morning. The silver gray coffin with the body was shoved into a rectangular crypt. Two men sealed the grave by cementing a black marble slab with the maid's name (*Liwayway*—dawn) and death day into place. Carlos Lucas, Mayang, and the children watched in silence, Carlos now and then checking the sky for rain clouds. It remained clear and blue, intensifying the heathen cemetery's air of exile.

Mayang never returned to Carlos Lucas's room. In the gray pall of her mother's death, she and Carlos Lucas reached an understanding. A new routine was imposed on the household. Mayang, being undisputed señora, searched frantically for someone to take her mother's place. She hired and fired a succession of servants, liking them at first sight because of some ineluctible quality, disliking them intensely when the month's bills with their steadily increasing totals came. Carlos Lucas, on the other hand, slept until noon, got dressed, had his breakfast, and hied himself off to the taverns, returning past midnight. A vast indifference caused his eyes to glance away from the faces of his wife and children who seemed no more than a play of color and shadow in his path. He reserved his life for the taverns where strange, dark-skinned men breathed into his ear, along with alcohol fumes, the strategy and tactics of war, the superiority of one gun over another, and promises of unlimited manpower for the second revolution. Each of them lurched away with a share of Carlos's money, leaving him barely enough to pay for the drinks but delirious with thoughts of a coming chaos. The tavern waitresses winked at the men as they stripped Carlos Lucas of his wealth and themselves wrote down impossible sums on little squares of paper which were sent to

Mayang every Sunday. Years later, when Luis Carlos opened an old pirate chest in his grandmother's room, he would be puzzled by a mound of paper squares and their mathematics and would spend fruitless nights trying to ferret a code from what he took to be a secret language.

Every end of the month, Mayang made for the streets of rented houses, a huge black purse slung over her shoulder. Before Luis Carlos was old enough to walk, he was already familiar with the route, for Mayang insisted on his being with her. Held by his nanny's arms, later straddling her back, he trailed in his mother's wake, from one greasy door to another, in her attempt to collect money from tenants who were invariably not home, or who met her with tales of the most impossible calamities.

The taxi dancer suffered rapes and muggings every last week of the month; the dockworker had been on strike since his first day of work; the students just had to have money for this very last semester. Disaster struck everybody at the same time and without fail. Mayang, speaking in her most courteous Tagalog, was so overwhelmed by the tragedies of existence it was a relief to approach the twentieth door of the boarding house. Here, the lanky American always welcomed her with a cup of coffee and the month's rent, a Coke for the maid, and biscuits for Luis Carlos.

"Rest your feet, señora," he would say and she had no reason to refuse such courtesy.

The small room was always neat, the floor shiny with wax, the tiny table with its two chairs set with the wherewithals of an afternoon snack. The American spoke impeccable Spanish and was working on his Tagalog, which he practiced for half an hour with her. Slowly, the conversation veered toward her difficulties with the tenants.

"But you can sell the houses," the American said. "You don't need the aggravation. You can deposit the money and live off the interest."

At first, she had shaken her head, saying no, that would be a betrayal of her dead mother-in-law, certainly not, but somehow, whenever they left one boarding house for the next, and the equatorial sun stamped the asphalt roads with its relentless rays, the idea was not as shocking. By the end of two years, it had become a ritual, this playing with the temptation, the American teasing her for her reluctance to be freed of burden.

"But this is so typical of your people," he would say, "confess it. We haven't really changed you, despite clothes and makeup. You'd rather carry on with suffering than move to rectify the order of things."

He was an anthropologist and spent his summer months in the mountains, among tribes which had remained marginal. Soon, he would finish his studies, write his book, and return in glory to his country. His dedication to an academic pursuit impressed Mayang so much she took to calling him Señor Doctor, over his protests. If she dared, she would have baptized him a doctor twice over, for his bravery and his daring.

"The things I've seen," he would whisper, thrusting his fingers through his faded cornsilk hair. "The tribes—they'd make your refined skin crawl, señora. They starve a dog for days and days, then give it soft rice. The poor animal. It would eat and eat and eat, half-mad with pleasure, not knowing what was coming. Of course, as soon as it could eat no more, *wham!* The pagans cut its throat and roasted it while they danced around a huge bonfire. And guess what the prized part was, the delicacy, eh? The intestines, with the half-digested rice, fermented by stomach juices. Too strong for you, señora? Eh? But they love that and go on dancing, dancing, beating gongs, their gold necklaces, gold bracelets, gold anklets blazing. What a sight, señora! What a sight!"

For a moment, he was back in the mountains, the glare of gold in his eyes, his mouth open with lust. Mayang shared that vision of barbarity and wealth and thought herself wise to have earned the trust of a man who was obviously on his way to success. She shifted in her chair, glanced at Luis Carlos, who was intent on his biscuit. Deftly, she brought the conversation to the houses and how difficult it was to collect rent.

"But you don't have to sell," the American interrupted her. "You can mortgage them—not for full value, of course. Maybe half, or a

third, so you won't be saddled with debt. I know the manager of the
Far Eastern Bank and he'd be happy to arrange it for you. The
mortgage payments—well, they can collect the money from the tenants. Everything should be easy."

"But—"

"Let me do this for you, señora, since you've been so kind to me.
So I can repay my obligations to your household."

Put in those terms, the request could not be refused. Mayang
smiled, said neither yes nor no, announced it was time for them to
proceed, and had the nanny pick up Luis Carlos. But it was a lost
battle, both she and the American knew it. Two months later, she
signed the papers that mortgaged all four houses and the land they
stood on; Carlos Lucas signed as well, mesmerized by the wad of paper
money the American banker laid on the coffee table in the living room
of the Binondo house. The same evening, he was back in the tavern,
demanding whiskey and doling out the payroll to an imaginary army.

In the foolish belief that the pirate chest had magic of its own,
Mayang decided to hide the cash there, under the household bills. She
hummed happily as she set the bundles, each neatly held by a strip
of yellow paper, at the bottom of the chest; she could not help
imagining them breeding, turning into an inexhaustible supply of
wealth, one paper bill identical to the next, each bringing its own
brand of freedom. She would be a wealthy woman, was already a
wealthy woman, and would never have to fear the future. So, the
dream having become a certainty, she covered the money with bills
and left the room to check on the household. As she passed through
the living room, she glanced out of the windows and saw, as though
it had never been there before, all the litter and chaos of the front
yard, the pieces of the dismantled shed, the earth-encrusted bottles,
bits of iron, old packing cases, and other relics of the distillery's busy
years. They were suddenly offensive to her eyes; she shouted for the
servants and demanded that the yard be cleaned—now, at once. It
seemed then, for that day and months after, that the Binondo house
was to live again, what with the maids calling in their sweethearts to
haul away the garbage, uproot the cogon grass, and prepare the soil

for respectable plants. Not content with the bustle, Mayang exchanged her leather shoes for wooden clogs, grabbed a coconut-rib broom, and began sweeping, clearing debris away from the stone steps and setting such a pace that, now and then, a servant forgot herself and sang, letting loose a phrase or two of an old serenade song, about a woman who said she'd rather not, would rather not . . . until Mayang, scandalized, biting her underlip to keep from laughing, shushed the offending one. At twilight, the youngest maid appeared with a pail and half a coconut husk and proceeded to scrub the great stone steps, scattering soapsuds and water while the others, caught by the spray of her cleaning, screamed and laughed in protest.

Mayang would love the garden—the most beautiful this side of the *estero,* all red roses and white St. Joseph's Canes, and gardenias and orchid sprays hanging from the branches of the tamarind tree which had managed to survive the chaos of the distillery. By the time the garden reached its full magnificence, it would be nearly five years, Carlos Lucas had been felled by a stroke, all the mortgage payments were in arrears, and Luis Carlos, sitting on the stone bench under the tamarind, wore the Capuchin school's uniform of white shirt and blue pants and blue necktie as he breathed gently into a recorder flute, the first of many wind instruments he would learn to play, and coaxed fishing tunes from its slenderness. Mayang, hearing the fragile music, would lean her elbows on the upstairs windowsill and look at her son, so small, so innocent. It would seem then that she had planted and cared for the garden for just this moment, when the sunlight grew to such robust gold and the canal boats passed in their stillness in the distance and the music wove itself as a silver brightness in the air. She would allow herself to think of her one great love, of the man of the brittle dance, who she knew lived in one of the thousand islands of the South, breeding grapes in the hope of wine, and answering to another name. The last piece of information had cost her the proceeds of the warehouse's sale but it was worth it—this being able to whisper his new name at this instant, her lips and tongue shaping the syllables: *Chris. Chris Hansen.* The boy piped on.

7

The leaf-slim boats disappeared. Though the Binondo residents ran-
sacked their memories, no one could say exactly when—last Tuesday
perhaps or Friday of the previous week—they stopped coming. Suddenly, they were no longer there, probably hadn't been for some time
but because they were so much a part of the landscape, no one had
remarked on their absence. Carlos Lucas, on his way to the tavern at
six on a Sunday afternoon, was the first to be struck by the canal's
stillness—no eddies, no waves, only the momentary mud spurts of
burrowing crabs and catfish at the bottom of the water aflame with
the remnant orange light of the sun. His eyes pushed north to where
the canal vanished in a bend and then south to where it stretched
toward the sea. Nothing, nothing there. He couldn't remember when
he had last seen a skiff; yesterday, the day before, and all the days of
his immediate past, the canal appeared to have been thus—still and
empty, the leaf-slim boats gone.

When he mentioned it at the tavern, as he was sitting down, his left hand cupping the top of his hat, it became a fact. Where could they have gone, what had happened, was the last boat sighted on a Monday or a Thursday, did they all sail to the heavens? The tavern habitués whispered about the omen, between gulps of rum and beer, and while chewing on slivers of dried beef, trying to recall when the last boat sailed by. One man recalled purchasing a blouse from the wandering vendors but when—Monday or Saturday—escaped him completely. Another had been at the *estero* on a Sunday to watch the children swim between and among the boats—but which Sunday, heaven help him, he couldn't say. There were enough canal recollections to weigh everyone with a massive headache, which fortunately could be cured by downing a glass of beer in honor of each lost dear and familiar boat. Carlos Lucas wept over a blue-painted skiff with the name *Estela* on its bow; he had haggled with its master—a stocky, bare-chested, white-haired man—over a basket of unhusked oysters and a dozen blue crabs. A month ago, perhaps, or six weeks, he couldn't tell. Suddenly, the canal was still.

Because this was true sadness indeed, it had to be acknowledged with music. A girl started it, singing about the vanished boats, one of which—a blue-and-gold-painted skiff—set sail for a land of starlight, carrying the woman who tucked her skirts between her knees and said—here, the entire company joined in the refrain—no, no, she'd rather not, thank you but no . . . Carlos Lucas smashed a hand on the table, sending glasses jumping, and rudely ended the song. Because the worm of foreboding was writhing in his heart, he seized the battered hat off his knee, jammed it on his head, and having tossed a fistful of paper money on the table, rose to leave. He stopped for a second at the tavern door and turned choleric eyes on his friends. That was how they would remember him until they, too, lost their faculty for remembrance: as a stooped, graying old man, shoulders pulled down by his paunch, his hat low on his brow, his bloodshot eyes gripping the room in accusation. "Son-of-a-goat," he said, "how can things happen without our knowing? Ignorant louts that we are." In the silence, he peeled himself away from the light and the music and entered the dark.

By the time he reached the *estero,* the last cloud had passed on to the sea and a double moon—one above, the other its reflection— transformed the canal water into silver milk. Momentary thoughts of mermaids and nymphs, of the Pasig River muse who cast her silk net each midnight to harvest star droppings came to Carlos Lucas and he felt himself held by an unbearable longing. But the next instant, he had to blink his eyes, for it seemed to him that the water in the canal was less than before, that its surface was a good foot beneath its usual level and that the scuttling of crabs and catfish at its bottom was panicked. As he watched, the water level fell again. A giggle rose, distinct and obscene, from the gray and silver houses on the opposite bank. *I'm losing my mind,* he muttered and, enraged, aimed a kick at the canal's edge. His foot slipped; for a second, he rocked back and forth with one leg in the air and was almost on this side of safety. Alas, he was too old, too stiff, and had drunk too much this night of all nights. There was time only to let go of a fearful yell before he toppled over in slow motion, his eyes transfixed by the sheen of water rising to meet his face.

In his child's bed, Luis Carlos awoke to a terrific clamor of bells. Church bells, trolley bells, ice cream bells; bells big and small. They rang out—on and on as he lay frozen, his eyes on the open window which seemed curtained by the October moon's brilliance. In the strong light, the acacia tree's leaves, snagged by the moon, looked like slim boats, miniaturized by distance, sailing the skies. He lay stiff and frightened, listening, wondering what had provoked the bells. He whispered his mother's name; a wave of relief washed over his body. His fingers touched the flute which was always in his bed at night. He grasped it and, compelled by a terrible foreboding, lifted it to his mouth and was soon sitting up, searching through the instrument's thin wail for the roots of his sudden sadness.

Mayang, who slept in the next bed, reached him first. She called his name once, twice, not daring to touch him as he improvised a song of nostalgia, down to the last note, before lifting his eyes to her face.

"Now, we must look for Papa," he said calmly and put the flute down.

Such was the understanding between them that Mayang did not hesitate. She called the servants, set them to gathering torches, candles, and storm lamps, and saw them off to trace Carlos Lucas's route to and from the tavern while she and the children, bundled in flannel blankets, waited in the living room. At dawn, the servants returned, carrying Carlos Lucas, soaked to the skin, his flesh blue and cold, in a blanket sling. He had drifted nearly five hundred yards downriver, helpless and drowning, until his hand had scraped against a crack in the canal wall. An impossible salvation—but Carlos Lucas, with the strength of desperation, wedged his right hand into the opening, dug his fingertips into whatever hold he could find, and held himself there, alternately vomiting and swallowing water until help could arrive.

In the foyer, as Mayang bent to check his breathing, Carlos Lucas opened one eye, spat a bubble of saliva, and rasped: "Fire them all; they came too late." Then, he turned his head aside and convulsed. He never spoke again, though he tried as he lay on his bed like an upended crab for many, many months, working his lips in an effort to warn them of the disappearing water. But this was weeks later, for he was immobilized first by double pneumonia and a series of small strokes, with his right hand in a cast, his huge body transformed into a crumple of mounds and valleys under a bedsheet, his breathing a constant rasp that distressed the house until it became familiar noise, receding into the background along with the children's voices singing *Ferdinand Magellan, the crazy old coot, took five ships and circumcised the globe . . .*

"No, darling," Mayang would say to Luis Carlos, "circumnavigated—"

"It doesn't fit, Mama," was Luis Carlos's reply. He tried it on his flute but the tone stumbled.

"It is the right word."

"But what is circumcised?" Clara asked in her innocence.

"Well—well, you'll know when you're old enough. And so will Luis."

"When will I be old enough?"

"When you're twelve."

"But, Mama," Clarissa said, "it really doesn't fit."

So the children went on singing their error, as children would, the same way that at street corners assorted brats swung jumping ropes to the rhythm of a historical error. *Ferdinand Magellan* . . . Clara, Clarissa, and Luis Carlos sang it sotto voce as they played in Carlos Lucas's room, crawling under and all over the bed, transforming his inert body under a white cotton sheet into terrain for their games. On his broad stomach, aquiver with breath, Luis Carlos set his toy blue soldiers, his tiny artillery pieces, while Clara, propping up Carlos Lucas's right leg, balanced her toy white soldiers and cannons on the gentle slope of his thigh. Clarissa claimed his shoulders and launched her attack down his breastbone. *Fuego, fire, putok!!!* After a good war, the children would pat his cheeks and murmur, *good Papa, good Papa,* and retrieve their demolished armies. Carlos Lucas worked his lips, in the anxiety of his news about the canal, the disappearing water, and the leaf-boats that had sailed to the sky with the woman who said no . . .

The few times Mayang noticed the children's sacrilegious game on their father's paralyzed body, she brushed it away with the thought that it was good for him to be surrounded by such joy. The truth was she could barely spare him her attention. Times were difficult; for some inexplicable reason, factories were closing all over the city and the sale of rope and sugar, on which the country depended, had come to a standstill. It was as though no ships were sailing the world, none at least that required Manila rope, made of the finest, strongest hemp ever, famous for defying the sea's teeth. As a consequence, the seven thousand one hundred islands were blighted by a hot wind of poverty.

Fields lay fallow beneath the drought; peasants bundled their pots and pans, rolled up their mats, and, loading their buffalo-drawn carts, made for the city to escape the drought. Overnight, slums mushroomed, became bloated; the city's sewers leaked from the impossible burden of carrying the refugee's discards. Through her maids, the winds of foreboding reached Mayang. Water was contaminated and in the maze of the neighborhood of the poor, disease passed from one house to the other, touching men, women, and children with fever, issuing from their bodies in bloody, watery stools, snatching the hair off their heads, and wracking their limbs with convulsions until death itself was a relief. "As though I didn't have enough to worry about," Mayang muttered to herself, thinking of the money in the pirate chest, money that dwindled, even as she ordered the drinking water boiled, the food steamed twice, and the children guarded. She found these precautions inadequate, and had clothes and bedsheets boiled as well, the floors scrubbed daily with hot water and soap, until the whole house was fogged over by a warm mist of cleanliness and the neighbors gossiped about her venturing into the laundry business, the poor señora. All the commotion failed to allay her foreboding; she walked through the house, the haze and noise of the cleaning, with her left lip corner drooping with discontent, for the thought of the rapidly dwindling money gnawed at her. Not even the garden, with its magnificent white roses, could give her peace.

One afternoon, as she stood under the lone tree in the front yard, a tree that carried the weight of half a dozen hanging pots of orchids, all in their full bloom of white, purple, and speckled yellow sprays, there was a soft knock on the gate, a hesitant scratching almost. She raised her eyes to a brilliant smile, a child's painting of a sickle moon on a face. A man dressed in a dazzling white suit, impeccably pressed, stood there, his eyes nearly lost in the crinkle of the soothing, reassuring smile he was aiming at Mayang. At her look, he stepped back from the gate and folded his hands, one on top of the other, on his belly. Automatically, surprised and delighted, Mayang identified him: "A Chinaman!"

How the Chinese learned of her predicament, she would never find out. Nor did she even think of her mother's blood legacy until she was herself old and dying, and the murmured legends of her time were pressing in on her brain for a last lick of memory, among them the iron truth, questioned by none, whether native or Westerner, that the Chinese cared after their own. It was only then, as she was dying, that Mayang realized that her mother had made provisions for her beyond the grave, that she had made sure that Manila's Chinese knew of her daughter and her marriage to Carlos Lucas. On this afternoon, though, Mayang was simply enthralled by a visit from an alien and, moving quickly to the gate, she drew the latch herself and let him in. With quick, tiny bows, with many salutations and inquiries after her health and the household's well-being, the Chinese explained his presence. The father of his father had died three days ago, may the world sing his praise, and he, as son of the son, was beholden to mourn his passing as magnificently as possible. His grandfather, he said, loved roses and to honor that lifelong dedication to living beauty, he would like to rent pots of white—the mourning color—roses, in full bloom please, for the wake and the internment. At a reasonable price, of course, he added, half down now and half to be paid at the end of the funeral when the plants were returned.

Mayang dashed into the house after the transaction, clutching the money the Chinese had given her. He had brought a jeep along and carted away six giant and six small pots of roses, to be returned in a week's time. To Mayang, it was incredible luck and the beginning of an enterprise that kept the household afloat through the depression years. For the white roses proved irresistible to the Chinese community and they came, one after the other, to lease the flowers. Pots of them stood guard about the biers of patriarchs and matriarchs; more were scattered about the mausoleums which the Chinese preferred to the simple aboveground crypts the natives used for their dead. Once in a while, Clara would find it disquieting that her roses—which were always returned in full health, along with full payment—were witnesses to rituals she herself couldn't watch. But there was no helping it, these were hard times and the money in the pirate chest was ebbing quicker than the canal water.

It ebbed. The canal dried up slowly, having been dammed upstream, even as bulldozers and trucks waited with landfill to erase its existence. The lanky American anthropologist, passing by one sweltering afternoon with his surveyor's tools, explained and made her understand what a waste it was for water to be occupying prime real estate. His manners were so impeccable, his efforts at Tagalog so comical, that Mayang forgot her resentment at the loss of her own lands.

"But how will rainwater get to the sea?" she asked in her ignorance.

"It will find its way," the American replied. Then, almost as an apology, he added: "It is a new age, señora."

After giving him the glass of iced water he asked for, she walked with him to the canal, listening to his exposition on the coming great times. But the sight of the panicked crabs and catfish moved her to tears, though the Binondo men were rolling up their trousers, preparing to lay siege on the silvery mass slithering on the canal's muddy bottom. The American suggested she return home, as this was no happy vision. That evening, over the front gate's top, a stranger delivered a brace of crabs and a dozen catfish to her youngest maid. "Compliments of the *Señor Americano*," he said.

A week later, Mayang awoke with the certainty that she was dreaming, that the ceiling's rafters on which her eyes rested were merely a play of shadow and light, insubstantial as smoke; that her life had all been an illusion; that none of the things that had happened had really happened and time was at a standstill. She felt the sun in the blast of heat roasting the house and the unnatural silence. Rising, she threw a robe over her shoulders, cast a glance at Luis Carlos, who slept like a soldier, straight on his back, his chin at a precise angle, and assured herself he was safe, singular issue of her singular love that he was. She had a sudden yearning for cocoa, as though that frangible morning of her destiny many years ago was back. She crept out of the room, past the closed door behind which Clara and Clarissa whispered, past the door of Carlos Lucas's breathing. She glanced out of the living room windows, searching for the blue canal and the leaf-slim boats. Thick dismal mud lay there, between the cement walls, hurting the eyes. Downstairs, in the front yard, her youngest maid moved like a black shadow among the plants she was hosing, the hiss of streaming water accompanying her slight voice as she sang her grief for the men who were gone, along with the water and the boats, to yet another landscape of death.

Mystified, Mayang sought out the kitchen maid and found her also in black.

"What's this? What's happened?" she asked.

"Another war, señora. The peasants have taken up arms."

She crossed herself. The maid offered her a steaming cup of cocoa and as she accepted it, slipping her forefinger into the cup's ear, her left hand balancing the saucer, as she raised the cup and pursed her lips to blow on the hot liquid, the words reached her like an echo and she said them aloud, not knowing where they had come from:

"Pray, then—everyone. And see that you all get pregnant. We'll lose many, many good men."

The peasants' uprising wound and rewound itself through four provinces of Luzon, spewing from its miasma of blood and death, noise and smoke, a thousand and one legends—of warriors who found the lost *anting-anting* of ancient priestesses, amulets which rendered them invulnerable to bullet and steel; of fanatical disciples of a crypto-priest who descended upon towns as swiftly as smoke, overran American garrisons, and vanished just as quickly; of women generals more ferocious than their male counterparts. Tales brought to the city by refugees who fled both poverty and artillery, cramming themselves, their wives, and their children into sweltering slums and finding, in the Ever Loyal and Ever Noble City of Manila, no relief at all, no relief. The factories remained closed, workers were marching beneath union flags, and discontent was general.

Because the slums were now nudging the southern perimeter of Binondo, strangers could be seen in the afternoons, standing by the canal's lip, watching the mud bake, and flicking sidelong looks over their shoulders at the nearby houses. Mayang had the gates double-barred, the front door locked. She kept the keys in a massive keyring tied to her waist and herself opened the gates in the morning, when two of her servants would leave for Quiapo, bearing bundles of cut roses for the retail vendors who lined the sidewalk near the church. This was now part of the house's ritual, for aside from leasing white roses to the Chinese Mayang had expanded her business to delivering flowers wholesale.

She had, in her garden, two hundred pots of roses, twenty-five of which were white (she reserved those for the Chinese), fifty orchid sprays, twelve varieties of ferns, and assorted plants of the more banal species, in addition to the tree in the front yard and the tree in the back. Because they bloomed in turns, seemingly determined not to fail her, she could harvest the flowers in rotation, rising at dawn and wielding her heavy shears even before breakfast, cutting and pruning ever so carefully, checking leaves and stems, while two maids wrapped the long-stemmed blossoms, some the color of blood clot and just as fragile, with fresh banana leaves and craft paper, tying them into manageable bundles with green ribbons. Mayang let the maids haggle with the vendors over the price of the flowers, by the dozens or by the bundle, her instructions limited to a minimum amount for the lot. She never knew whether the maids remained honest or cheated her, outrageously or in small ways, for the truth was the business pained her, this decapitation of plants, this stripping of the garden she had built so meticulously for the return of her faraway love. It sufficed that there was enough to cover the expenses for food and the maids' pay.

The maids returned at mid-morning, bearing provisions they had purchased at the market. At their knocking, Mayang opened the front door and the gate, let them in, and relocked the gate once more, noting how the number of strangers by the canal increased each day. Dusky men in straw hats and slippers, in ill-matched shirts and pants, their hands in their pockets, staring dully at the empty canal on which work had stopped. Mayang would mutter a short prayer, a plea for the house's safety, before she withdrew and locked the front door.

In the kitchen, as the cook degutted fish and poultry, crushed ginger and garlic, the two maids emptied their pockets, laying wads of bills and change on the table, along with abused pieces of paper on which they'd done their tallies. They maintained an incessant chatter, mixing their accounts of the flower sale with stories picked up from vendors and at the market, stories about the uprising, about the slums, about the city, about movie stars, until Mayang was caught in the paradox of feeling herself an eyewitness to events even as life passed her by.

Through the maids, the slums reached her—a vast maze of desolation, with its sun-bleached wooden walls, its roofs of rusting corrugated iron, its rooms built upon rooms, boxes on boxes, an impossible tower of existence where a packed humanity eked out the impossible lives of rats, feeding one another with dreams and hallucination. She heard about a couple who, driven mad by the transfer from the calmness of open fields to the city's frenzy, convinced themselves of their own children's metamorphosis into monsters. They committed the unspeakable crime of killing their own brood—two girls and a boy, all below the age of ten—by cutting their throats, draining the blood from their bodies, and stuffing their orifices with crushed garlic to prevent their rise from death. Mayang shuddered but the younger maid assured her that everything was in order; the parents had been seized and a trial was to be held, all in accordance with the law, at which the murderers were to be prosecuted by a brilliant new lawyer by the name of Adrian Banyaga.

"Who?" Mayang asked, wrinkling her forehead.

"Ay, señora, you're so behind the news. He was the one who married Miss Estela."

"Miss Estela who?"

The maids broke into giggles and gave up. Mayang unrolled the paper bills, separated fives and tens from ones, and ironed each with the palm of her hand before counting them. It was a tidy sum. She sighed.

"When will it be over?" she asked aloud.

The maids said soon, soon, but not before masses of people reached the city; the migration was going on, an eternal procession, it seemed, of buffalo-drawn carts on the highway. Appalled by this influx, the city residents could only transform the event into a celebration. Thus every twilight the Manilans packed dinner hampers and hied off to the city boundaries to watch the refugees enter.

"It is a beautiful sight, señora," the maid said, confessing to an indiscretion.

How it came about, Mayang didn't know, but plans were suddenly afoot for the whole family to witness the parade of refugees. She hemmed and hawed, putting it off week after week, making excuses as the maids pressed her gently, teasingly. One Friday, she could protest no more. The food was prepared and wrapped, the route back

and forth by trolley and bus worked out, the children's clothes prepared, and the task of guarding the house assigned. Clara, Clarissa,
and Luis Carlos, returning from school in the afternoon, found themselves hustled out of their uniforms into everyday clothes and led out
of the front door, through the garden, and out the gate by triumphant
maids while Mayang, wearing a shin-length shirtdress and false pearls,
brought up the rear with three other servants who carried the food
hampers.

Though the journey took longer than Mayang had expected, there
was only the minor mishap of Clara throwing up on the bus. Luis
Carlos tried to soothe her by playing her favorite melodies on the flute
but the stink and sour taste of her own vomit had made Clara irritable.
She spent the rest of the ride with her head on her nanny's lap,
whimpering into her skirt folds, while Mayang massaged her nape.

Just outside the city, they passed a camp of six carts on the roadside.
Luis Carlos stopped playing to stare at the men who were weaving
rattan strips into chairs and tables. Mayang pointed to the makeshift
stove to one side of the circle and reminded the maids of their luck.
There was an inordinate number of toddlers, half-naked and barefoot,
which caused Clarissa to sniff with disdain. "They will get worms,"
she declared. But they were leaving the scene already and an astonish-
ing spread of land was rushing toward them.

A few minutes more and they reached the picnic site, recognizing
it instantly from the cars parked by the road. They disembarked,
walked self-consciously up the land's rise, debated about the proper
spot, and finally chose one that gave them a clear view of the road.
Already, the first carts were visible, rolling in slowly with a side-to-side
motion. The maids spread mats and unpacked the hampers, while the
children, freed from restraints, burst into motion. Luis Carlos forgot
his flute in his fascination with space and began to run to and fro,
chased by his two sisters, their laughter sweet as birdcalls. For the first
time in many months, Mayang smiled, her lip corners lifting. A maid,
ladling food onto plates, caught her breath at this glimpse of the
mistress's past beauty.

By the time they finished eating the sun had gone down, and in the purple twilight they saw, down the road, a trail of tiny lights, swaying, as though germinal stars had fallen to the earth. Luis Carlos found a melody in his head, one that mimicked the slight quiver of those lights, and he raised his flute. The music rose in the stillness. Mayang watched her son fondly, with pride, in her own head a gentle remonstrance to Hans for his neglect. Flute notes ran down the hill and joined the rhythmic whoosh of the water buffalos' breathing, their abrupt snorts, and the swish of their tails as they lumbered down the road, their swaying gait making the carts and the hurricane lamps hanging from their woven roofs dance. One after the other, in the soft dark, they came as though to sneak into the city.

Clara gave a sigh and crawled to where her mother sat. She slid downward and laid her head on Mayang's knees.

"Don't you like the carts?" Mayang asked.

"No," she said, "I'm cold."

And rising to her knees, she threw up again. Mayang shrieked. She had the terrible certainty she was about to pay for the past hours' tranquility. Catching Clara in an embrace, she felt the fever in the child's body. Too late. It had spread through her limbs, was now sucking at her bones and twisting her intestines into impossible knots.

Three weeks later, Clara died, leaving behind such an unbearable memory of pain that Mayang, until the next war, wore only black.

8

It was Luis Carlos who explained everything to his father—the funeral, the canal, the buffalo carts, the stars on the road—when no one else dared, fearing the shock would lead to a double burial. On his own volition, one Sunday while the house was yet prostrate with mourning for Clara, he slipped into the master bedroom, his flute under his arm, and perched on the bed's edge, close to Carlos Lucas's chest.

"I'm sorry, Papa," he said, "the bells gave no warning."

Carlos Lucas's eyes blinked, ran over with tears.

"Sssh, Papa, there's nothing we can do," Luis Carlos said, wiping the old man's flabby cheeks with a corner of the bedsheet.

And with his flute, playing with all the skill of his virtuosity, he wove for Carlos Lucas all the scenes of what had happened. The frantic sewing of funeral costumes, the household in black; Mayang terrible in silent grief, not daring even to weep lest the commotion disturb Carlos Lucas; the gray thing that had been Clara, wearing a white tulle gown, a perfect white rose in its clasped hands. The music brought Carlos Lucas the clear morning of the burial, when the small coffin was carried down the stone steps, through the garden, and out the gate to a black hearse while Mayang, swallowing the sounds of her weeping, fell down, first at the front doorway, then under the front-yard tree, then again outside the gate as they were loading the coffin. The hearse didn't head for the cemetery. Instead, twisting through streets, it drove toward the San Lazaro Hospital, propelled it seemed by the hawk screams Mayang released at last this distance from Carlos Lucas's bed, until it found the crematorium behind the main building and here stopped for the culmination of an agonized quarrel between Mayang and the new American health authorities. Despite the intervention of the Capuchins, the Americans had decided that burning was cleaner, safer for victims of the epidemic.

For a long time afterward, Mayang's knees would buckle and she would slump to the floor, until her knees and shins were mottled with bruises, whenever Clara rose in her memory. The child was always alive to her, walking in her white gown and lace gloves, her lip corners drooping in her usual dour expression, while flames licked at her bare feet, her elbows, her hair. Mayang thought she was seeing her daughter in hell.

The household heroically resumed its daily routine, moving around Mayang's intermittent falls. The maids cooked, cleaned, clothed the children, gossiped with neighbors, fed Carlos Lucas his pureed meals, and bore Mayang's distress stoically. It was while watering the garden that the youngest maid discovered the cure for Mayang's loss of balance. Running the hose out in the garden, as the morning still hung moist in the sky, wrestling with the sprinkler head that writhed like a snake and dousing herself in the process from head to toe, the maid was petrified by the sight of heaped petals on the ground. All the flowers had been stripped; only the stamen and pistil remained attached to the plants, ugly and naked. At the foot of each pot lay a scattering of red, yellow, white, and pink petals. Mystified, afraid she would be blamed for this new disaster, the maid wondered whether she had made an error while mixing insecticides or a strong wind had blown in from the South China Sea. But no, everything had been ordinary the night before. Shrugging, she marched into the house and announced a miracle.

The flowers never returned. Mayang could ease her chagrin at the blasted buds that took their place—buds edged in brown, stunted, failing to reach full bloom—by saying that surely this was hint indeed of Clara's welcome in heaven. She had to turn away her Chinese customers who, receiving no explanation, concluded that the household had no need for extra income anymore.

On the contrary, Clarissa and Luis Carlos still attended exclusive Catholic schools, where fees increased regularly. They outgrew their clothes as rapidly as they were bought and in the case of Clarissa, the cost was tripling because she was gently but irrevocably becoming a young woman. Mayang dug deep into the pirate chest, often panicking at the meagerness of her resources, and finally, in despair at the price of a silk dress for Clarissa who was caught now in the school's social whirl, she walked into the master bedroom, opened the wardrobe, and took out the emerald necklace.

Carlos Lucas's eyes were open and he saw how, with a kitchen knife, she pried off a stone, leaving the setting blind. In the vast silences of his body, he realized suddenly that this was not the first time she had opened the wardrobe. His eyes brimmed over; he wept, begging forgiveness of the Chinese-Malay maid, and finding her in the labyrinths of his memory, also found his mother in the cemetery and realized he had failed to reserve the plot next to her tomb.

The thought galvanized him enough to struggle with his body, willing his mouth to form words. Words. Clarissa, entering the room with his midday soup, was so startled by a volley of snorts and gasps that she dropped the tray and rushed out, shouting her papa was dying. Mayang and the maids came running, and clustered about the bed.

"He wants something," Mayang declared.

"He's dying," Clarissa countered, "and you still in black! Call the doctor."

"No, he wants to say something."

The truth was Mayang had conceived such an antipathy for doctors since Clara's death she had vowed never to let one attend her family. They were all ignorant, she thought, and worse, they wouldn't admit it.

"Well, what are you going to do?" Clarissa shouted finally.

"We'll wait for Luis Carlos."

"For Louie?"

"For Luis."

"He'll be stiff by then. On your head be it!"

Luis Carlos arrived at twilight, skipping innocently through the gate a maid held open and up the stairs toward the front door. He had good news, gathered from his friends. The war was over; a dozen peasant leaders were in jail while the rest had returned to the fields which held promise now, what with storm clouds forming over the Pacific. He was midway up when a cry slammed onto his chest and he froze. The cook grabbed him and pushed him toward the master bedroom.

"What now?" he demanded as he caught sight of the six women ringing Carlos Lucas's bed.

"He wants to say something," Mayang replied.

"He's dying, imbeciles," Clarissa snapped.

Luis Carlos calmly bent over his father and noted the blinking of his eyes.

"Hush," he said to the old man who calmed down immediately. Then, turning to the women, he shooed them away. "Go, go. He needs air."

Obedient to the male voice, they made for the door, even Mayang who threw a backward glance at her son, a stripling yet whose slim ankles thrust out of the pants he had outgrown. His authority was already undeniable. She sent an unvoiced remonstrance to Hans for his indifference. Luis Carlos, she thought, was such a beautiful child, true son of a true love.

The women's obedience, more than anything else, made Luis Carlos aware of changes in himself. He no longer asked what circumcision was, having undergone it the year before, choosing his own herbalist and river, and the forked guava branch over which his foreskin had been drawn, and going through the procedure without Mayang's knowledge. He had managed even to reach the house without howling in pain though with an indescribable grimace to Mayang's fright and Clarissa's disdain that he would be so stupid as to risk infection. But as he smoothed the bedsheet over Carlos Lucas's stomach and hips, he felt the household roost on his shoulders and knew he would never be a child again. He gave his father a wry smile.

"Sorry, Pops," he said in the new manner of speaking he had picked up from his friends, "women are so hysterical. I have a new tune for you."

And he played a popular song, one that resounded now from the houses along the canal, from women washing clothes at public faucets, though the bands and professional singers hadn't caught on to it yet. A song about a boat in the sky bearing a woman who said no, she'd rather not, thanks but no . . . Silent laughter ran through his body as the risqué words thrummed in his head. That he should be playing this for his father!

The tail of another melody thrust into the song and Luis Carlos couldn't help but follow it, in its loops about itself, its twirls, its rise upward, as though it were smoke in the wind, curving toward a place where Carlos Lucas, healed and in white ducks, waited, sitting on a strange tomb in a strange cemetery, a fishing pole at his feet. The old man nodded knowingly and threw a glance over his shoulder at the name on the tomb. That was how Luis Carlos learned of the Don's wish for a burial plot in Bulacan.

"Well, buy it yourself," Mayang snapped, not believing but insulted nevertheless by her husband's desire to creep back to his mother.

She marched into the bedroom, opened the wardrobe, and without ceremony pried out another emerald, leaving the necklace twice blind. She dumped the gem into Luis Carlos's palm, challenging him. The youth raised his eyebrows, curled his fingers about the green stone, and withdrew.

The task did not faze him. By incessant questioning, he learned from friends, first, what the reasonable price for the emerald was; second, the name of a reliable pawnbroker; and third, how to get to Bulacan. It took several weeks to work out but one Saturday morning, when only the youngest maid was up and about, he crept from his room fully dressed and told her he was off. None too soon as it turned out for Mayang, pitying her son, was about to ask for the emerald to see to the plot herself. But when she rose for breakfast, his bed was empty.

In his absence, she felt his presence the more strongly. As she went about her chores, laying out Clarissa's clothes, washing Carlos Lucas, her thoughts remained on him. He had been, he was, a happy child—not raucous, never noisy except with his flute, but happy nevertheless, as though he had discovered the secret of perpetual tranquility. He was the most reasonable of the children, despite having been spoiled shamelessly by herself and the maids, who, one and all, were in love with his fragile good looks, his fair skin, gray eyes, and reddish-brown hair. He was still filling out, his bones stretching for their true height though he was already taller than most of his classmates. Still, the tentativeness of youth conferred an air of gentleness and consideration upon his movements. Once, at dinner, Clarissa had teased him about a friend of hers who had fallen under the spell of his lambent eyes. Luis Carlos had broken his silence to say only that there was but room in life for one passion. At which Clarissa had turned merciless, demanding to know who this was. But Mayang, sitting in Carlos Lucas's chair, had understood—for the flute was on the table, beside Luis Carlos's plate. It would take an impossible woman to come between him and music.

As the day wore on, Mayang's pride melted into fear and then into certainty that Luis Carlos had met with an accident. She questioned the youngest maid over and over again, lost her patience when she was given the same answers, and screamed at the girl.

"Why didn't you ask when he was coming back?"

"He's not my son, señora!"

"Impertinent slut."

The girl flinched. "If I am, then I am," she muttered, and without further ado marched to the back room and bundled her things.

"Well, where are you going now?" Mayang asked when she reappeared in the living room with her reed suitcase.

"Off to be a slut," the girl said. "There are bars for Americans all over the city. I'll get more money and less aggravation."

Clarissa broke into a wail. "My God, everyone will know we had a whore working here. Mama!"

"Don't say such words," Mayang snapped. "Well, go—"

The girl's eyes swung between the front door and the kitchen. She inhaled, raised her chin, and took a step.

"You can send my wages to my parents," she said in parting.

Clarissa shouted no but with a look Mayang held her to the rocking chair until the girl had reached the front door. The sound of bolts being drawn reached them. Mayang called the cook and gave her the house keys.

"Open the gate," she said, pitiless in her guilt, "let her go. Then lock it. I won't have her back."

They watched from the living room window as the girl, thirteen years old, issued from the gate with the suitcase under her arm. She stopped for a second, her head turning this way and that; then, she moved westward, away from the canal, toward the downtown area.

"It's not going to be an easy life," Mayang murmured, though she asked quietly whether what the girl had said was true. If so, how had she known it?

The evening meal was dismal. The maids were subdued, Luis Carlos's chair was vacant, and Mayang was well launched into a general condemnation of the times. In her youth, she declared, no one even dreamed of talking back to one's elders and certainly not to one's superiors. All this corruption came from watching the movies, the *zarzuelas,* and listening to the radio while not heeding the Church's teachings enough.

"That stupid Louie!" Clarissa muttered.

"Who?"

"Louie, your son."

"His name's Luis Carlos and he's your brother."

"Luis Carlos, Luis Carlos, Luis Carlos, my ass. Even the priests call him Louie."

"Clarissa!"

But the girl, gripped by some passion, yanked the napkin off her lap and slammed it on the table.

"His classmates, his friends, everybody—he's Louie to them. Sissy Louie, Louie the limp wrist. And if you don't watch out, he'll be wearing high heels when he grows up! Perfect Louie, the wimp!"

She stood up so abruptly her chair overturned. For a terrible moment, Mayang and Clarissa looked at each other. Clarissa's face was dead white at her own effrontery. Mayang shuddered. How ugly her daughter was—with a bump for a nose and fat, quivering cheeks, a chin which eased back too soon, and narrow shoulders that sloped with perpetual dejection. How such an ugly daughter could have been born to her was certainly one of the world's great mysteries.

Clarissa turned away and walked toward her room. Mayang took a deep breath, ordered the maid to prepare a tray for the girl, and followed. She found Clarissa snatching clothes out of the bureau drawers, tossing them to the floor.

"But what are you doing?" Mayang asked.

"You don't have to send me away. I'll go. I'm sorry. I'll leave—like—like . . ."

She burst into tears. Mayang smelled danger and, wrapping her daughter's plump body in an embrace, pulled her to the bed. Rocking back and forth, caressing her tangled hair, Mayang poured reassuring words while her mind searched for the roots of this disturbance.

"She was a maid," she said, "you're my daughter. Don't be silly. I'll never send you away."

At last, when the girl had calmed enough to fall asleep, Mayang retrieved the scattered clothes and began returning them to the dresser. That was how she found the dozen signed photographs of a *zarzuela* matinee idol tucked under sheets of terrible love poetry, smudged with tears, in Clarissa's hand.

"Holy cow," she murmured, "she had to choose a handsome devil!"
The last photograph was of Clarissa and the young maid standing

under the marquee of the Teatro Ideal. The two had connived to escape her vigilance. No doubt Clarissa, with the maid in tow, had been inside the dozen or so theaters downtown. Mayang sighed as she returned Clarissa's secret to its hiding place.

At midnight, the cook who slept in the garage was awakened by a banging at the gate. With many whispered curses at the pain in her bones and complaints about the tactlessness of neighbors, she hobbled out. "What d'you want—we're asleep!" she rasped out.

The thin old man outside waved familiarly, whispered her name, and grinned. It was Luis Carlos, mission accomplished, though his hair and eyebrows had been whitened by road dust.

He wouldn't eat, wouldn't even sit, until he had entered Carlos Lucas's room and waved the rolled-up title to the burial plot before the Don's open eyes. With great tenderness, he placed it on the pillow, near his father's right ear.

"There you are, Papa. All signed and sealed. It's all yours. Ready for you."

A quiver of contentment washed over the Don's body; all his doubts about Luis Carlos were leached out of his bones by the affection in that voice. Carlos Lucas closed his eyes and surrendered himself to his memories, closing his senses one by one, departing the house even before he was dead. He joined Juan Itak once again, in the mornings of his childhood, when the very river smelled fresh and everything was new and in its proper place, the world still all broad lines and color and tiny sounds, and not yet insane with details. Slowly, through the weeks until his death six months later when he was curled so tight about his memories he was the size of a fourteen-year-old, he sank deeper and deeper into the universe of his past, vision and odors returning with such clarity he could believe he was still a child: the earth's wet scent in July, the pungence of tamarind, the tobacco odor of Maya's skirts, October's roasting corn, and through it all, antiphonal, that seducer, the perfume of hot cocoa.

As Luis Carlos ate his belated dinner, his eyes misting over with sleep, so fatigued was he from the journey, Mayang inspected him, Clarissa's words still in her ears.

"Go to sleep, Mama. It's late."

"I'll wait."

The examination puzzled Luis Carlos and he felt in his mind for what, if anything, he had left undone. He had gone to the parish priest, walked with him to the cemetery, pointed out the plot, determined the landmarks, and while the title was being prepared had even found a bunch of wildflowers for his grandmother's grave. He had paid and . . .

"Oh!" he said. "Oh. I forgot."

He dug into his pocket, took out a wad of bills, and pushed it across the table.

"You should have reminded me," he said. "It didn't cost that much." He found a few coins in his shirt pocket, his bus fare change, and gave them to Mayang.

She accepted the money without interest.

"Your friends call you Louie?"

Surprised, he was quiet for a second. "All the time. There's an American teacher at school. He called me that—uh, I don't remember when. And everyone sort of took it over."

"You like it?"

He shrugged. "It's shorter. I don't mind."

"How come your friends never visit you?"

By this time, he was completely mystified.

"We never—I don't know. I don't visit their homes either."

"Do you have female friends?"

He picked up his glass, took a gulp of water.

"Clarissa again? I'm just a kid, Mama. I'm too young."

Mayang lost control. "At your age, I was already married. You should have some interest in women."

He rose from the table. "So I'll be as stupid as Clarissa? She chases that actor all over the place! Hasn't been to school in weeks!"

"Santa Maria!"

"Sure," he went on as he edged away. "It's the talk of the town. Fat Clarissa's nuts over an actor's mustache." He laughed, threw her a measuring look, and said he had to go to the bathroom.

Mayang was speechless.

The next day, as she laved Carlos Lucas's feet with warm water and dried the skin between his toes, she prayed for him to rise from the bed. "Carlos, my heart, what am I to do? Clara's dead, Clarissa's panting after an actor, and Luis Carlos—oh, he's too young to fight a duel over his sister's honor. Which he'll certainly have to do if I don't do something. Or you don't do anything. Can't you go to the theater and inquire what this man's intentions are? Carlos, Carlos, honored spouse, husband, wake up. It's bad enough they sing about us all over the place—though how the devil they found out about that, I'll never know—"

But the Don heard Mayang's voice as the complaint of a hungry mosquito and, sighing, he lost himself deeper in the green fathoms of his past. Mayang rolled the Don to his side, checked the suppurating sores on his back, lanced a few bad ones, and covered them with a poultice of macerated guava leaves on a sheet of gauze. There was no helping it, she thought as she carried towel, basin, linen, and the Don's dirty clothes from the room, she would have to confront the man herself.

Dressed in her best black silk dress, a black lace shawl across her shoulders, her feet choking in black patent leather pumps, she took her cook's arm—the cook being the most senior of the maids—and made her sally to the *teatro*. She was bumped and elbowed so many times in the course of the journey that by the time they reached the Ideal, she had lost all her self-confidence and was clinging with desperation to her maid. A stream of rebuke accompanied their passage, for the cook, even more used to their monastic existence than Mayang was, steadily decried the loss of, first, the horse and caleche, then the car . . . "We shouldn't have sold them, señora," she said gloomily, as they inched down the sidewalk, dodging pedestrians. "The instant we lost them, the times changed."

At the Ideal, Mayang summoned enough courage to inquire at the ticket booth for the actor. She couldn't see behind the window, though, so that the reply reached her as a disembodied voice and confused her even more. "Autographs after the matinee," the voice said, "back stage. If he's feeling good." Two tickets were thrust out, followed by fingers which waved demandingly. Mayang, frightened silent, held out a peso bill which was snatched rudely. As she turned away, the tickets in her own hand, the voice called out: "*Hoy*, your change!" She took back the few coins and murmured at the miracles of science, that it could make a ticket booth speak and rubber hands move.

The theater's interior was even more awesome. She and the cook could only stare open-mouthed at the oversized chandeliers, the velvet carpet and curtains, the friezes on the wall which were a repeating pattern of the masks of tragedy and comedy.

"No wonder there's no money left; they used it up here," the cook muttered, shielding her eyes from her exaggerated sense of the chandeliers. A subtle noise, restless and excited, rose from the seats. They managed to find their seats and, still clutching at each other's arms, sat down.

"What do we do now?" Mayang asked.

"Beats me," the cook answered. She felt her brow. "I'm getting a fever."

A crash of cymbals, horn toots, spasms of music shook the theater. Mayang held on to her maid, certain that the ceiling would cave in. Instead, the lights dimmed, the curtains parted slowly, and in the space of a heartbeat she was in a different world. For three hours solid, she wandered among cardboard coconut trees and a waterfall, agonized over a love born, defeated, and finally triumphant amidst the cacophony of an offstage war as the breathless *kundiman*, the love aria, became a duel of passion between the slight, bare-shouldered heroine by the name of Esperanza and her handsome lover, Bayani. The wedding scene finale, held while the hero was as yet bleeding from wounds at the hands of the villain he'd dispatched in the great sword fight of Act III Scene IV, found Mayang's eyes streaming with tears, the cook hiccupping into a corner of her shawl, while all over the theater cheers erupted and cries of *bravo!* thundered. As the curtain fell, Mayang applauded, smacking her thin hands together until her palms hurt and, tremulous yet with the emotional bath of the operetta, she turned wet eyes to her cook.

"Wasn't that silly?" she asked.

The cook, rearranging her face back into its usual smirk, nodded and wiped her cheeks and chin. "Quite silly, señora. I didn't understand everything that was going on, so much noise— Who was the young man . . . ?"

Mayang shook her head. "Neither did I. We'll have to come back, get better seats, and really find out what all the furor's about. Clarissa might marry an actor and . . . "

"Oh, señora! Not that one, not the—"

She nodded. *"That* one! The scandal of it!"

There was no chance of it, the actor told them firmly. Mayang and the cook, confused and bedazzled by the light bulbs of the dressing room, taken aback by the fact that the actor was so much smaller, so normal away from the stage, though his glorious voice remained the same, cringed at such forthrightness. They had been ushered in immediately, for the actor had recognized the family name of the chairman/president of his dozen fan clubs and at once understood the danger he was in. Seated on a battered sofa, entranced by the globs of cold cream the actor was smearing on his face, Mayang could only haltingly express her trepidation, her fears of the ruin of a girl—one who came from an honorable family—by the ephemeral attractions of the theater . . .

"There's no chance of that," the actor interrupted her.

Mayang was taken aback. In her surprise, she dropped both her English and her indirection. "But you've been seen all over the place."

"Not all over, ma'am. Certainly not. I've taken her out once or twice, only in the afternoon and only to the ice cream parlor."

"The what? For what?"

"To eat ice cream," the befuddled actor said. "She's too young for alcohol. We have an ice cream cone apiece and I thank her for her work on my behalf. All those fans, those letters . . ."

"But you're betrothed," the cook cut in.

"I am—to my heroine."

There was dead silence. The women didn't dare look at each other.

At last, feeling sorry for Mayang, who was flushing as red as his sofa, the actor explained gently: "She's too young, ma'am. And also, also"—he gestured delicately—"she's not exactly, well, you know, attractive. At least, not yet. When she grows up, maybe, who knows—"

Only by a miracle, Mayang thought as she gathered herself for an exit. I'll kill that benighted— She couldn't complete the sentence.

But the actor went on: "Perhaps she'll lose fifty, thirty, maybe ten pounds. She's still chunky right now." Then hurriedly, for the cook's face had contorted beyond description: "But you, madame, ten years less and I'd fall on my knees before you and beg you to elope with me."

Later, on the bus, Mayang said dreamily: "Someone in that profession—well, you know . . ."

"Señora?"

"—he would know real beauty."

The cook snorted and pushed a curl off her forehead. She was sure he had been talking to her.

"At least, at least, we can rest easy about Clarissa. He was right. She's not very attractive. Charming but not—not—"

"Yes, señora."

"Nothing will happen to her."

And so she forgot all the dangers attendant to her daughter's sex; she lost her fears in the noise and light and music of the theater, its many plots and adventures, its impeccable heroes and heroines, and its bloodless wars—stories which she remembered aloud as she washed and fed Carlos Lucas, hardly seeing him, until of course the day the sponge bath, the linen and clothing change, and the operetta were finished, all at the same simultaneous moment, which was also when she noticed he was dead, had not breathed all throughout the procedure, and must have died sometime that strange, diaphanous morning, perhaps at the instant she appeared in the doorway, her salt-and-pepper hair still loose and tickling her ankles. She forgot Clarissa's perils in the complexities of the funeral, of her move back to the master bedroom, of the sale one by one of the emeralds until only two were left, such forgetting becoming an impossible guilt the day Clarissa did elope with a half-breed magician. But that was after war rumors were rife again and Luis Carlos had already fallen in love.

9

In 1846, when Adolphe Sax finished putting together the instrument, he had no presentiment at all of that moment when, in a monstrous country of seven thousand one hundred islands—a conception certainly beyond even his restless imagination—a seventeen-year-old youth would fall thoroughly and irrevocably under its fascination. From first sight of the thing, that ugly hybrid woodwind with its bell-maw sprouting from an obscene snake curve, Luis Carlos couldn't think of anything else. The noise in the bar receded, the faces of his friends who had dragged him from school to the American hangout disappeared. His flute struck him as inordinately delicate, a child's toy, feminine beside the intrusive ugliness of this gold instrument, with its infinity of stops, its very massiveness. And when the young black musician, holding center stage, blew into the thing, the hoarse note, powerful as an organ's, ran up Luis Carlos's spine, tickling his vertebrae. At once, he was convinced that no other sound, no other voice, could carry the song of his house as well as this one filled with pain, with complaint, with graveyard echoes and wails of the sea, with the coolness of rain and the crackle of sun rays falling on galvanized iron roofs. He heard Carlos Lucas's bellows, Mayang's morning harangues, the maids flittering through rooms and corridors, plants thrusting roots through packed soil, the gate creaking open, trucks roaring as they dumped landfill into the canal, the house beams' groans at the blows of the seasons—in short, all the sounds he'd lived with and by, in his seventeen years, including, oh but miracle of miracles, the bells—belfry bells, altar bells, school bells, ice cream bells, trolley bells—which rang out in mad cadence with the instrument's cavort. Absentmindedly, he lifted the glass before him, took a gulp of brandy, and nearly asphyxiated to death. But he couldn't spare the time and went on watching with streaming eyes, as the jazz band went through its paces, piling melody upon melody, until he was sure the top of his skull had unhinged. Near midnight, when his friends tired of the amusement, he was drunk to the gills and in love.

He lost appetite, dropped eight pounds, and looked even more of a stripling; he could not summon any enthusiasm for school where hitherto he had been considered somewhat of a scholar, a little too Germanic perhaps in his earnestness, but a scholar nevertheless who excelled in chemistry. He could not even be happy for the aging Superior whose pet he was and who was pleased as a puppy over the modest success of the Capuchins' new product, a "mild" gin called the Archangel since it brought comfort to the afflicted, peace to the distraught, and generally slayed the demons of sorrow—or so the ads said. Luis Carlos went about in a haze of melancholia, confusing his Pythagorean theorem with Aquinas, perking up only with the last school bell at which the gates were opened and he could dash out, catch the bus, run into the house to dump his books on his bed, change clothes, and dash out again to meet the neighborhood's young men, all sassy in plaids and bell-bottom pants, so together they could make their way toward Ermita's cluster of American bars. Escape was no problem, what with Mayang and the cook lost in the theater and Clarissa locked in her bedroom, composing bad poems for who knew what actor. The house paled away, retreated to an insignificant corner of his mind whenever he sat at one of the tables or the counter stools, waiting for the band or, more important, the saxophonist.

By this time, he had read everything on the saxophone he could lay his hands on and, theoretically at least, knew enough to play it. But astute musician that he was, he also knew that unless he could lay his hands on the instrument, unless he could own one to tinker with, there was no way to tell whether he was the man for the instrument. Unfortunately, though he always had odds and ends of money, given by Mayang or slipped into his pockets by the maids, he did not have enough. Since he was a responsible child, he could not bring himself to demand that Mayang buy him a saxophone, knowing as he did the precarious state of the household's finances. Thus, like the eternal lover yearning, he stood at the sidelines with his friends and watched his beloved.

It was a fortuitous evening when Jake—as Jacobo Montreal, his eighteen-year-old friend, was now called—came up with a new way to torture dear, delicate Louie. Whispering to a waiter, he convinced the older man that Luis Carlos was a famous musician, the lead in a band playing at a ritzy club outside Clark Air Force Base. He was in the city to pick up new tunes and would be pleased to play something for the bar customers. Thus, during the intermission, Luis Carlos heard the manager announce the presence of a world-renowned musician, whose flute was truer than Arthur's sword—or something to that effect. A terrible suspicion dawned on him when he caught sight of Jake's grin, a suspicion confirmed by the thunder of his name over the speakers: Louie "the Hun" Villaverde.

"The Hun? The Hun?" he muttered, aghast, as his friends pushed him to his feet and thrust his flute into his hands.

"Well, you had to have a name!" Jake replied, giggling and clapping his hands, drumming on the table along with the rest.

"Mama, help!" Luis Carlos said as someone led him to the stage. The band was out of the lounge room now and clustered about the stage. The bass guitarist came up, offered his hand. Luis Carlos, nearly dead from stagefright, shook it. "I'll tag along with you, son," the black man said. "What're you playing?"

In his confusion, he could only remember the song of boats in the sky. "S-s-s-skyboats," he stuttered, giving the tune the title by which it would be known forevermore.

"Well, start and I'll move in as soon as I get the rhythm. Okay?"

He nodded miserably, raised his flute, cocked his head for the tiny bell that always rang in his ear to give him the key, heard it, and felt a wave of calmness drench him. He lunged into the melody and unwittingly gave the first public performance of the song of his father and mother, seeing in the sky beyond the bar's roof, that sky that was blue now, the boats sailing on waves of laughter, following a blue-and-gold skiff that bore the woman who said no, thanks but no, she'd rather not . . . Dimly, he heard the bass guitar enter the song and, after a while, the drums and, later, the piano. Much, much later, the wail of the saxophone that gave full body to the fragile, chortling tune. His debut lasted twenty minutes.

When he returned to his seat, he was a professional. His friends clapped him on the shoulders; Jake was nonplussed; a hovering waiter whispered that drinks were on the house. Then, to Luis Carlos's awe, the saxophonist came and asked about the tune.

"It's a great one," he said. "I've never heard it before."

"Just composed," Jake snapped, "special for my friend here."

"How long are you gonna be in the city?"

"Uh—a week or so. Uh."

"Maybe longer. He's looking for gigs up here. Bored with Angeles City. Too small-time." It was Jake who answered.

The man was impressed. "You think you can have sheets made for me? I like that tune."

Luis Carlos couldn't believe his luck. "Certainly, sir. Most certainly. I'll write it out, sir. Most happy." He shook the man's hand with great enthusiasm, thinking of how he would bring the music sheets, would maneuver the talk to musical instruments, would confess his admiration for the saxophone and finally get his hands— hallelujah!—on the instrument.

"Well," Jake said, when the furor had died down, "a toast to the world-renowned musician."

They all drank, Luis Carlos as usual choking on the brandy.

He woke up late, a sledgehammer in his head, and, moaning and groaning, submitted to Mayang's ministrations. "You're not man enough to drink," Mayang shouted, slapping a wet towel on his forehead. At noon though, he revived enough to work on the tune, note by note, amplifying and correcting. For years afterward, until the bombs of a new war destroyed all memory, Manila's evening crowd would jitterbug, Charleston, foxtrot, and even waltz to the tune in its many variations, all under the title "Skyboats"—a tune truly modern for its non sequiturs and craziness, for its utter lack of meaning that rendered it so, as one Manila debutante said, "full of it"—while Mayang tried to close her ears to the anthem of her married life which, unlike Carlos Lucas, showed no signs of fading into oblivion.

That evening, at the same bar, Jake told him to forget the music sheets. He had found a job for Luis Carlos, playing at a competing nightclub.

"I used the same trick. World renowned." He laughed. "Said I was your manager. I get free drinks, at least."

Six months later, Luis Carlos bought a saxophone, secondhand, true, but serviceable, and commenced his study of the instrument. Which was to his good fortune, for having missed so many classes and exams he flunked out of school to Mayang's and the Superior's hysterics. But despite tears and threats of eternal damnation, Luis Carlos refused to promise to do better. He had decided. He could work now, he'd found his calling, and he could ease Mayang's financial burdens. "What dreadful stubbornness," the Superior said, "but there's no helping it though his father would be most distressed. He had such a good head for chemistry." At this, Mayang eyed the Superior with suspicion, not sure whether he meant Luis Carlos or— Perhaps the friar, now tottering to the end of his life, knew more than he'd ever let on.

Luis Carlos's decision left a new wake of grief in the household. Even the maids, whenever they brought him his newly pressed clothes, turned up their noses at the plaid jackets, the wide pants, the purple and red silk shirts he now wore. He suffered the opprobrium in silence, waiting for the ill wind to blow over. He would not even remonstrate with Mayang who, to show her displeasure, left whatever money he brought home lying on the altar in the living room.

One morning, Mayang found herself having breakfast alone. Irked by this show of sloth, she had the maid knock on Clarissa's door. Five minutes, ten. Mayang pushed back her chair in irritation and rose. The maid was still standing before the closed door and rapping steadily on the wood with her knuckles.

"She won't get up, señora," the maid said, abashed.

Mayang let fly a kick; the door sprang open. The fresh wind that played about Mayang's face told her, even before she walked in, that the room was empty, the bed not slept in. The dresser drawers were all half open, as was the closet door. Clarissa's clothes were gone.

"Holy Lord," Mayang muttered, hearing the sky crash. "She's gone and done it."

Clarissa left a note, handwritten on perfumed stationery, sealed and addressed to Mayang. *I have gone with the only man I've ever loved and will ever love. Don't try to stop us. I can't live without him anyway and he can't, without me. Your most loving daughter.* Mayang had to rinse her mouth after reading it. "Such terrible prose," she spat and went to Luis Carlos's room.

"Wake up!" She shook his shoulder, noting grimly how firm his muscles were. "You have to fight a duel."

"A what?" Luis Carlos bolted upright.

"Your sister's ruined. You have to right that. You have to kill the man."

"Is she in trouble?" Luis Carlos blinked and shook his head.

"She's eloped, idiot. Go kill the man and bring her back." The finales of several operettas ran through her mind. Luis Carlos would run him through with a sword. Easily.

"Uh, I have to find them first." With great reluctance, he dragged his body out of bed. "Who in God's name bothered? You know anything? How about the maids? Go ask them. One of them, for sure, knows something. How'd she get out of the house, who packed her clothes? And so on and so forth."

"All right. Be sure to challenge him first. Jacobo can be your second."

"Holy bananas," Luis Carlos said as he headed for the bathroom. "Kill a man? Blast him to the death with my sax, maybe."

"With a sword! With a sword!" Mayang shouted. "Nothing as uncouth as a gun. A sword."

"I don't even own one," Luis Carlos muttered as he closed the bathroom door.

But because he was a magician, the man made Clarissa and himself vanish into thin air. They couldn't be found, despite Mayang's relentless interrogation of the maids, her astute assembling of bits and pieces of information until she had the man's name (Pedro), his bloodlines (sturdy Malay), his work (sleight-of-hand), his habits. He was wont to hang out, said the maids, by the canal, amusing the construction workers and earning a few pesos from their sympathies. He was an itinerant, with no known address, though surely he must have had a place to lay his head and to keep his paraphernalia, which included paper flowers, a rabbit, two doves, an umbrella, scarves and hats, rings, odds and ends, and a folding table.

At first sight of Clarissa, one dusty afternoon when she and the laundry maid had wandered over to the canal, he'd said clearly, even as the king, queen, jack of hearts flew out of nowhere and fluttered about Clarissa's hair, that there, God willing, was the woman for him. Clarissa had turned red to her hair roots while the maid, askance, had snapped "Tse! Barbarian!" and would have added a few choice words had not Clarissa begun preening. At which, encouraged, the man had gone on, calling her the plump gooseling of his eyes, well cushioned, full of soup—here he'd licked his chops, while Clarissa's eyes moistened and she flushed once more.

"Holy mother," Mayang said, crossing herself. "He knew what to say."

Since then, for six weeks running, while Mayang and the cook basked in chandelier fantasies at the *teatro*, Clarissa had ambled over to the canal, first with the maid, later by herself. She had taken to saying that, compared to the magician, the actor had no salt in his blood, was indeed a sap lacking in that strange virility which only lower-class men seemed to possess.

"Holy mother," Mayang interrupted the narrative.

"I told her she was stupid," the maid said. "And since he was such a poor prospect—I mean, we wouldn't even consider him, penniless as he was—I didn't think, didn't think . . ." And here the maid, being in the solemn years of her maidenhood, began to cry.

Mayang could only shake her head. Luis Carlos, treated to this narrative again and again, marveled at the wiliness of a man who could find metaphors for his sister's many shortcomings. "It must've been love," he told his mother and was rewarded with a filthy look.

Once more the house nosedived into grief, for not a trace of the two could be found. Luis Carlos escaped from the melancholy by sleeping most of the day, getting up in midafternoon to open the garage where he and his band now practiced. He equipped the place with chairs, music stands, a sofa to rest his friends' backs, and an icebox for beer, though he himself was content with *kalamansi* juice, the sharp citrus tang of the tiny green fruit easing his throat which was often sore from the bar's cigarette smoke. He had his flute, his saxophone, and his clarinet, though he played more often now with the second. But it was on the clarinet that he composed the music of "Chattering Flowers," in memory of Clara. He played the piece for Mayang, listening with delight to the roses as they resolved to undress, letting go of their petals one by one in homage to the innocence of a dead girl. Mayang remained dry-eyed to the last note, and then, without comment, vanished into her room. Hours later, she reappeared and handed Luis Carlos a scribbling of lyrics in English for the tune. It became a favorite of the bar's regulars, especially when sung by the Eurasian chanteuse who came to the club now and then—"only as a diversion."

She was the mistress of the American military governor, it was said, and as a consequence was well financed. She sang infrequently, more to exercise her vocal chords and to freshen memories of her sultry, passionate contralto, which suited her slim, high-breasted, lithe body, her blue-black hair piled high on her head, crowning an oval face of incredibly delicate beauty. She was exquisite, there was no other word for her. And she was also, at the hour she sang with Luis Carlos's band, afire with lust for his own brand of beauty.

Jake was the first to discover her secret and, being the shrewd manager that he was, arranged for them to be alone in the bar's dressing room. The following day, though, he was summoned to her house by a chauffeur in a white Bentley and here, in a voice hoarse with weeping, the Eurasian told him that nothing, but nothing, had transpired.

"I was a band member to him," she said angrily, her fingers flicking outward so that she seemed to be unsheathing claws.

"Did you tell him?" Jake asked.

In so many words. She'd talked of romance, of youth, of bloodheat; he'd countered with woodwinds; she'd regretted the passing of time and told him how, in old age, love memories could be great comfort; he'd detailed for her the intricacies of a new song; she'd mentioned flowers; he had anecdotes of his flute.

"I'm not used to such treatment," she said, inhaling deeply while Jake's eyes nearly popped from watching how her breasts, bare certainly under the silk, further strained her cheongsam's bodice.

"You'll have to be more direct than that," he said, licking his underlip. "He's never had a woman."

She lost her breath. "Never?"

"Virgin," Jake confirmed, grinning.

"Holy mother of God!" She had to sip water to stop hyperventilating.

A week later, Jake asked Luis Carlos to meet him on Sunday night at the Eurasian's house. "She has a job to discuss with thee and me."

"Hey, that's your role, *pañero.*"

"Uh-uh. She wants to commission new songs. I know nothing about that part of the show."

Luis Carlos shrugged. "Sunday's the only night I have dinner at home. Mama will kill me."

"After dinner. See you there."

He thought nothing of it, merely tucking a reminder somewhere in his mind. When Sunday came, he presented himself at the door of her Ermita house, gave his name to the uniformed maid. He was ushered into an upstairs dressing room, all white and lilac, where the Eurasian waited. She handed him a glass of brandy.

"I'm giving a party," she said in a cold voice. "I want to inaugurate a new song at the party. Everyone who's anyone at all will be there. It's the chance of a lifetime. You understand?"

He nodded.

"I want a record made afterward. I don't care how much it costs. Money's no object. Drink your brandy."

So used was he to obeying older women, he didn't protest. She pretended not to notice how he choked and his eyes streamed.

"Do you like my dress? I'll be wearing it at the party."

He looked at her. She was wearing something that looked like wet black paint. He shrugged.

"Won't it rip?" he asked innocently.

"Perhaps," she said, "shall we try?" And putting both hands at the high collar of the dress, she yanked with all her strength.

Luis Carlos dropped the glass. The dress had slit open neatly, down the middle to the waist, freeing her magnificent breasts.

"You'd better enjoy it," she said.

He gulped and managed to croak: "Why?"

"Because a war is coming."

Two years later, when the jeeps, tanks, and armored personnel carriers of an invading force roared into the open city of Manila, in an expected but still surprising swift attack, Luis Carlos would remember this moment of discovery. Only then would its peculiarity hit him, and he would shake his head over this mingling of pleasure and death, of flesh and disaster, of beauty and blood. At the time, though, his first experience left him unmoved and when queried the following day by Jake, he said only that everything had been fine.

Not so with the Eurasian beauty. Her memory of that night was eloquent, the seven curtain calls Luis Carlos took unforgettable, each in a manner different from the preceding, now with a long-drawn

excruciating gentleness, then again with the vigor of the knowledge-
able, or with the swift poetry of the very young. She pursued him
henceforth, as much as she dared considering her status, from nightclub to nightclub, until, along with the American High Command,
she had to be evacuated to Bataan and from thence, by submarine,
to Australia and to the United States where, treated as a shameful
secret by her lover who was deathly afraid of his Bostonian mother,
she pined away in obscurity and narcotics.

Luis Carlos never denied her anything, nodding calmly at her
whispered request for a rendezvous except when the latter interfered
with his job schedule. When it did, he was always courteous enough
to suggest another day, making sure she was not humiliated. He was
never familiar with her in public, always respectfully distant as befitted a young man's demeanor toward an older woman. The problem
was he also never thought of her, except in tiny reminders as to date,
time, and place, for he kept a neat calendar in his head. Worse,
though he made no move to be rid of her, neither did he pursue her.
He just forgot her the minute he went out her house's gate, his mind
surrendering once more to music. Thus, in his innocence, he inflicted
an unspeakable torment on the Eurasian beauty, one she would remember in her sojourn abroad, recalling how in his easy availability
he was all the more inaccessible.

Jake was the recipient of the Eurasian's complaint, a role which,
after a time, he found most tiring. To the woman's ecstatic recounting
of her nights with Luis Carlos, Jake's sly answer was that, to men his
age, this prowess wasn't uncommon. The words passed like wind
between them—an indictment no less cruel for its being tacit. Jake's
underlip curled; he told himself to wait, wait, until the mammoth
party and the recording were over—after which he would come into
his own. He had started Luis Carlos's career, by a fluke, true, but his
management of it since had been inspired. Having no talent of his
own, he dreamed of owning a stable of the talented—musicians,
actors and actresses, even a Eurasian beauty or two. The party, he
surmised, would be as great an opportunity for his recognition as for
Luis Carlos's. Gently, then, not letting his impatience show, he prod-
ded Luis about the new song.

In the Binondo house, between the end of his day's sleep and the band's arrival, Luis Carlos sat at his desk, hunched over music sheets, his saxophone at hand. On this, he was creating Clarissa's song, "Plump Goose"—a song which, despite his irritation at her continued absence, was still a song of fondness. Every so often, he would call the maid who had been Clarissa's conspirator and ask her for more of the man's words. With her memory so taxed, the maid resorted to invention, dreaming of how she herself would be addressed by a man, some man, any man.

"Arms as white as cotton bolsters," she said, squirming on the edge of Luis Carlos's bed. "A torso vast as sails and as magnificent; thighs—" She hesitated, wondering if that would be too much for the boy. She decided to drop it. "Dimpled ankles, sweet as flan."

Luis Carlos let go his pencil. "He said these?"

"Most assuredly, the barbarian."

"In public?"

"Ay, that's the shame of it."

Mayang, overhearing, concluded that Luis Carlos was persevering in the search for Clarissa. His tenacity pleased her, as did his asceticism. None of her fears about his bar work had materialized. He didn't smoke, didn't drink, and no woman hovered about him. A twinge of fear touched her at the last thought. She hurried to the garden. The plants were still healthy enough, though without flowers, and as she moved from pot to pot, inspecting leaves and stems, she wondered whether she should buy new ones.

What with the indescribable noise from the trucks which rushed by nose to tail in their eagerness for the canal, Mayang could be forgiven for not hearing the gate's creak as a man pushed it open, nor his admittedly stealthy footsteps as he circumnavigated the garden until, by a circuitous route, he reached the front-yard tree at the same instant that Mayang did. He loomed so suddenly before her that she reared back and screamed. He snapped his fingers and a paper bouquet materialized under Mayang's nose. Her jaw fell.

"It's him!" she shrieked.

Her hand snatched up the coconut-rib broom that always leaned against the tree trunk. Holding it firmly with both hands, she flailed

at his head and shoulders, cutting off his escape and herding him
toward the stairs, then up the steps, as she screamed for Luis Carlos.
Cowering, the man tried to stem her rage by conjuring handkerchiefs,
rings, a duckling, balloons from his sleeves, managing only to leave a
colorful trail as they went up, crossed the front door and foyer, and
entered the living room where Luis Carlos found them circling each
other warily amidst what he construed to be a cloth peddler's wares.

When he learned who the man was, largely through Mayang's
incoherent tirade, he burst into such laughter that his mother was
scandalized.

"Well, aren't you going to slap him?"

"What for?"

"That's how you start a duel."

Such a look of fear crossed the man's face that Luis Carlos had
another laughing fit. Then, from outside came Clarissa's frantic
screech, begging her mother not to cut her husband's throat. Luis
Carlos doubled up again, laughing loud enough to raise the roof, while
Mayang rushed to the window and screamed for Clarissa to come up,
for God's sake not to create a scandal in the middle of the street, there
were decent people in the neighborhood. Still shaking with laughter,
Luis Carlos rushed to the steps to embrace his sister, noting how her
skin gleamed with happiness. Then he returned to the living room
and, ignoring Mayang's barks for him to slap the stranger who was
alternately turning red, turning white, took his brother-in-law's hand
and shook it. He left them to settle everything by themselves. The
truth was, a tune was playing in his mind, a companion piece to
Clarissa's song: "The Magician's Duel," in which rabbits, ducks, red,
orange, and blue scarves, metal rings, and top hats redeemed a man's
name in honorable battle.

10

The bells. As soon as he opened his eyes, they were there, distant but insistent, an ominous whisper. Tiny bells, big bells, silver and brass bells. He shook his head, trying to rid his ears of the sound but they remained, sometimes all together at once, often petering out to one hollow note lasting for hours, mimicking a faraway belfry bell, only to be joined by another, higher note, then another and yet another, until he thought he could hear all the bells of the city softly but determinedly pealing, warning him of danger. Before he did his ablutions, he checked the house warily, tiptoeing from room to room, lest he wake the specter that had disturbed the bells. In the kitchen, the cook bent over the old wood stove, her face sheathed by smoke and the sizzle of eggs and sausages. In the living room, two maids sang *fat girl, you're everywhere—geese in the river, sails in the sea* as they danced to and fro, half-coconut shells, dried and unhusked, under their right feet, polishing the floor. Mayang was in her bedroom,

gold-rimmed eyeglasses on her nose; she looked up from her sewing
to frown a question. He smiled, waved reassuringly, and checked
Clarissa's and Pete's bedroom. His heart jumped. It was empty. But
they were merely in the garage, half of which Pete had taken over for
his rabbit and duck cages and magic props. The two were bent over
three large wooden boxes on the floor, studying them intently. Pete
had a large saw in his hand.

"He's going to try to saw me in half," Clarissa said in an awed voice.

Gently, Luis Carlos loosened Pete's hold on the saw.

"Not today," he said. "I had a bad dream."

"Oh, for—" Clarissa flared. But Pete stopped her. He was a firm
believer in omens.

"Tomorrow. We can practice healing today."

Clarissa giggled. "He thinks he can become a faith healer," she told
Luis Carlos proudly. "More money in that. So you won't have to work
so hard."

"It's nothing," Luis Carlos said hastily, for Pete looked wounded.
"I like working and I don't have much use for money."

"Someday, we'll return the favor," Pete said grimly.

"I'm sure you will. Think nothing of it."

He slipped out, followed the footpath to the backyard, and here
found two maids washing clothes at the faucet. They were singing
*out came the army of rabbits and ducks, with banners of red-blue
scarves.* Their movements, as they rubbed and squeezed the clothes,
synchronized with the tune's beat. Luis Carlos smiled but a silver bell
cut off his pleasure and he turned away.

It was the day of the party—the monstrous gathering promised by
the Eurasian beauty, postponed many times for many reasons, not the
least of which was the woman's fear it would signal the end of her
trysts with Luis Carlos. During the delay, Luis Carlos had composed
half a dozen tunes she'd found unacceptable, though of course all of
them, silly and perky songs, were invariably hits, making the rounds
of nightclubs, corner stores, and public faucets. Luis Carlos was somewhat surprised by his affinity for music that worked on a wide range
of listeners. But what truly pleased him was hearing his songs rising

from the city's nooks and crannies, sung by men and women weathered by intense labor and poverty. He couldn't make heads or tails of the Eurasian's desires, until, of course, jolted from sleep one early morning, he smelled the wet sky and found both words and tune for the ballad "Lovely Stranger." It was a song for and of his neighborhood but the Eurasian surmised she was the central metaphor and took it to be proof of Luis Carlos's affection. Thus, the plans for the party were put into operation.

Despite the band's noise that mid-afternoon, the bells remained in Luis Carlos's ears, throwing a pall on the excitement. His drummer remarked on this but the bass guitarist, a man nearly twice Luis's age, merely shrugged and whispered that the evening's hostess must've been riding the boy hard. Their concern collapsed into laughter. They were in high spirits, for the Casa Español had been hired by the Eurasian, who'd practiced the song with Luis for months. Well, among other things, as Jake said with his wry grin. The band was to be in tuxedoes, as the beauty had demanded; they had to look first class for the five hundred or so guests, the wealthiest and most powerful individuals in Manila, including the American High Command. The military governor would grace the occasion as a favor to his mistress.

The bells. As Luis Carlos prepared, checking the band's repertoire (they would play only his songs this evening), listening to the entrances and exits of the guitar, the drums, the piano, the bass, sifting the roughness out of the music, he heard the bells. They would not let go, even when he called a halt to the warm-up, shook hands with everyone, and saw them off, with the understanding that they would be at the Casa Español an hour before the party's official start.

He sipped his *kalamansi* juice lazily, gave his mother a hug. In his room, the laundry maid was fluttering over the laid-out costume: black pants, black tails, frilly dress shirt, lavender cummerbund, lavender bowtie. Luis Carlos had to shoo her away so he could get dressed, though he found himself slowly but inexorably sinking into melancholia. The costume seemed inordinately thick and heavy when he felt the coat's lapel. The color, morose as a funeral, repelled him. He sat on the bed's edge and finished his juice. From outside, seeping into the sound of bells, came Mayang's harp. She was picking the tune of "Lovely Stranger."

She had not heard the song before and, during the band's practice, had been struck by its uncertain yearning. It could, it did, sound almost classical on the harp. She plucked notes out of her memory, her fingers echoing them on the harp strings, even as she wondered why such a sad song should come to her happy son or why he hadn't shown it to her. In a few minutes, she lost herself in the tune and could almost believe that boats were once more plying the canal and that the failing light outside was a dawning, that instead of easing into night, the world was moving into morning, a morning as fragile as a dream.

Then, a presence cut the light from the doorway to the dining room. Mayang looked up; her heart kicked against her ribs. *I'm dead,* she thought, *my past is loose in the world.* Without realizing it, she was crying silently.

"I look that bad?" Luis Carlos asked.

He had come to show her his costume. But what Mayang saw was Hans, dressed exactly as he had been on the nights of her thrice-held wedding, his hair slicked back from his forehead, his eyes cool as a December sea. But this was a younger Hans, tentative in his manhood, still vulnerable. She felt a sudden rush of love for her son, love which, amidst the thousand mundane details of existence, had lost its glint and been nearly forgotten. Wiping her eyes on her sleeve, she vowed that nothing short of death would separate the two of them; no, not all the disasters in the world.

"You look so grown up," she told him.

But Luis Carlos sat down abruptly, with such a morose look Mayang was alarmed. "I don't feel that way, Mama. I think I'm still a kid."

"Are you feverish?"

He shook his head. "No."

"For a child," she said, "you have so many dependents."

He would not be comforted. "I'm tired, Mama. I've been working three years straight now. Maybe, I should have a vacation."

"There's enough money. Why don't you go back to school?"

"After this party. When this party's over. I'll take a week, two weeks, a month off. We can go to Bulacan. Visit Papa's grave." He stood up and flung his arms overhead, stretching his torso. He seemed taller than Hans. "Will you come with me, Mama?"

"Of course," she said. "Wherever you want to go."

When the Eurasian beauty's white Bentley let him off, with his clarinet, flute, and saxophone cases, at the Casa Español, Luis Carlos noticed what an inordinately warm December it was. The weather, it seemed, had conspired with the chanteuse to assure the party's success. In the clear night sky, stars as huge as a man's hand burned fiercely and a sickle moon swam over the sea, that sea of unbearable perfumes sending out a breeze that now smelled of roasting corn, now fresh grass, and even hot cocoa. Crossing the Casa's threshold with its hundred torches, seeing the glitter of chandeliers within the main ballroom and the fifty roast pigs still embracing the bamboo spits of their demise lined up like knights' lances against the wall behind the buffet, Luis Carlos suddenly felt that he had been here before, that all this had happened before, and without exactly knowing why, his gaze swept the floor in search of some trinket, inadvertently dropped, which shouldn't have been dropped: a tie tack, sleeve stud, or—.

The bells. They were louder now. He heard them even as the Eurasian, resplendent in white silk and emeralds, approached and took his arm. Pleasure intensified her beauty and, for a minute, Luis Carlos had the disquieting feeling that she was not who she was, perhaps because, for the first time in public, she wore her hair loose, falling in vine curls to her hips. She steered him gently toward the stage where the other band members waited.

"Everybody's coming," she whispered. "All except for that tiresome Estela Banyaga. The shrew."

"Who?"

"Old blood," she said. "Said she and her husband wouldn't eat with the likes of me." She laughed. "But her son's coming, though. At least, the eldest. Tiresome shrewish old blood."

"I never heard of them."

The bells. They pealed on through the band's opening number "Skyboats," and through all the numbers thereafter, as the guests poured in, flinging coats, hats, and canes at harassed attendants, and heading straight for the dance floor, edging into the mass of whirling, twisting couples while sweating chefs took down the roast pigs one by one, yanked out the bamboo poles, and laid the unfortunate creatures on oversized chopping boards to be reduced to edible pieces. Dancers broke away from their partners for a quick trip to the bar in the next room or to snatch a plate from a hurrying waiter so they could stand in line before the buffet and get their serving of the thirty dishes prepared for the occasion. There were basins of scalded oysters, husked; rolls of *morcon;* an endless stream of stuffed milkfish; *enceimadas* from Valenzuela; prawns and crabs from Cavite; chicken cuts in *adobo;* gallons of *paella,* sautéed string beans, noodles, four different kinds of sweets . . . The bells catalogued the gargantuan feast as Luis Carlos and the band hit the opening bars of "Chattering Flowers," a favorite dance number despite its rather morbid content. Cheers broke out as the familiar tune floated over the rabble and there was a mad move toward the dance floor.

When the moment came for the *pièce de résistance,* Luis Carlos's shirt, inside the tuxedo, was soaking wet and he was ready to drop from exhaustion. The bells were louder. But everything had been arranged; he could not beg off at the last minute. He signaled for a halt to the music and nodded at his bass guitarist, who always spoke for the band, Luis Carlos being too shy. Into the sudden quiet, broken by murmurs and the clink of glasses and silverware, the old man announced the formal launching of a new song—to be performed by the band with the evening's hostess.

To enthusiastic applause, the Eurasian mounted the stage and waited for Luis Carlos to cue her. He cocked his head, straining for the single altar bell that gave him his key and heard instead a deep thoroughly unnatural boom. This jolted him so much his saxophone bleated. A ripple of laughter followed—which the Eurasian stilled by charmingly saying this was a new song, they hadn't quite mastered it.

Then she threw Luis Carlos a killer glance that said *get on with it.*
Luis Carlos aimed a plea at the heavens, *please,* and there was the
key, a tremulous harp note in his ear, cool and strengthening as rain.

In the darkness of the war that was to follow, the memory of this
song, the chanteuse's voice and trills of the saxophone, the way it
happened this night, would return to those who had been present. For
in the six minutes that it took to begin and finish the song, the Casa's
roofs and walls disappeared and it seemed that the entire archipelago
lay before them, all seven thousand one hundred islands, and they
could focus on that hallowed place—mountainside, seashore, city or
town—wherein their birth pillows (as the placenta was called in the
native language) had been buried, in a tradition older than the Spanish walls of Intramuros, linking them inextricably, despite tortuous
journeys, to the stones, dust, and trees of their childhood which called
for their return, in accents so fraught with love that not a few of the
women shivered and dropped their *yes* to their suitors.

Quiet followed the song. Then, applause. The beauty took her
bows, as did the band, and, finally, Luis Carlos could climb off the
stage and edge to the buffet table, shaking hands and accepting
shoulder claps. The bells were still now; during the song, not one had
pealed out.

"You wrote it for her," a girl blurted out as he passed her. Abashed,
she added: "Is this true?"

At other times, he would simply have nodded. But . . . "She
commissioned it," he said curtly. "It's actually about Binondo. Or the
city. Or perhaps, even the country." He smiled and pushed on, not
noticing how the Eurasian had overheard.

"Did you hear that," the girl said in a loud voice, turning to her
escort, "it was written for the city! How lovely."

To the Eurasian's mortification, the information spread throughout
the Casa, often in the same words the girl used—*For the city? How
lovely!*—and she could barely smile as she held on to the military
governor's arm. In her distress, she failed to notice the uniformed man
who, with nary an excuse, wedged himself through the crowd until
he was before his superior. She barely caught his words—but it was

enough. The blood drained from her face and before she could stop herself, she had repeated them aloud:

"Clark Field! Bombed!"

Luis Carlos had found a quiet back room in which to have his dinner and he was at one of the tables, hunched over his meal and his melancholia, when six men pushed into the room. He recognized the military governor. Fear froze him in his chair. The six, though, perhaps mistaking him for a Casa staff member, ignored his presence and, clustering in the middle of the room, proceeded to argue.

"We'll declare Manila an open city," the governor said. "Can't have the buildings and the houses wrecked. Intramuros alone is irreplaceable."

"But, Excellency"—this from one of the two natives in the group—"the enemy won't accept that. The military command's stationed here."

"We'll withdraw," he intoned.

"Withdraw," his aide repeated. "To Bataan. We'll make our stand there."

"But the supplies, the—"

"We won't have long to wait. Reinforcements will come from the United States. By submarine, if necessary. By air, most certainly."

"When?" The other native looked cynical.

The two glanced at each other. Luis Carlos could almost read their faces. *What about the rest of us?*

"Excellency," the first now said smoothly, "we can understand your wish to spare lives. Fight in Bataan, if you believe that wise. But please, let us help you."

"How?" the governor asked.

"Distribute arms. To everyone," the man said. "We won't let the enemy occupy Manila. At least, not in peace."

The military governor bent a cold eye on the speaker. "And when you finish with the enemy, on whom are you going to use those guns?" There was no answer. The man dropped his eyes before the governor's scrutiny. His mouth twisted, as at the taste of something infinitely vile. "But we will reassure the populace, gentlemen," the governor went on.

"How?"

"We shall give them a promise of our return." The governor threw back his head and smiled at his men. "We have work to do."

The white men swept out of the room, leaving the two Manilans. Suddenly, one turned to Luis Carlos.

"Remember this, son. This American *loco* chose to leave us defenseless before the enemy."

"Reinforcements, bah!" the other cut in. "My spy network's better than his. I *know* Pearl Harbor has been demolished."

"Tough times, tough times." The first shook his head. "Well, I'm off. That was a beautiful song."

"Very apropos." They waved—gestures of despair—and left the room.

Luis Carlos, alone once more, couldn't be certain it had not all been a hallucination. Carefully, he picked up plate, spoon, and fork and found his way back to the ballroom. There was no dancing now, despite the relief band's efforts; the crowd had broken up into small groups, intense in their conversation. Luis Carlos surrendered his plate to a waiter and circled the room. The words were everywhere: *bombs, Clark Field, war* . . . He made his way to the stage and, waving his excuses at the band, picked up his clarinet, flute, and saxophone.

"But where are you going," the Eurasian stopped him.

"Home," he said. "My mother, the war, bombs . . ."

She sighed. "I'll have to go with them, you know."

He understood. She would go to Bataan. "I know." He sounded so forlorn her eyes misted.

"Don't worry. I'm used to it. I've been all over—born in Hong Kong, raised in Holland, etcetera, etcetera. Tell you what, we'll promise each other—" Here, she raised a hand to her right ear, unclasped the emerald-and-diamond earring she wore, and slipped it into his coat pocket. "We'll bring them together when we meet again. Meanwhile, meanwhile—" She laughed gaily. "I'll just wear one earring. Perhaps start a new fashion."

No arrangements had been made for his ride home. In the dead of night, under the clearest evening sky he'd ever seen, Luis Carlos had to catch a bus, lugging his instrument cases and wearing a superb tuxedo. It was the only way, he thought, to end a bizarre day.

He did not sleep at all. He paced in his room, between the bed and the windows, now and then looking at the canal that was a dark gash under the sky. Question after question raced in his mind but he couldn't complete a single one. He thought he could hear the whine and thud of distant bombs, but that was only his imagination. Not until Manila was bombed would he find out what those things were.

As soon as he heard the maids laying out breakfast, he slung a towel over his shoulder, went to the bathroom, and doused his face with the cold water of the cistern. Wide awake now, though still in his striped pajamas, he entered the dining room. Mayang nearly dropped her fork. Even Clarissa and Pete stared. But Luis took his seat, unfolded his napkin, bent his head in a seeming prayer, and without preamble gave them the news.

"We're at war," he said. Just as abruptly, he corrected himself. "The Americans are at war. *We* are being invaded. Manila's an open city—which means they'll march in and take over."

"Take over what?" Clarissa asked.

"Who knows? Maybe everything. But we have to prepare."

"I'm not a stranger to war," Mayang said. "I'm not afraid."

"Food," Pete said. "We have to stock up. There'll be a riot at the stores. Money. All the money in the house. We have to buy rice—a truckload maybe."

"Ah, it won't last that long," Clarissa said. "Maybe, just a sack or two."

"One truckload," Luis Carlos said firmly. "Salt and sugar. Cocoa. Coffee beans. Dried fish."

"I'll go," Pete said, gulping down his coffee.

"You'll get killed," Clarissa wailed. "Mama!"

"Stupid! He's not going to war. He's going shopping." She held out her bunch of keys to Luis Carlos. "In my room, in the wardrobe, top shelf. An old cashbox. Hurry."

They had five thousand pesos all in all. Without ceremony, Pete shoved the cash into a brown paper bag. "I'll go to the waterfront," he said, while Mayang nearly had hysterics at the thought of how he had made himself and Clarissa vanish. But Pete, rolling up his sleeves good-humoredly, reassured her by throwing his arms around the weeping Clarissa and peppering her cheeks with kisses.

"My tidbit, my incomparable morsel, my love, I'll be back with enough food to see you through a thousand-year war." He snapped a blue nosegay into existence and offered it to her with a bow.

Entranced, Clarissa watched him from the living room window. "I'm so lucky," she murmured.

Mayang, looking at her shapeless figure beneath the loose housedress, could only shake her head. "How lucky—you don't even know."

They were all lucky indeed to have Pete in the house. Indefatigable in the emergency and aided by a peasant wisdom, he brought home, day after day, so long as there were some to be had in the city, sacks of rice, salt and sugar, cocoa and coffee, baskets of dried fish and shrimp. He fought his way through mobs at warehouses, bribing when necessary, charming storekeepers with his scarves and paper flowers, showing the threat of his massive arms when nothing else worked. He and Luis Carlos cleaned out the garage, reinforced its walls against rats and the damp, and thus managed to turn it into a storage for their provisions. The rabbit and duck cages were moved to the garden where Pete built a shed under the tree, not knowing a shed had stood there once before, a long, long time ago. Mayang was reconciled to her uncouth son-in-law at last; she even breathed thanks to him—for they were by themselves now, the five maids having packed up at the first public announcement of the war.

Tearfully, Mayang gave each a gift of money and her blessing, despite Clarissa's rage.

"Give my regards to your parents," she said, "and take care of yourselves. If there's too much trouble at home, come back to me. I have been your second mother, after all."

"Madness," Clarissa screamed. "They'll never make it."

"Sssh," Pete calmed her. "If I were far away, wouldn't I make my way back to you? They love their parents, brothers, and sisters . . ."

"Oh, Pete! What about you?"

"Fortunately, my parents are dead." He plucked a coin from her ear. "I have only this house to take care of."

Luis Carlos remained silent and grim. He made his way to downtown Manila to watch the military convoys roaring out of the city. He didn't know why he watched; perhaps, he hoped for a glimpse of the woman who'd loved him so much. Or perhaps, he wished he too could leave, such was the dread that shrouded him. Or perhaps, he wished merely to fix this in his memory: jeep after jeep appearing and disappearing while on both sides of the road men and women watched helplessly, empty hands at their sides. Sometimes they craned their necks at the sky to follow the flight of strange airplanes.

After a while, he tired of counting the jeeps and walked to the Ermita nightclub where his band had played. The place was closed but the back door was open. Inside were Jake and the manager demolishing a last bottle of brandy.

"Can't give you any," Jake said. "The Americans took the whole caboodle. This"—he gestured at the bottle—"was in this man's safe. Precious cargo."

"I don't drink anyway," Luis Carlos said, pulling a chair to the table. "What are we going to do now?"

"I'm closing the club," the manager said. "Though I'll probably be forced to open it." He shrugged. "To amuse more soldiers."

"Holy Christ," Luis Carlos muttered. "Play for them?"

"No, friend," Jake replied. "We aren't doing that. Definitely not. That would make us collaborators. And believe me, this imperial army's a flash in the pan. The Yanks will be back. They promised."

"No," Luis Carlos said slowly. "I don't have any music left in my head."

"What you and I will do, hey, listen here," Jake went on, "what we'll do is go to Laguna. My cousin's putting together a guerrilla unit. Fight the Japanese. Hit and run. Do them in here, do them in there. Disappear. Easy. And when the Yanks return, we get military ranks and back pay, not to mention retirement pensions. Then, we can go make music."

Luis Carlos didn't answer. He picked a few peanuts off the dish on the table and chewed earnestly.

"Hey, really. My cousin's sent word to me. He's got couriers waiting in our village. What say you?"

"When do you go?"

"In a week's time. Got to say good-bye to my girlfriends. Sunday, definitely."

Luis Carlos nodded. Listless, he stood up. "I'll see you before then."

"My pleasure, captain. Maybe, major?" Jake laughed.

Chances were Luis Carlos wouldn't have gone had it not been for the Japanese captain who showed up four days later at the Binondo house. Speaking impeccable Tagalog, he reduced Mayang to an indescribable state by accusing the household of the crime of hoarding. He then demanded that half of everything in the garage be donated to the Japanese Army. Clarissa had to drag Pete to their bedroom, gag him, and finally sit on him, so intent was he on assaulting the foreigner, while Luis Carlos, pretending to hug his mother from behind, calmly placed a hand over her mouth.

"This is a big house," the Japanese said, his eyes roaming the living room. "We can billet four or five soldiers here. You will be happy to lodge friends, yes?"

Luis Carlos smiled at the officer. "Certainly. But we will need the food to feed them. There are four of us and with three of your men, why, our stock won't be enough."

"You are a clever man," the officer said. "Perhaps we shall revise the amount of your donation."

"Perhaps we won't donate at all."

"In that case, we will take. Tomorrow. Half. There are other houses."

Mayang wriggled loose. "But I know you," she said, "you used to work in the barbershop. At the corner."

The officer smiled. "Ah, true. The vagaries of war."

And he left, marching smartly out of the room. Mayang was so dumbfounded she stuttered for a while. But Luis Carlos's face, its slow-blossoming rage, stopped her tirade.

"What are we going to do, son?"

"I'm going to Laguna, Mama," he said, the words costing him so much pain he nearly wept. "I will join the guerrillas. There's more danger here for me."

To his surprise, Mayang nodded. "Of course. There's nothing else to do." After a while, she added: "I will go with you."

"Mama!" He looked at her.

She stood before him, slight in her felt slippers and robe, her hands clasped near her womb. But her eyes were steadfast and he understood that, far more than any danger, it would kill her not to be with him.

Then she made the one offer he couldn't resist.

"I will carry your saxophone while you fight."

11

The reinforcements never came. Bataan and Corregidor fell, and what was to be a short, happy war became a deadly four-year struggle. By the time Mayang and Luis Carlos began their journey to Laguna, six months had passed. The transportation system, never stable under normal conditions, collapsed totally in this state of war. With reed suitcases and provisions of rice and dried fish, they trudged to the highway, flagged down buses, cars, water-buffalo carts, went on foot when necessary, joining the hundreds who were making for their hometowns by hook, crook, and wiles, stopping along with the others whenever planes skirmished in the sky—for it was the way of the people to seek out the amusing and ridiculous in the most terrible of events. Bets would be laid as to which plane would suddenly veer away, black smoke spewing from its tail, and drop, like a crippled duck, to the earth. Until once, at the edge of a rice paddy, spewed debris from an exploding aircraft neatly took off an onlooker's head and that was the end of that.

The town of Saray where Jake had agreed to post a guide was on a mountain plateau, the first hills of the mountain ridge that ran like dinosaur fins through Luzon—the Cordillera which, in the great War of Resistance against the Japanese, as later this period was to be enshrined in history, served as headquarters, sanctuary, and launching base for the guerrillas, in much the same way it had functioned and would function in many other wars. Their arrival in the village was heralded by an ear-splitting cockcrow. It was the cry of the *labuyo*, the wild mountain rooster which, though nearly an extinct species, retained its fame as a cockfight champion. A boy of ten, barefoot and thin, peasant shirt slipping off the sharp clavicles of his shoulders, grinned a welcome, his breath misting in the cool morning air. "Someday," he said, "I'll trap that son-of-a-bitch."

After an hour of rest and breakfast of fried rice, sausages and ginger tea, the boy led the way through a labyrinthine footpath past gigantic fern and grass patches. The path burrowed into bedrocks of ancient boulders covered with lichens and lost itself now and then in the soft clay of abrupt springs and tiny brooks. After nearly half a day of wading through the melancholy twilight of a rain forest, they reached the camp: a few tents and lean-tos of nipa fronds on stripped branches, a makeshift stove of three rocks, and twenty men all as young as Luis Carlos.

Commander Manny, as Jake's cousin was called, turned out to be long on ideals and short on skills. Their first ambush of a Japanese patrol led to their grief, with five men dead and Jake suffering a flesh wound in his thigh, into which, frightened nearly out of his head, he poured what little sulfa powder was left in his medical kit.

"Rats," he said to Luis Carlos, "they didn't fight fair. We stood square across the path with our guns, *mano a mano*, cutting their escape. But they didn't have the decency to shoot it out. First thing we knew, they were diving for cover, flat on the ground, and were lobbing hand grenades. We had to retreat."

"But where are your rifle sights?" Mayang asked.

"Took 'em off," said one of the men. "They made us cross-eyed."

"Holy bananas," Luis Carlos muttered.

Commander Manny, fiddling with the ham radio, managed to contact a larger guerrilla unit and was told that three men from the Chinese Wang Chai Division were fighting their way through enemy lines, fording the gaps between towns and mountains, slipping past fortifications to reach Laguna. They had started a week ago and were expected any day now.

"Three men?" Luis Carlos scratched his head. "You're sure they're still alive?"

Mayang cautioned her son with a smile. Having found a dry enough spot for their things, she stepped back into the forest to gather palm fronds and fallen branches—materials for their own lean-to. Automatically, as she circled farther from the camp, the local names of berries and ferns returned, and she began to catalogue what was edible and what wasn't, what virtue each had, not noticing how, by this simple act, she was already reverting to her unwedded days. Whenever she spied and bent to pick up a usable discard of the forest, the fingers of her left hand went to her chest, pressing back the cloth of a remembered wide-neck peasant blouse though she wore a man's shirt and trousers. Catching herself in the gesture, she had to smile ruefully, thinking how strangely indeed time had looped, so that she found herself in her old province once again, breathing that impossibly pure air and wondering how it all would have been had the Spaniards not arrived three hundred years ago. Just then the *labuyo* shrieked again and from below the mountains, distant but true as bell peals, came the answering chatter of domesticated hens. The *labuyo* crowed twice more. In the abrupt silence that followed, Mayang's heart kicked thrice in her ribs. The worm of foreboding stirred and told her she would not survive the war.

"Nana." The voice scattered her thoughts.

Whirling, she found a man standing to her left, camouflaged by forest shadows. A disquieting familiarity, as though she had seen him before, flitted through her mind. Then, she was clapping her hands in childlike delight. "A Chinaman," she said and remembered her roses. But this was the forest and the slim youth was soon joined by two others, all of them mud spattered and in the last throes of exhaustion. As she led them to the camp, she was haunted by the feeling that she had something important to remember but all that came to her was the insane chattering of hens from some village below.

"But how," she asked, just to ease her mind, "can you teach them how to fight? You're not old enough to be warriors."

Even as she asked, the last of the three, walking behind them, was straightening broken fern leaves, propping grass blades, and, where the bald earth showed through, carefully sweeping away footprints with a twig, erasing traces of their passage. From time to time, he circled away from the path, in an odd complex dance, and Mayang was about to laugh at this madness when she realized he was removing the signs of her foraging as well.

"Nana, you mustn't be careless," their leader said.

Abashed, she kept quiet after that.

The three stayed for two weeks, at the end of which even Mayang was familiar with the short, full-powered blow—with a dagger, if there was one; with the outer edge of the fist, if no knives were on hand—at the nape's base, which disabled the motor nerves; the graceful glide of blade across a neck, destroying the vocal cords; and the bunt with the rifle butt which cracked the ribs and drove its broken ends into the heart. She watched bemused as the twenty young men learned how to flit like deer through the forest, to safeguard the secret of their comings and goings, and, more important, to catch hold of the rhythm of sounds—birdcalls, rustle of butterfly wings, fall of dew on leaves—that spelled the difference between danger and safety. Often, to while away the afternoon hours, two of the three Chinese would give an exhibition. Mayang, convinced though she was that she would never understand men's need to kill each other, would have to suck in her breath as the pair circled, danced, flew, and struck in stylized combat.

One afternoon, on her return with a pail of water from a nearby spring, Mayang found the men huddled at the camp's center, studying marks which a Chinese was making on the ground.

"This is the fort," he said, laying a stone down, "and this, the river." He drew a line with a pointed stick. "A frontal attack is impossible. The river is the only access. A hundred men inside. In groups of ten. Guards here and here. We're more than par. Rifles, grenades, ammos, medicine. We'll take it at dawn. Now, who can swim?"

"I can swim," Luis Carlos replied.

Mayang's hair tried to stand on end. But it had been said and Luis Carlos was chosen to be with the first assault team of the sneak attack, swimming across the river, wearing only a coat of soot mixed with coconut oil, and with his knife between his teeth.

"Holy mother of God," Mayang said and went off to huddle at a tree base in prayer and tears.

Moments later, a hand touched her head.

"Nana," the Chinese leader said gently. "He'll be fine."

"How do you know?" Angrily, she wiped tears off her cheeks.

He shrugged. "Presentiment. But you must eat." He disappeared and returned with a spoon and rice gruel in a tin bowl. Settling on his haunches, he would have fed her but she snatched the food away, still furious with him.

"I don't smell death on him," the Chinese said.

"Don't humor me, child."

"We've never done that, Nana."

His tone said he meant neither her nor himself. After a while, he sighed.

"You have never trusted us. We were trading with you before the Spaniards came. Your ancestors were buried in porcelain kilned in our land. Yet at the white man's word, you razed our districts and massacred our uncles." He shook his head. "We'll never understand you." He exhaled audibly. "Trust me, Nana. He will be safe."

"You can talk. You're not swimming the river stark naked."

He laughed. "But I am. I go with the first group. I promise to keep your son by me. Will that make you happy?"

Mayang, head bent, hid her relief by blowing on the gruel.

"Of course, I know he's special. I played the flute!" He laughed again at Mayang's astonishment. "I've known from the first day who he is. But since it's not supposed to make any difference . . ." He hummed the opening bars of "Chattering Flowers." "Lovely song. Nana, perhaps when we begin to treat you like the white men do, you'll trust us at last. He shall be by my side. All right?" He rose to his feet. "But then again, if you knew me, you wouldn't want him beside me."

"Stop! Why are you doing this? Why do you do this?" She swung a hand to take in the forest, the country, the war.

The question hung in the air. The Chinese youth, for he seemed even younger in the phosphorescent glow of the forest night, shrugged.

"Some say because of Manchuria. Some say because any ground where our forefathers are buried is hallowed ground. Can you, with your blood, understand that? The others don't; your people do not. So we say because of Manchuria. This country—it has no continuity. It is only a country of beginnings. No one remembers. Not the burial jars, at least."

When he walked away, sure of foot despite the dark, it did not occur to Mayang that he could be lost to her forever. But three days later, when the men returned from the attack, having cached their loot in mountain caves, the Wang Chai men were not with them. The three had taken leave of the unit, for some secret destination. Commander Manny's unit, in their estimation, had enough skills to survive, and they would learn more by surviving. In addition, the group now had supplies taken from the fort and such confidence as could only come from an unblemished victory. "Expect retaliation" were the last words from the Chinese. Sure enough, two weeks later, black smoke roiled upward from the lowlands. The Japanese had torched the October harvest.

Luis Carlos was caught in the dilemma. Each attack on the enemy was visited on the hapless villagers. Public executions, rapes, vandalized homes, even crop burning became the enemy's standard response. The towns emptied as the peasants fled to the forest, hauling pots and blankets, dragging roped pigs, goats, and children, until Luis

Carlos feared that the lowlands would melt back into the primeval forest out of which they'd been carved. Miles of ricefields lay fallow now. "The whole country's sinking into barbarity," he said to Mayang. "I don't like this war. Any war!" Pained and angry, he would stalk away from the camp, with only his saxophone for company, and hie off to the waterfall whose noise masked the bull wail of his lament.

Mayang had no time for discussion. From dawn, when the *labuyo*'s cry roused her, to nightfall, when she threw dust on the cooking fire's last embers, she was intent on foraging. Picking berries, scrounging for sweet potatoes, discovering a wild banana grove, setting traps for monkeys and bats, she roamed through the forest. Now and then, she would come across itinerant vendors with their bamboo poles and woven baskets. A furious haggle would then ensue, she with her rare green coconut or two, a banana bunch, or sweet potato shoots; the vendor with the needed jacket or blanket. At such times, Mayang could believe that nothing at all was left of the world, except for this jungle in which they lived no better than the monkeys they ate stewed in tamarind leaves.

She could not know that in the enemy's territories she was a legend, that the old native title of respect, Nana, had been construed by the ignorant aliens as a guerrilla alias and that they had set a price on her head. Jake had started the lie, explaining to Luis Carlos that it would protect the identities of the rest of them while enhancing the band's reputation, for it was here, in the self-same place, that two female generals had discombobulated the Spanish garrison during the Revolution many, many years ago. "Besides, it's a good joke," Jake said, laughing, "and your mother's never in the battle zone anyway. She's safe." Luis Carlos had to agree. Thus Manny's guerrilla unit became famous for two things: its musician, said to summon water spirits with an instrument of unspeakable sadness; and its ferocious leader, *Generala Nana* or General Old Lady.

It had been almost a lark, this war, the first year when the peasants, whose own sons and daughters were scattered in guerrilla units throughout the archipelago, gave willingly of both food and information. But as Japanese reprisals—swift and merciless—increased, an essential weakness in the national character surfaced, and the towns-people found themselves betrayed by men who wore paper-bag masks, with torn-out holes through which the informers peeped at and iden-tified those who served the guerrilla network. In Saray, one early morning, the Japanese descended in armored personnel carriers and, kicking doors open, hustled the villagers from their homes to the town's central clearing, a miserable plaza. Standing shoulder to shoul-der, men, women, and children watched with incredulous eyes as a man wearing a reed-bag mask and speaking in their own language and their own accent aimed his forefinger at one individual after another: "This one, this one, this one." It was death for a boy of eleven, fleet of foot, who carried messages to and from the guerrillas; an elderly woman who went to the town market near the Japanese fort; a brawny peasant who, for the sheer pleasure of it, occasionally unearthed his guns from the ricefields' dried-up irrigation ditch and joined a guer-rilla sally. The three, speechless at the betrayal, were pushed to their knees before an executioner and summarily beheaded.

Hard times descended then, for the Japanese stationed sentries at the dust roads leading to the village. They also confiscated fowl and grain, three silver lockets, and two gold-capped teeth from the village elder who had to submit to the bloody and rude ministrations of a Japanese soldier wielding pliers. When two families slipped away under cover of darkness, determined to die rather than live so imposed upon, the sentries had the entire village line up from the oldest to the youngest. They took turns slapping the villagers' faces.

Meanwhile, the rest of the enemy force spread out through the forest searching for the guerrillas and gunning down whatever moved in their path: wild boars, roosters, monkeys and lizards, an unfortunate refugee family or two. Warned by the villagers who had escaped, the guerrillas were already on forced march, wading upstream to conceal their footprints. After two hours of walking, they slipped back into the forest cover, diving under tangled vines, between giant heads of fern, careful not to disturb even the littlest pebble between green-bearded boulders. They traveled, having hidden their provisions in caves along the way. True to her word, Mayang carried only the saxophone, the first thing she had snatched up at the alarm, while Luis Carlos had his rifle, two guns, two daggers, and two ammo belts.

They never set up a permanent camp again, for the enemy proved tireless and stalked them through the forest. Once they ran into a patrol and had to fight their way through, Mayang on the guerrillas' heels, her body curved about the saxophone to shield it from bullets. They lost three men but managed to cut the enemy down.

The forest seemed to stretch forever. Submerged in a perpetual green twilight, they found themselves yearning for the sea. Luis Carlos felt he was caught in some nymph's net and was walking the riverbed, as he chewed on the unripe mock apples Mayang had found along the way. The forest clutched at his body, and from head to foot he was covered with thorn and leech bites and was chewed up by vines and ferns, by supple branches that clawed at his face, swung back when pushed and stung his nose. "Mama," he called out, "I'm dying." In truth, all felt themselves to be at their last breath, soiling themselves as they marched, for the berries they plucked and the green bananas they stole from groves so offended their bellies that their bodies emptied themselves as they ate. Monkeys scolded them, trees creaked with imitation, and, to make matters worse, ghost voices from all the wars which had been fought in the forest buffeted them from all sides. Luis Carlos at first thought he was hearing the distant boom of artillery. He threw himself down, digging his face into the green slime underfoot, certain that he was dead already when he realized it was the bells—deep, bass-voiced bells, cathedral bells, ringing all at once. He propped himself on an elbow and saw how the others had thrown themselves down as well. His heart stopped then rushed again, skipping in time with the bells. "Mama!" he called out and realized Mayang was no longer with them.

She was bent over, still cradling the saxophone swathed in a blue cloth like a baby, near the green-bearded boulder where she had stopped to catch her breath. Now, she looked up into a face full of hate and had to force herself to think, to separate the words which it had marked out in a rush.

"Old woman, let your son go!" Jake had said, his voice hoarse, dead.

He stood over her, his rifle in his hands, his chest rising and falling with the agony of breathing.

"You'll get us all killed, old woman," he said in a low voice, mindful of the fact that the others were searching for her.

"But what are you saying?" Mayang whispered back.

"Stay behind; surrender. Or just—just leave us. You're the one they're looking for."

"Who? What are you saying?"

Losing his patience, Jake bared his teeth in a dog-grin and jiggled his rifle.

"Are you going to shoot me?" she asked.

He gave a despairing groan as she hoisted herself to her feet. Catching sight of the rim of the saxophone's mouth, its mocking gold, a flare of rage lit up Jake's face.

"Stupid—," he muttered, and reversing his hold on the rifle, he struck.

Mayang barely had time to turn her torso. The rifle butt caught her on the side. Something cracked. A spurt of pain ran up and down her chest; she rocked on the balls of her feet, the forest spinning crazily. But she held on to the saxophone and heard, clear as sunlight, her son's voice calling her name.

"Don't go tattling to him," Jake hissed. "I'll shoot both of you." Straightening up, he yelled for Luis Carlos. "I found her." His dog-grin snared Mayang again and then Luis Carlos was there, taking her arm.

Breathing hurt her. "I'm sorry," she said, "I'm too old."

"This is too heavy," Luis Carlos replied, taking the saxophone from her. He had Jake tie the instrument to his back, using the blue cloth as a sling. "We'll have to stop and think. Some plan, any plan." He slipped an arm about Mayang's shoulder. "Next time, holler if you have to stop. You scared us half out of our minds."

The search though was lucky for the guerrillas. One of them stumbled on a patch of wild tomatoes and sweet potatoes. Commander Manny, in sudden good spirits, called a halt to the march, stationed Jake and two others as sentries, and told the rest to prepare for an attack on the vegetables. Laughing, they drew their knives, hacked away at the creepers, and unearthed the plump, succulent tubers. Mayang hobbled off, looking for firewood.

Breathing hurt her. As she inhaled, exhaled, fire raced in her chest in tiny spurts. She tried to keep her chest as still as possible, breathing as shallowly as possible, so as not to disturb the broken thing within her. When she bent to pick up a dry twig, flames filled her chest. The ground spun like a toy top and, for a second, she was on the brink of fainting. But she pulled herself back and discovered that if she knelt, very carefully, she could just reach down to pick up odds and ends of wood on the forest floor. Once, she coughed and spat and saw a drop of red in her sputum.

Despite all her precautions, she grew weaker by nightfall. Luis Carlos, alarmed by her silence, studied her pinched face by the campfire's light. She seemed distant, as though listening to the bells which pealed solemnly now, one by one. But whenever he asked her what the problem was, she merely smiled and shook her head. He took the blue cloth off the saxophone and, ignoring her protests, wrapped it about her shoulders. Then, still uneasy, he unbuttoned his shirt and laid it over the palm fronds and banana leaves they had gathered for bedding.

"Sleep here," he said, stretching out on the ground a few feet away. This way, he could hear the rasp of her breath in the darkness.

When he opened his eyes to the pale-green dawn, she was already up, sitting with her back against a tree trunk. He was so surprised he nearly cried out. It was a young woman who smiled at him with such eager love. She had thrown the blue cloth over her hair, like a peasant, and her skin, beneath the mantle, was so smooth, so clean, that Luis Carlos had to blink to convince himself she was Mayang. He rose and hurried to her, dimly aware that the others were still asleep. He bent to touch her. Suddenly, her body convulsed with a horrible cough, her face puckering into a mask a thousand years old. Horrified, Luis Carlos seized her hands. They were cold.

"But what have you been up to?" he cried out, feeling her forehead at the same time.

She was burning. She saw him through a haze of flames, exactly as she had seen Clara, though he was no youth but a man. Flames licked at his feet, his elbows, his hair, and she understood that the vision of long ago—so very long ago—had not been of her child in hell but of her own death. She held on to his hand, feeling a wail rise in her, in a hundred different voices, clamoring for the bequeathal of knowledge. But his skin was too harsh, his mind too closed. He was a man. Regret touched her briefly at the absence of Clarissa who, for all her stupidity, would have been transparent to the touch of centuries. She would have learned this way, the only way to knowledge, flesh to flesh.

They carried her in a blanket slung between two stripped acacia branches, setting off in their desperation for any place at all. If Mayang had qualms about her status among these young men, they were stilled. Even Jake was subdued, now and then peeking down at her as though about to ask a question. After two hours, one of the two scouts who had raced ahead returned. A kilometer to the east, he said, lay what seemed to be refugee huts. Without a word, Manny gestured for him to lead the way.

It was nearly noon when they reached the lean-tos. Luis Carlos parlayed with the head of the three families which had joined forces in their new life as forest dwellers. In exchange for news and for his two daggers, the man agreed to Mayang's being left in his care. Thus, she was laid gently on a mat on the shack's slat-wood floor though she shook her head and called Luis Carlos's name again and again. A peasant woman came, felt her forehead, and said, "She has a fever." She hurried out to prepare a poultice.

Luis Carlos sat beside her for a few minutes. "We'll be back, Mama," he said, pushing back stray hair from her cheeks and chin. "You'll be well by then and come with us."

"Leave the saxophone then," she answered, smiling. "Just to make sure you return."

He thought at first she was kidding, but no—. He nodded and set the instrument by her side. "We're leaving now," he said.

"So be it."

When he left, she pushed gently at the wall until her head was near the doorway and she could peer out. There they were, marching in single file, already a distance away, their rifles slung on their shoulders. Their voices rode the wind through the cogon grass as they sang the guerrilla marching song. She listened, trying to catch Luis Carlos's voice, and automatically heard the song in three languages. *Difficult indeed was the guerrilla's life; always in the mountains and forest; at stake our lives, all for our country's sake; often, we have to fight; with machine guns, rifles, and grenades* . . . She nearly laughed out loud. The day the guerrillas had a machine gun, she thought, would be the day they won.

12

After the war, Luis Carlos would burrow thrice through the jungle in search of Mayang's grave. It was so vivid in his mind, so unmistakable as to detail, that each time he set out to look he was certain he would find it: the crude wooden crucifix a hundred yards to the lean-to's side, past a clump of wild *ylang-ylang,* near a tree of immense proportions which assuredly had contributed its branches to the grave's marker. But he never did. Perhaps the peasants, at war's end, had dismantled their lean-to; perhaps, a Japanese straggler had killed them and erased all signs of their existence to hide his crime; or then, again, perhaps the forest had simply swallowed everything, lean-to, crucifix, and all, the way time nibbled on memory, rendering imperfect what had been precise. In any case, after his third failure, Luis Carlos had to reconcile himself to his mother's resting apart from Carlos Lucas and Maya. What he couldn't accept was his inability to create a song for her, which he blamed on the loss of the harp, because only harp notes, he thought, could sing of Mayang's quiet courage. He couldn't know that her song had been composed and sung many, many years ago, and the harp actually made music only for a German scholar.

He had known the exact moment of her death, for the bells rang out then—a knell of alternating high and low single notes, one brass, one silver. Despite Manny's objections, they had abandoned a raid on a Japanese patrol and instead half walked, half marched through the forest, with Luis Carlos, guided by the bells, leading them through the maze of trees and vines, until the lean-to had hovered in sight, dancing in summer's heat waves. He smelled her rain scent at once and, nearly weeping with missing her, burst into the peasant clearing to the raucous crows of an insane *labuyo.* She was dead, dying to the minute the bells had begun. She had grown worse, said the women, as soon as the guerrillas had vanished from sight—coughing out blood, sinking into a delirium. Still she had lingered, completely out of her mind, conversing in Spanish with someone only she could see. She had seemed happy. But on the last day she had recovered her senses and, calling to the man who spoke for the families, she had made him swear, on his children's heads, that the saxophone would be kept in a safe place and returned to Luis Carlos.

So, they gave him the instrument.

"There's no helping it, *pañero,* " Jake broke in, "one goes when it's time to go."

The eldest of the children, a boy of fifteen, offered to show him the grave. To his relief, Manny held back the others and allowed him to go alone. On the way, Luis Carlos stared so intently at ready landmarks that the boy grew wary and edged closer. Shrubs, Luis Carlos was thinking, tree, and, a half-mile away, a pointed rock of reddish hue. Abruptly, it was there, the rude crucifix, and he shivered.

"Strange thing," said the boy, "but once I saw a man here. My mother said I was dreaming."

Preoccupied, Luis Carlos barely heard the words.

"In a black coat. Like in the old books. Very tall. Looked American but I can't be sure. Didn't see his face. Know what I think? He was

an American pilot, his plane downed. We could have hidden him—"
He grinned.

"*Loco,*" Luis Carlos said. "It will take a long time before they come
back. A long time."

He shooed the boy away and knelt at the grave. "I'm sorry, Mama,"
he said, unconsciously repeating his words to Carlos Lucas. "But
there's no helping it." Suddenly, the boy's words rang in his ears and
a vague memory of his old nanny's chatter surfaced in his mind—
about a man who'd lived at the Binondo house before his birth, a man
who resembled him, Luis Carlos. His heart turned over. With a
forefinger, he poked at the heaped earth. "Well, Mama," he said, "I
hope he's with you." He rose, renewed by this discovery of his origins,
and rejoined the guerrillas.

He thought he would be with them to war's end and, indeed, they
would go through a hundred and one adventures, zigzagging from
village to village, burying their dead, treating their wounded, recruit-
ing new comrades, and always watching, watching the skies for the
promised airplanes. The time came when Luis Carlos, looking at the
faces by the campfire, saw only Manny and Jake of the old group, all
the rest being newcomers. He himself, despite being a veteran, had
not even been nicked, for the bells warned him on the eve of each
battle, ringing so consistently he had learned to tell whether the
danger was his or someone else's. He could not always forestall the
other's fate, but whenever the bells rang for him he was very careful.
Once a peasant commented on this, saying Luis Carlos must have a
virtud, a quality that made the gods protective. Jake, irritated,
snapped that it was simply the unit's superior training, that was all
there was to it.

Once in a while, they would meet another unit and exchange news.
But it was the same all over: hard times in the lowlands and no sign
of the Yanks. The enemy's noose had encircled the archipelago and
was choking it to a slow but sure death. Famine, disease, and war
casualties. In some towns of Luzon, the guerrillas had won, securing
territory against the Japanese and, now, villages were run by peasant
leaders. This made Jake uneasy.

"This war will turn us into a country of peasants," he muttered.

Luis Carlos had to laugh. "We are a country of peasants, *pañero*. You and I are aberrations."

But Jake didn't like that at all, not at all, and, from that instant, what had been a mute transformation since they had abandoned their Saray base became obvious. Once, Luis Carlos, as they were walking to yet another camp, reached out to tap him on the shoulder. A companionable gesture, usual between them, but Jake dodged and such an angry glance shot from beneath his brows that Luis Carlos withdrew his hand. From then on, Jake kept counsel with himself, always five feet away from the others. His eyes turned shy, avoiding the others'. Luis Carlos suspected he was having death omens. But even news of other guerrilla victories failed to relieve Jake's dark mood.

It only lightened when Manny agreed to loop back to Saray, in an effort to get at their cached supplies. Jake was sure the sentries had been withdrawn and that troubles elsewhere had caused the Japanese to pull back. "It's such a flea village," Jake argued, "they wouldn't bother holding it when they're getting clobbered in central Luzon." In the ensuing argument, Manny, exhausted by their day's march, threw down his rifle and snapped: "Verify, verify, verify. Have you forgotten the Wang Chai's instructions? Verify information. If you can, then we'll go." He stripped off his shirt, wriggled out of his pants, and proceeded to swim in the creek they had found. "God, I'll never be clean again," he muttered as he clambered up the bank. Luis Carlos and the others laughed while Jake's face closed up in anger.

Two days later, returning from his usual marketplace foray and bearing, to the guerrillas' delight, nearly two kilos of rice and three cans of sardines—"donations," he said, "from the parish priest!"— Jake claimed he had found a Saray trader who had confirmed his suspicion. The prospect of having medicine at last, for their arms and legs were pocked by ulcerating sores from insect bites, convinced the guerrillas to try for it. Only Manny and Luis Carlos were reluctant; the first because of the memory of the bag-masked man and the latter because of the stirring of the bells. But Jake forced a vote and there was no helping it, they were to go to Saray.

That night, as they ate the incomparably rich dinner, smacking their lips at the sardines' tang, Luis Carlos busied himself, between mouthfuls, with checking his weapons. Rifle loaded, guns loaded, ammo belt filled, his grenades and new daggers easily released. Around him, the others were in high spirits, their stories of war mingling with bells in Luis Carlos's ear. He heard them like distant artillery, dull and ominous. *Madre de Dios,* he thought and crossed himself awkwardly. Jake caught sight of this and eyed him intently.

"Is something wrong, *pañero?*" he asked. "You're not eating enough."

"I'm not used to such fare anymore. Sticks in my gullet." Luis Carlos averted his face.

"Try to keep it down. You've got to eat to survive. And that's our primary duty: to survive."

Luis Carlos made a noncommittal sound.

Jake became expansive. "When we get to Saray, ay, such living we shall have. No more dysentery, no more—"

"The war's not over yet," Manny broke in.

"I was just dreaming," Jake said with a giggle. "Just dreaming."

"I hope this Saray thing's no dream, *pañero.*" Luis Carlos couldn't help the words.

Jake's eyes narrowed. "We'll have to watch you. You're losing your balls."

In the sudden silence, the hard butt of the gun he had just checked dug into Luis Carlos's palm. All movement had stilled. With his peripheral vision, Luis Carlos saw the others staring open-mouthed at Jake. After a while, the eyes swung to Luis Carlos. It was an iron rule never to question a man's courage. Even Manny stirred uncertainly. Jake, suddenly aware he had gone too far, looked sick; he gave Luis Carlos a sheepish smile.

"Everyone does, now and then," he said. "I didn't mean anything." He stretched out his arms to show he had no weapon.

Luis Carlos nodded and the tension broke. Everybody spoke at once, Manny berating Jake for going about unarmed. Luis Carlos veered away. He had lost his standing among the group. But the bells had warned that this was no moment of reckoning.

It took them a week to reach the foothills of Saray and, by this time, the bells had petered out to silence. Luis Carlos, though still uneasy, heaved a sigh of relief. Perhaps, the danger had abated. Nevertheless, a heaviness remained with him; something, a worm perhaps, writhed in his chest, a foreboding of further sadness. He would have liked to play the saxophone but instinct warned him against encumbering his hands.

They were nearing their first cache—a small natural cave snuggled against an abrupt rise of the mountainside, hidden by ferns rooted on boulders—when leaves rustled, and a strange sound came.

"Look at that son-of-a-bitch," Manny cried out.

A *labuyo* stood to one side of the path, atop a boulder, preening its wings and cocking its head now and then, the better to inspect the men with a glistening, dark eye. It was as iridescent blue as a peacock, though its tail was shot through with red-orange feathers. Jake drew his gun but Manny stopped him.

"Don't waste meat!" And compelled by a freak sense of humor, he pointed to Luis Carlos. "Go get him, Louie. That's our supper!" The guerrillas broke into laughter. Luis Carlos, with his weapons and his saxophone, was the least agile of them.

He sprinted for the cock, though, and felt the wind of its sudden flight between his fingers. Behind him, the guerrillas laughed again.

"Don't come back without it," Manny yelled.

"Come on, come on. It's just a stupid bird," Jake said.

Instead of disappearing into the forest, the rooster stopped fifty feet away and crowed. Luis Carlos circled warily, legs and arms wide apart, his torso in a half crouch. To his amazement, the rooster lowered its head and dove straight for him, a comical bullet that zoomed between his feet, leaving a long, curving feather in his hands.

"Jesus," he said in surprise, "a suicidal chicken."

Two yards away, the *labuyo* stopped once more and eyed Luis Carlos, as though waiting for him to follow. Luis Carlos did and the rooster led him into a merry dance, farther and farther away from the others, teasing him with its nearness until, sweat-soaked and raspy-breathed, he cornered it in the crotch of twin boulders by a spring.

"Got you!" he said, grabbing its body. He caught its frenetic legs and turned it upside down. "Dinner!"

In that instant, a terrible fusillade erupted, the noise shaking loose dead leaves and sparrows from trees overhead. Luis Carlos threw himself to the ground. The rooster escaped and, with one last trumpeting crow, lifted its wings and soared. He barely caught the magnificence of its flight, one befitting the king of birds who served as the ancient priestesses' sacrificial offering to ancestral spirits, before it was gone and silence descended. He heard the bark of a foreign language and nearly wet his pants. Then, a familiar voice came, pleading, saying one had escaped, go search for him, only to be met by guttural laughter and the swish of a descending sword. Jake screamed.

Then followed the nightmare of his flight through the forest, his steps haunted by an imagined battalion of enemies, from dream monsters to Japanese patrols. He had never been alone. To be alone was madness. He crawled, walked, climbed, waded rivers, dimly recognizing places where he, Mayang, and the rest had camped a long, long time ago. At night, using his dagger, he hollowed out a nest in the earth and curled in like a fetus, not daring to slap feeding mosquitoes off his body. He was saved only by his rage, a deep-seated hatred that would well up, like a lazy spring, to overwhelm his thoughts, his body, and end with an explosion of curses and the vow that, someday, Jake's debt would be settled, if not on him then on his brood, for assuredly such a snake could only breed asps.

Without knowing it, he crossed the boundary to the next province and it was here that another guerrilla unit found him, licking dewdrops off leaves. They fed him, questioned him, and comforted him at the loss of his companions. He stayed with them throughout the war and was partially healed of his sadness, for they were a peasant unit, kind and warm-blooded. He served them faithfully until the moment dawn broke with a thunderclap and, rising from their sleep, they saw row after row of black bird shadows, already in their downward sweep toward the city, and heard the shrill whine of bombs as they fell, and the roar of an injured earth—hundreds of them, mother of God, row after row of airplanes, latticing the sky from horizon to horizon, with more crowding in, dropping their unspeakable cargo on a defenseless city, while black smoke boiled upward and Luis Carlos felt his eyes water at the thought of Manila burning, the Binondo house burning, the cluster of American bars, the Eurasian beauty's elegant parlor, the Capuchin school where he had sat in classrooms and memorized the English alphabet, the San Augustin church, the cathedral of the dawn masses at Christmastime, the bamboo stalls selling steamed mashed purple yams with grated coconut toppings, the public faucets where women gathered to scrub and rinse clothes, the cobbled walks, the walls of Intramuros, the gas lamps glowing at twilight, just when Mayang, in her velvet needlepoint upholstered seat, drew the harp closer to her body, as though to warm it with her heat, her hands caressing the nearly invisible strings so that they, Clara, Clarissa, and he on the floor, Carlos Lucas in the doorway to the dining room, were drenched with the cool sound of rainfall, rain falling, though no rain would suffice to quell that monstrous fire eating now at the city, chewing up houses, boats, and buildings, one by one, scenting the air with the smell of blood and roasted flesh, mocking Luis Carlos with the truth that, though he and everyone on the seven thousand one hundred islands rebuilt with ferocity, they would never have that same grace again, never again the grace that only came with antiquity.

"We will have new things," said the peasant leader of the unit, seeing Luis Carlos's wet cheeks.

Then they fought their way through straggling lines of Japanese soldiers gone berserk, down to the lowlands, to meet the Yanqui forces and register their brave deeds. In the newness to come, it was important, they all felt, that a little of history remain.

Three weeks of the bloody walk, marching and fighting—for the entire Japanese force seemed to have become suicidal, rampaging through villages, killing everyone in sight—before they broke into the Yanks' camp in their filthy and blood-spattered clothes, joining what appeared to be all the guerrillas in the world, coming down the mountains, dragging their rifles by the barrel, and singing *a guerrilla's life is hard indeed; stuck in the mountains and the forests . . .* They were making for an American sergeant, dazzling in his cleanliness, seated behind a makeshift table, paper and pencil at hand, listing down the names, units, and area of operations of each guerrilla who came before him. To his right, a mound of rifles grew as the young men—for they were all young men—divested themselves of weapons, dropping their warrior disguise, to become simply men again, now thinking of loves and homes and the future.

After Luis Carlos identified himself, he was handed two chocolate bars, a bath soap, and cigarettes. He gave away the last since he didn't smoke, unwrapped the chocolate, and, sucking happily on the divine gift, asked for directions to the river so he could bathe. He was turning to leave, his thoughts already on the agreeable feel of water and soap, when he heard his name barked out by someone.

"Hey, hey, Louie! The Hun! Hey, Louie, the Hun!"

Pivoting, he confronted the oldest American he had ever seen, certainly the ugliest: a yammering death's head at the end of a turkey neck protruding from the stiff khaki wings of a collar bearing a colonel's insignia.

"Christ, you survived the war! Luis Carlos Villaverde! I knew your mother! I rented a room in her boarding house! I knew you as a baby! The Hun!" The man gestured for him to come close. "A guerrilla, eh? Listen, I need an aide. You're drafted. Come along. War's not over yet. Another one in the offing. But first, we have to go open the brewery. We need beer!" He laughed, winked. "Of course, the good ole general's part owner of the goddamn brewery but that's neither here nor there. The Hun, I can't believe it. Play for me, son; play for me—all the way to Manila."

That was how Luis Carlos returned to the city: playing "Skyboats" on a flute supplied by Mad Uncle Ed, as the colonel was known, the two of them in the back seat of a jeep driven by a drunk private, while the colonel ranted about all the things he had seen and done in the archipelago, from filling in the canal to filching gold anklets from savage tribes. Suddenly, Luis Carlos stopped playing and gaped; he had caught sight of Manila.

"But I can see the sea!" he shouted.

"Flat as a pancake, son. We always do a thorough job." Mad Uncle Ed chortled.

The jeep stopped at what seemed to be the only extant house left, a house already crawling with Yanks and women. Here, Mad Uncle Ed gave him a three-day leave to search for his sister, warning him to stay clear of the debris and rubble for the Japanese had mined every inch, it seemed, of the land and the unwary were still losing legs and arms. Feeling helpless without his guns, Luis Carlos made his way to Binondo. He had to circle twice and start all over again, for all the familiar landmarks were gone; there was only the topography of devastation. He found families huddled among the ruins; potbellied children eyed him from beneath half-fallen house beams amidst the pungence of ripening corpses. After a while, he came to the canal, recognizing it because it still lay lower than the ground proper, though its surface was covered over with burnt wood, torn galvanized iron sheets, cement slabs, and loose slate tiles and bricks. From there, he traced the remnants of the streets to their house and found only the stairway thrusting upward amidst an impossible tangle of wood, slate, dismembered furniture, and half the roof.

"Is she dead, too?" he asked aloud.

"Lord, it's Louie!" Clarissa shrilled behind him and he was caught in a spasmodic embrace, pounded on the shoulders by Pete's fists, and, smelling the soot odor of his sister's hair and clothes even as he caught sight of a naked, brown toddler standing behind her, his fist caught in the folds of her skirt.

"Our first," Pete said, leading the boy forward.

Luis Carlos was speechless. For the first time, he added up the years: three and a half, all in all. *Madre de Dios!* He swallowed the dryness in his throat and said: "Mama died."

"But we knew. One night the pots in the garden broke into two and fell apart," Pete said, shaking his head. "We couldn't replace them."

The bad news out, the two now regaled Luis Carlos with their adventures. The carpet bombing had driven them out of the house, just in time, for the roof was stoved in by a terrific bomb while they were a mere block away. Along with hundreds, almost dead with hysteria, they had gone south of the Pasig River, to vacant lands at the city's edge. Here, compelled by the instinct for survival, they had gathered planks and plywood sheets for a shack and eventually managed to fence off a garden. They returned to Binondo now and then only to salvage what they could: a chair, a lace curtain, serviceable wood and roofing, nails, a basket of fragrant and healing oils, plaster saints—which they loaded in a pushcart for their new home.

"They say there are still Japanese hiding in the ruins," Pete said. "It's not safe yet."

"I will never return!" Clarissa snapped. "Those bombs! Live in the city! Never again!"

It had only been an exaggeration, Clarissa would later admit; how was she to know that the heavens had taken note and would see to the truth of it? None of them had objected. Pete dove into the ruins to ferret out their old life's leftovers while Luis Carlos, galvanized by this reunion with his family, ascertained the exact location of their shack and hurried back to Mad Colonel Ed. Having mollified the crazy colonel with twenty minutes of the saxophone, playing "When the Saints Come Marching in," he got permission to raid the head-quarters' supplies and use the jeep to boot. In haste, before anyone changed his mind, Luis Carlos loaded chocolate bars, tins of corned-beef hash and milk, cigarettes, bath and laundry soap, two blankets, vitamins, and whatever he could take away safely, including candles and an oil burner, for the city was still without electricity. All went into the jeep and he drove recklessly through the bombed-out streets until he reached the vast refugee camp where Clarissa, Pete, and their child were. It was a tangle of clapboard houses, but at Luis Carlos's arrival the residents poured out, mistaking him despite his tan and because of his gray eyes and reddish-brown hair for an *americano*.

"Joe, victory Joe! Don't be stingy, Joe!" The voices hammered at him as he waded through a forest of raised palms. The maimed, the wounded, the dying rose to their elbows, as though he could instantly cure their injuries, and cried out in that bird whine: "Victory, Joe!"

"Shit," he muttered, shooing them away from the jeep. For a moment, he considered batting them away with the axe he had brought for Pete.

Fortunately, the commotion drew Clarissa. She screamed at the sight of her brother set upon by beggars. "Get away," she shouted, "that's my brother! You shameless thieves!"

"How come he doesn't look like you? Your mother slept with a 'cano?"

"Yours slept with a monkey. Get away from there."

She was more than a match for all of them and cleared a path for Luis Carlos while Pete, with two young men who had been promised cigarettes, carted the jeep's treasure into the shack.

The visit raised Pete's standing in the community. He had direct access, he would boast, to the American command's kitchen pantry. As a result, his patients doubled, for he had become a healer now, deftly opening this man's or that woman's belly with his thumbnail, extracting white stones and bits of knotted tissue, sealing blood vessels and the skin so magically that, afterward, when a wet rag was passed over the wound, wiping away the blood, not a sign of the operation could be seen.

Luis Carlos watched with his mouth half open. Later, in the quiet of the kitchen, when the last patient had finished slobbering his gratitude and had left his payment of a piece of bread, a velvet skirt rescued from the ruins, or a woven mat for the floor, he asked Clarissa:

"It's all sleight-of-hand, of course."

Clarissa's smile, by the candlelight, was enigmatic. "He's done wonders for the sick."

"Holy cow," muttered Luis Carlos, "I have a saint for a brother-in-law."

Clarissa giggled. "Oh, he's not that at all."

She patted her belly and it was only then he noticed the slight swell of it. For a dizzying moment, he imagined the whole shack—the whole city!—peopled by Pete's miniatures; he grew faint at the thought of the army of children he would have to support for he was sure now that Pete would always be this way, at society's periphery, picking a living off scraps of superstition and the people's impossible need to believe in magic. It made up for their helplessness.

"I have to go back now," he said.

Thus it was that, immersed in the task of meeting their requirements of survival, they forgot all about the Binondo house while Luis Carlos drove from one Yank camp to another, salvaging what he could of the soldiers' rations, Clarissa roamed the streets, her swollen belly swaying, and sifted through ruins for usable items, and Pete did marathon operations on twelve to sixteen patients each day. By the time they all sobered enough to think of rebuilding in Binondo, it was too late. A barbed-wire fence cut off five blocks of the district including a length of the canal.

"A sign said *Property of the Banyaga Estate,*" Pete reported.

Not even Mad Uncle Ed, to whom Luis Carlos appealed, could recover what had been stolen.

"All the records went *kaput!*" he said, "and the Banyagas laid claim to the title. They are connected."

Clarissa spent a whole day weeping, blaming herself for having brought about this new calamity. But there was no helping it. Luis Carlos, twisting his mouth at the vile taste on his tongue, gathered odds and ends of clothes and other gear and made ready to leave with the colonel for central Luzon, a place he thought he would never see again, now that the state of war was over.

13

The ambush was well planned. The neat rows of marching men, five abreast, fell in a confused mass of heaving bodies as machine gun bullets rained down from the land rise on both sides of the dirt road. Mad Uncle Ed laughed and laughed, slapping his right knee as he watched from behind the second machine gun nest, his Army jeep nestled under the trees ten meters away. The parade's tail had shattered into individual men running for shelter, and Luis Carlos, standing four feet from the Yanqui officer, could see that they were peasants—or guerrillas who, after surrendering their weapons, had reverted to being peasants. Shivering, not knowing what this new war was all about, he wondered if he had known any of the dying and the dead down there—a good two hundred men, still sunburnt and brawny from the four-year War of Resistance against the Japanese, spilling blood, urine, and vomit on the golden dust.

One man broke away from the chaos and ran for the hill com-

manded by Mad Uncle Ed. Luis Carlos almost heard the man's
fingernails snapping off as he scrambled for a handhold, his body
squirming like a worm, his bare feet clawing the earth. He nearly
made it; indeed, his head rose nearly to the level of the colonel's feet
but Mad Uncle Ed, eyes so huge they nearly ate his face, drew his
service pistol and aiming carefully, shot the man between the eyes.
Luis Carlos saw the back of the man's skull fly off, specks of brain and
flesh staining the earth below before the body completed its arch
through the air to plop on the road's edge. Mad Uncle Ed laughed
and laughed.

"It is the best kind of war," he roared later, as he sat in the jeep
and was driven toward the camp.

"What kind?" Luis Carlos asked politely.

"The kind against your own kind." The colonel pursed his lips
obscenely, as at an inordinately saccharine taste. "I shall teach you to
make war on your kind."

"But the war is over." Luis Carlos knitted his brow against a
headache.

"Not yet. Your peasants are restive."

"That will pass."

"Perhaps, yes; perhaps, no. But I don't have the time to wait, son.
There are fortunes to be made. I grew rich on this land and so will
others. Mark my words and know which side your bread is buttered
on." Mad Uncle Ed laughed.

Luis Carlos raised the flute to his lips. The *pan de sal,* he thought,
was a fist-shaped bread; one slit it open with a knife and buttered it
inside. The thought soothed him. He played "Killer Joe" for the
colonel.

Thus it was that he would wend his way through central Luzon,
weaponless except for his flute, sitting in the jeep behind Mad Uncle
Ed and puzzling the whys and wherefores of a war treading on the
heels of a just-concluded war in a country of beginnings. The old
Yanqui, his boss, had been reactivated to deal with an incipient
insurgency, his genuis at dealing with skittish natives being well
known even in the Pentagon. And indeed, despite bouts of nausea,

Luis Carlos could bow to the old man's inventiveness. He treated his own men well, turning their weakness into strength, their perversions into military tactics. To this end, he established an elite battalion, called the Nenas—a pampered, much publicized unit of handsome and photogenic soldiers. Privately, though, Mad Uncle Ed laughed his head off at official adulation of his unit, for the word *Nena* (he had to remind Luis Carlos who had forgotten along with the rest of the country) was Tagalog slang for faggot.

Set loose upon villages barely recovered from the Japanese occupation, the Nenas' passage was a swath of terror and destruction. They would dress in civilian clothes, knock on peasant homes, pretend to be guerrillas, and kill whoever received them kindly. A chance meeting with peasants on the dust roads ended with the latter losing their heads to the axe that the Nenas' captain preferred. Through it all, Mad Uncle Ed laughed with approval and hummed along with Luis Carlos's music which, as the months passed, grew more and more strained.

It was in Floridablanca that the depths of Uncle Ed's madness made itself known. The Nenas caught a seventeen-year-old peasant fishing in the river. The lad, stuttering with fright, was brought to Mad Uncle Ed who ordered him worked over with rubber hoses. "Until I say stop!" he said. He never did and, seven hours later, the lad was dead, though without a mark on what had been a sturdy, deep-brown body. But he did not die before implicating everyone, from the eighty-year-old elder to a ten-year-old boy, in his village. Then, to everyone's surprise, Mad Uncle Ed had the entire unit hunt for a bat: "Just one! I need just one!"

When the rodent was caught, Uncle Ed stabbed the corpse twice in the neck with an icepick. He wrung the bat's neck and ordered the men to take corpse and bat to where roads from four villages converged.

"Spread him there," he said, "and put the bat on his chest. Scraps of superstition! We've never changed you, you people. You still believe there's something stronger than money and bullets. Obligations and spirits, honor and monsters!" He grinned at the corpse sprawled on a jeep's back seat, the bat on its lap. "That should scare everyone out of his mind." To Luis Carlos, he muttered: "A panicked town won't think of self-defense." Laughing, he headed for his tent. "We march at dawn."

For the first time in many months, the bells stirred in Luis Carlos's ears. But there was no helping it; at dawn, he was in the colonel's jeep, trying to soothe the old man's hangover with flute music. He was still playing when the soldiers kicked hut doors open, roused all the inhabitants, dragged out the male residents, and, with gun-butt blows, herded them to the river. Here, they were lined up on the bank while the Nenas, four at a time, practiced their marksmanship. They marched to a spot a hundred yards away, wheeled to face the agog peasants, fell smartly to their knees, brought their guns up, and shot the unfortunate villagers one by one. The bodies toppled back into the river and Luis Carlos, still fingering his flute, tried to close his eyes to the scene. But all he could see was a red river aswarm with brown crocodiles.

Afterward, Mad Uncle Ed and the men returned to the village. "For some sport," he said, grinning. Luis Carlos begged off, saying the heat was getting to him, and thus he was by himself, near the river, when one of the bodies stirred, swam ashore, and hoisted itself out of the water. For a moment, he thought his vision of crocodiles had come true. But it was only a boy, maybe eleven or twelve years old, and he gave a cry of despair when he caught sight of Luis Carlos. He would have thrown himself back had not Luis Carlos, bending over quickly, seized his forearm.

"Sssh," Luis Carlos warned him. "Not a sound. Quickly. Downstream. They went back to the village."

The boy wept then. "My mother, my sister," he said between sobs. He glanced at the river. "My father."

"There's no helping them now. Go quickly. To the next village and warn them."

Shivering, his skin peppered with goosebumps, the boy nodded. "Yes, sir. Thank you, sir. I will do so, sir."

"Don't use the road. Go through the fields."

"Yes, sir. But why? Why, sir?"

Luis Carlos shrugged. "Some war. The landowners returned with the Yanks. I don't know. Wait. What's your name?"

The boy hesitated. Then smiling suddenly, his eyes focused on the name tag on Luis Carlos's uniform. He was committing it to memory: Villaverde. "I am Ismael," he said softly. "Ismael Guevarra." He ran then—a supple animal cutting across the open cogon field toward rows of sugarcane. Minutes later, he was gone and Luis Carlos could look innocent when Mad Uncle Ed and his driver, a jar of sugarcane wine between them, returned.

He would have abandoned this crazy war right there and then— were it not for the thought of Pete and Clarissa and their brood who lived on his salary. Mad Uncle Ed insisted on their driving to Angeles City to meet his newest counterinsurgency expert. It was Jacobo Montreal, incipient wrinkles on his forehead and under his eyes, a cane in his left hand to make up for his wooden right foot, and an arm around a swarthy, very pregnant woman.

"Jake!"

The sight of Luis Carlos appalled him as much. But he was older now, quicker to recover. He swept the arm off the woman's shoulder and extended a hand to his enemy.

"The Hun! You survived the war!"

He shifted the cane to his right hand when Luis Carlos, frozen by an incredible surge of hatred in his body, didn't move. Three bells rang a warning in his ear, followed by three harp notes, and it was the latter that drew his eyes to the men in the room—men as still as snakes. Luis Carlos shivered but could not bring himself to be even vaguely polite to the traitor.

Jake waved his men nearer, introducing them to Mad Uncle Ed. "This one—a real viper," he laughed, pushing forward by the shoulder a slim, wiry young man with jet-black hair. "Funny thing's he's got a beautiful name. Amor. Urbano Amor. Good enough to be a musician's, eh, Louie? He's my favorite."

Uncle Ed had tossed a swift glance at Luis Carlos, catching the tension. "You knew each other?"

"Even before the war." Jake grew expansive. "We served in the same guerrilla unit. But an ambush wiped us out. I lost my foot then. Louie, though, was luckier. He was chasing a wild rooster for our supper. Not even a scratch. Lucky devil!" He joined in the sudden laughter.

Luis Carlos was helpless before the man's temerity. The foot had been lopped off by a Japanese sword, his only reward for having betrayed his companions. That and his life. But Mad Uncle Ed had already brushed aside his suspicions and yelled for his driver to bring the sugarcane wine. Sitting at the only desk in the room, pouring the brew into glasses the men held out, he outlined his plans for the rice lands: crop burning, dawn raids, and death. "Death, death, death," he said. "A festival of death. This is a war of attrition," he said. "All possible supplies to the guerrillas must be destroyed."

Luis Carlos left the room. Outside, the sun was a murderous white ball in a sky one could swear was the bluest God ever made. In the distance, the sole mountain, Arayat, abode of spirits, hoisted its immense bulk out of the horizon. Luis Carlos's eyes misted and he slid down, folding his knees, his back against the barracks wall, and hugged his legs. The bells rang: silver notes of danger.

That night, he took pen in hand and, in his confusion, composed a letter to Clarissa. *There's no understanding this war,* he wrote, *I thought it was over but it seems that just as it had no beginning, neither shall it have an end. Find me a band, sister, and I will play again. I don't like having to kill children to feed your children. I don't like having too many murdered men in my dreams.* He couldn't know that Clarissa, with the letter in her hand, would revile her brother aloud for the spoiled sissy that he was, being so ready to lose chocolate bars, a good salary, a military rank, and an important connection. It was Pete who would take the letter and hide it among the oil miniatures, yellowing photographs, scorched letters, and odds and ends rescued from the Binondo ruins and now stashed away in the garage of their one-and-a-half bungalow, a neat, middle-class home paid for by Luis Carlos. He kept Luis Carlos's letter, ignorant of that moment in the future when it would reduce the musician's only child to such pity that she would swear never ever to become involved in any war at all, big or small, just or unjust; never, never at all. Neither did Pete know, when he began willy-nilly to ask about job possibilities for Luis Carlos, that he was starting the process by which the latter would be permanently exiled.

The truth was Pete would save Luis Carlos, for the day following his meeting with Jacobo Montreal a deadly duel commenced, masked by a seemingly friendly competition for Mad Uncle Ed's favors. Luis Carlos was at a disadvantage. Jake had the constant protection of his men who, singly and together, made him understand that his presence was not at all welcome. The opening salvo of the struggle came from Jake, as Luis Carlos expected. His water canteen was tampered with. But at the last minute, in the midst of an encounter with stray guerrillas, his throat parched with disgust, fear, and summer heat, as he raised the canteen to his mouth, a bullet had zinged through the air, punching a hole right through the thing. Smoke rose from the few drops that sprinkled his trouser leg while, on the ground, the spilled water hissed and steamed. It was battery acid and would have eaten away his lips, his tongue, his palate, his throat. The cruelty of it stunned Luis Carlos.

Jake's tent was always guarded by Amor, whose dog-grin flashed each time Luis Carlos passed by, on his way somewhere else it would appear, though the truth was he was waiting to catch the man by himself, to deliver that deadly chop to the nape's base he had learned years ago in the Saray forest. But no, neither in sleep nor awake was Jake ever alone. Two or three of his half-dozen men were always by his side. On the other hand, though it would have been an easier solution, Luis Carlos could not bring himself to lay the matter before Mad Uncle Ed. Not even when his tent was peppered with holes one rainy night or when his rations appeared dusted over with glass shards, or when he was set upon by two men the night he was careless enough to pee in the field outside the camp's perimeter. He kept counsel with himself, watched his back, and listened to the bells.

No one was more surprised than Mad Uncle Ed when a guerrilla unit they had thought demolished looped through the fields and assaulted the Nenas. Because the season's first typhoon, blowing in from over the Pacific, was in full fury, they had battened down their tents for the night and were already huddled in their regulation olive-green blankets when the whoomph of a mortar shell hitting the makeshift kitchen threw them to their feet. Luis Carlos, shirtless in his cot though still wearing his boots, lunged for the Coleman lamp, knocked it off its perch on his army duffle bag, and in the sudden darkness found his gun and his dagger. Crouching, he slipped out, pinpointed the general direction of the colonel's jeep, and slowly, letting his eyes grow accustomed to the intermittent flashes of explosions and lightning, began a careful half crawl, half run for the vehicle. He heard exuberant shouts and knew the guerrillas had pierced the temporary barricade of sandbags and barbed wire the soldiers had strewn about the camp that afternoon. In a few minutes, they would be overrun. Over the whine of bullets and soldiers' curses, he heard the kick of a motor and deduced that the colonel had reached the jeep. Bad luck for him. He had no recourse now except to make for the open fields and hope he survived long enough to be plucked by reinforcements. Still crouching, he pivoted and nearly keeled over when blue light burst overhead. A dozen paces to his right, a soldier spun three hundred sixty degrees before dropping, assuredly dead, face-down on the mud.

To his surprise, sandbags at the camp's rear had been pushed aside, the wires cut to make a passage. He hesitated, cocked his head for the bells, but there was only silence. Still careful, with the least noise possible, he slipped through and inched along on his haunches—a trick he had learned in his guerrilla years. He breathed easier when he felt the first sugarcane stalk before him. But something else was there—moving with thick animal gasps, stumbling among the sugarcane, frenetic in its haste. Not a guerrilla, he decided at once; they usually moved like greased shadows. Still, he was not prepared, when another lightning bolt came, for the sight of Jake hopping stupidly on one foot, his hands clutching wildly at the cane stalks. The man had lost his prosthesis and his walking cane. A single silver note echoed in Luis Carlos's ear and as he mulled over this incredible coincidence, wondering whether it was right to do in a helpless man, both wind and rain died abruptly, the storm's eye slid overhead, and to his stupefaction an orange moon, misshapen and strange, drenched the field with light. It was now or never. Almost automatically, his body poured forward, all tensile grace, in the learned reflex of his war years.

When he rose in Jake's path, cutting off his escape, the man yelled. But he was armed; Luis Carlos had not anticipated that, and for a minute the universe went still as he stared at the black hole of the gun barrel's mouth.

"Leave me alone, monster," Jake shouted, saliva spewing from his mouth, "my wife's about to give birth." Then, he grinned.

The silver note rang out again. And as the dagger's tip left Luis Carlos's fingers, its weight perfectly balanced in a flight straight and true, homing for Jake's neck, he felt a tremendous blow on his shoulder, a blow that snapped his body back. He was suddenly looking at the sky while somewhere near him a giant snake thrashed and writhed, snapping sugarcane stalks, crushing, it would seem, the very earth underneath. Luis Carlos lay back, and looked at the impossible moon. Sudden relief cocooned him, the same he had felt once before, when his hands, reaching upward, had touched the opposite banks of a warm black river through which, with a knife clenched between his teeth, he had swum stark naked. "I don't know why men kill," he said almost dreamily, addressing the body that still heaved, "nor why they betray. But if your child's you, then your fate is his as well." There was no helping it, he sighed to himself, and promptly lost consciousness.

It took a month for his bones to set though the round scar on his chest and back marking the bullet's passage would remain. Mad Uncle Ed had given him up for dead and, indeed, Luis Carlos would have perished in the storm had not a peasant boy, already called Guevarra by his friends, found him. Whatever he thought of the scene he came upon—the corpse with the knife in its gullet, Luis Carlos covered with blood, his clavicle broken—he kept to himself. It sufficed that he bound Luis Carlos's wound and with the help of reluctant friends, all young orphans like him, he had constructed a makeshift stretcher on which they had taken turns dragging him, none too gently for he was still a soldier, to the highway where they flagged down a bus and convinced the driver to take the wounded man to Angeles City's military camp. Here, Mad Uncle Ed, his own body threatening to disassemble at any minute, accepted the delivery and hustled him off to the camp hospital. Later, it was all Luis Carlos could do to dissuade him from searching for the kid or kids—"to do them justice," as he said. Jake was dead and would be buried with full honors. His woman had disappeared. "She wasn't married to him, anyway," the colonel said, "not entitled to his pension." He winked.

It was at the hospital that Pete's letter found him and Luis Carlos wept with gratitude at the news of a job possibility. When Uncle Ed came again, hurrying him to get to his feet, Luis Carlos asked to be released from his commission. "I want to attend to my life," he said and Mad Uncle Ed, exasperated at his stubbornness, finally agreed. The guerrillas were on the run, anyway. The rebellion was broken and it was time for young men like Luis Carlos to enjoy themselves. "Make yourself some money, son," he said, as he heaved himself to his feet. "Though I don't know what for, you die just the same. Well, Amor can ride in the jeep with me." He patted Luis Carlos's right shin and left.

Thus it was that one afternoon, with his bags and his saxophone, flute, and clarinet cases, Luis Carlos stood on a Manila pier and gave Pete, Clarissa, and their three children farewell kisses. Docked behind him, waiting it seemed for this severing of his ties to the city, was a luxury liner, on which he and his fellow band members would make music as it plied the shipping lanes of the Pacific. Luis Carlos gave a last look at the Manila skyline, the melody of "Lovely Stranger" in his head. Already, new buildings shielded the war's relics and, even as he watched, trucks carting away rubble rushed toward the city dump. Nothing, it seemed, not even a spasm of memory, would bring those terrible years back.

"Don't forget to write," Clarissa said. "And come for Christmas and Lent and—whatever."

He nodded. In that instant, all the remaining church bells rang out, the city hall clock struck six, and the ship belched thrice. Luis Carlos picked up his bags and embraced his sister a last time, certain that, as he would never write another song again, neither would he return to the Ever Loyal and Ever Noble City of Manila.

He was wrong. Just once more, two years later, before his final voyage as ash and bits of bone in a porcelain urn, Luis Carlos came back, bringing a most exquisite creature, the last Chinese girl to be foot-bound in the world, sixteen years old and seven months pregnant with his child. She was a creature of despair, raised on hallucinations of the impending collapse of China's new government and the return of the Manchu emperors, trained by her obsessed grandmother in the subtle but totally useless arts of a court lady. She spoke nothing but pure Mandarin, imperial in its precision of grammar and pronunciation. Her meeting with Luis Carlos had been heralded by a laughter of bells, the very last time Luis Carlos would hear them, as he strolled one late afternoon through a Kowloon side street with its unspeakable tenements and flea-sized restaurants, its scabbed she-dogs with teats grazing the pavement. She had fallen out of a narrow doorway into his arms, quite literally, in her panic and confusion as her grandmother lay felled by a massive thrombosis in the tiny room upstairs. How she had managed the stairs, Luis Carlos would never understand, but he had understood her cries, the mad music of her speech, for he spoke Mandarin by then, and, taking her by the hand, seeing her pitifully tiny feet, he fell completely and irrevocably in love.

He buried her grandmother in the old custom and married her, giving as his wedding gift the diamond-and-emerald earring another beauty had handed to him many years ago. He had found it intact in his old tuxedo's breast pocket, where it had rested through all the war years—a garment Pete had carefully kept safe, believing Luis Carlos would find use for it again as a musician. It was fitting, this transfer of the artifact, from one beauty to another beauty—and though Luis Carlos did not realize that the stone had come from his grandmother's necklace, a rare joy, as pure as any he had ever felt, touched him when his wife dropped the earring into her antique jewel box, her grandmother's only legacy: a curious miniature Chinese pirate chest, inlaid with flowers of soapstone and filled with gold hair ornaments, pearl clasps and necklaces, combs studded with red and green stones, rings and earrings and even a gold shoe buckle. These were supposed to be the granddaughter's implements for her assault on the Manchu court, if and when it reascended to power.

She had learned well, even Luis Carlos had to admit on his wedding night. Though he himself excelled, taking her nine times in twenty-four hours, it was she who led him to paths of exquisite tenderness, curving her body around and about him, her little sighs as murmurous as caterpillars' songs, her fingers, the inner skin of her thighs, as fluid in their touch as water, until Luis Carlos could almost believe that the rest of the world had disappeared and the bed they lay on was a skiff adrift on a wayward current, floating between unknown lands of smells which, wafting round and about them, nestled between her toes, in the twin skinfolds under her breasts, and in her armpits. Lightly, to the singsong of her language, she stroked the calluses off Luis Carlos's soul until he shivered in his nakedness and lying on her, beside her, under her, in her, he let loose his first-ever cry of happiness and passion.

They were never to be happy again. Her confrontation with reality failed to enlighten her, to Luis Carlos's chagrin. Everything about it—the noise, the number of people, the speed of traffic, the abundance of goods and the cacophony of half a dozen languages—merely confused and frightened her, driving her deeper into her inherited dreams of order and ceremony. She would lie the whole day on the silk-upholstered settee of Luis Carlos's apartment, her swathed feet on a pillow; with all the window curtains drawn, she would open her jewel box, would run her treasures through her fingers over and over again. When she became pregnant, Luis Carlos's mention of a doctor so terrorized her that by the time he came home, he found her with her hands clinging to the settee's back, as though she was about to be bodily dragged outside. It was an impossible situation. He had a month's contract to play in Tokyo and could neither leave her to her devices nor abide her constant distress. Finally, he convinced her to sail with him to Manila, barely managing to do so by lying through his teeth, saying all the Emperor's relatives resided in splendid exile in the city.

Clarissa, of course, was thrown into hysteria by the prospect of caring for a stranger who could not speak a single comprehensible word. "What do you expect me to do?" she shouted at her brother, thrusting her own swelling belly at him. Worse, her own loudness compared to the Chinese girl's fragility scared her. She was convinced the girl would break in her hands somehow, like one of those painted, empty eggshells one didn't dare hold too tightly. As usual, it was Pete who allayed her fears, and soothed the girl's own panic by leading her to the sofa from which she would never stir again. He assured Luis Carlos that everything would be fine. The latter, relieved, stayed long enough to hire a maid for his wife, purchase a layette for his child, and check out the city's nightclubs before taking a plane back to Hong Kong. Three months later, Pete phoned him for the good and the bad news: his daughter was fine but his wife had died.

"How're her feet?" Luis Carlos said after a while.

Mystified, Pete answered: "They're still bandaged."

"My daughter's? Who did that? Take it off at once."

"No, your wife's. Your daughter's feet are fine. Small."

"Holy bananas, she's inherited—"

"No, no, no," Pete cut in, "they're tiny. She's only a baby. She can't have full-size feet."

"Oh my poor, poor, poor—"

"No, her feet are fine! Five toes, good arches!"

"—anachronism."

A silence. Pete realized Luis Carlos was crying.

"What do you want me to do?" he asked gently after a while.

"What? What the hell does one do with a corpse? Bury it. Wait. You know any Chinese?"

"Tons. All the corner stores are owned by them."

"Ask one—ask one to help you. My poor, poor—. Pete, buy her a plot in the Chinese cemetery, a good one. I'll send you the money. I'll send you all my money. I don't need anything anymore. Is she pretty?"

"A little pale. The undertaker hasn't worked on her yet. But she will be, with makeup and lipstick."

"No!" Luis Carlos shouted. "My daughter. My baby. Is she pretty?"

Pete hesitated. "Uh—yes. No. Can't tell yet. She's newborn. All wrinkled and with tiny hands and feet."

"Oh, the poor thing. And I can't leave, I can't—"

"Clarissa wants to name her Maya."

"No. No. Something else. Let's see—first letter, A. Anna. Anna. Maybe she'll be the start of better things. Anna. The poor, poor—"

He hung up. Pete, who had borrowed a neighbor's telephone, for phones were still scarce in the city, walked home bemused by Luis Carlos's question. Was she pretty or not pretty, this Anna? In his simplicity, he made straight for the crib, bothered by his inability to answer Luis Carlos's query, and checked. The baby lay quiet, with eyes closed, fists clenched, and toes curled. It had been an obstinate birth, sixteen hours of labor wracking the slim bones of the Chinese girl, while the hapless midwife, whose presence had driven the girl into the most horrible screams, tried to staunch the blood seeping between the girl's thighs, soaking the newspaper wads under her buttocks. To make matters worse, once out, the baby refused to cry, despite the many whacks on her haunches, merely frowning in anger and jerking her arms and legs. Finally, the midwife had given up. The child was breathing normally and, having dressed her in the delicate little silk shirt and diapers Luis Carlos had bought, the midwife laid her down on the crib. "What dreadful stubbornness," she said to Pete.

But was she pretty? They would never find the correct answer, both yes and no being too imprecise, in the years to come, even to the last day when she left them, cradling her father's saxophone, for her husband's home. And because they couldn't quite define her, they forgot her even as she was growing up, cared for by a nanny paid by Luis Carlos and left to her own devices in the garage which Pete had refurbished as a nursery. It was not that Clarissa or Pete neglected her. It was more like the child saw to it that nothing beyond necessary attention was given her. From the very beginning, contrary to the elusive answer to Luis Carlos's question, she was a creature of precision, crying at specific hours, give or take a few minutes, for her food, sleeping in between.

Such self-will in a baby bothered Pete. He bought her a radio which every morning he would turn on, keeping the volume down, and turn off at night. He did not know what good that did her, though, after a time, Anna's nanny reported that the child seemed to rest better whenever she tuned in to the Spanish broadcast in the morning, the English one in the afternoon. She herself spoke only Tagalog, of course, and busied herself with cleaning the room, washing Anna's clothes, and helping Clarissa with her increasing brood.

Pete checked on the child at least once a day, taking note as well of the garage's contents, for it would not do to have anything stolen. Not that there was anything of value among the remnants of the Binondo house. Nothing at all. Even the Chinese girl's treasure box had contained junk jewelry. He had taken the precaution of having two pearl necklaces appraised but they were simply paste, of all the rotten luck. Thus, assuming the same for all, he missed the diamond-and-emerald earring which would catch Anna's eye when she was but ten years old and which she would secrete away, until in her twenty-seventh year she had a sudden need to purchase something from Hong Kong and pawned the jewel.

As it was, the years passed calmly, with Pete doing both magic and surgery, Clarissa getting pregnant and giving birth with tedious regularity, and Luis Carlos's checks arriving every first of the month. There was a tense moment when Pete had considered joining the army because there was a war overseas in which all good men were supposed to join, but Clarissa had a fit and there was no helping it, he stayed at home. In due time, that disturbance calmed down as well, though another war was brewing, but Pete had no inkling of it and by the time it became full blown he was too old to be a warrior.

They lived simply, preferring to forget the past, and even the strange child fitted into that simplicity. Until, of course, one morning, as Clarissa stood in the kitchen, debating whether to plug or not plug in Luis Carlos's most recent gift, the first-ever electric stove in the city, not sure she would not be electrocuted, die on the spot, and burn the house down to boot—she had the plug in her hand and was inching it toward the wall socket when she felt a most unnatural silence fall on the house, light itself turning diaphanous, and every-thing—wall, kitchen counter, window, and sink—was suddenly bathed in a nacreous shimmer, so that Clarissa thought she had awakened into a dream moment, a moment filled with this presence, a presence that stood behind her and watched as her hand advanced, pulled back, advanced again with that ugly plug and its equally ugly diagonally striped black-and-white cord. She whirled around, nearly pulling the stove off the counter. In the doorway was the child and Clarissa was suddenly guilt-stricken at the thought of how they had neglected her, not exactly neglected, but paid no attention, so that they had even forgotten to have her hair trimmed, letting it grow undisturbed since her birth, that blue-black hair falling in successive curls to the child's hips as she stood there, in her tiny denim overalls and bare feet, one hand on the wall as though she did not trust her sense of balance yet. Then, to Clarissa's utter fright, the child, who had been so silent for so long they suspected she was retarded, opened her mouth and said:

"It was morning when the Spanish long boats sailed from Cebu to Mactan." She paused, looked thoughtful, and went on: "Everything in this country happens in the morning."

Shocked, Clarissa could only ask: "Why?"

And the child replied: "Because it is a country of beginnings."

She giggled while the strength went out of Clarissa's knees and she oozed to the floor.

That was how they discovered that between the radio and the stock of memorabilia in the garage, Anna had taught herself to speak and read Spanish, English, and Tagalog. More than that, by prodigious deduction, she had learned the identities of everyone in the oil minia-tures, old photographs, and unfinished sketches. She could name Maya, and Mayang, Carlos Lucas and Luis Carlos, the child Clara, and even a hitherto anonymous oil of a Spaniard dressed as a Capuchin, though she insisted that one portrait was missing or had never been done and thus the family line was incomplete. Pete was delighted and considered letting her join his show, suspecting she could tell the future. Futile hope, alas; she knew only the details of the past and could prattle endlessly about the Four Roses Gin and the wedding at Casa Español but went mute whenever she was confronted with questions about the morrow. This phase lasted many months until one of her cousins, a girl of eight, hating the excitement about this strange girl, the sight of her at the dinner table under the scrutiny of Pete and Clarissa, slipped into the garage while Anna's nanny was helping with the laundry in the backyard and, seizing the girl by the hand, hissed into her face to shut up about grandmothers and grandfathers and boats in the sky, and shoved her into a closet.

They did not find her until four hours later. Those hours of darkness must have traumatized the poor soul, for since then, though Clarissa and Pete bombarded her with questions, she could only repeat:

"Everything in this country happens in the morning."

The Book of Revelations

The Book of Revelations

1

The tally, by the second day of the Festival, was twenty thousand bottles of beer, five thousand bottles of gin (the Archangel), a thousand-odd bottles of wine, whiskey, rum, etc., consumed, along with a veritable lava of food, not to mention rooms occupied, souvenirs purchased, plane and ship fares paid. The number ricocheted back and forth, across the governor's dining room, over steaming cups of coffee, platters of ham, bacon and eggs, and bread slices—numbers which were doubled and tripled by accountants on both sides of the table, the governor's and Adrian's father's; which didn't help his headache any nor the conviction that he had misplaced half of his mind the previous night. Speculations of wealth this early, premised on the construction of the resort, were not to Adrian's liking.

He had awakened to sunlight behind the lace curtains of french windows in a strange bedroom. He was naked beneath the sheets. The discovery was unsettling enough to make him keep still, his eyes scanning the room for his clothes, a familiar object, a clue perhaps, but finding only the disquieting pattern of the curtains' greenish shadows on the floor, on the edge of the bed, and on the back of his left hand. He knew this wasn't an altogether strange situation; enough tales from his male friends told him that as much could be expected after all-night binges and while it had been hilarious in the telling, it was no longer as amusing now that it was happening to him. He had belched, his stomach muscles bunching painfully, and tried to dredge up an image—any image—of what had transpired the night before. Then, this girl had materialized in the doorway, breakfast tray in hand, and he had to search his memory for a name to fit the face framed by bangs, hair cut so short it slithered away whenever she inclined her head, showing off her cheekbones. When she laid the tray on the dresser bench, pushed it toward him, snatched a pack of cigarettes off the vanity, shook one loose, and lit it with a silver lighter, he knew he did not know her at all. Laughing, she had informed him she was the governor's daughter, this was her bedroom, and their betrothal—Adrian's and hers—was being worked out in the dining room below, between his father and hers. Adrian's headache had started then. He had shooed her away, found his clothes, and dressed, nursing his tender belly. Then he had made his way downstairs.

There were too many soldiers. Appearing singly or in pairs at various doorways, their presence seemingly accidental, their inspection of the scene within casual. But Adrian would feel their eyes rest on his being, inevitably, at the end of an arching glance about the room. Too many soldiers, in combat uniform, gun belt, ammo pouches, M-16s. Now and then, a man in white showed up with them; his eyes, too, reached for Adrian—an intent, studying look that always ended when he looked back.

Abruptly, he pushed his chair back, ignoring the startled faces of the others. He walked to the windows—more curtains—and catching hold of a fluttering, serrated cloth edge, drew it back. Instantly, his eyes closed. The light was too strong. He blinked, eased himself back before looking again. In the distance, leaf-slim boats sailed a sea of molten gold and sapphire. It was morning yet. The thought broke

over him, a wave of joy. There was enough time. Time enough to find
Anna and end the Festival.

She was as snagged by morning as he was, seeing the town roofs fluted
with gold, the yellow flash on a seagull's wing. Morning; her hand in
Eliza's hand. Eliza whose beauty as usual drew its own audience.
Children this time, open-mouthed, now and then bending their heads
to take counsel with each other, wondering who she was—a movie
star, perhaps; a town official's wife. Their voices, snatched by the
wind, carried to her, though they maintained their distance. Tiny
gurgles of laughter, small mouthfuls of words. Quite clearly now, she
heard herself as she had once sounded, her own child's voice, clear
as harp notes: *It was morning when the Spanish long boats sailed from
Cebu to Mactan.* And another voice, older but still a child's: *forget!*
What was there to forget, she asked the other. It was nothing more
than a fact, learned by rote if not by heart. The long boats did sail
from Cebu to Mactan on a morning of beginnings.

Just like the morning she stood among the wreckage of her home,
thinking she had awakened to step into another dream, the living
room, the broken furniture, the smashed vases and ashtrays bathed by
a nacreous light so intense she was convinced nothing was solid,
everything was color and shadow. No more. Even the soldiers who
poured in through the doorway, past the door hanging half off its
hinges, were no more than a pattern of forest shadows pouring in,
splitting into two, surrounding her. The sense of unreality was such
she had to stretch a hand to the sofa, expecting her fingers to go
through the blue upholstery. But another hand, hard, skeletal, intercepted her hand. She was caught. Terror drew one sharp gasp from
her. That was all. It was morning again and she was at the Festival,
her hand stroked by Eliza.

With an effort, she brought her mind back to Amor. If she could
find the house of the gun shipment, find it, trace Rafael, she could—
She jerked her hand from Eliza's grasp.

"I have to find—"

"—Adrian!" Eliza cut in. "We've forgotten him. We have to find him."

She pulled Eliza down, seating her on the grass. "Stay," she said. "I'll find him. You wait here. Wait." And ignoring her friend's protest, she walked away, stepping carefully among the dancers lying on the grass, felled by tiredness and the sun's heat. A few waved, called, asked her to stop by and share a drink but she ignored them. She jumped over the low cement hedge separating the lawn from the sidewalk and plunged into the Festival.

Two hands wrapped themselves immediately about her waist. She was lifted off her feet, arched in the air, and set down again. She had barely time to bow her thanks to the stranger before her right arm was hooked and she was dancing, borne along by the current and the drums. "Drink, love," said a young man with bloodshot eyes, his mustache quivering. "Drink." She sipped at the bottle, handed it back, and found six more being offered. Not to give offense, she took a sip from each, shutting her mind to the taste. Beer and gin and rum and Coke and whatnot. She would round the plaza, keeping an eye out for anything remotely familiar. A doorway, an alley, a gap between the houses.

A commotion behind her. The crowd parted for twelve young men, marching, bottles in hand, boisterous with a newly invented song. *Ferdinand Magellan, the crazy old coot; took five ships and circumcised the globe* . . . On and on, the refrain winding through the story of the sea of typhoons, rhythm stamped out by feet pounding the asphalt as the men pranced first on one foot, then the other, yelling about the boats and ships and the men on the shore one morning. Anna laughed, couldn't stop laughing at the mangled history. She remembered: visions given her by printed words, by sensuous chants, women's voices wailing in her sleep to the tinkling of gold anklets. One morning a long, long time ago. She pressed the young man's arm against her body, raised a bottle to her lips, forgot the action, and looked at the sky instead. The sun entered her eyes. The Spanish long boats did sail from Cebu to Mactan, one early morning when the archipelago's song was just beginning, in a still-young world of un-

charted seas where already the possession of seven thousand one
hundred islands was a passion which would not yield even tiny Mactan, though the Portuguese Magellan, with his Spanish flags, threatened and stomped his feet in rage; the young chief Lapu-lapu
wouldn't allow such a travesty and in the heat rush of blood that was
the archipelago's song, he lined the shores with half-naked men and
dared the Spanish cannons, fighting desperately, with the rage of his
love, until he skewered that poacher-vagabond Magallanes (she shivered; death at the beginning) while typhoons scattered Spanish expe-
ditions and sent men scurrying into monasteries to escape the terror
of memory, the sea of storms, until the Spanish king tricked Fray
Andres de Urdaneta out of church walls and threw him aboard another ship, this time with Miguel Lopez de Legaspi and Martin de
Goiti who burned Manila's palisades, erecting forever in this part of
the globe the memory of the good ship *Victoria* and the eighteen men
who survived the Magallanes expedition, the first to circumnavigate
the earth, while De Goiti impregnated women of the northern shores
and more besides, in punitive excursions inland, into the legendary
kingdoms of Luzon, and his offspring would grow up, through four
hundred years, to become the most beautiful women on earth, blood
confused, diluted with the semen of all races, Chinese, Malay, Indian,
British, not to mention the *norte americano* who came, led by Commodore George Dewey, with cannons blazing, sending to the sea
bottom of its own hallucinations the Spanish fleet, where it still lies,
visible through blue-green fathoms with the sea like a piece of glass
from a cathedral window. So it began—the islands' confusion over
language and memory, so that in this Festival of commemoration
there remained no more than this mangled song, as ridiculous as those
tiny English classes where little brown boys, their minds stuck between the pages of the English-Pilipino-Spanish dictionary, stood up
and announced to their New England Baptist teachers, a gift from
Arthur MacArthur, a man whose forefathers were so besotted with
themselves they had to name him with his name twice over, boys
standing up to announce that the melancholy Portuguese-Spaniard
had circumcised the globe, that son-of-a-goat; making no distinction

between the girding of the earth and the girding of one's instrument
of manhood which every full-blooded son of the archipelago underwent in the twelfth summer of his life, with the old man herbalist
choosing a guava branch for chopping board and spitting chewed-up
leaves and roots on the bloody wound while the boys twisted their
faces against the pain, minds flashing through a litany of curses in half
a dozen languages, and could hardly keep still for the splat of poultice
on their tools before rushing off to the river, there to wash themselves
in some recollection of a baptism at the font which in turn was
another recollection, going back to the river Jordan, and before that,
much much older, going back to immersion in the river Ganges. Thus
it was that one entered maturity through pain, the boys with their
wounds, the girls jumping down steps to set the duration of their
blood cycles, young minds already twisted by the many histories to be
learned, beginning with the *barangays,* large canoes which brought
the first exiles to the archipelago, Malays fleeing persecution, their
boats hugging the shores of peninsular Southeast Asia to reach these
islands, known now in English as the pearl of the Orient seas, pearls,
my ass (she muttered, giggling), if pearls were green, possibly, in a blue
sea, that sea where the children, sometimes girded about the loins,
often naked, called out for coins tossed by the visitors aboard ships
cruising the tamed sea; they would dive, true as fins, after the shimmer
of money, catching coins with their teeth, bobbing up again like
buoys, the coins flashing in their hands in triumph. Or where there
was no sea, up in the mountains, they stood at the edge of precipices,
calling for money, no, not really money, but for a chance to exhibit
their loveliness, their swift, sharp grace, their precise eyes as they
marked where the coins fell, thrown by tourists who raised cameras
in anticipation as the children plunged into the abyss, leaping from
rock to rock, toes prehensile as monkeys', bodies held from death by
sprigs of fir and tendrils of *cadena de amor.* How wise and beautiful
were those faces, eyes brown enough to seem black, heads of hair
bleached red-brown by the sun, truly beautiful even when they were
just staring at the city while resting atop the gapped walls of Intramuros, watching men and women promenade through the rebuilt

romance of another age, through the Gate of Isabela, to cobbled walks and gaslight where the air was a compound of seawind and jasmine breath and perfume, how Manilans loved perfume, the city covering itself in all the world's odors, a trace of yesterday in the scent of horseshit, today in carbon monoxide, and tomorrow in the gaseous spit of the stars, their simultaneous presence a testament to the existence of possibilities, where one could choose one's own amiable time, even such a time when the world was young and women were named Maya, or Miss Estela, women so loved that an embrace of them went beyond the body, went beyond even the now, and, understanding all through a four-hundred-year-old song, accepted all, past, present, and future, and the seven thousand one hundred islands of a fractured history.

Surely that couldn't be diminished, notwithstanding this Festival of drunks, misfits, and aliens (once more love, about the plaza, which is all that's left of our world) staggering about in a parody of celebration, no, no, no, couldn't be diminished, not by gin and rum and Coca-Cola, nor by losing one's self in the drum's rhythm, pounding the earth with one's feet, in a rage for oblivion, nor even by the shit and lies growing thicker each day as the Commander's proclamation of power entangled itself in letters of instructions, general orders and decrees, all intended to be part of the archipelago's constitution, said document growing fatter by the minute as more and more laws and bylaws came, all signed by one man who believed he could rule, regulate, manage, and control seven thousand one hundred shrapnels of a boisterous celebration of man, controlling these with one signature, it's a lot of bullshit, notwithstanding his men who together and singly have decided to speak in four-syllable words, becoming more confused and confusing each day, so that a new troop of servants had to be created to tote dictionaries and define each word for the rest of us who knew only the simple language of love, freedom, and life, the same that drove our forefathers to brave the monsoon, harness the trade winds, and settle along inhospitable shores, from whence sprung the generations of the god Bathala, created from wind and water and clay, so that the bones of the archipelagic man were held together by the breath of liberation and he could not be returned to the bamboo prison from which the islands' first man and woman came, bamboo being the only object which could ford the titan waves of the Great Flood of Gilgamesh. And if he dared touch the children, whose bones breathe the same breath, if he dared touch them, harm them, murder them—why, we would remember, we who awoke to find his curse woven in the barbed wires before our windows, held by the guards before our doors, in the cement walls which turned cold with each scream of pain wrung from a body of too vulnerable flesh, God, if there's one, don't let all of us die (the house! the house!), allow one to survive and wear down the eternity of the dictator; if he lives to a hundred, let us last a hundred and ten, long enough to spit on his grave and drown his corpse in the lagoon of our contempt; if he lives to two hundred, let us survive two hundred and ten, just long enough to fertilize the gardens with the shit of his memory; and if he's thinking of living through his sons' sons, allow us to outlive them all, just for the pleasure of being alive when he dies, before we bury him in the amnesia of our relief at his passing. After that, why, after that, there will be time for everything, time to lift this drink to one's lips, time even to turn our faces to the sun's fragrance in the unbearable fragility of this country's morning.

In the Festival of memory, all Eliza could remember was how her mother, the Hansen woman as she was known then, would watch without rancor the final exit of the last lover. Then she would run to her upstairs bedroom, fling open the window shutters, and lean her torso out, her arms spread open as though to gather in the hour, the day. She would murmur, *oh now, we have to do something; something has to be done; something, something . . .* She never discovered the nature of this obligation, which, undischarged through the years, now roosted on Eliza's shoulders. All the younger Hansen could think of was to wait. Wait. The word remained, an immovable boulder at the bottom of her befuddlement. She straddled the low cement hedge, her eyes passing from one soldier's face to another, soldiers in combat

uniform. There were too many; six about her now, four more over
there; a flash of the same olive-green and ocher colors at street corners
and intersections. The soldiers near her held out hip flasks and bottles,
inviting her to partake. *Drink,* said one, *and be merry for tomorrow
you die.* His English was heavy, newforged. His remark, though,
amused him and he brayed with laughter, the beer bottle shaking up
and down with each guffaw. Eliza took his offering, wiping the bottle's
mouth with her shirt's hem. The others pummeled the lucky one's
shoulders, poking his ribs. Eliza drank, her eyes squinting against the
sunlight. It was still morning. Time enough. Wait. *Come dance,* said
the chosen soldier, grown bolder now. She shook her head; she had
to wait. Wait. Such a trust should not be betrayed.

"There are too many of you," she said.

We have to be here, they said.

"Why?"

But they turned from her, elusive now, shrinking into their dark
brown skins, their uniforms. Just then, the crowd roared. She lifted
her eyes and saw how, beneath the town hall clock, which was permanently set at six o'clock, a half-dozen men had appeared, dressed in
the formal *barong* shirt of embroidered pineapple fiber and black
pants. They paused on the top step, waiting, too, it seemed, for they
kept glancing over their shoulders toward the building's interior. Each
had one thing askew with his costume, in honor of the Festival: a
garland of seashells, a leaf instead of a flower on a collar, a purple scarf.
She recognized the mayor, the councillors, the provincial commander—the powers of K——. As one, the crowd below the steps retreated, creating an emptiness, a path running down the center of the
road through which the authorities would pass. It was the promenade.

Another roar. From the shadows of the building's pillars came a
woman, in a fuchsia, ankle-length gown with butterfly sleeves, a
matching parasol held above her head by a male flunky. She paused,
holding out her face—that face of one perfect, flesh-tinted oval, with
deep black wing eyebrows, blue-tinted lids, mascaraed lashes, and a
red, impeccably etched mouth. As a concession to the Festival, a
perfect red heart had been stenciled on her left cheek. She held it out,

that face, like a banner of challenge and from below, from the men and women straining against an invisible barrier, came a responding roar. Whether of approval or rage, it was impossible to tell. Then, slowly, she came down the steps to precede the menfolk on the promenade. The Commander's wife. Behind her, the flunky kept a precise distance and, behind him, the town authorities. Eliza, watching the boiling at the back of the crowd, wondered what kept them from spilling over, from filling up that emptiness. Tradition, habit, fear? She didn't know. She knew though it needed but one person to cross that divide, to violate the sanctity of authority, for all of them to be in the middle of hell.

*A*drian suffered the hiss of his father's anger. In the foyer of the governor's mansion, with the voices within muted by walls, he kept his face still even as his father thrust his own face forward, his nose six inches away from Adrian's nose, and called his name. *Adrian, Adrian!* He shook his head, said no once, twice, then repeatedly as the whisper turned insistent, words cascading. *Adrian, Adrian!* He said no again. *You're the only grandson,* his father said, keeping his voice low. Adrian shook his head.

"In these times, we need protection," his father said finally. "We do not have political power."

The words were separate, distinct, each given its full weight. His father sighed. He stepped back, passed a hand over his face, cupped his mouth and chin, and eyed Adrian. Adrian shook his head. He could not trust his voice. His father was calling on his allegiance.

"In that case"—his father turned toward the inner doorway— "wait here."

He was back shortly, pushing Julius before him, Julius who smiled sheepishly, foolishly, at Adrian.

"He'll tell you," his father said before ducking back into the living room.

"Friend, why not?" Julius asked.

"It's not possible," Adrian replied, offended by the other's knowledge of a family problem.

"Because of the—? She's . . ." He groped for a word. "Pretty?" He made a face. "Passable?" Another grimace. A glance at Adrian's impatient face. "Vivid. Truly vivid. Reminds me of that, uh, transcendental girl, your old passion. Though come to think of it, she resembles the Hansen woman somewhat. Now, that other one. I can understand that one, *pañero*. I can appreciate that one." He whistled.

But Adrian had stopped listening. Vivid. The right word, he thought; vivid. With her blue-black hair which, when loosened, fell to her hips, a sight rarely seen; and her skin of impossible colors, golden where it had not been touched by the sun, dark brown in the exposed areas. Her face—he remembered Transcendental suddenly, moon of disasters, and flinched with regret at his own words of denial. What did that have to do with him, he had asked. Her face. A cross between Transcendental's (what was her name?) and Eliza's.

"I see you never caught it, friend," Julius was saying. "I knew it the minute I laid eyes on her. You're obsessed with a memory. Illusion. That's all."

Adrian glanced away. "You tire me, friend."

"But wait. A solution. Your father's right. A proper marriage, a passionate side dish. Who would know? Who would care? It wouldn't be the first such arrangement. Nor the last. For my sake, friend." He snickered.

"I said no."

"Never say no. Your family motto, friend. Stamped under the corporation's flag. Never say no. She—" He jerked a thumb toward the inner rooms. "She will agree."

"I say no."

"The other one won't agree? I bet you she will."

Adrian sighed. He placed a hand on Julius's shoulder, squeezed the flesh beneath the cloth. "Friend, you don't understand." He searched for the right words. "I say no. I won't agree. I have—I have room in my life for only one passion."

"Holy shit! That bad?" Julius stepped away from his grasp. "In that case, pal, you'd better know everything." And he held out a brown envelope.

"What's your stake in this?" Adrian asked, taking the envelope, turning it in his hands. It was sealed.

"A job in your corporation. Perhaps, public relations for the resort." He shrugged. "I'm not as rich as you are, Mr. Banyaga."

Adrian ripped the envelope open. Papers, stapled together, slid out. His eyes scanned the first words. Incredulous, he looked at Julius, who shrugged and lifted his hands, palms up. A gesture of helplessness.

"Your father thought you should know."

"And you, too, should know?"

Julius shrugged again. Then quietly, with more decency than Adrian was willing to credit him, he left. Adrian weighed the sheets of paper in his hand. It was a report on the interrogation of one subject, female, age twenty-five, by the name of Anna Villaverde. What did it have to do with him? At once, he cringed at the familiar words and heard his grandfather's creaking voice saying: *someday, we'll do away with the extraneous and confront the enemy.* The old man's laughter as he followed that with a question: *but what if the enemy is us?* Adrian dropped his eyes to the paper, willing himself to read slowly, not skipping a word of the quasi-scientific text, feeling its coldness seep slowly into his bones. The electric shock sessions; the water cure; sensory deprivation sessions; nights without sleep; days without food and water; the insane questions and answers; the psychiatric probes which had ruled out brute pain; the musical chair rapes . . . In the report's darkness, he searched for light, desperately, refusing to acknowledge his rising pity. A man could love only what he respected, not pitied. He should not have been told. Searched for and found it—the light!—in the report's last entry: *subject did not break; returned to Camp C——.* Truly, she was transcendental.

He flicked the pages over, throwing a pitying look at the direction of the voices within. He didn't know what to do now, not even with the report, which he shoved back into the envelope and carefully laid on the little marble-top table holding a vase of flowers. He was sure of only one thing. No one had the right to add to that nightmare. As he walked to the front door, he wondered vaguely, uneasily, whether he would draw the soldiers in his wake.

The house was empty. Only an upended Styrofoam icebox, marked with the Coca-Cola logo, remained, to one corner of the inner room. Nothing else to show that the place had once been occupied. The guerrillas were thorough. She scanned the floor, the walls, blinking her eyes to clear them of sunlight, of memory's vision. But there was nothing. Unwilling to admit failure, she walked out slowly. Perhaps there was a clue outside. A dislodged pebble, a twig bent in a certain direction, a flower growing where it shouldn't grow. The hidden language. She looked around carefully, going down the footpath slowly. Nothing. The path began to lose definition, its edges gnawed by weed clumps. A gray streak appeared. Sand edging in, widening as she moved away from the town, and spreading abruptly into a low dune. She climbed it, her foot slipping, her ears filling with the lapping of waves. She stopped, catching voices in the wind. They seemed far away, those voices, and she resumed walking. Suddenly, the sea was there—spread out flat and yet restless under a sky red-orange with sunset. She was surprised to see the sun so low. It had been morning just a while ago. It still felt like morning, with an impending vast stretch of time. Without end. But even as she thought this, seeing the ships docked nearly prow to prow, clustered to her left, the sun slipped, its flames rippling forward from the horizon. In that instant, the moon bodied forth from the sea, pale orange, full. She was transfixed; the sun and moon, nearly of equal dimensions, shoulder to shoulder at the horizon. She inclined her head, half expecting a raucous cockcrow, but instead, the voices came—the irrepressible singing of three girls who ran, holding their skirts' hems up, strands of their hair floating in the sea wind. Their bare feet marked the wet sand. They ran up to her, passed her, hardly acknowledging her presence, leaving her but a few words of their song: *Ferdinand Magellan, the crazy old coot; took five ships* . . . And came to a full halt a few yards away, in some enigmatic understanding of what was right.

They let go of their skirts abruptly, spilling what they had collected to the sand: seashells, coral bits, plastic beads. They squatted then, chins on knees, and began to sift through their loot. Once more, compelled by a strange sense of rightness, their singing changed and Anna found herself listening to a song about boats sailing the heavens, one of which was carrying away the woman who said no, thanks but no thanks . . . Her knees sagged; she herself sank down. For she remembered, Lord, how she remembered, the memory that had been her birthright rising to reclaim her. The bells. The rain of harp notes. The woman screaming her way to death on a sofa, as noisy as her child was quiet. The magical nosegays and rabbits. Infinity's odor in a hot cup of cocoa. A monk's bones, torn from their crypt by the flood of '72, washed clean now by river currents. An omen come true. The tobacco stink of velvet skirts; the harsh scent of a distillery. Chains of female voices, emerging from the secret niches of her brain, linked her to the years, back, back, back, even to a time when the tinkle of gold anklets was a message, herald of a passing, one morning of beginnings in a still-young world of uncharted seas.

2

Sun and moon shone on Eliza who, at that instant, was wading, shoes in hand, pants rolled up, in another part of the beach. She had acquired a small backpack, a gift from her transvestite friend who filled it with all kinds of Festival knickknacks, strips of gayly colored cloth, a bottle of the local wine, saying that no woman as beautiful should be allowed to leave without mementos. Laughing, Eliza had traded a kiss for the things. Then, seized by feelings of aloneness, she had run away, cutting through the dancing. There was no place save the shore for her mood. The town was too noisy. Thus, she was on time to witness that terrifying moment when sun and moon nearly touched. She fell to her knees, forgetting the waves, and lifted her face to the twin light's benediction. The waves splashed against her chest, soaking her, spraying her cheeks, her hair, but she did not flinch, waiting until the two orbs strayed apart—one sinking, the other rising.

It was, she thought, an omen and her witnessing it had been no accident.

It was a pestilential sight, the Loved One thought, catching a glimpse of it through an open window he did not dare approach. He remained instead in the room's center and watched, hands clasped behind him. From the rooms below and all about him, the noise of his sanctuary's demolition rose. He mouthed a curse. Because of that stupid goat Adrian Banyaga, he would have to face the dark. The sun and moon, now, together in the sky, boded no good, as far as he was concerned. He would have liked to go to the window, lean his hands on the sill, and examine the phenomenon. But that would not do at all, not at all. The memory of one night was still fresh. One evening when, as was his wont, he had had himself driven to his mistress's house—that stupid, silly woman whose hysterics afterward had provoked that unfortunate gun-butt blow on her skull top—for an hour of release. The doorbell had rung. Luckily, his aide, a lieutenant of the same height and build as Amor, had opened the door, only to be saluted by six .32-caliber bullets discharged right into his face. Rest in peace. Since then, Colonel Urbano Amor stayed away from open windows and doors. The enemy was always on the prowl outside. He had gotten rid of the mistress as well. What remained of her, anyhow, with her twitching hands, dragging leg, and drooling mouth. He had had his wife taken away, too, that sterile female bonded to him by law. She was on a small uninhabited island now, in the north, guarded by soldiers, surrounded by luxury. It would take a destroyer to assault that fort.

Not that he cared, stupid woman that she was. But it would not do to give the enemy the satisfaction of touching anything remotely his. He had no doubts they would try. Sooner or later, it did not matter. They would—for he himself had no compunction about touching what was even remotely theirs.

They, theirs, the enemy. He disliked the vagueness of those words. He needed a face (faces), a name (names), a body (bodies) of flesh and blood. An identity (identities) he could hook his claws into and dissect into information. Growing angrier by the minute, he stared back at the sun and moon, wishing it was the day's beginning instead of the end, so he could pursue her. Her face swam upward behind his eyes: the firm, smooth cheeks, the hazel eyes, the small, succulent mouth with its hint of corruption, the fair skin. An asset. He could let her loose among more powerful men and siphon off their strengths, using her, though she would be of full use only if she agreed. And she would agree only if she let go of her stupid vestiges of sentiment. Friendship, duty, obligation. These people never changed, he told himself, the words echoing a familiar thought. They still believed labels sufficed to confer a value on the intangible. Amor sighed; he made a mental note to speak to the Commander. Language had to be changed; names had to be changed; places had to be re-baptized; all moral and ethical signposts eradicated. Call the sun, the moon; the moon, the sun and no one would be able to find his way out of confusion's labyrinth without guidance. He, Colonel Urbano Amor, shall guide the way. He would be the truth, the way, the life. He smiled at this relic of his past. But how pleasant the thought was. The truth, the way, the life.

His brow knitted. It was a pestilential sight, nevertheless, boding no good for the morrow's undertaking. He would have to take a sleeping pill tonight but no—the stupid governor would wait for him, together with the town mayor and the provincial commander, stupid one and all. He jerked back, straining his shoulders, feeling the very air restraining him. Of all the stupid luck, she had to be a stupid officer's mistress. Batoyan, the stupid, whom Amor himself had approved to be the Commander's aide, precisely because of his stupidity. Now, he had to proceed slowly, carefully, for touching what was another officer's was frowned upon. The others would say he was getting too big for his breeches. They would mass against him. And working insidiously, relentlessly, they would strip him of his privilege and his protection, leaving him to the enemy outside. His shoulders strained again. He groaned—a terrible sound that momentarily stilled the commotion outside the room. Proceed carefully. With caution. And take full measure of this pestilential omen.

*A*drian knew it was coming, this conjunction of moon and sun. The children had told him. Squatting at a roadside food stall, driven by hunger to purchase two boiled plantains, he had peeled the brown soft skin back to reveal the steaming, golden flesh within. As he ate, thinking he had never had better food—or as right a kind of food at as right a moment—he returned the children's stare. A dozen of them surrounded him, keeping their distance, but intent upon him never-theless. Now and then, two would lean their heads together, take counsel from each other. Despite their care, his name slipped out from among the jumble of incomprehensible hisses and titters. *Adrian, Adrian.* He chewed calmly and when he finished the first plantain, he threw the skin at the nearest group of children. They scattered, screaming with laughter, but merely ran in circles and, like disturbed doves, returned when it was obvious he planned to go on eating. He peeled the second plantain. *Adrian, Adrian,* the children's voices whispered.

"Goddamn kids," he said to the old man vendor. "They know everything."

He rose, tossed the other banana peel toward the trees.

"You!" he called to the nearest child, a boy, barefoot, half-naked, his penis a fat brown worm. "What do you know?"

The boy grinned, showing missing front teeth. "Today, the sun and moon hold hands."

"Hold hands! Crazy. What does that mean?"

The boy glanced at the old man, who nodded. "It means tomor-row—" He collapsed into giggles, collected himself, and went on, struggling against laughter. "Tomorrow the sea will collect tribute. From the Festival!" The last was shouted. The boy fled.

"See," Adrian said. "They know everything."

The old man smiled. He, too, was missing his front teeth. "Will they be building the resort?"

Adrian shook his head in wonder. "You, too, brute?"

The old man shrugged. "Everything is known."

"And you read it off leaves, I bet. Listen, I don't know. And listen, I don't care."

He was thinking of Anna and Eliza and the problem of finding them among the two hundred thousand benighted creatures in the town. Find them before his father did, for he was sure the game was not over; traps were still being laid along his path. Old Andy, help! He called to his grandfather in his head, even as he moved down the road toward the town. Help. Bring the sun and moon together.

This was the moon's dominion now, its milk flooding the streets, house walls, and roofs, lapping like the tide at shadowed recesses, boles of trees, coconut fronds, licking the buntings overhead, the bamboo arches, and the electric poles. Men and women chased their shadows through the town, the Festival broken and scattered. Anna joined a stream of people heading for the wharf where the steel boats scurried between ships and shore, ferrying passengers. Coleman lamps had been strung along the pier and, by their unsteady light, the visitors formed a queue, steadying one another against wind gusts and the slickness of sand and salt water underfoot. From underneath the pier, darkness crawled up, retreated, bodied forth again, with each swaying of the strings of lamps. The noise was terrific. The uncertain footing lent a sense of adventure to the waiting and each tremor of the pier at the waves' impact set off a volley of shrieks and laughter among the passengers. Out in the sea, ship lights blazed—a beacon to ferryboats which carried their own Coleman lamps.

At the landward end of the pier, the noise was loudest. It was here that Anna saw Eliza, barefoot, shoes tied by their laces to her belt, a knapsack on her back. She was, by this time, in the queue's center, fixed in place by the woman in front and the man behind. She waved to Eliza, calling her just as another wave hurled itself against the pier. Anna slipped but the man behind caught her by a shoulder and steadied her. Glancing back, she saw Eliza veer away and head for the water, stopping now and then to dig her toes in the sand. Did she mean to swim to the ship? But Eliza went on pacing back and forth, stamping her feet, and after a while Anna realized she was trying to make escape canals for seawater trapped in sand furrows. Just then, the pier shuddered; a boat had scraped against its pillars. Screams. Laughter. The line was moving. Anna found herself staring down at the boat's bottom, a good four feet below. Two men stood there, their arms held upward. She was shoved forward and fell but the men caught her deftly, a little hard around her waist and ribs, but they set her on her feet gently enough, steadying her against the boat's swaying. She made her way forward. Despite the primitive way of loading, the boat was filled quickly—men and women standing on spread legs, some holding on to the boat's walls, others to one another. Crammed thus in the hold, Anna couldn't see whether Eliza had made it. She prayed she had boarded the right boat, that she would not find herself in a strange ship. She was hungry and exhausted.

By luck, it brought her to the proper ship. She climbed the rope ladder, pushed by hands from below, pulled by hands from above, so she had no time at all to think of falling. She reached the deck, gasping with relief. It was easy passage to her cabin, for the ship was half empty, most of its passengers having elected to stay on the island. In her cabin, she laid out clothes, soap, and towel, and was about to undress when someone knocked. It was a steward, with a message from Adrian. He was in the radio room and if she wanted to, she could join him. Otherwise, they would meet for dinner. She thanked the man, and locked the door carefully before unbuttoning her right sleeve and loosening the knife's cords. She thrust it under the pillow. Adrian was probably calling Manila. Business. He was always on business.

It was not that at all, he said to her later, looking hurt at this summary judgment. He had tried to contact his grandfather. But the connection kept failing. He thought he recognized the maids' voices in Old Andy's mansion, but there had been a painful sputter and the voices had waned, grown loud, waned again. Interference, the operator had said, probably from a nearby military base.

To Anna's relief, only a dozen or so couples were in the dining room, scattered among the tables. She and Adrian had been given the best location—beside the glass-paned windows through which the island lights were visible. "But what happened to you?" he asked. "I didn't see you the whole day."

"Nothing. Nothing unusual. Where did you go?"

"Here and there," he said, as careful as she was not to cause distress. "I wish we were on the way now—back. Back home."

"What will you do then? Make more money?" She laughed.

He picked up the menu, ran through the list quickly, found something for her and for himself. Then, having given their orders, he turned back to her, setting his arms on the table. Anna shifted in her chair.

"I want to go away."

She nodded.

"To Hong Kong maybe. Or Tokyo. Anywhere. I'm tired. For a month, at least. Two, maybe."

"What're you running from? Me?"

"I want you to come with me."

She was surprised. "What're you running from, Adrian?"

"Don't tease," he said. "I want you with me. I want you to—" He flushed. "Help me. I'm no good at this."

She shook her head. "I'm too old for you."

His hands clenched, unclenched. He had the impulse to throw himself on his knees.

"Really," she said. "Too old. You don't even know anything about me."

He opened his mouth but a spray of laughter fell on their heads. It was Eliza, soaked to the skin, waving her shoes.

"You abandoned me," she shrieked, sliding into a vacant seat at their table.

"Not true," said Adrian. "We held on to that chair for you."

"Uh-uh. The place is certainly crowded." She looked about the room mockingly. "But I had such great fun, running around with the transvestites. We danced ourselves silly."

"Good for you," Anna said.

"I met Colonel Amor, by the way." She said it easily enough, keeping her eyes on the centerpiece orchid and blade of fern. Something beautiful to shroud her lie. A movement across the table. Adrian had reached for Anna's hand, covering it with his fingers. Eliza, surprised, gave him a covert glance. He knew.

At Adrian's touch, Anna had looked at him as well. He knew. Though Adrian made no other move, his expression was eloquent. It was in the eyes, she thought; one could always tell.

"He's here because that son-of-a-goat Commander will be here tomorrow."

"Sssh! Keep your voice down." Anna picked up a spoon.

"Well, okay. That goat of a Commander. I don't know what for. But Colonel Amor's in charge of security—or security intelligence. I forgot what. He sends his regards. Most civilized of him, I should say." She felt the wet hair on her nape. "I should take a shower. You order for me, Adrian. I'll be back. And don't gossip about me while I'm gone."

It was done. Seamlessly. In her cabin, she slid the backpack off her shoulders to the bed. It was only after she had unzipped it and thrust in a hand to ferret among its odds and ends for the .22-caliber carefully wrapped by the transvestite that she noticed the envelope on her bed. A radiogram from Batoyan. His request for a leave of absence, having cleared the military's first level of command, was stuck somewhere in the intelligence division. *Wish you were here,* said the note. Eliza smiled. Silly old man. She raised the gun and sighted. Small, the transvestite had said, but sufficient at close range. Aim for the head. Or the crotch. Her hand shook. Sighing, she lowered the gun. There was no helping it, she thought. Amor would never let her go. He had said as much during their accidental encounter in a side street. It was just lucky she had danced before then and was sober enough when he had come up behind her, tapping her shoulder with his swagger stick.

He smiled at her surprise. "Having a good time?"

He wore civilian clothes—a white shirt, a pair of black polyester pants. This close to him, she realized she was taller. Or nearly his height, though Amor's way of craning his neck forward gave the impression he was addressing someone two inches taller.

"Come, come," he said, "you can't fail to recognize me!"

"No," she said.

"I've been waiting and waiting. I showed myself to you at the balcony. Too bad your friend had to see me. But there's no helping that now. Perhaps, it did her good. The soul has to be taken by the shoulders and reminded. Now and then. Otherwise, we end up mired in sloth."

"Your words or—"

He laughed. "Don't tease. Even though I have a military rank, I'm a true scholar of the human psyche. Someday, you'll find out. I'm not as stupid as you think I am." He cupped her elbow and led her away from the plaza.

"No one would make that mistake, Colonel."

"Pah!" He smacked the swagger stick against his left thigh. "Words. Nothing but words. What do you have for me?"

Her bones ached. She was too rigid. She inhaled, forcing her heart to calm down.

"Why don't you leave her alone? A poor kid—"

He snorted. "She would tear me apart with her hands if she could."

"And she has no reason to do that?"

He stopped. "How sharp you are! My mistake. You'd tear me apart. If you could. With your bare hands. But what frightens you? The loss of your home? Your Mercedes? Your servants? You can have twice that and more. More!" He raised his fists. "More! Just give me, give *me* that man. I need him. Oh, how I need him!" He writhed.

"For what?"

He bent his head, catching his forehead with a hand. "I've gone as far as I can go. If I don't move soon, I'll have to wait forever." He looked up, bared his teeth. He sighed. "But pay no attention to me. I'm just—just tired. Vigilance is tiring. I need that man because he has important information. That's all. Or think of him as a step. Unfortunately, I can't jump over that step. I have to take it." He straightened his shoulders. "But why do you ask? I serve the Commander; this man's an enemy. And it would give me great pleasure to bring him to the Commander. There's pleasure in service, Eliza. The discipline of suppressing the ego in the name of duty. There's joy in being empty, clean, so that one can be filled with nothing more, nothing less than obedience." He laughed. "Wasn't that delightful?"

She shivered. "I don't think she knows. Really. All she's ever wanted was to walk around carrying her father's saxophone . . ."

"Her fa—!" His eyes glazed. He scanned an interior country. It was only a second, then he was laughing. Laughing. He leaned against the wall of a house and wiped his eyes. "Remarkable," he said, weakly. "Dear, dear Eliza. Remarkable. We're fated to keep on meeting each other through time. What a war!"

She watched open-mouthed, afraid she had betrayed Anna. But how?

"How could that have escaped me? Oh, but this is truly delightful! I must check that. And check her husband's family. Delightful. Oh, don't look so scared. It's nothing. An old memory." He jerked himself forward. "But now I must have her as well. How do we manage this? The moment of truth."

Her belly roiled. He was reaching for her again, taking her hand, walking.

"Tell me, tell me."

She twisted, whining, saying there was nothing to find out, nothing to discover. His fingers about her hand tightened, tightened until she thought her bones would crack. She bit her underlip's inner skin.

"We could place a bullet between your middle and ring fingers. And with pliers, we could . . ."

"Aaaah!"

He let her hand go. She flexed her fingers, closed them, flexed them again.

"Amazing," he said. "You react instinctively. Checking functions at once. No tears. The pain already behind you. Amazing. But that won't save you."

"I'll find out tonight," she said evenly; in her head, a sinkhole swallowed her cries of pain. "It's difficult to talk. The Festival—"

"Ah!"

"I'll meet you tomorrow."

"I was right, then. He's here. That's why she's here." He smiled, folded his arms.

"You're right," she lied. "He's here. But where—I don't know. Tomorrow. When the Commander arrives, I'll slip away from the confusion. I'll meet you at the—the . . ."

"The belfry. Built by the Spaniards. A proper place to sell one's friend."

"Spaniards! By native you mean, supervised by Spaniards. Possibly conscripted."

"How sharp you are!" He considered for a moment. "Right. Six o'clock. No, six-thirty. I have to meet that tiresome old fool. Here, ha? Maybe, I'll let him take the Commander." He laughed. "Then, I'll take him." He dropped back, motioning for her to go on. "The belfry," he said.

The transvestite had promised to be there as well. On the morrow. Six-thirty. With a rifle. In case she failed. She slipped the gun under her pillow, along with Batoyan's radiogram. A weight slipped off her shoulders. For all his cruelty, Amor was stupid. Cruelty was stupid.

In the dining room, the guests were on their feet, necks stretched out the better to see the fireballs rising from the island.

"To the deck," Adrian said. "Let's go. It'll only last for a short while."

With the two women in tow, he dashed out, calling to the steward to save their dinner. Anna shivered as the sea wind boiled about her, threatening to unpin her hair. But she made it to the rails, and with Adrian's body shielding her from the cold, she could lean her arms on the salt-encrusted bars. In the distance, beyond the moon-touched waters, the town lights glimmered, the double string of lamps at the pier distinct while over the darkness of the plantations globules of white light floated upward, skimming coconut fronds. The peasant's festival.

"Swamp gas," Adrian said. "Or something as mundane."

"It's beautiful," Eliza breathed.

Anna smiled, remembering the luminous parade in the sky. The island now, with lights below and lights above, seemed to float in a silver sea, like a monstrous leaf-shaped boat, stirring white foam in its wake.

"One could almost believe," Eliza said, "that there are, uh, things beyond"—she shrugged—"beyond now."

"Swamp gas," Adrian said. He was wondering if those were the souls his grandfather spoke of, the wandering dead who manned mountain passes and laid a question on each mortal who came by.

"Ghosts?" Anna teased Eliza.

"Why not?"

"Logical," she said. "Before the Spaniards came, nothing in these islands went away. Our ancestors' spirits were supposed to continue roaming the forests."

"You mean I could've met my grandfather?" Eliza laughed.

"More likely, your grandmother. The women were the intermediaries then. The—priestesses. What an ugly word."

Adrian shivered in mock horror. "I don't want to meet my grandmother."

The passage door opened and the steward stuck his head in the wind. They had to finish their dinner, he called out; the hall was to be cleared for dancing. There was no helping it. They turned away from the island with regret and returned to the dining room.

By a coincidence, they all decided to retire early, in preparation for the Festival's last day. Though Eliza hesitated, casting covetous glances at the band tuning up, she had barely made it through dinner, yawning between bites of broiled milkfish. Anna definitely wasn't dancing anymore. She went to her cabin and, stretching out on the bed, sifted through Guevarra's cryptic message.

Be happy, he'd said, *it's preordained.*

"But what does that mean?" she had asked Rafael, finding him at last perched on a stool in front of a corner store. He had a Coke bottle in his hand. His eyes had warned her away—a warning she ignored, walking straight up to him to thrust her face toward his face. *Amor's here,* she had whispered, *tell Guevarra to call it off.*

But he had merely nodded. "Yes. We know. The *pendejo* is here.

So don't forget. The cemetery. Beside the chapel. Inland. There's
only one road so you can't—"

"Call it off."

He snorted. "How? Dismantle the stage? You're dreaming. The old
man knows. That's enough."

"What old man?"

"Him. He. Now, leave me alone." And he slid off the stool. She
seized his arm then.

"I don't understand."

"Let me be, Anna."

"Don't. Please. Don't just walk away."

"All right, all right." He looked around and jerked his head toward
an alley. She let him precede her, following a minute later. He was
there, haunches folded, drawing with a piece of stick on the ground.

"What's happening?"

"It's Guevarra's show. The first luxury he's allowed himself. At
least, as far as I know." He peered at her. "Ever wonder why he was
taken that time?"

She shook her head. "We never asked questions then."

"Nor even later, it seems." A pause. "His wife and son betrayed the
routes."

"Shit!"

"It happens. When you least expect, from where you least expect
it: betrayal."

She had nothing to say.

"Amor broke them. He turned the woman over to the soldiers and
let the kid watch. And listen. A fourteen-year-old. I'd pulverize Amor
myself." He lifted the Coke to his lips. "But don't repeat this or I'm
dead. We only found out recently. Since then, Guevarra's gone—
deep. Submerged. Deep, deep."

"What happened?"

"They were executed. Guevarra cast the first death vote. Nobody
else would." Another silence. "You've never seen an execution. Bullets aren't wasted on informers. The men used a crowbar. Guevarra
watched."

She opened her hands helplessly.

"He had a message for you. Be happy, he said, it's preordained. Don't ask me what that means. He's been into cryptic remarks lately."

"Like what? And what does that mean?"

"Time at his heels. Settling old debts. Mostly about time. And something about meeting everyone again and again through time. I don't know. Once he said we knew one another before the war made us strangers; that we were all kin." He shrugged. "We love him, though."

"To be loved that way!"

"Be happy, he said." He rose to his feet, stretching his torso with a pained grimace. "Remember: the cemetery."

But it was Guevarra's words—*be happy*—she held now, as Adrian walked into the cabin. He slipped into the narrow space beside her, his body's curves fitting against hers. It was painless, easy, without doubt. She could trace in the clean lines of his young body the origins of his need—his grandfather spending a fortune on old records, searching for his name, rasping how impossible it was not to know one's name, or even the name of the four-hundred-year war which couldn't be won until its nature had been deciphered, baptized, understood, his wheeze an undertow in Adrian's harsh whisper of *his* own dreams, nothing beyond the simple language of a home and work, "a house by the sea, Anna, which we'll keep clean ourselves, without confusion, the hell with all these games, and you'll heal there as I will. . ." Yes, Adrian, yes. Lulled by the waves, the ship's rocking, she was almost asleep when he laughed suddenly, loud in that small room.

"Whatever shall we do with my grandfather's money?" he asked.

She patted his head. "Give it to our favorite charity." The corners of her mouth twitched. He'd be surprised to know what that was.

Thus, they slept, Eliza with the gun under her pillow, Anna and Adrian with their arms around each other, within the ship rocked by a wayward current, and under the wakeful eyes of Colonel Urbano Amor who, standing well away from a barred window, the moon casting vertical shadows on his face, looked out to the sea, to the one ship among ships, and wished himself in possession of the most singular, most beautiful thing he had ever encountered in his life.

3

The Festival awoke to a Latin mass celebrated by three priests at the town's main church. Bells, whistles, and drums. As the din rose over the town, the barbaric throng within the church swelled and spilled to the outside veranda, down the steps, onto the narrow strip of grass lying between the sidewalk and church property. It became impossible to line up before the altar for communion. The two assisting priests and their acolytes had to thread their way through the crowd, handing out the holy wafers. Thus, with forbearance and a long wait, all who wished for the sacrament received it: warriors and urbanites, transvestites, the malformed, the soldiers, the children. The odd congregation bent its head, fist striking the breast thrice in a confession of frailty.

As the bells signaled the mass's end, men and women plunged through the church portals and threw themselves back into the Festival, dancing even without the drums, their music human shrieks and laughter. Anna, Adrian, and Eliza, borne by the celebrity tide, found themselves arm-in-arm with strangers, pounding the earth with their heels. *Jump, step, jump, dance away a little.* They passed a clump of young men, beer bottles in hand, bawling lustily to an old man's guitar. Anna caught the song's lyrics: woman in black, shrouded by her own black hair, walking the darkness. She recognized it at once, the words appearing in her mind as wriggling black ink on yellow music sheets: "Lovely Stranger." Something survived, she thought; something real survived. To her surprise, Adrian himself was singing the lyrics, stamping his feet in rhythm, his voice collapsing into trills of laughter. To her right, Eliza picked up the refrain—woman in black with blue-black hair, searching for a black shroud for her grief— and bent the melody into a faster beat, turning it into a silly excuse for dancing. On and on, about the plaza, the drums now joining them, they whirled, feeling the plants wriggling through the earth's layer, the globe itself wearing down a track in space, the galaxy turning on its axis.

They passed Rafael once. Perched on top of a garbage bin, he favored Anna with the sight of his tongue, sticking it out as she went by and then looking away, ignoring her pointedly. She was so surprised all she could think was how obscene, really, that organ was—red, slick, and wet, not meant to be exposed to dry air. Automatically, she tensed her right arm against the "toy"—a hardness against her skin.

They circumnavigated the plaza thrice, until Adrian, panting, yelled "halt!" and jerked them suddenly and efficiently out of the crowd. He ignored Eliza's protests and herded them to the market-place, a vast temporary shed, inadequately lit, with aisles narrowed by piles of woven baskets, wooden gods flung carelessly in grocery car-tons, bead necklaces redolent of plastic, black whistles.

"Pah!" Eliza said. "Shoddy, shoddy, shoddy."

But she tried on a brass corset with a fringe of bells and laughed with pleasure.

"Oh, perfect," she shouted, picking up a headband of boar teeth. "I look barbaric. Primitive when I meet—" She seized a comb of seashells, shaped like a peacock's crest, dyed blue and green. Holding it against her head, she turned to the two. "How do I look? How do I look?"

"Beautiful, Lord," Anna replied.

"I'm scared to look at you," Adrian said.

Eliza was pleased. When the storekeeper drew near for the payment, she batted her eyelashes at Adrian, pretending to charm him. He laughed; picking up a necklace of tiny skulls—carved wood, painted white—he threw this over Anna's head. "In memoriam," he said.

"I don't want it," Anna said, retreating one step, looking at the skulls nestled between her breasts.

"It's not nice!" Eliza shook her head.

But Adrian was already counting the money onto the storekeeper's palm. Eliza preened; arching her fingers, she stalked down the aisle.

"Make way, make way," she intoned mockingly, thrusting her head forward. "Make way for the matriarch. I am the protector. Protecting!"

The vendors shrieked with laughter. Anna, walking slower, lifting the necklace away from her chest, squinted at the sunlight. "It's too bright," she said.

"Too hot," agreed Adrian. "And it's morning yet."

"Hey, you mortals, hurry up!" Eliza waved.

They stirred reluctantly, drawn despite themselves by the commotion in the streets. A fat man wearing diapers and an oversized bib rattled by in a cart drawn by a goat. He sucked on a huge wine bottle capped with a rubber nipple.

"What's that?" Eliza screamed and, reaching over, patted the creature on the head. The fat man gurgled and lunged, his teeth snapping inches away from her fingers. Eliza veered away, laughing.

"Yummy, yummy," the fat man said as his cart moved on.

The heat was terrific. Jostled, shoved this way and that, they wandered through the Festival, feeling the sun sucking at their strength. Adrian stripped off his shirt again and wound it about his head. He wished the Festival were over, that they could leave for Manila, resume old routines, carry out new plans. Now, in its last hours, the

Festival was dragging, though the dancers leapt higher, the drums played with greater frenzy, and the warriors marched with more bravura, brandishing spears now, and chanting *hala, bira! hala, bira!* while wine bottles traveled the route of the plaza. It was the energy of desperation.

Anna, too, was touched by that sadness—a grief as stealthy as the rush of waves, a quiet, remote, and yet insistent noise trickling into the silent spaces of the Festival. She danced on leaden feet, never missing a beat for all her hesitancy. An automaton making merry. Beside her, Eliza, arching her neck to the sun, whispered, asking what was happening, what was wrong. But she danced nevertheless, in her loose blue peasant blouse, blue jeans, and blue sneakers. All three were in one color this day—blue all the way—quite by coincidence, though they had bantered about their uniform throughout the boat ride from ship to shore. Blue they left, thought Eliza, and just as blue would return at the setting of the sun.

Thus, they spent the day, hurled by the Festival from one mood to the next, until the sun lay low enough to be speared by the town's roofs and shadows slanted across the plaza's lawn. Anna awoke to the time of danger quite abruptly, seeing the plaza with inordinate clarity: church and municipal hall, facade of houses, the central spread of grass with six desultory trees, the kiosk. Northward, beyond the eastern intersection, a side street had been barricaded, a temporary stage erected. This was where the Commander, flanked by the island's officers, would give the salute to the Festival.

"It's just a speech," Eliza said, "probably four hours long. Boring, boring, boring."

"True," Anna agreed. "We should find a friendly house and proceed to dinner."

"But I want to see him," Adrian said.

"In which case," Anna countered, "we should stay right there!" She pointed to the church steps. "He'll pass by, in his car."

"It'll be too quick. His car never stops. It just goes—zoom!"

"Not in this crowd. Not possible. How do you clear the road? He'll go by very slowly. It will be a promenade. It's supposed to be lucky." Anna laughed.

"Oh? How?"

"Add five years to your life." Anna shook her head. "He's superstitious. Won't be able to resist that."

"In that case," Eliza jumped up, "so am I! I'm making my promenade."

"Hey, hey!"

Adrian grunted. "Let her go. But come, I want to look at the stage." Anna shook her head. "Just look. I swear. We'll be at the church steps by the time he gets here."

He began walking toward the intersection. Anna cursed and followed quickly. She wore no watch and the town hall clock was permanently set at six o'clock. Adrian was walking too fast, dodging the crowd which was moving southward, in anticipation of the Commander's appearance. She could not keep up with him. As they neared the boundaries of the plaza, a loud, wordless roar swept toward them. A minibus appeared at the far end of the short road, inching through a rush of bodies, ignoring hands raised to its tinted windows. Impossible to tell whether noise and gestures were in greeting or in rage. Now, Anna could see the soldiers—six rows deep, eight abreast—who preceded the bus, M-16s at ready, held low, at the waist. More soldiers on foot behind the bus, followed by a military jeep with a machine gun. There were more—still lost among the narrow back streets that fed the plaza's main road.

When she turned to Adrian, she saw he had reached the intersection. She was about to dash across when a phalanx of men came out of the side street. They were all in immaculate clothes and garlanded with purple flowers. She recognized the governor, the mayor, the provincial commander—those who had done their promenade the previous day. But with them was another man, one who gestured imperiously and called out "Adrian!" *Adrian, Adrian.* The group stopped and now, as one, looked at Adrian who himself stopped moving. *Adrian, Adrian.* "Adrian," the man called, "come here. The governor—" Adrian's head turned slowly, his eyes finding Anna and there was that plea. Understand, the eyes said, not in public; one couldn't shame one's father in public. Anna caught the contempt that the older man flicked her way—a careless whip of a look. She swayed, stunned both by that look and by the anger surging through her body. But she was already suppressing it, automatically, keeping an eye on the minibus and the crowd, men and women passing between the vehicles, ignoring the soldiers, forcing the two vehicles to spread farther and farther apart. Adrian shrugged and half turned toward the group. *Adrian, Adrian.* "Hurry," she called out, "come back quickly. I'll be by the steps." And watched him join the group as it disappeared in the direction of the stage.

She was counting. Twenty-four. Twenty-five. The minibus continued its snail pace. Thirty. The military jeep had entangled itself in a knot of people at the road's head. The soldiers on foot brandished guns, shooing the crowd back, but the young men and women merely gestured amiably, shook their heads, linked arms, and danced about the soldiers.

Midway down the road, suddenly aware of the distance between itself and its escort, the minibus stopped.

"It stopped!" Anna shouted.

The Festival flung itself at the bus. Men and women—a human wave—rushed forward even as soldiers quickly deployed themselves about the vehicle. More soldiers appeared, running from side streets, and from the trapped military jeep in which only the driver and gunner remained. At the far intersection near the church, a black van appeared, sirens screaming. An ambulance.

She was running, dodging strays from the Festival, the children who could not get through the crush of people. They thought it was a game, this sudden flight of hers, and like a flock of pigeons on the wing they ran with her, laughing. Stunted, potbellied, half naked, barefoot. Snot running. Dust and soot streaks on cheeks, on arms; scabbed wounds on shins and toes.

"It stopped, it stopped," she was crying, remembering suddenly Guevarra's wife and son, and his vote of death. He could have said no. *She* could have said no. Don't go.

She was nearly in time. The road bent into a sudden vacant lot. She saw the stage, photographs of the Commander and his wife tacked on the back wall; the lectern, the microphones; the buntings overhead, the wires twirled with *cadena de amor,* its pink flowers still fresh. She saw Adrian standing between the stage and the row of chairs on the ground, chairs reserved no doubt for the town officials. He was looking at his father who was on the stage, looking down at Adrian and saying something, while the governor, the mayor, and the riff-raff powers of the island milled about, some on stage, some on the ground below, checking the sound equipment, the video cameras . . . "Adrian!"

He turned. In that instant, as though his movement and the noise were synchronized, the church bells pealed—the big, low-voiced one and the three small, silver-voiced ones. Six o'clock. A slow smile bloomed on Adrian's face and he took a step away from the stage.

The lectern rose, the stage floor bucked and splintered upward; a force swept the chairs back, toppling them at one blow. It scooped Adrian up and flung him against the nearest bamboo pole, which snapped at the point of impact, dragging down light bulbs, wires, buntings, and the *cadena de amor.* Then, the ground shook beneath Anna's feet and she was on her hands and knees, a ringing in her ears, staring at tiny kernels of dust on the ground with the cold certainty that Adrian was dead.

Seconds later, she was at the intersection. A terrible wind was stirring the crowd. Heads bobbed, arms flew. The minibus plowed through the Festival. The soldiers all had their guns aimed at masses of bodies which jerked, stirred, jerked back, disintegrated into individual men and women running, running. There were things on the sidewalk, things trying to climb trees and walls, things dangling from windows. A stream of people came toward her, passed her, their mouths open but she couldn't hear. There was only this whine in her ears. She raised a hand to her head, felt a wetness. It was blood. She'd been cut.

A half-naked woman ran up the town hall steps, struck a pillar, bounced back, then ducked into the building. Two men were pinning another woman down on the grass near the kiosk. A blond man came up, kicked at the two, but suddenly jerked back, whirled, and fell face down.

"But how truly marvelous, Manolo," she said. "They're fighting back."

Eliza came out of the chaos, saw Anna, and calmly walked toward her. Anna, frozen at her corner, stretched a hand out, as though she could pull Eliza forward. Quick. Quicker. She nearly made it. A soldier materialized and swept his rifle butt at her. Eliza fell. He bent down, slinging his M-16 on his shoulder, and seizing her right arm, began dragging her away. Eliza raised her head, screamed something at Anna, and pointed, pointed, toward the sea. Over there, over there. Another soldier appeared, running on bent knees, stooping to catch hold of Eliza's legs. The other soldier stopped, turned around, took her left arm. Eliza swung between them—a butchered pig, ready for flaying.

She ran then, away from the plaza, into the side streets, meeting soldiers who, deploying for their assault on the town's center, not knowing who the enemy was, ignored her. How she made it through the confusion, she didn't know; but suddenly, she was at the town's edge, at the beginning of the only road inland and the whine in her ears was abating—slowly, but enough to enable her to hear explosions, gunfire, glass shattering, and, like a voice of reassurance, the deep bark of a BAR, Guevarra's preferred weapon. "The cemetery," said Rafael's voice in her head, "near the chapel. Inland." She repeated the words, holding herself, hands on elbows, shoulders hunched. The hard edge of the knife's hilt dug into her flesh. One thrust, straight and true, just above the nape, severing the medulla oblongata from the spinal chord. Instant paralysis. "But how marvelous, Manolo," she murmured. "They fought back. You would've been so proud."

Run, walk. Run, walk. Behind her the darkness crept, paced her, overtook her. But the moon, its fullness marred by a bite from the night, rose, its light etching the road clearly. She didn't know how long it took her, for she scurried into the fields at the first noise ahead and waited, hunched against tree trunks, among weeds, until whatever it was had passed. She nearly missed the chapel—it was a small shed, really—but a red altar candle signaled its presence in the moon's silver light. She approached carefully, making no noise at all, and circled the place, making sure the lighted candle was no trap. Reassured by the silence, she walked in, looking at the pitiful pews and the raw, wood body of Christ on the cross. It was bloody, unvarnished. Two thousand years of crucifixion. Weary, she slid into the last pew, near the door, letting go of her body. Two thousand years and *he* was still up there. The pew was rough and splintered, the hand rest bleached by the sweat of many wrists, many fingers clasped in prayers. They had come here, the peasants, day after day, pleading. Four hundred years. Where was the end of it, this war, where the day of peace? Four hundred years and all those prayers, asking, asking, only for the simplest of joys: to know what the miracle of being alive was; to survive with the least pain. She stole a look at the Christ again— deaf, dumb, unresponsive wood. If *he* appeared now, would they sing hosannas and wave palm fronds? Or would they, in the grim pleasure of anger, nail him back to the cross in retribution for those centuries of silence? Bang, bang, bang. Mallet in fist, nails in hand. Another thousand years for you, indifferent friend. She could see it: the village elders picking themselves up on withered legs, hoisting their threadbare pants; the children laughing like seagulls, women peering slyly, the men holding down the body. Well, well, well, here you are. Back to the cross with you. She laughed.

And heard a rustling outside, as of an animal dragging its belly on the ground. She rose, quickly, smoothly, sliding out of the pew, her eyes darting. To the left was another icon, beside a massive collection box. She flew to it and wedged herself in the space between the box and the wall. Tight but a good hiding place. She breathed a prayer. Let it be Rafael; let it be Rafael.

A jackal, one leg scraping the ground. Brown and ocher skin, mimicking the pattern of foliage on the forest floor. The animal turned its head this way and that. It held a white bundle in its hands. Slowly, it slouched toward the pew, sat down, one leg held straight, and laid the bundle on the seat. It peeled its shirt off, loosened the bundle, and shook out a white shirt and slipped it on. Carefully then, it started undoing its gun belt, the laces of its boots, its pants. It inspected its damaged leg—no blood there, just cloth wound about the ankle—and inched itself up, drawing to its full height. It ran its hand through its hair before turning, turning, to inspect the church. Breath exploded from Anna's mouth.

Instantly, a gun was in the creature's hand. "Out," the voice—oh, that familiar, so-valued memory of a voice—said calmly, "come out!" *Manolo!* She rose to her feet and showed herself, tears already spilling down her cheeks.

"Anna," he said, lowering the gun. There was no denying the pleasure in his voice.

She took a step forward; stopped. It was Manolo. And he had worn a jackal's uniform. She wiped the tears off her cheeks; her eyes shifted to the gun.

He caught the look. "Oh, this?" He tucked the gun back into its holster, picked up the belt, and wrapped it about his hips. "A precaution, that's all. It's me, Anna."

"You're not dead," she said.

"Never was." He laughed. "But how marvelous. You're here. Good. You can help me. My ankle's busted. We'll have to make our way to a village, find a boat."

"The photographs . . . ?"

He laughed again. "Wasn't me. Someone who looked enough like me. With rigor mortis and blood, you couldn't tell. Amor's clever when it comes to those things. But we're wasting time. There's a war going on in the town—house to house. Shit! Was Amor surprised! Turned out the whole fucking place was a nest of insurgents—every single resident. It was funny. Transvestites whipping out sawed-off shotguns from under their skirts; half-naked warriors . . . Lord, those spears were real! I was half laughing all the time. Shooting and laughing."

"Stop!" Anna's hands clenched at the sound of her voice. The knife's hilt bit into her skin. "Stop, Manolo. Explain. Please explain. They took me. Did you know that?"

He shifted uneasily, looked around. "All right," he said, running his fingers through his hair. "But it's too open here, too open."

"The cemetery," she said. "Behind the chapel."

He studied her, silent. She did not flinch. "All right," he sighed. "You lead the way."

She shook her head, waved vaguely. "No. You go ahead."

"You don't trust me? Anna, it's Manolo."

She held her silence. Waited. He sighed again, then limped toward the door. "At least we can sit on a tomb or something. My foot's swollen."

She followed, keeping the distance between them. If he ran, she would let him go. Run, Manolo. But he was damaged, could not run. Run, Manolo. My slim, young rabble-rouser, all good intentions and wisdom. Run. He was damaged. Damaged. Manolo in a jackal's uniform. In the dark, she held her wrist against her side, jerked her hand, and felt the knife slide down. Smoothly. No hitch there, no tugging at the cord. Blessed be Rafael. She waited, palming the knife, leaving the blade sheathed.

When he turned at the perimeter of the graveyard, she slipped into the shadows.

"Anna," he said.

In the moonlight, she could see his hands were empty. She took a step, gestured with her left hand. "A little further, love. Just to make sure no one sees us."

He stopped again when they were surrounded by graves—white, rectangular tombs of cement, set aboveground, topped by crosses, angel heads, stone wreaths. "Good enough?" he asked.

"Yes," she said, peering at him from behind a cement crucifix. "Far enough, ghost."

"Don't make fun, Anna." With his hand, he dusted a corner of a tomb, sat down. "My foot's killing me. That's better. I don't like graveyards."

"They suit me fine."

"You were always the serious one."

"Explain, Manolo. Tell me. It's me, Anna." Her voice caught. Anna who cleaned your books, put your test papers in order, cooked your meals, scrubbed the floor you walked on.

"I went, as you know, with the guerrillas." He snorted—a bitter sound. "I lasted only six months. Some things no man should be made to go through. Dried leeches for breakfast. Christ! The forest night. Monkey shrieks for music. The infernal rain. Drip, drip, drip. We were always wet. Everything damp, moist, wet. Fungi chewing on our elbows, crotches, and feet."

"But—"

"Sssh. That wasn't the worst of it. Not the worst of it. We were doing two tactical offensives per week. Two! With old guns, World War Two grenades, knives, wooden stakes. Week after week. The casualty rate was unbelievable. The only thing was we never lacked for manpower. We could replace men as fast as they were being killed off, maimed. But what replacements! All young, inexperienced, straight out of the city. Students. It was enough to make you weep. Bury the dead; take the new ones through the routes."

"But—"

"You sing songs to forget. Peasant songs. But you never forget. Sixteen-year-old eyes, blank, below the neat hole on the forehead. And always, the enemy was there, with his bazookas, his machine guns, his grenade launchers, his inexhaustible supply of weapons. The best money could buy. Made in U.S.A. It got so I would start quaking from head to foot at the chug-chug-chug of helicopter propellers. The noise would drop from the sky, from all directions. My toes would flail; every muscle in my body would bunch up and my rifle—a stupid, antique hunting rifle—would sway this way and that. I was trembling so much. Finally, after one particular bad encounter—the military made a mistake; mortared a village and we had to clean up the mess, picking up arms and legs, shoving intestines back into the bodies, trying not to retch but heaving nevertheless, nevertheless, puking carefully so one didn't dirty the bodies . . . After that one, I had nightmares. Nightmares. Then, the enemy came in a counteroffensive. We had been warned. We were ready, deployed for ambush. I heard the choppers. Chug-chug-chug. I fled. Abandoned my position. They found me later, as they were retreating. I had dropped my rifle and wrapped my arms around a coconut tree. I was crying and trembling and hoping the tree would open so I could hide myself."

He sighed.

"After that, well, there was no point to my remaining. The others pretended nothing had gone wrong. But there was no forgetting it. We talked among ourselves. Reached a consensus. I would surrender. They gave me some money so I could bribe the checkpoint soldiers. I didn't want to take it, they were so poor, but they said it was for my own safety, so I wouldn't be harmed. That was the way it was. I came down the mountain, out of the forest, and gave myself up. Amor arrived at the provincial fort and took me three days later." He stopped. "But why are you so far away? You're making me shout this. It's difficult enough without my having to shout it to the world."

She sighed and approached him. She sat beside him, making sure the gun holster was pressed between his body and hers.

"Amor took you," she prompted him.

"By that time, you—" He made an ineffectual gesture.

"I'd gone through tactical interrogation."

"Yes. I was sure in due time you'd be freed. But of course the escape happened and you—"

"Had to go through it again."

"I can never understand how you withstood it."

"What do you mean?"

"I'm sure you knew how they escaped. But you kept the knowledge. How did they escape? It's still not known."

She smiled. "You're wrong," she said. "I didn't know. I don't know."

"Oh, you poor child!"

She shook her head, held herself rigid against the arm he placed about her shoulder. With her left hand, she groped for his free hand, entwined her fingers about his fingers.

"Yes. It was all a mistake. But Amor took you—"

He leaned his forehead against the side of her head and whispered: "I broke." Whispered like a phrase of endearment.

"I gave him everything I knew—names, routes, addresses. Except the Hong Kong address. In return, he let me live, found some use for me. He had the strange idea that since I was a scientist, I could devise better ways of"—again, the voice dropped—"getting at the truth."

She nodded.

"I helped. There was no avoiding it. He was my only sanctuary. Outside, because of, of . . . I was a hunted man." He shifted his weight. "It was somewhat strange. Mixing chemicals, trying this or that combination. Drawing up a pattern of afflictions. A little of this, a little of that. Very removed from the reality. Except once. He had me do it to Adrian—"

"Adrian!"

"Amor said he had to be careful not to leave a trace. Of the tampering. And I had to do it. Very strange. Amor's sense of humor. Come to think of it"—he stretched out painfully—"he must have known. He wanted me to know it was all useless. My sacrifice; yours. Funny how— But listen, Anna, it was the old man, Adrian's grandfather . . ."

"What?"

"He set up the Hong Kong trading company, shipping in arms, trying to make sure everything was not swallowed up by one man. A bumbling, incompetent, senile old man. Feeding money, arms, and believing he was the center. Stupid, stupid. And we holding in that stupid address. I, thinking I would escape some day, make my way to another country, and from there help out, via that Hong Kong address—salvage a shred of respect. Shit!"

"What do you mean?"

"We're all peripheral. The war—it's always been between men like Amor and that guy who escaped. Between them. No more, no less. We just got sideswiped. What we should have done was remain neutral; just gone on living our lives. Like you wanted. You were right all the time. I was stupid."

"I—"

"Sssh!" He was on his feet at once, despite the injury. He thrust her behind him. His gun was out now.

Anna listened. Only the wind; crickets. The moon. But Manolo was motioning for her to get behind a tomb. He was already folding his body into a crouch. Anna, mesmerized, watched the transformation. He was becoming an animal again.

"Anna?" Harsh whisper. Rafael.

Manolo tensed, unwound from his crouch. Anna jerked her right arm back. A double click. The hilt unlocking, blade sliding out, the hilt's halves locking once more, tongue of metal bare now. She touched the back of his head with the fingers of her left hand, felt his irritated shrug, then his surprise as she increased the pressure. She pulled back a little, drawing in her breath, and with the full weight of her body behind the blow, she rammed the knife in.

4

ITEM: Though crippled, Adrian Banyaga survived. He replaced his grandfather in wheelchair perambulations through rooms and corridors of the ancestral mansion, Old Andy having died in his sleep one night. The doctors held out hope that in due time, with the proper therapy, he would recover. At least, physically, for there was the minor problem of his mind. The explosion seemed to have hurled Adrian into a time warp, fixing him forever in a maze of words, a verbal account of four hundred years, tortured and tormenting. Now and then, a coherent story would leap from his mouth, like a page of clear writing in a book of errors. He would rant for hours, about the legend of a half-boy, born with half a head, one arm attached to one shoulder of a half-torso, one thigh and one leg, and how this creature searched through the seven thousand one hundred islands for his completion. But his other half turned coy and disguised itself, first as a boulder jutting from a cliff, a bird piercing the mountain air, a filigree of clouds snagged by a volcano, a fern probing the earth with its toes, a green lizard asleep in the cool recesses of a banana plant, a wild boar slinking through the jungle. It eluded the seeker, taking on shapes of earth, sea, and heaven in the archipelago, in the process conferring upon each a sanctity which the seeker recognized and worshipped. He had no recourse but to love them all, for they were parts of his soul, even that female form that took on a host of names, calling itself Maya, Miss Estela, Liwayway, and even Anna.

ITEM: Eliza Hansen's body washed ashore four days after the Festival. The fishermen who found it waited twenty-four hours. When no one claimed the body, they poured gasoline over the decaying flesh and set it afire. The village children watched from the safety of coconut trees fringing the coastline. They smiled at the flames. And waited for the fire to die and the high tide to rinse the sand of the scorch mark. The bones they gathered and took home, to be split and carved into wind chimes which would hang at windows and doors. It was said that the remains of the Festival's tribute to the sea brought good fortune.

ITEM: Colonel Alejandro Batoyan fell ill a month later and succumbed to a systemic disorder that saw his organs attacked by chemicals his own glands produced. Liver, lungs, spleen, kidneys, and heart, particularly the heart, disintegrated at a terrific pace in the toxic broth flushed through the body by the veins. The heart's rate of breakdown fascinated his doctors, who couldn't know that the colonel was a true romantic. He had striven for the possession of beauty in his own awkward way and having sojourned briefly in its glory, found it impossible to live without it.

ITEM: Guevarra was wounded and captured. Again. Nothing more was known. His friends resigned themselves to his absence. First, they said he was probably dead. Later, that he was dead. From the south, from one of the islands of the Central Philippines, came some comfort. A fledgling guerrilla group overran and destroyed a military base. The leader, a young man of few words, had named himself after a great man. He called himself Guevarra.

ITEM: Colonel Urbano Amor survived, minus his left arm. He completed a dissertation and was conferred a doctorate in the behavioral sciences. The labored-upon manuscript, a distillation of so much human pain, was read by the university examining committee whose members, it was said, were so horrified they waived its oral defense and abruptly passed the colonel. Then they had the manuscript microfilmed, destroyed the paper versions, and had the only copy placed among the restricted files of the library. Researchers of the future, when all this trouble is over, may perhaps discover it there, with its perverted truth. But considering the volume of materials under this code, it may lie there forever.

The loss of his arm having made him unfit for military life, Urbano Amor was appointed chancellor of the Academy of Man, a new institution generously endowed by government and dedicated to the study of perfection. At his investiture, Colonel, no, Chancellor Amor delivered a two-hour speech of great erudition, before two thousand hand-picked students who were all on scholarship. The speech dealt with the seven virtues of the Commander's Society, namely, patriotism, loyalty, integrity, intelligence, compassion, simplicity, and sacrifice. It was loudly applauded and praised. But students being students, and the young being young, the joke circulated later that the long-winded treatise could be reduced to a single sentence: "Man is a dog and has no right to happiness."

ITEM: Anna Villaverde made it back to the Ever Loyal and Ever Noble City of Manila. She and Rafael managed to stay but a step ahead of the wolves unleashed by the Loved One. Perhaps it was grief over the loss of his arm; or perhaps, as some said, he had taken the attempt on the Commander's life as a personal affront . . . No matter. Colonel Amor laid siege on the urban resistance, the most vulnerable link, cordoning off one district after another. One house of safety after another was hit in that phase of the war and nearly a thousand men and women were swallowed by the detention camps.

But Rafael matched the colonel's anger. He guided Anna through the danger—a full month of scuttling between houses, from district to district—at the end of which, if Anna had bothered to make an accounting, she would have been able to say she had slept in nearly all the city's neighborhoods.

It came to a finish, though—for the enemy's actions were based on a momentary spasm of rage. Against this, the resistance poised infinite patience, a steadfast passion that knew full well the nature of both the enemy and time. The enemy saw the resistance as an irritant, a disruption in the normal conduct of its affairs. The resistance, on the other hand, saw only the enemy. It had no festivals to celebrate, no career to worry about, no property to protect, no manuscript to finish. It absorbed its losses, withdrew its people from exposed positions, clothed itself in anonymity. In due *time,* it saw the flagging of the enemy's zeal, saw its attention waver and, at last, turn to other matters. Then, the resistance stirred and reached out.

In due time. Rafael and Anna were plucked out of the city. She was brought to a small village in Laguna. Rafael went somewhere else, though with the promise that he would always know about her, remember her, for he had promised Guevarra that. And who knew what would happen, the vagaries of war being what they were? Perhaps, they would meet again.

Anna's arrival at the village, after two days of walking through hill trails to avoid the main roads' checkpoints, was heralded by an odd, raucous sound—a cry that split the air and made her guide smile. "A *labuyo,*" he said. "I gotta set a trap." As though to taunt him, the rooster crowed again.

He never caught it—at least, not in the week that he stayed, seeing to Anna's getting settled. She had a task now. She was to teach the children. So many of them, even in this flea-sized village: dark and sturdy, small because of the food but with eyes like polished onyx. The villagers built a shed for their use, touched by the resistance's gift. Already, they were calling her *maestra*—teacher—and from their poor homes brought her odds and ends: a stool and a table for her own hut, a mat, woven blankets, pots and pans. Her offer of money embarrassed them and, after a while, she learned to accept and let her pleasure be gratitude enough. They would not take payment, not even for the batteries they brought, whenever one or the other went down to the town. They never forgot the batteries for her radio/tape recorder. She found a way to repay that, though, carrying the thing to the corner store at dusk and leaving it so they could gather and listen. To music sometimes, to the news often, and, even oftener, to a soap opera where the heroine was always named Esperanza and had to go through a million and one threats to her integrity and chastity.

She taught the children in the morning. With the mountain sun soft on the windowsill, the children's faces a garden of flowers before her, she was almost happy as she listened to their singsong: *It was morning when the Spanish long boats sailed from Cebu to Mactan.* In the forest, the wild rooster let loose its cry of triumph.

At noon, she ate her frugal meal before walking to the corner store, picking up her radio/tape player, and hiking to a nearby spring. Here, she played Guevarra's tapes, taking pleasure in his voice. "My name is Ismael Guevarra." He had no identity except for that name which he had screamed out, over and over again, in the Loved One's romance room. No one had believed him. "The problem with Amor and his men," said Guevarra, "is that they can't distinguish the true note from the false. Thus, they conferred heroism on a simple man. Which was good, for the times needed heroes, no matter how illusory."

She heard him speak of her father, not knowing who he was; the music and that act of kindness, never forgotten, in the midst of cruelty. They were, Anna thought, ordained to meet each other again and again, through time, reenacting stories of love, of abuse, of kindness, of betrayal. But of kindness above all, which enabled them to survive, which in turn allowed the archipelago to keep on dreaming its history.

A rustling among the leaves. The *labuyo*—iridescent shape among the shadows. It preened itself, grooming its feathers while she held still, letting Guevarra's voice meander through its tale. How, still a child, he had gathered the remnants of the army of the poor, those who had survived the years, and carried on the war which was no less ferocious for its being invisible. On and on, to the trial of his wife and son. "It was with pride that I cast my vote. The rules were clear. Death to the traitor. I looked at my wife. Once, long ago, she had helped me in my loneliness. But she was old now, tendons standing out on her arms, spatulate fingers restless under my scrutiny. I looked at my son. He was merely another barefoot, filthy child littering the landscape, lost in ignorance. He had absorbed all the ugliness of my flesh. No nobility there. I had been away from the two of them too long.

"The rules were clear, are clear. I could give a hundred unassailable reasons for my verdict of death. None would be any good at all. No good at all. I had no answer to my own questions. I still don't. For no man acts according to rules but simply, according to the dictates of his heart. When I looked at them, didn't I—but for a moment, true, just as it was true that the thought had been there—wish for a better wife, a better son? What woman, what child, came to my mind then? Was my verdict heroic or base? I have no answer. We begin as accidents and end as the sum of accidents. The rites of this land seize us by the hair and force us into a design begun a long, long time ago." A shy laugh. The *labuyo* stirred. A cloud moved in the sky and, from the village, the voices of the children rang out, chanting *Ferdinand Magellan, the crazy old coot; took five ships and circumcised* . . . Anna sat up slowly, for silence had fallen, bird and insect calls gone now. She shivered in a sudden cool breeze, while the children's voices went on and on, and bushes, tree leaves, and water trickling from the spring shimmered with a nacreous light. She thought she had fallen asleep and was waking now, stepping into yet another world of dreams. She rose to her feet, her joints slipping smoothly into place; the wild rooster stopped, inclined its head sideways, and studied her. As in a dream, she felt her own hand touching her neck, the space between her breasts, her belly, her navel. And she knew. Instantly. She was pregnant, the child was male, and he would be born here, with the *labuyo*—consort of mediums and priestesses—in attendance. He would be nurtured as much by her milk as by the archipelago's legends—already, she was tucking Guevarra's voice among other voices in her mind—and he would be the first of the Capuchin monk's descendants to be born innocent, without fate . . . She knew all that instantly, with great certainty, just as she knew that her son would be a great storyteller, in the tradition of the children of priestesses. He would remember, his name being a history unto itself, for he would be known as Ismael Villaverde Banyaga.

Time passes.